Chinese Society on the Eve of Tiananmen

of Tiananmen

The Impact of Reform

Harvard Contemporary China Series 7

edited by

DEBORAH DAVIS
and EZRA F. VOGEL

Published by
THE COUNCIL ON EAST ASIAN STUDIES/HARVARD UNIVERSITY
Distributed by the Harvard University Press
Cambridge (Massachusetts) and London 1990

Chinese Society on the Eve of Tiananmen

The Impact of Reform

Printed in The United States of America
Index by Katherine Frost Bruner

The Council on East Asian Studies publishes books in four series and, through the Fairbank Center for East Asian Research and the Reischauer Institute of Japanese Studies, administers research projects designed to further scholarly understanding of China, Japan, Korea, Vietnam, Inner Asia, and adjacent areas.

Library of Congress Cataloging-in-Publication Data

Chinese society on the eve of Tiananmen : the impact of reform /
    edited by Deborah Davis and Ezra F. Vogel.
        p.   cm.—(Harvard contemporary China series : 7)
    Papers first presented at a workshop held at Harvard University in
May 1988.
    Includes bibliographical references (p.   ) and index.
    ISBN 0-674-12534-7 (alk. paper)—ISBN 0-674-12535-5 (alk. paper pbk)
    1. China—Social conditions—1976—   I. Davis, Deborah, 1945–
II. Vogel, Ezra F.   III. Series.
HN733.5.C45   1990
306'.0951—dc20   90-1960
                                                          CIP

CONTRIBUTORS

YVES CHEVRIER, Co-Director, Center for Research and Documentation on Contemporary China, Ecole des Hautes Etudes en Sciences Sociales, Paris

DEBORAH DAVIS, Associate Professor of Sociology, Yale University

THOMAS GOLD, Associate Professor of Sociology, University of California, Berkeley

GAIL HENDERSON, Assistant Professor, Department of Social Medicine, School of Medicine, University of North Carolina, Chapel Hill

CHARLOTTE IKELS, Assistant Professor of Anthropology, Case Western Reserve University

RICHARD MADSEN, Professor of Sociology, University of California, San Diego

JEAN OI, Associate Professor of Government, Harvard University

STANLEY ROSEN, Associate Professor of Political Science, University of Southern California

HELEN SIU, Associate Professor of Anthropology, Yale University

EZRA F. VOGEL, Professor of Sociology and Clarence Dillon Professor of International Affairs, Harvard University

ANDREW WALDER, Professor of Sociology, Harvard University

TYRENE WHITE, Assistant Professor of Political Science, Swarthmore College

MARTIN KING WHYTE, Professor of Sociology, University of Michigan

Chinese Society on the Eve of Tiananmen

The Impact of Reform

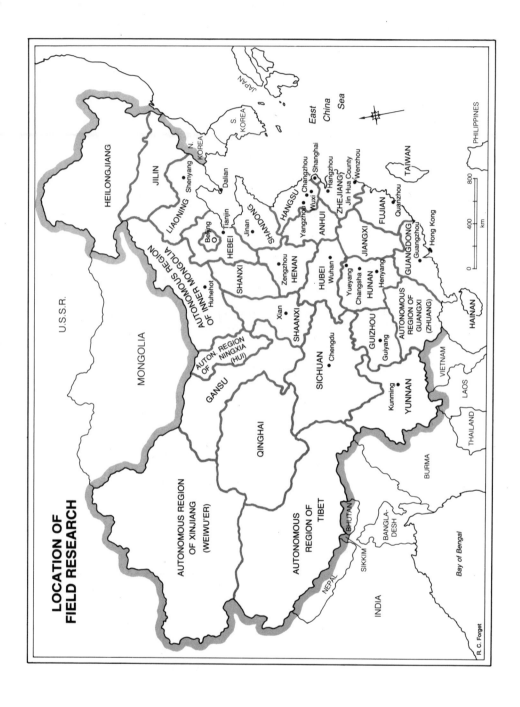

LOCATION OF FIELD RESEARCH

CONTENTS

Introduction: The Social and Political Consequences of Reform 1
DEBORAH DAVIS AND EZRA F. VOGEL

PART ONE   RURAL SOCIETY AND POLITICS

1 *The Fate of the Collective after the Commune* 15
JEAN C. OI

2 *Political Reform and Rural Government* 37
TYRENE WHITE

3 *The Politics of Migration in a Market Town* 61
HELEN F. SIU

PART TWO   URBAN REFORMS AND URBAN WORKERS

4 *Urban Job Mobility* 85
DEBORAH DAVIS

5 *Micropolitics and the Factory Director Responsibility System, 1984–1987*   109
YVES CHEVRIER

6 *Economic Reform and Income Distribution in Tianjin, 1976–1986*   135
ANDREW G. WALDER

7 *Urban Private Business and Social Change*   157
THOMAS B. GOLD

PART THREE   URBAN SOCIETY

8 *Changes in Mate Choice in Chengdu*   181
MARTIN KING WHYTE

9 *New Options for the Urban Elderly*   215
CHARLOTTE IKELS

10 *The Spiritual Crisis of China's Intellectuals*   243
RICHARD MADSEN

PART FOUR   NATIONAL TRENDS

11 *Increased Inequality in Health Care*   263
GAIL HENDERSON

12 *The Impact of Reform Policies on Youth Attitudes*   283
STANLEY ROSEN

Appendix: Chronology   307

Notes   315

Glossary   375

Selected Bibliography   381

Index   391

A C K N O W L E D G M E N T S

The twelve core papers in this volume were first presented at a workshop on "The Social Consequences of the Post-Mao Reforms" in May 1988 at Harvard University. Kathleen Hartford and Merle Goldman played the major role in organizing the conference, and Sally Kolodkin and her staff provided the essential administrative muscle and talent. Financial support came from the Fairbank Center for East Asian Research of Harvard University and from the Mellon Foundation. In addition the authors are indebted to Anna Laura Rosow and Laurie Scheffler for their help in preparing the final manuscript; to Jackie Dormitzer for her skillful copyediting; and to Laurie Spillane for her organization of the notes and bibliography. Throughout the project, Nancy Hearst, librarian at the Coolidge Hall Library of the Fairbank Center, identified and located documentary treasures not only for several of the authors but also for the editors as they developed the chronology and reviewed the separate chapters. We are indebted to our conference participants and to our rapporteur, David Wank.

Deborah Davis
and
Ezra F. Vogel

INTRODUCTION

The Social and Political Consequences of Reform

DEBORAH DAVIS and EZRA F. VOGEL

By the end of the 1970s state communism was everywhere in retreat. In the Soviet Union, Eastern Europe, China, and even in Vietnam, communist leaders found themselves leading economies that could neither compete in international markets nor satisfy domestic expectations. And so, first in Eastern Europe and then in China and the Soviet Union, party leaders were compelled to devise fundamental departures from the economic procedures and structures they had confidently installed at the outset of their revolutionary victories. In each country these economic reforms marked a distinct break with past practice. But perhaps no country departed more rapidly from the institutional core of the preexisting economic order than China. (See Appendix for chronology.)

Within five years of Mao Zedong's death (1976), the reformers led by Deng Xiaoping had dismantled the people's communes as the basic economic and political unit in the Chinese countryside and created a range of markets that established the institutional foundations for a new form of socialism. But unlike the Soviets and the Eastern Europeans, the Chinese reformers refused to consider parallel changes in political institutions. Even after a decade of experimentation and radical innovation, the national leaders remained uncompromising and repeatedly refused to legitimate new political procedures and behaviors.

The explosion of demonstrations in Beijing and other Chinese cities during the spring of 1989 made clear that, despite the leadership's refusal to implement political as well as economic reform, the post-Mao economic policies had had unavoidable political consequences for the society and for the top leadership. Nevertheless, it is not possible to identify a single causal link between the economic reforms begun in 1978 and the events in Tiananmen Square in May and June 1989. The decision to shoot down the demonstrators and bystanders in Tiananmen was only one of several options open to the leaders, and one that probably is best explained through an analysis of conflicts among the political and military elites—subjects that are beyond the focus of this volume and outside the research interests of our contributors.

And yet the unrest on display in Tiananmen in May 1989 was deeply rooted in the social consequences of the post-Mao economic reforms. As the twelve authors in this volume document in their individual case studies, decollectivization and decentralization of the economy proceeded unevenly. In some sectors, most notably agriculture, the departures were national in scope and the changes profound. Elsewhere—for example, in industry—departures from past policies were partial and often limited to a specific sector or region. As a result, there was a great diversity of social and political outcomes, some of which were even contradictory. Yet even when structural innovations were partial, they still altered popular expectations. Thus, to the extent that the events of June 1989 were the consequence of a revolution of popular expectations, one can identify a connection between the subjects of inquiry in this volume and the turmoil in Tiananmen.

All the chapters in this book were originally presented as papers at a conference at Harvard University in the spring of 1988, and although none analyzes fieldwork done after the massacre, a number of the authors did revisit their field sites in the summer and fall of 1989. Their sources suggest that, despite the political crackdown, the attack on private entrepreneurs, and the restrictions on credit, there is no indication that the basic developments described in this book have been reversed.

DISMANTLING THE MAOIST ECONOMY

In the first three years after Mao's death, the Deng leadership abandoned several ideological mainstays of the Cultural Revolution era. In their rhetoric they overtly endorsed a more individualistic and materialistic reward structure, and they explicitly renounced class struggle as a vehicle for economic mobilization. Yet in practice their words ran ahead of their actions. Before 1980 Deng and his colleagues were slow to dismantle core institutions or even to renounce such orthodox Maoist priorities as self-sufficient local economies, price controls, the primacy of the command economy, or government restraints on geographic mobility. Instead, in the first phase of post-Mao reform, priority was given to consolidation of power at the upper reaches of the Chinese Communist party (CCP) hierarchy.

Beginning in late 1978 Deng Xiaoping moved quickly to rewrite Maoist history. First came a formal reversal of verdicts on the Tiananmen incident of April 1976 in which hundreds had been killed and arrested for their public mourning of Zhou Enlai, and after which Deng himself had been purged. Shortly after came the reevaluation of the 500,000 who had been pilloried as rightists in 1957 and the rehabilitation of Peng Dehuai, whom Mao had banished from the party in 1959. A year later Liu Shaoqi was posthumously returned to the CCP pantheon.

While those at the highest reaches of the party were rehabilitated, however, and official rhetoric switched to endorse material incentives and individual striving, the most outspoken voices of contemporary dissent continued to be methodically silenced. In 1979 the human rights activists Fu Yuehua and Wei Jingsheng were arrested, tried, denied appeals, and sent to solitary confinement. The democracy wall where thousands had hung big-character posters during 1978 and 1979 was initially restricted to government-controlled spaces, and in December 1979 permanently closed. During November of the same year, the National Writers Conference reaffirmed the principles of the 1942 Yan'an forum stating that artistic expression should serve the party. And with no apparent trace of irony or embarrassment, the same delegates who had unanimously approved the rehabilitation of Liu Shaoqi rescinded the constitutional article that protected free speech.

The years 1978 to 1980 were years of political realignments and consolidation. During this time the Deng reformers laid the ideological groundwork for subsequent institutional changes, but overall structural reform was modest, and the societal conflicts that would erupt in spring 1989 were still latent or inchoate.

After the sentencing of the Gang of Four in January 1981, however, the reformers proceeded with extraordinary speed. Within three years people's communes, the institutions that for twenty years had been the cornerstone of Chinese socialism, were replaced by a "household responsibility system," which essentially was the functional equivalent of family farming. Private trade and artisan craftsmen flourished under direct government encouragement in market towns, and throughout rural China the ideological commitments that had dominated the countryside for two decades were in disarray. But new policies were often implemented by old leaders, and new structures were rarely entirely new. Thus, while there was a revolution in ideology and in some basic institutions, the transformation was incomplete. The immediate consequence was a tangled skein of new and old networks of influence and authority.

In urban areas the post-Mao reforms were even less complete. There was no structural parallel to the elimination of the communes, and no comparable surge of private entrepreneurial energy. Large state enterprises continued to be the main employers (see Table 1 in Chapter 4), and the first stages of reform were limited to wage adjustments and increased opportunity for bonus pay. Nevertheless, even without fundamental institutional transformations, the policies of the early 1980s did have a major impact on urban society, primarily in terms of citizens' attitudes and expectations. The ideological shifts sanctioning individual and materialistic aspirations directly undermined the values of collectivity and asceticism that had dominated urban politics and education since 1949. In praising the initiative of independent entrepreneurs, the reformers supported privatization and commodification, with the expectation that such shifts would increase worker productivity and enthusiasm; inadvertently this retreat from Maoist "idealism" legitimated massive cravings for personal possessions and strong preferences for privacy and individual choice. The shift in popular attitudes thereby fostered defections from public obligations and ultimately weakened the ability of the party-state to command popular obedience to the leadership's blueprint of reform.

SOCIAL AND POLITICAL CONSEQUENCES
OF THE POST-MAO REFORMS

Decollectivization, privatization, and commodification unleashed social forces and personal ambitions that had remained dormant throughout most of the Mao era. Their sudden release challenged the preexisting relationship between the Chinese party-state and Chinese society. But even before the events in Tiananmen, it was clear that the party-state remained preeminent and that market reforms were still viewed as a secondary "corrective" by the top leadership and by most enterprise managers and municipal planners. Nevertheless, the party-state's bureaucratic powers varied markedly by region of the country and sector of the economy. Thus any account of the impact of the reforms must recognize that what is true for one segment may not be true for another.

In Part One of this book, three scholars (Jean C. Oi, Tyrene White, and Helen F. Siu) who did fieldwork in rural China in the 1980s begin the process of disaggregating the social and political consequences of a macrolevel national reform on microlevel behavior. Through their observations they not only help us understand the social unrest that precipitated Tiananmen but also prepare the way for an understanding of China in the 1990s.

After several visits to industrialized communes in north China, Jean Oi concludes that the reforms can spawn a new "redistributive corporatism" when most members have left agriculture for employment in rural factories and the new prosperity is redistributed among all households by controlling employment in the collective factories and by upgrading village social services. Oi makes very clear, however, that the strong collective economies of the communes she visited are atypical; in most areas the predominant pattern after the breakup of the communes has been greatly to weaken collective forces. But Oi also emphasizes that the successful redistributive corporatism she observed is a direct consequence of the reformers' policy of promoting local entrepreneurial initiatives and releasing communes from grain quotas. Moreover, probably many of the new "community enterprises" *(xiangzhen qiye)* that have prospered under the control of local towns and large villages have in part thrived because of a continuity with past collective leaders and a basic identification with the locality rather than just with the enterprise.

By contrast, Tyrene White, observing political as well as economic consequences in Hubei, identifies less positive outcomes of decollectivization. Even among several relatively affluent areas outside Wuhan, she saw little new collective wealth despite a good deal of leadership continuity. Instead what most impressed her was the increased number of rural bureaucrats and the increased estrangement of ordinary peasants from rural cadres. The party apparatus had been formally separated from government organs, but the result of this separation was the creation of two parallel channels of party power rather than a reduction of political supervision. Quite clearly in this region the reforms had produced a bloated but weakened state apparatus. The losers were both the ordinary citizens, who had to negotiate an even less efficient local bureaucracy to secure the key inputs that continued to flow through administrative channels, and the provincial leaders, who had less effective control over local representatives of government and party offices.

In Helen Siu's work in the Pearl River Delta, we gain yet another perspective on how the collapse of the old commune structure only partially altered the Maoist distribution of power and status. From 1958 to 1980 Chinese citizens with rural household registrations (*hukou*) were uniformly denied a vast array of government subsidies and services that were routinely available to almost all those with urban registrations. In Siu's field site this was true even when the distance between a rural and an urban household was no greater than the width of a narrow creek or a dusty country road. After the collapse of the communes, the reforms somewhat lessened these past inequalities between rural and urban residents. Many rural residents earned higher incomes than urbanites, and within limits they could ignore the much resented policy of a one-child family. Nevertheless, in 1986 Siu still found that delta residents without an urban *hukou* perceived themselves as disadvantaged, and she concludes that the reforms barely altered the bureaucratic privileges that perpetuated the basic hierarchies of social prestige created in the Maoist era. Thus, even in the Guangdong "showcase" of economic liberalization, those who held rural household registrations continued to face political and social exclusion.

The next two parts of the book discuss the impact of the reforms on urban China. Because there has been no structural shift as central or dramatic as the dismantling of the communes, it is not surprising that several authors, most notably Deborah Davis and Yves Chevrier, stress the continuities between the pre- and postreform years. In the case of the urban workers and factory managers analyzed by Davis and Chevrier (Chapters 4 and 5), the key to continuity was the unchanging role of administrative controls in the urban workplace, ideological resistance to a labor market, and the limited ability of the Deng reformers to achieve economic efficiency without changes in political control. Chevrier, who is especially interested in the "statecraft of modernization," analyzes how efforts to create a new class of managers failed because the Chinese state was in fact too weak to institutionalize new power. A historian by profession, Chevrier also notes an interesting parallel between CCP inability to cede an autonomous role to management and the hostility of Qing emperors to challenges from an autonomous merchant class. The parallel suggests that some of the continuities between the Mao and Deng years are as rooted in a shared Chinese bureaucratic past as in a shared commitment to Leninist democratic centralism and communist rejection of labor markets.

Not all the contributors to this volume who observed the urban scene, however, emphasize the limited impact of urban reform. Using a 1986 survey of income trends in Tianjin, Andrew Walder (Chapter 6) documents a dramatic decrease in income inequality among urban employees after 1976. Thomas Gold (Chapter 7), analyzing the emergence of urban entrepreneurs *(geti hu),* also stresses change rather than continuity. In the cities where he has conducted his fieldwork, Gold has found the *geti hu* to be a new social stratum of wealthy consumers whose reliance on a cash nexus not only engenders enormous envy but also suggests the potential for a "fundamental change in Chinese social structure."

Although both Walder and Gold note considerable change, their observations lead to somewhat different implications for social solidarity. Among workers in Tianjin, reduced wage inequality brought less rather than more social differentiation. By contrast, the *geti hu* interviewed by Gold earned incomes three or four times higher than that of an average worker; therefore he documents the emergence of a more heterogeneous and perhaps even economically polarized urban society. Moreover, Gold goes beyond his immediate data and cautiously hypothesizes that contained within this emerging stratum of urban entrepreneurs are the seeds of a new civil society that could challenge the ideological and political hegemony of the CCP. Little wonder then that those committed to socialist planning who emerged stronger after June 1989 should have tightened control over these emerging entrepreneurs who absorbed wealth, materials, and even labor power that might otherwise have gone to established state enterprises.

In the two chapters on family relations, Martin Whyte (Chapter 8) and Charlotte Ikels (Chapter 9) explore private domains of urban life that in most cases have been only indirectly affected by the major economic reforms. In both cases the authors found little evidence of an increasingly empowered or even significantly altered civil society. Instead, what most impressed Whyte in his study of marriage practices in Chengdu was the apparent "stalled convergence" in mate choice. In the first decade after the CCP victory, Chengdu couples quickly moved away from traditional practices of arranged "blind" marriages and began to converge toward the Western pattern of love matches. In the 1960s and 1970s, however, this convergence "stalled," and after nearly ten years of Deng reform Whyte could still find no major departures from the Maoist practices of the 1970s.

In her study of the elderly and their families in Guangzhou, Ikels also found little evidence that the policy of the Deng reforms—in this case as expressed through increased cost-consciousness and the rapid shift to a more commercial and expensive life style in Guangzhou—had directly affected the position of the elderly in their families or the quality of the care they received. Inflation, greater mobility, and the rising cost of medical care had, however, appeared to heighten concern about future arrangements, and Ikels writes in some detail about innovative community programs that Guangzhou residents have envisioned.

Even the authors in this volume who have observed social changes after 1978 found little evidence that any nonparty, nonstate agents offered alternatives to the existing hierarchies of party and state power. Instead in both rural and urban contexts, most evidence suggests that in this first decade of reform many people became more concerned with personal and family advancement, and few overtly or directly challenged party or state authorities.

In Chapter 10 Richard Madsen looks at those whom one would most expect to present radical new visions, the urban intellectuals and artists, who in Eastern Europe and in precommunist China have been among the first to envision and create alternative viewpoints. In his interviews in 1988 and early 1989, however, Madsen found that among those whom one might expect to be most articulate there were instead high levels of ambivalence and confusion. Madsen attributes this outcome partially to shifting government policy toward intellectual dissent, but primarily to the contradictory self-image of Chinese intellectuals who find themselves torn between traditional expectations of the intellectual in service to the state and a modern ethic promoting professional and intellectual autonomy. Among his respondents Madsen witnessed a high level of ideological and psychological conflict that often left them with an "aimless, fragmented liveliness" and prevented them from finding coherence in the cultural turbulence created by the collapse of Maoist institutions and ideals. Yet in the months since June 1989 Madsen has also been impressed by the power of the intellectual critique emanating from the exiled intellectuals who took refuge in Western Europe and North America, and by the strength they draw from their membership in a transnational community of professionals. When they can link up with their colleagues in China, Madsen is confident that the Chinese polity will be fundamentally changed. Thus, while in the short term he finds little evidence for a basic realignment of social power, in the long-term view he, like Gold, sees a new civil society beginning to take root.

The last part of the book considers the impact of the reforms on national-level constituencies. Gail Henderson (Chapter 11) evaluates the impact of the reforms on the cost and quality of medical care. Stanley Rosen (Chapter 12) analyzes their impact on the attitudes and ambitions of youth. In both cases the reforms produced clear departures from the Mao years. Henderson found that the decentralization and privatization of medicine changed the distribution of and access to health resources. New investment in high-technology equipment, renewed focus on hospital-based care, and increased commodification created a wider range of services. But because these advances were coupled with reduced insurance coverage and higher charges, the greatest benefits have gone to the wealthiest; those in the poorest regions or with few personal or organizational resources are more disadvantaged now than they were in the 1970s.

Rosen, while briefly noting the impact of the reforms on the distribution of educational opportunity, focuses primarily on how the reforms have affected attitudes among college and high-school students. Like Madsen, he observes that economic liberalization has fostered ideals and ambitions that simultaneously challenge Maoist orthodoxies and the ideological priorities of the Deng reformers. Official praise of private entrepreneurs and reduced control over school and job choices allow young people coming of age in the mid-1980s to hold views radically different from those of youth in the Mao years. These young people of the late 1980s are blatantly materialistic, and they perceive themselves as individuals who deserve options different from those of their parents and older siblings. Many actively reject the old choices of the military or the Youth League as reliable routes to adult success, thereby leaving the CCP leadership with the difficult task of ensuring political loyalty through manipulation of material rewards. Rosen is uncertain whether these trends will be reversed by the policies adopted by the central leaders after June 1989, but his extensive review of Chinese surveys of youth in the early and mid-1980s gives strong evidence of a direct link between the reformist policies and student opinion, and of the volatile nature of this social stratum.

China's efforts to decollectivize and spur entrepreneurial energies have many parallels with the experiments begun in Eastern Europe in the 1960s. In both situations communist bureaucrats tried to graft components of market choice and competition onto a command economy in the hope of improving efficiency and productivity. In Eastern Europe the result was a dual dependency in which markets shaped some economic decisions but hierarchies dominated, and entrenched bureaucrats alternated between cycles of relaxation and repression. Among Eastern European intellectuals who have addressed the limits of market reform, the works of the sociologist Ivan Szelenyi and the economist Janos Kornai bear directly on the societal shifts in post-Mao China.

For Kornai the key to persistent bureaucratic power is the ever-present "soft budget constraints" that prevent the harsh messages of the market from changing the behavior of socialist firms. Whenever a firm that would face extinction in a market economy flounders, the state budget comes to the rescue and prevents the firm from effectively changing its behavior. Even in periods when the leadership overtly strives to increase market guidance or rationality, bureaucratic controls do not disappear, because government administrators, even as they push others to cede control to the market, act defensively to guard against their own loss of power or privileges by adding new layers of regulation or by shifting their attention to previously unregulated areas.[1]

As Szelenyi emphasizes even more than Kornai, behind any reform of prices and firm behavior are prior political problems that emerge whenever reform challenges the exclusionary property relationships of a communist party-state.[2] Party bureaucrats come to the rescue of inefficient state firms because they themselves are functional owners of these enterprises, and it is not in their own long-term interests to extinguish these enterprises. Therefore, to reduce fundamentally the preeminence of bureaucratic party power, a reform must realign existing hierarchies of class relations and allow new political alliances. In Hungary, Szelenyi found that the drive for this level of change comes largely from employment outside the state sector and, in particular, from the rise of new entrepreneurs in private agriculture and the service sectors. In the transition phase one finds an emerging dual class structure, with cadre elite at the apex of the state "redistributive" economy and entrepreneurs at the apex of the emerging market sector. Szelenyi's optimistic reading of this increasing social differentiation is to hypothesize the emergence of new class alliances that will ultimately produce both prosperity and democracy.

Overall, Kornai's and Szelenyi's analyses of the persistence of bureaucratic power are relevant to Chinese reform. Support for greater commodification and decentralization altered popular expectations in China and in some cases changed performance. But as the studies in this volume suggest, these shifts away from state coordination were also frequently slowed or obstructed by the prereform authority and power structures.

The Deng reforms produced a new distribution of wealth and power within villages, within factories, and among regions. Although the final tally of winners and losers was unknown by the spring of 1989, it was clear that the status quo ante could not continue to go unchallenged, and both among the elite and the general population there were increasingly sharp disagreements about how to distribute the costs and benefits of the economic reforms. Relaxed controls over private markets and greater commodification of goods and services had increased the role of money in social exchanges. Not unexpectedly, financial corruption emerged as a national issue as it had not for nearly forty years. The reformers' efforts to establish markets and to monetize also created new price structures and unprecedented shortages of key consumer goods that fueled inflation. By the standards of many nations the rate of inflation had not reached astronomical heights, but because under CCP policies from 1952 to 1982 Chinese citizens had grown accustomed to virtually no inflation for basic goods and services, the escalating prices for grain, clothing, and vegetables aroused great anxiety. Thus, even when the reforms succeeded in unleashing unprecedented economic growth and diversification, they also aggravated social tensions that divided Chinese society and frightened the leaders in Beijing.

The twelve chapters in this book address these varied responses from a range of different vantage points. Some of the authors emphasize change; others stress continuities. Yet when read as an overview of Chinese society in the mid-1980s, the collective voice of this volume describes conditions that not only distinguish these years from those of the 1960s and 1970s but also identify underlying societal forces that are unlikely to be fully extinguished by short-term retreats from full-scale reform.

PART ONE

Rural Society and Politics

The Fate of the Collective after the Commune

JEAN C. OI

Just two years after the death of Mao Zedong, the December 1978 Third Plenum of the Eleventh Party Congress opened the door to a new era of rural development. Within less than a decade of the Chairman's death, the structural features of collectivized agriculture that defined Maoist socialism were gone. In rapid succession the government reopened markets, turned to economic incentives to procure agricultural goods, diversified the rural economy away from its singular emphasis on grain production, replaced the communal system of agricultural production with the household responsibility system,[1] and abolished the system of unified procurement in favor of contract purchases of grain and cotton.[2]

Much like land reform, land parcels, tools, boats, fishnets, tractors, even entire factories were redistributed to peasant households in millions of production teams (and brigades) throughout the People's Republic of China (PRC) in the early 1980s. But unlike the first land reform, after the property had been redistributed, ownership of the major means of production—land, factories, and large pieces of equipment—remained with the original owners, the collective. Individuals acquired the right merely to *lease* the use of this property for specified amounts of time. Only tools and smaller equipment were sold or apportioned to individual households.[3]

While ownership remained collective, the division of property spelled the death of the production team, which had been the basic unit of accounting and production. Offices stood empty, the team became obsolete as a level of administration and eventually was abolished, replaced in some places by what is called the village small group.[4] Officially it still owned all the land and most of the property, but team cadres no longer directed production; and, most important, the team no longer had any legal claim on the harvest. The household became the official unit of accounting and production.

For the individual peasant household this allows, to a degree unprecedented since collectivization began in the 1950s, the right to decide the division of the harvest. No longer are peasants dependent on the collective for their basic food supply; no longer do ceilings exist on the amount that peasants can consume. Work points, grain rationing, and state-set limits on consumption are relics of the past.[5] No longer is the collective allowed to retain grain for fodder, seed, rations, or local grain reserves. The reforms nullified the local grain reserve system and put stricter limits on the amount of funds that villages had to expend on public works projects, which during the Maoist period had used up substantial amounts of a team's reserves. The collective no longer stands between peasants and their harvests. The village gets only the grain that the state provides, that peasants might voluntarily contribute to the village, or that it can illegally squeeze from the peasants through ad hoc surcharges.

The central state still competes as a claimant for the harvest, but the terms are more in the peasants' favor.[6] The agricultural tax remains as inevitable as ever but is decreasing relative to the increasing size of the harvests. In 1983 it was only 4.1 percent of the total grain output; after tax remissions and reductions, the actual rate was only 3 percent, which is the lowest in the PRC's history (21 percent of the tax levied in 1952).[7] In poor areas that do not meet minimal levels of production and distribution, the agricultural tax has been reduced and in some cases eliminated.[8]

Although peasants must still sell grain to the state, and although the contract-purchase system is essentially the same compulsory sales in new guise, the state now pays peasants more for the grain it procures. In 1979, for the first time in over a decade, the state increased procurement prices, paying 20 percent more for basic procurements and 50 percent more for overquota procurements. Initially sufficient to induce peasants to grow more grain, procurement prices later failed to offset the high costs of inputs that make grain production unprofitable. Overall, in spite of continued shortcomings, the situation has improved over the Maoist period, when sales cut into peasant subsistence. The reforms mark a dramatic shift from a strategy based almost exclusively on administrative measures to one that features economic incentives, including increased procurement prices and production of consumer goods to secure a sufficient grain supply.[9]

The demise of the production team, the return to household farming, the policies encouraging some peasants to get ahead first, to "dare to stick out," all suggest that the family and the individual have become the all-important units. The question is whether this emphasis on individuals and entrepreneurship also means the demise of those mechanisms that redistribute income and provide social welfare—what I refer to here as the fate of the "collective," that often used but vaguely defined term that embodies the socialist ideals of community commonly associated with the Maoist period.

A related question is whether these reforms also signify the withdrawal of local governments from managing local economic activities. It would certainly be reasonable to assume that peasants now have autonomy to manage the land or enterprises that they contract. This certainly has been the case for land, as I suggested above. But can we make the same assumptions about the operation of the other collective properties, specifically the fast-growing rural industries?

Early reports of empty collective coffers as well as team offices, decreased collective welfare funds for village schools and clinics, the end of health insurance, the decay of village irrigation systems and roads, and the marked inequality of income with the emergence of 10,000-yuan households that have resulted from the responsibility system suggest that the era of the "collective" as well as the power of local governments ended with the reforms. My own research, however, suggests that such a conclusion may only describe a transition period and may hold only for certain types of villages. Such is not necessarily the fate for all villages under the reforms.

There is no simple, direct correlation between the post-1978 reforms and the demise of the collective. My research in the Chinese countryside in 1985, 1986, and 1988[10] found that some villages remain strong corporate entities, where local governments intervene in the economy, redistribute substantial amounts of income to their members, provide impressive social services, and generally give villagers a stake in remaining part of the collective.

The fate of the collective is linked not to the structural reforms as such, but to the *sources of income* in a village, specifically the degree of industrialization in a village after the adoption of the household-responsibility system. My main contention here is that the fate of the collective is correlated with the level of industrialization. The higher the level of industrialization, the more likely that local government will act in a corporate manner to intervene, extract, and redistribute income.

Villages that rely exclusively on agriculture, particularly in the more remote areas—those with little or no industry or other income-generating activity—are left with few (legal) income sources because they get neither a share of the agricultural tax nor the profits from peasant sales of grain to the state—the only major assessments on farm income—for both go to the central state.[11] Peasants have autonomy over the management of their work and direct control over the profits from their harvests. Hence villages that rely primarily on agriculture are the most likely to have experienced a decline of the collective in both fiscal and organizational terms.

Villages that have nonagricultural enterprises, in contrast, are able to exert considerable administrative and fiscal control. Income from industry, which in some villages may be many times greater than that from agriculture, provides a collective cohesion that some feared would disappear with the reforms. This further suggests that a village may have suffered from problems of empty coffers immediately after the reforms were instituted, but such developments, as the World Bank study also suggests, were in some cases only temporary setbacks.[12] Once it became clear which way the policy winds would blow, enterprises were established, incomes were generated, and previously existing local governments and local services were resumed.

The problem is that the development of industry has been uneven, not only within but among regions.[13] The World Bank, for example, has shown that the nominal value of the industrial output of rural enterprises rose by 415 percent in Zhejiang but only by 37 percent in Inner

Mongolia. Eight of China's provinces had increases in the nominal value of industrial output greater than 250 percent, but seven had increases less than 120 percent. Even in the coastal provinces as a whole, including all of Guangdong, Fujian, Jiangsu, Shandong, and Liaoning, the township enterprises employed only 27.6 percent of the total rural labor force. In contrast, in the most highly developed areas, such as Wuxi, Suzhou, Changzhou, Zhujiang Delta, and Yantai in Shandong, 70 to 80 percent of the rural labor force is employed in rural industry.

I should make clear from the start that the villages on which this study is based are in no way representative. If anything, they tend to fall into the categories of developed and highly developed.[14] All these villages were near or at least had access to major cities and were at least partially industrialized. Thus any generalizations I make apply primarily to villages that have taken advantage of the reforms.

Precisely because my findings are so strikingly at odds with earlier reports, I suggest that we have perhaps been too narrow in our focus, looking only at what has happened to the production team and to the agricultural sector to predict the fate of the collective. To assess fully the impact of the reforms, one must look at what has happened to the industrial sector of the rural economy as well.[15]

Moreover, my intention is not to argue for the continued use of the term *collective*. That only causes confusion because of the ideological baggage the term carries from the Maoist period.[16] I use the term here simply to provide a familiar frame of reference to gauge the current strength of local governments, at the township and the village levels, to intervene and provide for the welfare of the "group" rather than just the individual. The less tangible aspects of "collective," such as the general spirit of community, identification with the group, and so on, are amorphous, and I am not able to provide any measure of them here. Nor do my data allow me to provide "hard" measures of the strength of the collective; all I can do is point to trends and indications suggesting that village and township governments are taking steps that show concern for the "collective." As rough indices, I shall examine the ability of local governments to (1) extract a portion of the income of rural enterprises; (2) intervene in the management of enterprises and the use of profits to promote collective interests; and (3) redistribute that income to provide basic social services and care for collective members, and to minimize differences in incomes. Finally, I make no connection between the strength of the "collective" and equality of income.

TABLE 1   Agriculture as Percentage of Total Rural Income,
          1980–1987

Year	% Total Rural Income	Year	% Total Rural Income
1980	68.9	1985	57.1
1983	66.7	1986	53.1
1984	63.2	1987	49.6

Source: ZGTJNJ 1988, p. 214.

I use the township and village as my units of analysis because they are the two levels of rural administration that constitute the peasant community (successor to the brigade and commune) and within which peasants still conduct most of their social and economic business. They are the levels of administration with which peasants have routine contact and which interpret the state's policies.

INDUSTRY AS THE NEW BASIS OF THE COLLECTIVE

Collective coffers gained little from the agricultural sector after the institution of the household responsibility system, but agriculture is no longer the major source of income in China's villages. Nationally, from 1980 to 1987, agriculture dropped almost 20 percent as a proportion of total rural income, to the point where it was less than half by 1987 (see Table 1).

Nonagricultural enterprises have become the moneymakers, in terms of both output value and individual incomes. By 1987, nationwide, "the gross value of output of rural enterprises (including village and township enterprises) exceeded the gross value of agricultural output for the first time."[17] According to Xiang Zhongyang, vice minister of agriculture, animal husbandry, and fishery, from 1979 to 1986 rural industries contributed 25 percent of the increase in China's gross total domestic product and 57 percent of the increase in its gross rural domestic product. From 1979 to 1986, 20 percent of the peasants' increased income came from rural industry.[18] Moreover, these rural industries also earned more than 40 billion yuan in exports.[19]

Not only are rural enterprises the major producer of income, but they are fast becoming both the prime and the preferred employers. As a consequence of the new mobility allowed by the reforms, and as work in

TABLE 2   Nonagricultural Production as Percentage of Total
Rural Income, 1980–1987

Year	Industry	Construction	Transport	Commerce and Catering
1980	19.5	6.4	1.7	3.5
1983	20.0	7.8	2.0	3.5
1984	23.1	7.4	2.6	3.7
1985	27.6	8.1	3.0	4.2
1986	31.5	7.8	3.3	4.3
1987	34.8	7.7	3.5	4.4

Source: ZGTJNJ 1988, p. 214.

agriculture becomes less lucrative than in industry and the service trades,
more peasants are leaving farming.[20] The numbers employed in rural
enterprises more than doubled between 1983 and 1987, rising from 32.4
million to 87.8 million.[21] From the beginning of the reforms in 1978
to 1986, 57 million new nonagricultural jobs were added; this number
equals the total number of workers hired in all state-owned enterprises
from 1952 to 1986.[22] The World Bank has estimated that between 1980
and 1986 employment outside of agriculture in rural areas grew 14 percent per year; during that period the nonagricultural labor force increased
by 124 percent, or over 30 million people. This figure, however, seems
to include only jobs in nonagricultural material-producing sectors, namely
industry, construction, transportation, and commerce, excluding the service sector.[23]

The category "rural enterprise" includes various types of ventures, from
factories to food stalls, and from collective to private owned. The growth
for this category as a whole is impressive. Their number quadrupled in
1984 alone.[24] By 1987 the total number equaled more than 17 million;
by comparison in 1978 there were a mere 1.52 million such enterprises.[25]

But, within this broad category, rural industry has been the driving
force that has fueled the economy. For the period 1980 to 1987, nationally, rural industry *(gongye)* produced more than double the income of
any of the other sectors (see Table 2). As Table 3 shows, even at the
level of the village where enterprises tend to be smaller scale, income
from industrial enterprises has grown fairly steadily as a percentage of
total product value for the country as a whole.

In the suburban villages I studied, industry is quickly becoming, if it

TABLE 3   Village-Owned Industrial Enterprises as
Percentage of Total Rural Product Value,
1975–1984

Year	% Total Rural Product Value	Year	% Total Rural Product Value
1975	6.4	1980	11.2
1976	9.1	1981	11.7
1977	11.0	1982	11.6
1978	11.7	1983	13.0
1979	12.5	1984	17.1

Source: ZGTJNJ 1985, p. 214.

is not already, the primary source of income. For example, in one village outside Shenyang, agriculture contributed 7.3 percent to total income, whereas industry contributed 63.6 percent.[26] One of the most extreme cases is a village outside Tianjin, where only 9 peasants still farm; the other 1,500 working members of the community earn their living in the village's 149 enterprises.[27]

The impetus to build factories is not only the increased profitability from a plot of land put to industrial use but also jobs for the surplus rural labor. Nationally, China has one of the lowest arable-land-per-capita ratios in the world, 1.5 *mu*, which is only one-third the world average.[28] The population-to-land ratios are particularly high in parts of China that are now highly industrialized, such as Wenzhou; there the land per capita is under one-half *mu*.[29] The land-to-agricultural-labor ratio declined from 8.7 to only 3.9 *mu* between 1957 and 1985. Currently, there are an estimated 100 million surplus rural laborers, all of whom the state hopes will soon be absorbed into rural industry.[30]

The private sector is growing in China but is concentrated in the services. According to a study done by the State Council, only 13 percent of individual entrepreneurs are engaged in industry. Furthermore, of those only a little over 4 percent have capital holdings over 10,000 *yuan*, and this includes those engaged in handicraft production.[31] Most of the large industrial concerns are owned in most parts of China by the collective, not individuals. In the remainder of this chapter, I shall limit my discussion to rural industries owned by either township, village, or the former team governments—industries known as "township (and town) enterprises" *(xiangzhen qiye)*.

TABLE 4 Number of People Employed in Township
Enterprises, 1982–1987

Year	People Employed (in millions)	Year	People Employed (in millions)
1982	31.13	1986	43.92
1983	32.35	1987	47.02
1985	41.52		

Sources: ZGTJNJ 1984, pp. 184–185; 1987, p. 205; and 1988, p. 287.

The number of these collectively owned enterprises, approximately 1.5 million, is only a small portion of the total number of rural enterprises. However, their importance and the amount of income they generate is far greater than their absolute number suggests. *Xiangzhen qiye* in 1986 and 1987 contributed 32.3 percent and 34.9 percent, respectively, to the total agricultural income.[32] By 1987, township enterprises employed nearly 47 million people (see Table 4).[33] As Table 5 shows, they are fairly evenly divided between township and village owned enterprises, with township enterprises gaining slightly.

TABLE 5 Percentage of People Employed in Township and
Village-Owned Enterprises, 1982–1987

Year	% People Employed		Year	% People Employed	
	Township	Village		Township	Village
1983	48.4	51.6	1986	51.8	48.2
1984	48.8	51.2	1987	50.7	49.3
1985	50.8	49.2			

Sources: ZGTJNJ 1984, pp. 184–185; 1985, p. 297; 1987, p. 205; and 1988, p. 287.

The Rural Enterprise Contract System

The key to understanding how local government is able to maintain effective control over the financial flows of village and township industries lies in the terms of the contract-responsibility system for rural enterprises. On the surface the responsibility system is deceptively simple: the contractor pays taxes to the state, a rent, and perhaps a management fee[34] or surcharge to the village or township government that owns the enterprise. Once those obligations are fulfilled, one might assume that contractors of a rural enterprise enjoy the autonomy of management and rights to profits similar to those enjoyed by peasants who contract farmland. Peasants who have contracted to manage enterprises have made huge profits, but the relationship between contractors of enterprises and the village or township is, however, much more complex than the bare outlines of the responsibility system would indicate. The managers benefit from the profits and bonuses, but they do not have the autonomy that one might associate with a leasing situation.

Local governments still exert significant control over their enterprises through a web of rules and regulations that go beyond the collection of rents or management fees. In contrast to their withdrawal from day-to-day management in agriculture, local governments continue to limit management autonomy, use of enterprise profits, access to credit, and allocation of investment opportunities and key inputs.[35]

The term *contract* is used to describe the relationship between the government and the individual entrepreneur but is somewhat misleading for a Western audience. A contract in this context does not necessarily denote a legally binding agreement negotiated by two parties of equal status. Village governments as owners of the enterprise are unquestionably the party with the power to determine the terms of the contract. They set the rents, determine the profit margins, and, as we shall see later, have the right to intervene in the internal management of the enterprise after it has been contracted out. Moreover, when they feel that the interests of the collective are no longer served by the terms of the contract, it is not uncommon for the contract to be unilaterally nullified and new terms drawn up. Contractors in this situation are often left with no recourse, even though in theory they are protected by law. This has been the case in those enterprises that have turned out to be unexpectedly profitable.[36]

Nationwide, in 1984 *xiang* (township) and *cun* (village) governments commanded overall 43.9 percent of after-tax profits from rural enterprises.[37] In highly developed areas, such as Wuxi, 45 percent of after-tax profits were submitted to the *xiang* government.[38] In 1988 one village in Shandong took approximately 70 percent of profits from enterprises, if taxes are included.[39] Regardless of differences in specific localities, overall the amounts were excessive enough that the press, in discussing reform of township enterprises, warned that "township enterprises should not be treated as 'small cash registers' from which money can be taken at will" by their local governments.[40]

A large part of the problem that underlies many of the current difficulties encountered by entrepreneurs is that contracts have been introduced in a context where planning still dominates. The plan, not the market, still reigns supreme. In those villages where I conducted interviews, economic enterprises, both those that have been contracted to individuals under the responsibility system and those that remain under collective management, are still subject to numerous plans, targets, and quotas set by the village and township governments. Granted there have been changes; only some plans and targets are to be strictly adhered to. Some are now "guidance plans" *(zhidaoxing jihua)* rather than the old mandatory plans *(zhilingxing jihua)*. The difference, however, is blurred.

One official in China who tried to explain the difference between mandatory and guidance plans said: "Mandatory plans are like putting a ring through the nose of an ox and pulling it where you want it to go. Guidance plans are like letting the ox go where it wants to go, but not feeding it if it refuses to go where you want it to go." Theoretically, mandatory plans are achieved through the use of administrative fiat, whereas guidance plans are achieved through the use of economic incentives. In practice at the local level, however, the distinction is not clear; guidance plans often seem to carry as much weight as mandatory plans.

Evidence of the continued importance of planning is found in the fact that some factory managers who have contracted an enterprise have no say in who is hired; they are forced to keep on the payroll unneeded and unwanted personnel. In an exhaust-fan factory near Tianjin, when workers are needed, the township government appoints and apportions the jobs among the villages and village small groups (former production teams). The township industrial company *(gongye gongsi)* takes care of labor allocation and administers qualifying examinations to workers when necessary.[41]

The plan is also felt in a factory's decisions with regard to product line. In some factories such plans are still mandatory; in others they are guidance plans. In those factories that produce "key items" and acquire supplies from the government at state prices, the plans for production and sale are mandatory. For example, the exhaust-fan factory outside Tianjin gets 80 percent of its supplies from the state, specifically the Tianjin Planning Commission, so the majority of its production is dictated by the state plan.[42]

It is much less clear how closely a factory must adhere to its guidance production plan. What is clear, however, is that those factories that adhere to what is desired by the local governments have the best chances of success. Local governments can give selected factories that decide to accept the carrot rather than fight the stick crucial assistance in the areas of loans, investment opportunities, raw materials,[43] and markets for finished goods.[44] The free market now exists, but the issue in China for so many items is not price but access and convenience, which often translates into having the proper connections *(guanxi).*[45] The result is a mix of regulation and continuation of the "iron-rice-bowl" paternalism that characterized the pre-reform urban state-owned sector.[46]

For example, one of the most coveted and profitable arrangements for rural industry is to land a contract with an urban unit. This usually is an industrial unit, but it may also be a "scientific unit," such as a university or a scientific lab developing new products. The urban and rural units form a "horizontal linkage" *(hengxiang lianhe),* whereby the rural partner does all or part of the production and assembly process. The urban partner is responsible for supplying the raw materials and agrees to market or purchase the output of the rural factory.[47]

Village governments can be instrumental in finding such opportunities. Outside Tianjin, for instance, village officials arrange special tours to their factories. In Sichuan, near Chengdu, various government offices, including those at the county level, actively seek cooperative relationships for rural industries.[48] Officials everywhere repeatedly said: "*Guanxi* is important in getting business. We have built up old connections and now use them."

This administrative power of local governments is translated into fiscal control through a number of different mechanisms, the most direct of which is the exaction of rents. But before describing the different rent systems, I should explain that in addition to controlling that portion taken out of an enterprise in rents, local authorities can control the profits that remain in an enterprise. A factory manager, like his urban counterpart, has little leeway to use the factory's profits as incentives for workers. Some regulations specify that 50 percent of the after-tax profits be plowed back into the factory to expand production, and only 20 percent can be used as bonuses and benefits *(fuli);*[49] others specify that 70 percent of a factory's retained profits be used for reinvestment.[50] Some local regulations further mandate that the remaining 30 percent of the profits go to the collective to subsidize agriculture and provide for village welfare.[51]

The Determination of Rents

There are currently three major types of rental arrangements by which individuals can contract from a township or village the right to work and earn profits from a collectively owned enterprise: (1) fixed rent, (2) floating rate calculated as a percentage of profits, and (3) factory-manager responsibility system.[52]

The first method is the one that was most commonly used, especially at the village level, in the early stages of the reforms. Villages simply set a profit target and allowed the contractor to keep any over-quota profit. But as the reforms took hold and governments gained some sophistication and saw how successful some of the enterprises were under private management, officials soon developed more effective ways of getting income.

Some governments turned to the floating rent or percentage system, whereby all profits up to a set amount are divided between the legal owner, the village or township government, and the contractor, according to a ratio set by local authorities.[53] For example, in a village outside Shenyang, originally contractors paid a fixed amount regardless of profits and were entitled to their over-quota profits. Beginning in 1985, however, this village switched to a floating percentage rent. The village set the ratio for the division of profits at either 7:3 or 8:2, with the collective getting the larger share. In this particular village the latter ratio is put into effect if the income is expected to be high.[54]

In addition, it seems that, regardless of whether the rent is fixed or a percentage of profits, there is a second set of ratios to divide the over-quota profits between the village or township and the contractor *(lirun baogan chaoli fencheng)*. Of the over-quota profits that a contractor can retain, a set percentage is designated to go back into the factory, with a portion given to the workers. In one village the ratio is 2:3:5—the village gets 20 percent, the contractor 30 percent, and the factory 50 percent.[55] In one township the ratio for township-owned enterprises was 1:1:3:5—10 percent for the economic commission; 10 percent for the contractor; 30 percent for bonuses; and 50 percent for reinvestment.[56] In yet another township the percentage changed depending on the size of the over-quota profits.[57] Through these mechanisms local governments are trying to assure themselves of a minimum profit and still get a share of any unexpected profits.[58]

A third and increasingly common alternative is the factory-manager contracting system, whereby the village or township continues to control all of a factory's profits and the contractors receive only a bonus wage. This arrangement allows the government authorities maximum financial control because it is essentially only a work responsibility system that fines factory managers if quotas are not met.

Under this system the enterprise is not contracted to an individual but to the factory as a collective entity, including both management and workers. Because it is difficult to deal with all members of the collective, the factory manager, and sometimes his top staff, act as the principal contractors and representatives of the collective in dealings with the outside and are given primary responsibility for meeting the quotas.

But unlike other contract systems, the factory manager and his staff, instead of getting a set percentage of the profits, receive a bonus from the village or township government if the factory meets the targets set by the industrial corporation *(gongye gongsi)*. This provides the manager and other cadres, such as the accountant, with a salary about twice that of the average worker. For example, in Nanjiao district outside Tianjin, the factory manager of a collective exhaust-fan factory makes a contract with the township to meet production and profit targets. He gets a bonus, including such items as a wristwatch, from the township if he exceeds the targets and his performance is considered outstanding.[59] In Shandong some villages limit the factory manager's salary to 20 percent more than the highest-paid worker's.[60] But in other townships in Shandong, the factory manager/contractor is allowed to make three to four times the salary of the average worker.[61] Contrast this to the situation in Da Qiuzhuang (village), near Tianjin, where factory managers/contractors earn as much as 10,000 to 20,000 yuan a year. Interestingly, this amount is less than the 80,000 some are entitled to. Apparently the local leadership decided that it was better to use more of this money for development and subsidies, especially because the managers were making more than they could possibly need.[62]

How should one interpret these changes in the rent systems? Obviously one reason is that both the percentage system and the factory-manager responsibility system allow local authorities a bigger share of the profits; and in the case of the factory-manager responsibility system, maximum control. Village officials justify such changes by citing a number of different concerns.

In interviews officials said that the factory-manager responsibility system was superior because they feared that if an enterprise were contracted to private individuals, they would not take care of the equipment but would merely try to make as much as possible off the factory the first year and be done with it. Officials also said that the majority of enterprises were too large for most individuals to handle, too much of a risk. Along similar lines officials also pointed out that the floating system would protect the contractor if problems arose that prevented him from meeting the set target.

Aside from profits and minimizing risks, there is an additional consideration that directly bears on our discussion of the collective. Both the percentage system and particularly the factory-manager responsibility system promote a greater degree of equality within a peasant community. A revealing article in the *Nongye jingji wenti* (*Problems of agricultural economy*) criticizes the individual contracting system for allowing an individual or a small group of management personnel, including factory directors, to earn much more than the mass of the workers and thus exploit their labor. It asks the question whether the value created by the labor of certain contractors is really worth so much more than that of ordinary workers; the answer was a definite no.[63]

Similar concerns were expressed when a village official explained the change from a fixed to a floating rate of rent, which reduces the amount of profit that an individual can obtain. He justified the change by explaining that the fixed rate had allowed entrepreneurs of particularly successful enterprises "to stand out too much." The set profit quota system was too unregulated. The three levels of interest—the state, the collective, and the individual—were not in harmony. The percentage rate would ensure more equality.[64]

THE NEW REDISTRIBUTIVE SOCIALISM

Having established that local governments have access to or can indirectly control substantial sums of profit from rural industry, let me now ask: Do they use this income to provide subsidies to promote the well-being of the collective, in addition to allowing certain individuals to prosper?

Direct Subsidies

Villages with highly developed industries have taken the funds they extract and the profits they make from such services as the sale of raw materials to provide impressive services and benefits to the villagers, whether they work in rural industry or remain in farming.[65] For example, highly industrialized, wealthy villages have built schools, apartments and houses, movie theaters, and clubhouses for their members. Some villages provide free water, electricity, and liquid fuel. A number provide subsidies for education, in one case up to 3,000 yuan, in another 1,000 yuan per student who tests into college, in another 600 yuan.[66] In the latter village 200 yuan is provided students who go to vocational schools; in another 2,500.[67] A village near Shenyang provides 60 yuan per student, 60 yuan in nursery school fees per toddler, 3 yuan per person for health insurance, and 20 yuan per month in old-age pensions for men over 60 and women over 55 years old. This village also provides each member free of charge 550 *jin* of rice *(shuidao)* as the basic grain ration, because most of the villagers are no longer engaged in agriculture.[68] In a Shandong village 150,000 yuan is spent each year to buy high-priced, free-market grain to sell to its members at the low rationed price because so few now farm.[69] In one of China's most industrialized villages, over 2 million yuan is spent a year on various subsidies, not counting all the services that members receive; this village makes over 30 million in profits.[70]

On top of direct subsidies to individuals, there are also general subsidies, such as those for agriculture. Under a policy called "using industry to subsidize agriculture" *(yigong bunong)*, local governments are mandated to take profits from industry to assist agriculture directly. This was necessitated by the growing disparity between the income from industry and the income from agriculture that has caused an exodus from farming, particularly from grain production.

National statistics show that the percentage of profits designated for supporting agriculture has been going down as a proportion of net profits.[71] The decline has been especially notable since 1984.[72] As late as 1981 commune enterprises were required to contribute 30 percent of their profits to aid agriculture. In the 1970s published guidelines for Jiangsu called for rural enterprises to set aside 50 percent of their after-tax profits to aid agriculture.[73] In absolute amounts, however, the dollar figure of investment since 1979 is not insignificant. A 1979 report states that a total of 11.6 billion yuan in profits from collective and township enterprises has been applied to agricultural production. Moreover, this figure is based on incomplete statistics.[74] Since 1979 in highly industrialized Wuxi, 1.1 billion yuan, which is four times the amount of state investment, has been taken from the profits of rural industry to support farming.[75]

Generalizing about the size of such subsidies is difficult because they take different forms, and it is unclear how these are accounted for. One form is payment of the agricultural tax or the management fee by the village for those peasants who still farm. Another way that "industry helps agriculture" is by starting factory work late in the morning, so workers can help with agriculture. In really rich and highly industrialized areas, villages subsidize the costs of agricultural equipment purchased by specialized farm households. Outside Shenyang, if a specialized household wants to buy a reaper for 4,000 yuan, for example, the village might provide a subsidy of 3,000, and the household would have to pay only 1,000.[76]

Subsidies for agriculture are only partially affected by concern over the collective. Whether industrial income is used to support agriculture or taken to expand the industrial base of the village is a separate issue from the strength of the collective. The very fact that there is a choice reflects the strength of the collective. The decision itself depends on other economic as well as political issues, such as the amount of pressure from the upper levels and the costs of letting agriculture die as more and more peasants move into the more lucrative industrial sector and buy grain on the free market.

Indirect Subsidies and Redistribution of Income

There are also indirect methods by which income can be redistributed and inequalities leveled. I have already discussed the different systems of rents and the terms of responsibility contracts, especially the limits on factory managers' profits, in this regard. Leveling can also be achieved through the distribution of jobs and the way that investments and loans are distributed and repaid.

JOBS. Because it is generally understood that the "high rate of increase in peasant income is maintained by income from industrial enterprises,"[77] an effort is made even in those areas that are not highly industrialized to have at least one member of each household work in an industrial enterprise.

A rather ingenious way of spreading wealth between those who work in industry and those who must still work in agriculture is to require those who are employed in industry, and who thus will be making more, to invest in or make "loans" to their enterprise. In parts of Sichuan, peasants who want to work in village enterprises pay 500 to 1,000 yuan to the factory. They receive 8 to 10 percent interest on this money, and the principal is returned if they work the minimum agreed amount of time.[78] Christine Wong also describes such a practice, what is termed *gongren daizi ruchang*. She found that in Wuxi workers were required to bring in with them 2,000 to 3,000 yuan.[79] The World Bank study similarly reports on the practice of requiring workers to make "loans" to the enterprises they want to work in. In Shangrao county, Jiangxi, for example, they found that workers brought in anywhere from 100 to 5,000 yuan.[80] In a Shandong village in 1988, one of the large metal works factories required new workers to pay 500 yuan before beginning the job. The money was returned with interest if they worked a minimum of two years.[81]

This practice is explained as a safeguard for factories to ensure that they do not waste their time and resources training workers only to have them leave to work elsewhere. While that may be true, it also gives factories extra funds, which the local authorities can eventually use.

LOANS AND INVESTMENT. Such income, in addition to the other sources discussed earlier, can then be utilized to further redistribute income through the selective allocation of loans to rural enterprises. Much like a large family or corporation, villages grant poorer enterprises loans, or new enterprises are started from profits taken from the more prosperous ones. In some cases funds are given to industries that are not particularly efficient or profitable, because they provide jobs for the village's surplus labor or because their existence gives "face" to the village.[82]

To get necessary investment funds, local authorities sometimes make the request to a single enterprise that is known to have substantial profits. It may be termed a "loan" or "rent paid in advance." In one township, for example, the local government took 400,000 and 200,000 yuan in two separate years from its wealthier enterprises.[83]

Similarly, debts are a collective responsibility. Interviews reveal that in a number of localities when an enterprise fails and defaults on its loans, the debt is paid off by the remaining industries regardless of the specifics of the contracting system. Theoretically the debt is the responsibility of the guarantor of the loan, but because most loans are guaranteed by the economic commission of the township or village government, the debt burden is divided among the remaining collectively owned enterprises. In other cases, an enterprise must find another to act as its guarantor, but even then local officials must approve, at least informally.

In one Shandong township in 1987, four of its enterprises closed, leaving a debt of 120,000 yuan. The economic commission had funds to repay the bank 60,000, but had to obtain the balance from its other enterprises.[84] The remaining factories pay, even if grudgingly, because their future depends on the good will of the local authorities who control credit and investment opportunities.

Individuals may contract to operate enterprises, but because these by definition are rentals, entrepreneurs will seldom if ever invest in these ventures with their own funds. All investment in collective-owned enterprises is therefore made by the collective, whether managed by the collective or by individual contractors. In this sense the real entrepreneurs are the local officials. They take the risks, make the investment decisions, and, when necessary, find ways to bail the collective out of financial trouble if an enterprise goes under.

Consequently, when factories want to expand production or buy new machinery, the contractor or manager goes first to the village or township government, not to the bank. Depending on the size of the investment or loan needed, the village or township will either provide the funds out of its accumulation fund or arrange for a loan from the local savings cooperative or branch of the Agricultural Bank for larger amounts. Loans are also available from the finance and tax offices. Whether or not these loans are approved depends less on the performance of the individual entrepreneur than on the good will of village officials and, in the case of larger projects, on the approval of higher officials at the township and perhaps even the county level. Through the intervention of village or township government, an enterprise may also receive a subsidy to pay the interest on a loan or obtain an exemption from penalty interest payments, an extension of the payback period, or even the opportunity to repay a loan before taxes (*shuiqian huankuan*). In sum, the relationship between banks, finance and tax offices, and township and village officials is very close; some have criticized it as too close.[85] Without a nod from these local-level officials, a loan is almost impossible.

THE EMERGENCE OF REDISTRIBUTIVE CORPORATISM

My research suggests that the diversification and particularly the industrialization of the rural economy that have followed the reforms can allow the collective to endure as a corporate entity.[86] Where this has occurred, the collective that results has diverse operations, some of which are more profitable than others. The economy of the township or the village perhaps should now be thought of as that of a *diversified corporation.* Instead of having a single source of income, villages as corporate entities now can use profits from one sector to support another. And as in a corporation, when a division is weak but seen as vital to the overall health of the company, profits are drawn from stronger divisions to maintain it, regardless of costs. This is the relationship between agriculture and industry. The relatively low profits in farming and, most important, the inability of the village government after the responsibility system to redistribute income from the agricultural sector have made the growing industrial sector the financial mainstay that keeps village finances afloat.

Like the bureaus that run urban industry, village and township leaders function like corporate boards of directors. Village leaders, township heads, and heads of economic commissions decide questions ranging from spending, investments, and loans to hiring, and also make provisions to assist their enterprises in acquiring credit and needed inputs. The reforms have decentralized farming, but they have done little to decentralize the management of rural industry to those who have contracted to operate the enterprises. This consequently has allowed local governments continued control.[87]

Where is the Communist party in all of this? I have been focusing on the role of local governments, but in practice that is only a shorthand, and in some cases a guise, for the work of Communist party officials, the local party secretaries. Contrary to the ideal of getting the Communist party out of the economy at the local level, the party continues to play the leading role. In fact, not only are the officials the real entrepreneurs in the rural economy, but in many, if not most, instances these officials are also the party secretaries.

Interestingly, however, even though party officials are clearly taking the lead, they do not advertise this fact. The behavior of one village party secretary clearly indicates the important but at the same time unsanctioned role of the party in developing the local economy. This party secretary had two sets of name cards, one listing him as the village party secretary, the other as the head of the village board of directors. When I asked him about the board of directors, he said it was nonexistent. He only created this body so that when dealing with the "outside," he would have a legitimate position, because he could not wear his "hat" of party secretary in the conduct of the village's economic affairs.[88]

Not only does the party play an important role, but politics and ideological considerations, such as the welfare of the "collective," continue to play a significant role in economic matters. Unlike the case in a true capitalist corporation, profits are not always the driving force. The former emphasis on strict egalitarianism has been rejected, but leveling of incomes still seems to figure in the decision-making process. The examples mentioned above of local governments dictating employment policies, production plans, and attempts to make sure that at least one member of every family works in industry, as well as limits on the amount that officials may receive based on the bonus system, are indications of this continued commitment to what can be called socialist planning of the economy.[89]

Byrd and his collaborators in the World Bank study put it nicely when they characterized the dilemma of community officials: they want to be good businessmen as well as good government administrators responsible for village welfare. Village and township governments try to maximize their revenues by promoting the development of rural industry, channeling increasing investments into industry rather than agriculture; yet they continue to be tied to their duty as socialist "governments."[90] These activities are not necessarily the harbingers of capitalism.

The extent to which local governments carry out their "government" functions and are able to provide subsidies varies greatly. The villages on which most of this study is based clearly are not the norm but are probably among the richest of the highly industrialized suburban villages and townships. Obviously not all villages are able to provide such subsidies. That is not my point. Rather, my purpose has been to show what *can* happen as a result of the development of rural industry and a conscious policy of support for agriculture. Local governments (i.e., party), both at the village and the township levels, have retained the ability to extract and direct investment and to allocate rural industrial profits, the mainstay of village income.

I have tried to show that the reforms do not necessarily lead to the end of redistributive socialism but can lead and have led to a new and perhaps stronger form of collective corporatism. It is precisely in those areas where the reforms have been pushed to the limit, where the economy is diversified, where agriculture is performed by specialized households, where the contract responsibility system is flourishing, and, most important, where industry is booming and peasants have been allowed to become 10,000-yuan households, that the collective has the most funds and is the strongest.[91] It is in this type of environment that the collective is able to draw on new channels of revenue and income to fund a type of redistributive corporatism.

Political Reform and Rural Government

TYRENE WHITE

During the 1980s rural Chinese society was buffeted by two sets of reform. The first, rural economic reform, had immediate and dramatic consequences for peasant households and villages freed from the constraints of collective agriculture. The second, rural political reform, was promoted by China's leadership as a corollary to the economic reform process, a necessary complement to institutional and policy changes in the economic sector. Apart from this facilitative role, central-level commitment to genuine and comprehensive political reform was as equivocal in rural China as it eventually proved to be in the cities.

Political reform therefore had less notable consequences for rural villagers than did economic reform, but its social impact was far from negligible. Organizational changes were implemented that created a formal division of authority among party, government, and enterprise organs. Power was decentralized and redistributed in favor of individual villagers and autonomous villagers' committees. Of course, formal reorganization proved much easier than changing the actual flow of power and authority. Moreover, tensions between competing reform goals (for example, governmental streamlining versus functional specialization, and village autonomy versus rationalized central planning) have endured, fueled by competing visions of a reformed economic structure still hotly debated in Beijing. Nevertheless, the process of reform slowly began to recast and redefine local-level political institutions and cadre-peasant relations, giving the peasantry greater leverage in political transactions. Equally important, the prospect and reality of political reform measures had a direct impact on the other key social group in the Chinese countryside—state and collective cadres.

To illustrate the problems and consequences of rural political reform, five reform goals will be considered: (1) separation of politics and economics; (2) reduction of staff size and promotion of younger, better educated cadres; (3) stabilization of rural leadership; (4) streamlining of rural administration; and (5) strengthening of village autonomy. The findings presented here are based on documentary sources and on field data gathered during 1982 and 1984 in Huashan Commune, a suburban commune in Wuhan Municipality, Hubei Province.[1]

SEPARATION OF POLITICS AND ECONOMICS

The centerpiece of rural political reform was the transformation of rural people's communes into separate organs of local government and economic administration. The commune system had embodied Mao's theory of political economy by "integrating government administration with commune management" (zhengshe heyi), but it was left hollow by the sweeping decollectivization of the rural economy between 1979 and 1984. The new political order envisioned by the post-Mao leadership stressed the withdrawal of the party from daily micromanagement and administration, and the separation of governmental and economic administration (zhengshe fenkai) in order to promote rural entrepreneurship and task specialization. Although decommunization was thus designed to institutionalize a division of power among party, government, and economic organs, the limited progress toward that goal has been offset by new problems. There is little evidence to indicate new patterns of interaction among cadres at each level. There is ample evidence, however, to suggest that a combination of leadership continuity, tepid implementation, and

TABLE 1 Rural Administrative Organization, Selected Years

Year	Communes	Towns and Townships	Brigades	Villages	Teams	VSGs[a]
1965	74,755	0	648,000	0	5,412,000	0
1975	52,615	0	677,000	0	4,826,000	0
1978	52,781	0	690,000	0	4,816,000	0
1979	53,348	0	699,000	0	5,154,000	0
1980	54,183	0	710,000	0	5,662,000	0
1981	54,369	0	718,000	0	6,004,000	0
1982	54,352	—	719,438	—	5,977,000	—
1983	40,079	16,252	550,484	199,657	4,575,000	—
1984	249	91,171	7,046	926,439	128,000	—
1985	0	91,138	0	940,617	0	4,760,000
1986	0	71,521	0	847,894	0	—
1987	0	68,296	0	830,302	0	—
1988	0	56,002	0	740,375	0	—

Sources: Zhongguo jingji nianjian 1981 (Almanac of China'a economy 1981), and *1982*, VI, 9; *Zhongguo nongye nianjian 1983* (Agricultural yearbook of China 1983), p. 21, *1984*, pp. 67–68, *1985*, pp. 120–121, *1986*, p.151, *1987*, p. 196; and *Zhongguo tongji zhaiyo 1989* (China statistical outline 1989), p. 21.

a. Village small groups.

conflict among political goals neutralized the attempt to separate political and economic power at the grass roots.

Between 1982 and 1985 rural people's communes were converted to township *(xiang)* and town *(zhen)* governments, with economic functions transferred to subordinate economic management committees *(jingji guanli weiyuanhui)*. Similarly, production brigades were converted to administrative villages *(xingzhen cun)* led by villagers' committees *(cunmin weiyuanhui)*, and production teams to village small groups *(cun xiaozu)*.[2] Tables 1 and 2 provide national and provincial figures for rural administrative units before and after the transition.[3]

This structural reform was the second major test of will between a post-Mao leadership bent on change and a local leadership that was skeptical and fearful of its implications for established patterns of power and authority. The first confrontation was waged over implementation of the responsibility system, a change that reduced direct cadre authority over the agricultural production process, but did so at a political cost.[4] Some cadres stonewalled or resisted the change, arguing that the new system

TABLE 2 Rural Administrative Organization by Province, 1982, 1985, 1986

Province	Communes (1982)	Towns and Townships (1985)	Towns and Townships (1986)	Brigades (1982)	Villagers' Committees (1985)	Villagers' Committees (1986)	Teams (1982)	VSGs[a] (1985)
Beijing	263	362	337	4,038	4,215	4,295	13,000	—
Tianjin	218	221	222	3,875	3,963	3,876	18,000	—
Hebei	3,651	3,674	3,665	50,405	50,434	50,448	297,000	289,612
Shanxi	1,890	1,920	1,927	31,689	32,291	32,330	120,000	—
Neimongol	1,379	1,533	1,548	12,654	13,628	13,700	69,000	—
Liaoning	1,142	1,211	1,222	15,757	15,656	15,658	104,000	—
Jilin	930	919	911	10,163	10,144	10,163	72,000	63,029
Heilongjiang	1,088	1,163	1,170	14,239	14,568	14,497	65,000	56,131
Shanghai	203	217	210	3,007	3,006	3,028	30,000	30,479
Jiangsu	1,923	1,923	1,905	35,928	36,117	36,093	349,000	340,075
Zhejiang	3,089	3,243	3,222	42,755	43,307	43,336	361,000	356,000
Anhui	3,324	3,407	3,366	30,385	31,495	31,360	373,000	337,746
Fujian	870	958	1,065	14,497	15,439	14,594	171,000	160,928
Jiangxi	1,672	1,748	1,746	22,246	20,103	20,110	242,000	195,569
Shandong	2,003	2,680	2,492	86,700	89,088	89,188	414,000	389,132

Henan	1,987	2,104	2,108	45,843	46,846	46,095	430,000	391,093
Hubei	1,260	4,709	4,555	31,769	32,438	32,734	273,000	258,501
Hunan	3,350	3,379	3,333	47,234	47,899	46,095	515,000	495,415
Guangdong	1,944	20,970	1,933	26,782	140,812	43,634	376,000	—
Guangxi	977	1,242	1,237	13,876	14,379	14,456	288,000	280,217
Sichuan	8,587	8,612	8,572	75,538	76,278	76,320	618,000	609,674
Guizhou	3,827	3,882	3,860	25,500	25,812	25,848	230,000	209,070
Yunnan	1,391	17,871	13,269	13,764	102,720	103,319	196,000	—
Xizang	2,063	2,090	2,105	—	5,362	10,115	10,000	—
Shaanxi	2,521	2,617	2,613	30,756	32,668	32,639	161,000	148,347
Gansu	1,506	1,517	1,509	16,785	17,530	17,536	109,000	100,392
Qinghai	420	453	454	3,729	3,933	3,940	21,000	16,959
Ningxia	256	279	281	2,307	2,393	2,418	18,000	—
Xinjiang	635	824	784	7,217	8,093	8,210	34,000	31,677
Total	54,352	91,138	71,521	719,438	940,617	847,894	5,977,000	4,760,064
% Change over 1982	n.a.	+68	+32	n.a.	+31	+18	n.a.	−20

Sources: *Zhongguo nongye nianjian 1983*, p. 21; *1986*, p. 151; and *1987*, p. 196.

a. No statistics were reported for village small groups in 1986.

was tantamount to private farming and fearing their loss of power.[5] Others appeared to delight in abandoning collective administrative tasks to pursue lucrative new economic opportunities.[6] Still others tried to act responsibly but were left baffled by confusing signals from Beijing, inadequate instruction, and an uncertain political environment.[7]

It was in this context that the commune structural reform was introduced in 1982. Aware that this new measure might contribute to confusion among cadres and "paralysis" of local organs, Beijing assured rural cadres that the reform would be implemented in a "well-guided, planned, and orderly way."[8] Although conceding that the reform would "inevitably affect the jobs of some cadres," one *Xinhua* commentary stressed that "proper arrangements for their placement" would be made.[9] In short, because rural stability was essential to the consolidation of the economic reforms, efforts to streamline personnel and reorganize power and responsibility within rural administrative units were to be pursued with great caution.

The immediate results of the commune structural reform were therefore more symbolic than substantive. The major target of the reform was to separate government administration from economic management by delineating clear responsibilities for government and economic cadres, but documentary evidence and field data reported by Western and Chinese observers suggest that the reform failed miserably in this regard.[10] As early as October 1983 Chinese newspaper reports were critical of the hollow nature of the changes.[11] Similarly, a 1984 *Liaowang* report on a model township conceded that for "a period of time" after the reform, cadres had "hung out their shingles, set up their offices, but work was still done the old way."[12] Elsewhere, peasants complained that there were "three signs but only one boss," the local party secretary.[13]

These impressions of empty reform are underlined by fieldwork data gathered in Huashan Commune, a suburban locality in the northeast corner of Wuhan Municipality.[14] Huashan was transformed into a township in January 1984, but a comparison of the prereform and postreform staffing patterns reveals that the leadership of Huashan Township was virtually identical to that of Huashan Commune.[15] The former director of the commune was elected head of the township government. It was claimed that he had relinquished his previous position of deputy party secretary, but he undoubtedly continued to exercise substantial influence within the party committee.[16] Similarly, all five commune deputy directors reappeared as township or economic committee leaders.

The same pattern was also found in the second tier of cadres who staffed the township government and the Economic Management Committee (EMC). Most township cadres held similar posts in the commune structure, and only one cadre from the commune group did not reappear in the township government list or elsewhere in the new organization.[17] In addition, twenty-eight of the thirty-three commune cadres employed in various aspects of economic work reappeared on the EMC, while one was transferred to the township government. Only four of the thirty-three commune cadres (12 percent) did not reappear.

Finally, the township party committee was reported to have undergone the greatest change, with a drop in membership from fifteen to seven. The question, of course, is what happened to the eight "retired" members. In all probability, most remained embedded in the new administrative structure, as did the township head, or were absorbed into the management structure for township enterprises.

In short, the result of the reform at Huashan was the retention of the vast majority of commune cadres in similar posts in the new structure. Although fourteen cadres were added, only eleven of them were fresh faces (17 percent of the total number of township and EMC cadres), and nine of those eleven were added to expand the industrial company staff of accountants, bookkeepers, and technicians. Thus the cadres who had worked years together as equals under a unified administration were now supposed to respect a new division of authority that subordinated all economic work to township government oversight. With such continuity of leadership, implementing that change could not have been easy.

At the village level the structural dilemma became more obvious. Caught between the demands to separate governmental from economic work and to streamline the administration, cadres gave priority to the latter, creating separate party, administrative, and economic organs but cross-staffing them with a small group of cadres. The typical pattern was to have a village head who continued to serve on all three committees simultaneously. In one Huashan village a second cadre also served on all three committees, and in others several or all cadres served on both the villagers' committee and the economic committee.[18]

Subsequent reports suggest that these early trends observed in Huashan were hardly atypical. In 1986, two years after commune reform was completed, a *Renmin ribao* article bluntly stated that "in some localities" the party committee was "acting as government," a complaint that persisted into 1987.[19] Since then, even the semblance of separation appears

to have fallen by the wayside, as township heads and economic committee directors serve concurrently as deputy party secretaries, deputy township heads remain party committee members, and party committees assign responsibility for government and economic work to individual
secretaries.[20] Although the political reforms adopted at the Thirteenth
Party Congress are targeted at this problem, township reform has been
delayed until after county-level implementation is complete.[21]

If the failure to withdraw the party from rural administration comes
as no surprise, there is irony to be found in examining some of the
unintended consequences of the structural reform. First, the reform has
encouraged some audacious government cadres to believe that they should
be able to run government affairs without party interference, thereby
increasing conflict among cadres. One report characterized the situation
as follows:

The relationship between the party committee and the government constitutes, in a
certain sense, one of leadership and subordination, and therefore actually constitutes
two administrative levels. Ordinary members of the party committee vaguely administer the deputy township level, but the deputy township director doesn't pay attention to the party committee, leading to an increase in disputes. Because of this . . .
relationships are not smooth, functions are unclear, and [cadres] have difficulty walk-
ing {bulu weijian}.[22]

In this case disputes were occurring even though the township director
concurrently held the post of deputy party secretary.[23]

Second, and conversely, reorganization not only failed to remove the
party from interference in economic administration, but in some localities it encouraged party secretaries and economic managers to coordinate
directly, squeezing out the township middleman.[24] Although the goal of
the reform was to remove party and government cadres from routine
administration of rural enterprises and agriculture, township governments were empowered to oversee the work of the economic committee
and engage in economic planning, and the party committee was given
final authority over local economic policy. In other words, government
officials were to administer economic work but not to manage enterprises
directly; party cadres were to oversee the work of the government and
develop local policy but not to administer economic work (a governmental function) or manage enterprises (an economic committee function).
This closely collaborative relationship between party committees and economic management committees threatened to undermine the intermedi-

ary role of the township between party and enterprise, to weaken the authority and status of government cadres, and to forestall the development of strong government institutions, all goals of the reform.

In Beijing's suburban townships, for example, economic committees and companies were nicknamed "the number-two township government" because they monopolized economic decision making.[25] The township government was left to administer public security and civil affairs, but it did not supervise the economic committee or oversee township economic planning. The result was a diminished status for the township government.[26] Elsewhere, the simple reclassification of the commune office as the joint service company ensured the second-class status of the township government, which was left to tend to the less lucrative and less prestigious agricultural sector.[27]

This problem resulted in part from the historic role of the party in the micromanagement of the rural economy, a deeply entrenched pattern of behavior that resisted change. More important, however, was the structural dilemma in which local party secretaries found themselves. On the one hand, party cadres had been told to withdraw from routine management of the local economy. On the other hand, they were still held accountable for local economic performance under the "guidance plans" delivered from above. Because economic performance remained a key indicator used by their superiors to judge their service records, few party secretaries were willing to place their careers in the hands of others. County-level officials reinforced their calculations by neglecting the role of township cadres in economic work, a pattern described in this *Xinhua* report:

According to many township heads, since the township governments were set up more than one year ago, county authorities have never held a meeting of full-time township heads. But they have held several dozen meetings of township party secretaries. Of those meetings, only a few discussed party affairs, while most dealt with purely economic and administrative work, such as agricultural production.[28]

Clearly, party cadres at both the county and the township levels were unwilling to relinquish control over routine production activities. Rather than work through township cadres, party cadres bypassed them in favor of dealing directly with economic committees and their specialized staffs. A *Renmin ribao* commentator even urged township governments to "assess their real situation" and "be equipped with cadres with the necessary [economic] specialties,"[29] and at least one scholar has urged that the economic committee be abolished in favor of an office for economic planning and administration within the township government.[30] These solutions, however, encourage the development of a duplicate set of township economic officials rather than restraint by party cadres.

REDUCTION OF STAFF SIZE AND PROMOTION OF YOUNGER, BETTER EDUCATED CADRES

A second goal of the commune structural reform was to effect an immediate reduction of the number of grass-roots cadres and to promote younger and better educated persons to cadre posts. By quickly reducing the number of grass-roots cadres, money spent by peasant households for local administration could be diverted to agricultural production. By promoting younger, more qualified persons to leadership posts, grass-roots economic management could be improved and the new work methods and relationships implied by the structural reforms could be more readily introduced.

To what extent were these goals met? First, between 1983 and 1985 scattered reports indicated that specific localities had reduced the number of cadres and promoted younger and more qualified ones as a result of the reform,[31] but in some places the number of township cadres increased.[32] These trends were confirmed by the results of a survey conducted by the Rural Policy Research Center of the Party Secretariat and the Rural Development Research Center of the State Council.[33] The report states that there were fewer cadres at the township level and below at the end of 1984, as compared with 1978.[34] The decrease, however, was attributed to a 69 percent drop in the number of cadres at the team or village small-group level. Since team-level units numbered over 4.7 million by 1985, a drop from 3 cadres to an average of 1.4 had a dramatic effect on the overall numbers. By comparison, the village-level units registered only a 12.9 percent drop, with the average number of cadres per village declining by 0.8 persons. At the township level, however, the total number of cadres increased by 9.4 percent during this period.[35] This pattern is supported by the case of Huashan, where the number of township-level cadres increased from 51 to 65, an increase of 27 percent. The increase was the direct result of bifurcating government and economic administration and increasing the support staff of the economic committee.[36]

A second personnel goal of the reform was to introduce younger, bet-

TABLE 3 Age and Educational Levels of Huashan Township
and Village Cadres Assigned before and after 1982

Cadre	Age		Educational Level			
	N	Median Age (years)	N	Senior Middle[a]	Junior Middle[b]	Primary[c]
Township						
Total sample	49[d]	39	48	73%	25%	2%
Assigned pre-1982	25	41	25	68	28	4
Assigned 1982–1984	21	32	20	90	10	0
Village						
Total sample	57[e]	36	56	39	43	18
Assigned pre-1982	33	41	33	33	46	21
Assigned 1982–1984	24	30	23	48	39	13

Sources: Interview Files, Huashan Township, 1982 and 1984.

a. Includes all cadres reported to have had a senior middle school education or higher (e.g., technical secondary school, university).

b. Includes all cadres reported to have had a junior middle school education.

c. Includes all cadres reported to have had a primary school education or less (e.g., junior primary, semiliterate, illiterate).

d. Total number of township and economic committee cadres in 1984 was 65, but data are not available for all.

e. This sample is taken from eight villages (formerly brigades). The total number of cadres in 1984 was 65.

ter educated cadres into vacated or newly created cadre posts. The report of the joint rural survey asserts that the cadre force is younger and better educated, but it does not offer any time-series data. In Huashan available data on the personal characteristics of township and village cadres provide such evidence. Table 3 records age and educational data, comparing the full sample of township and village cadres with those who began their current post (or its commune/brigade equivalent) before or after 1982. As shown, those recruited between 1982 and 1984 were significantly younger and better educated than the full sample. In short, data from the rural survey and from Huashan Township both suggest that between 1982 and 1985 more progress was made on the goal of promoting younger and better qualified cadres than on reducing their number, particularly at the township level.

TABLE 4 Annual Subsidies for Cadres in five Huashan
Commune Brigades, 1983 (in yuan)

Brigade	Party Secretary	Brigade Leader	Deputy Leader	Women's Leader	Accountant	Committee Members
Huashan	650	650	630	630	600	600
Donggang	504	504	420	420	504	420
Houshan	504	504	390	380	504	380
Hongguang	650	600	570	510	570(m)[a] 510(f)	570
Wuqiao	720	720	696	696	720	696

Source: Interview Files, March–June 1984.

a. Different salaries were paid to male and female accountants in this brigade.

STABILIZATION OF RURAL LEADERSHIP

The structural reforms were designed to bring an end to the phenomenon of "paralysis" and "semiparalysis" at the village level and below. With decollectivization, many village organs deteriorated as cadres and peasants alike concluded that they were irrelevant to the new economic structures.[37] Village cadres suddenly had opportunities they had never dreamed of to engage in entrepreneurial activities, taking advantage of their preferential access to human and material resources and their managerial experience to enhance meagre collective subsidies.[38] For their part, villagers were unwilling to foot the bill for cadres under the new conditions, particularly when cadres received equal parcels of "responsibility fields." But the result was often the breakdown of necessary collective services, generating renewed calls for stable and effective village leadership. Efforts to rebuild or strengthen rural organs, however, have been impeded in some areas, particularly poor ones, by the failure to provide salaries and other compensation for public service to offset the value of private market opportunities. Poor villages therefore lack the political representation and economic leadership they may need in order to improve the local economic base.

In order to strengthen village leadership, collective subsidies for cadres at the village and village small-group levels were reintroduced beginning in 1983. Table 4 outlines the subsidy schedule implemented in five Huashan brigades.[39] As shown, the level of income for individual cadres varied by brigade and post and was apparently linked not just to seniority but to the income level of the brigade.

Elsewhere, salaries tend to vary wildly depending on the level of local prosperity, with cadres in relatively prosperous areas typically receiving large subsidies, whereas cadres in poor localities are either inadequately compensated or fail to get subsidies at all. Thus, while some cadres in Jiangsu and Zhejiang receive subsidies as high as 4,000 yuan,[40] the deputy governor of Zhejiang Province reports: "In approximately one-fifth of the villages in the province, there is no assured source of funds to pay cadres, and some village cadres have not received pay for many years. In still another 10 percent of villages, the organization is lax, with no one to take responsibility for the work."[41]

Because subsidies are derived largely from the proceeds of village industry and enterprise, villages with a weak industrial base are unable to provide support, leaving cadres to rely on private income derived from agricultural production and on bonuses from the township. This encourages a continued neglect of industrial development, perpetuating the cycle of backwardness. Even worse, it has led cadres to sell collective property or take out high-interest loans in order to cover salaries and contractual obligations.[42] Where the industrial base is good, however, cadres can reasonably siphon off large subsidies from enterprise income. This provides an incentive to redouble efforts to develop the industrial sector, turning cadres into "industrial secretaries" who neglect agriculture.[43] This problem has persisted despite the organization-building efforts associated with rural party rectification.[44] In Zhejiang, county and municipal governments have responded by dispatching cadres to the villages to rehabilitate local organs.[45]

Beneath the village level, the reforms have done little to stabilize leadership. Prior to the reforms, production-team cadres played a vital role in the collective agricultural process. Decollectivization, however, made their job description largely irrelevant, so much so that national and provincial figures for village small groups (VSGs) went unrecorded for the first time in 1987 state statistical yearbooks. Provincial yearbooks for 1988 are inconsistent, with some reporting figures for village small groups and others omitting them.[46] Where they remain, the number of cadres has declined from five or even seven prior to the reforms to as few as one or none at present. Moreover, those who remain often receive no subsidy or an inadequate one.

TABLE 5 Annual Collective Subsidies for Team Cadres in
Eight Huashan Commune Brigades, 1983 (in yuan)

Brigade	Team Leader	Women's Leader	Accountant
Baihu	300	120	180
Huashan	220	110	110
Hedong	200	120[a]	80
Donggang	420	150	420
Lianhe	150	70	90
Houshan	210	50	120
Hongguang[b]	60	0	0
Wuqiao	480	300	300

Source: Interview Files, March–June 1984.

a. Women's leaders in Hedong received a larger subsidy than the accountant because they
served jointly as accountants. Thus the brigade paid women 120 yuan to perform two jobs
that were actually valued at 200 yuan.

b. In Hongguang cadres received a subsidy only if their income did not equal that of the
average brigade laborer.

In Huashan, for example, VSG cadre subsidies were set by the village
beginning in 1983, leveling income across teams. Table 5 gives a breakdown by cadre of the subsidies in eight brigades. The total compensation
awarded by the village to VSG cadres was set at approximately 1 percent
of total brigade distributable income from collective sources.[47] Thus VSG
cadre salaries varied by the wealth of the village, the total number of
VSGs, and the total number of cadres within the VSGs. How these funds
were distributed between the VSG leader, the accountant, and the wom-
en's leader, however, varied across villages.

The effect of this compensation system was to make service as a team
cadre undesirable in relatively prosperous areas where new entrepreneurial
opportunities were available to cadres. In one Huashan brigade, for example, all team cadres were provided subsidies of 220 yuan (team leader)
or 110 yuan (women's leader and accountant). At the same time, however, they were given a "responsibility field" that was 30 percent smaller
than that of the standard laborer. Based on crude calculations of the
average income from rice production per unit of land in each team, Table
6 compares the hypothetical income of an average laborer with that of
team cadres. As shown, cadres in teams that generate relatively high
income from rice production benefit proportionately less from the additional income a cadre subsidy provides than do those in less prosperous

TABLE 6 A Comparison of Hypothetical Peasant Income from Rice Production with Income for Team Cadres (in yuan)[a]

| | Income from Rice Production | | Income plus Subsidy | | Net Income Gain from Cadre Service | |
| | | | (220 yuan) | (110 yuan) | | |
Team	Peasants	Cadres	Team Leader	Other Cadres	Team Leader	Other Cadres
1	233	177	397	287	164	54
2	224	167	387	277	163	53
3	329	246	466	356	137	27
4	425	311	531	421	106	−4
5	477	351	571	461	94	−16
6	266	199	419	309	153	43
7	201	150	370	260	169	59
8	340	257	477	367	137	27
9	240	179	399	289	159	49
10	279	208	428	318	149	39
11	361	267	487	377	126	16
12	336	250	470	360	134	24
13	271	204	424	314	153	43
14	262	197	417	307	155	45
15	269	204	424	314	155	45
16	313	230	450	340	137	27
17	282	212	432	322	150	40
18	211	159	379	269	168	58
19	419	309	529	419	110	0

Source: Interview Files, March 1984.

a. Income from rice production is derived from average figures for team productivity, production expenses, and purchase prices. The figures are therefore hypothetical, not calculated from an average of actual peasant income. Details on the data used to derive these figures can be obtained from the author.

teams. And for accountants and women's leaders, the 110-yuan subsidy could not compensate for lost agricultural income. Moreover, the loss would be much greater if income from other crops besides rice production were added. In short, the more prosperous the team, the less valuable the cadre subsidy.[48]

In poor areas where brigades were unable to provide subsidies, the structural reforms provided the opportunity to reduce staff size and peasant subsidies by eliminating team-level cadres altogether. This left no formal buffer or representative between the peasant and the village (brigade-level) cadres, and it left villagers to fend for themselves in disputes with other VSGs, with higher authorities, or with one another.

In sum, to the extent that the reforms were intended to stabilize or strengthen village organs that were shaken by the process of decollectivization, results seem to have been mixed at best. Despite efforts to guarantee subsidies and rebuild village organs, many villages, particularly poor ones, continue to have no organization or an inadequate one, and thus lack any semblance of local representation.

STREAMLINING OF RURAL ADMINISTRATION

A fourth and key goal of political reform was to streamline rural administration, but all available evidence suggests that bureaucracy has expanded rapidly at the county and township levels of government. Nationwide, the total number of personnel in party, government and mass organs increased by 59 percent between 1982 and 1987, compared with a 20 percent increase in the labor force.[49] In the rural areas, however, the number of personnel quadrupled, jumping from 370,000 to 1.29 million, compared with an 18.3 percent rise in the labor force.[50]

This bureaucratic expansion was fueled in large part by economic reform, which motivated central-level organs (ministerial *xitong,* bureaus, commissions, etc.) and county governments to establish administrative branches and profit-making enterprises at the local level.[51] A second factor was the push to reform the cadre and personnel structure and the continuous pressure to reduce staff size at higher levels. Reform and streamlining at higher levels often took the form of cadre reassignment to lower levels.[52]

The result was a rapid expansion of bureaucracy at the township level. In some localities as many as 20 agencies were established at the township level to supplement the work of local cadres.[53] In Shandong, townships and towns under Laiwu City labored under the weight of 26 city agencies and "300 to 400 cadres."[54] Worst of all, the number of higher-level units established in one Anhui town totaled 72—6 prefectural units, 44 county units, and 22 district units.[55]

The proliferation of locally based personnel not subject to township control has created major headaches for township cadres. Because control over agency work, personnel, and funding rests with county or higher-level bureaucrats, township officials are constrained in exercising their rightful authority and complain that "what can be managed cannot be seen, and what can be seen cannot be managed."[56] Even the physical presence of these extratownship personnel can cause problems, as in the case of the water pipeline: "If the town government wants to arrange something, you must always get county or district leaders to lead the organization before you can carry it out. For example, in 1984 a supplementary running-water and drainage pipeline built by the town crossed the doorway of the dormitory for the county's transportation station workers; the workers did not agree, so there was no choice but to halt the project."[57]

The intrusion of the county into local government has also complicated relations among cadres within the township government. One young township party secretary captured the problems precisely:

Some departments at the higher level have continuously tried to take over profitable sectors . . . but shirk operating unprofitable units . . . [W]e at the township level have too many "immediate superiors," as new departments, offices, committees, and bureaus governing township authorities are being set up every year . . . Currently all offices and bureaus at the county level or even some companies at a level lower than the township level can directly issue directives assigning tasks to a township government. As most of these units . . . hold real power in certain fields, we dare not offend them . . . [T]here are currently many resident cadres in the township government, and quite a few of them are not under the control of the township party committee secretary and township chief because they belong to their own departments. In fact, as township cadres we have to work quite hard to assist these cadres from different departments in fulfilling profit-earning or procurement quotas. However, we would hardly be able to get what we need if we asked them to do something for us.[58]

In short, the tension between functionally *(tiao)* and territorially *(kuai)* defined arenas of activity is growing more acute, and the balance of power appears to be shifting to higher levels of administration as township officials get mired in red tape.[59]

STRENGTHENING OF VILLAGE AUTONOMY

The final goal of rural political reform was to enhance village-level autonomy and grass-roots democratic practices. To that end, autonomous self-managing villages and democratically elected villagers' committees have been constitutionally and legislatively mandated. Despite the attention to the language of autonomy and the form of participatory democracy, all available evidence indicates that political reform has not enhanced grass-roots democracy. At least three factors account for this. First, the definition of autonomy is too vague to override enduring authority relationships between township officials and village cadres. Second, the concept of village autonomy has been extremely controversial among county and township cadres who are fearful of its implications. Third, any tendency toward grass-roots autonomy has been overwhelmed by the rapid expansion of county-level power and bureaucracy at the township level and below.

The PRC constitution adopted in 1982 explicitly created a division between township- and village-level organs, with the township established as the lowest organ of state power, and the villagers' committee described as a "mass organization of self-management at the grass-roots level." [60] This construction was intended to turn the villagers' committee into a bridge between state and society in rural China and to shift the balance of power between township and village cadres in favor of the villages. At the same time, however, villagers' committees were called on to "assist local governments in administrative work and leadership over production." [61]

This dual mandate for villagers' committees created confusion as to their proper role. Were they to be extensions of state power into the village, or were they to stand as a buffer between state and community? Were village leaders subordinate to township officials, or did they have the right to refuse township directives and to promulgate village rules without interference? In short, was the relationship between township governments and villagers' committees to be "one between the leader and those who are led" or "one between those who guide and those who are guided"? [62] The former implies a continued obligation of village cadres to take orders from township cadres, whereas the latter yields more autonomy and independence to the village.

In Huashan it was the former view that held sway in 1984. When the township government was established early that year, brigades were converted to village committees, but this change was purely symbolic. Asked what difference the reform meant to his village, one newly appointed party secretary (and former brigade leader) spoke abstractly about the benefits of separating politics and economics but gave no concrete response concerning patterns of authority. But the village leader, who had heard the response of the party secretary, candidly said that the reform had made no difference in his work relationship with township officials above and village small groups below. In a second village, responses by the party secretary and the village leader were almost identical. At a third site, the party secretary himself said that the commune structural reform meant no change in the relationship between the village, township, and village small groups.[63]

To alter this state of affairs, the "Organic Law Governing Village Committees of the People's Republic of China (Trial)" was passed by the National People's Congress (NPC)) on 24 November 1987[64] and was scheduled to go into effect on 1 June 1988.[65] After three years of discussion and disagreement, the trial law upheld the principle of an autonomous self-managing villagers' committee, a model of grass-roots socialist democracy. Under the new law the villagers' committee consists of three to seven members, elected by a council of villagers composed of one adult representative per household. The village council may dismiss elected committee members, village regulations may be promulgated only with the approval of the full council, and expenses needed to "run public affairs and public utilities" must be discussed and approved by the council. In one case, for example, township regulations specified that agricultural expenses under 1,000 yuan could be approved by the village committees, those between 1,000 and 5,000 yuan required approval by the village council as well, and those over 5,000 yuan required the approval of the township government.[66]

If strictly implemented, the law could greatly enhance the power of villagers over the conduct of village affairs and convert village cadres from township-regarding to village-regarding incentive structures. This scenario, however, is troubling to local governmental officials who fear that township governments will "lose their legs" if they cannot rely on the villages to carry out their orders in the same way that production brigades followed commune instructions.[67] Not surprisingly, there is particular concern that autonomous village cadres will resist implementation of the unpopular regulatory and taxation functions of local government, such as family planning, conscription, and grain purchasing and taxation.[68]

On the other hand, advocates of village autonomy fear that local governments will seek to maximize control over village cadres, stifling local development through excess taxation, summary extraction of resources, and government by fiat, fears that are confirmed by frequent cadre and peasant complaints about overbearing government officials.[69] At one point during the extended process of revising the law, this fear translated into a suggestion by the NPC Law Committee that the draft explicitly state, "Villagers' committees are *authorized to reject undertaking assignments* handed down by any organ, group, enterprise, or institution"[70] (emphasis added). In the end a compromise was struck. The clause inviting villagers' committees to reject assignments from above does not appear in the trial law, but the principle of village-level autonomy and its supporting provisions survived a call for a constitutional amendment explicitly incorporating villages as subordinate organs of local government. Moreover, the trial law does state that the village committee "must not resort to coercion and commandism" or "take revenge."[71]

It is possible that, over time, the problems of ambiguity and local governmental opposition can be overcome.[72] In light of the countercurrents of cadre corruption, rural bureaucratization, and rationalized economic planning, however, the prospects for such an outcome are remote.

First, peasant vulnerability to corrupt cadres is well illustrated by the chemical fertilizer and diesel oil scandal of 1987, in which peasants were routinely shortchanged by village and township cadres.[73] In this case peasant purchases of chemical fertilizer and diesel oil were linked to sales of grain to the state. For example, a sale of 50 kilograms of wheat entitled peasants to 5 kilograms of chemical fertilizer. Yet in one locality peasants were promised only 1.73 kilograms of fertilizer for 50 kilograms of wheat and eventually received only 1 kilogram. Although shortages contributed to the disparity between promised and actual supplies in some areas, powerholders were charged with favoritism toward those with connections, and "lawless elements" were charged with corruption for using the goods "as 'capital' to exploit the peasants and seek exorbitant profits."[74]

More typically, township officials exercise arbitrary authority on the pretext of efficient management. In one case, for example, a peasant who had contracted for the use of 45.5 *mu* of land had his contract summarily nullified by the local township and village authorities. In 1986 the peasant had brought in three partners from neighboring villages to help him develop what had originally been barren land, only to have the contract nullified without compensation. Although the pretext for seizure was the development of large-scale agriculture and fulfillment of the wheat quota, the land was actually divided into strips for seventy-nine households, some of which were sown with crops other than wheat.[75] Such problems have led one scholar to call for the delineation of collective property rights for land at the level of the production team, a measure designed to prevent state and village infringements on "peasant collectives' rights."[76]

Second, the rapid expansion of bureaucracy at and above the township level has overwhelmed village cadres. Despite assertions of autonomy, they remain vulnerable to demands from their superiors and complain that they are "caught in the cross fire" between cadres above and peasants below.[77] When municipal or county officials need funds to complete special projects, township officials instruct village cadres to extract special "levies" or "apportionments" from local villagers.[78] Although village cadres have no choice but to comply, resentful peasants take out their frustrations on the messenger, particularly if he is an unpopular cadre. Retaliation is reported to take the form of poisoning chickens, destroying vegetable gardens, and throwing stones at the homes of village cadres.[79]

Third, concerns over the need for centralized coordination and management and the bulging cadre structure have been joined to fears of rural anarchy in the wake of designating villages as self-managing committees. The result is a call for the creation of an "intermediary link" between township and village. This link would be an agency established by the township with a "direct guidance role over the villagers' committee." As a "leg" of the township (to replace the ones cut off by making villages autonomous), the agency, also referred to as a "village administrative unit or leading group," would help township officials with local administration. How would it be staffed? According to one view:

Some people are worried about the question of how to obtain cadres if there are so many "legs." In our view, our present problem is that our institutions are bloated and overstaffed. If we want to overcome the serious question of bureaucratism, we should let a large number of cadres go down to the grass-roots level to work. In so doing we shall not only solve the question of overstaffed organizations but this will also provide "intermediary link" cadres between townships and villages.[80]

It is difficult to see how this formula will solve the problem of bureaucratism, but it is an excellent recipe for thwarting the intent of the villagers' law, imposing hierarchy and functional specialization onto the village, and creating a whole new brand of rural administrator, the village bureaucrat.

"A THOUSAND STRINGS ABOVE, THE EYE OF A NEEDLE BELOW"[81]

When rural China underwent decollectivization between 1980 and 1984, powerful centrifugal forces were set loose that shook rural political structures. Rural cadres and peasants, long bound to incentive structures that induced compliance through potent rewards and latent threats, were freed to test the value of those incentives against the tantalizing opportunity to command lucrative entrepreneurial territories. The dissolution of grass-roots organization that ensued provoked a centripetal response aimed at stabilizing rural leadership.[82] In that context political reform had important consequences, but the enduring primacy of economic reform and modernization has frustrated progress toward political reform goals.

Among the five reform goals discussed here, only the promotion of younger, better educated cadres has been successful. The creation of separate governmental and economic committees not only failed to eliminate party interference in the rural economy, but it encouraged direct collaboration between the party and economic committees and undercut the authority of newly established township and town governments. Efforts to streamline administration fared even worse, with the exception of the dissolution of team-level administration. Despite repeated bludgeoning, township-level cadres sit at the bottom of a bureaucratic apparatus that has continued to expand, with dramatic consequences for township government cadres. It is they who must coordinate the work of hundreds of resident cadres whom they neither know nor control, while simultaneously fulfilling their state-assigned tasks.[83]

Finally, the reforms have placed new burdens on village cadres, to whom all bureaucratic trails lead. Asked to trade the role of local overseer of economic activity for that of guidance counselor, while retaining the obligation to enforce unpopular state directives despite threats of violence (for example, taxation, grain requisition, birth control), village cadres are caught in a familiar but increasingly dangerous bind that reduces incentives for cadre service.[84] And for their part, peasants who delighted in the immediate benefits of the agricultural reforms now complain bitterly of unreasonable and arbitrary decisions that nullify their contract rights or escalate their tax burdens, impersonal leadership by cadres they have elected but never met, and favoritism by cadres for those with connections.[85]

None of these complaints are new, of course, but they are compounded by a growing sense of abandonment by the party, a view that some cadres share as well.[86] In the past the party played a vital role in unifying rural leadership and maintaining links between cadres and masses, but its continued ability to do so is eroding. As the cadre force has become more diverse, and cadre interests more divergent from those of the party apparatus, their complaints have multiplied. Their institutional arrangements were redesigned, their job descriptions rewritten, and their working relationships with peasants and other cadres made far more complex, but the expectations of their party superiors remained the same. As one insightful township party secretary put it, a township cadre

must fulfill all tasks assigned by the state and take the peasants' feelings into consideration as well . . . [T]ownship cadres have always been the scapegoats in the conflict of interests between the two sides, and principal leading comrades at the township level have to withstand pressure from their superiors and face protests from the peasants, a very awkward situation. We never complain about the heavy work load or some minor unfair treatments that we have encountered. What we cannot tolerate is that our hard work has not been appreciated by others but brought us a nickname—"local overlords." We are disliked not only by some cadres at the higher level but also by some peasants whose vested interests have been infringed upon.[87]

Nevertheless, he leaves no doubt as to who must be accommodated when these conflicts arise:

To complete these tasks [grain requisition, family planning, and taxation] we usually have to force people to obey the order. In consequence, some excesses are inevitable, which may involve violation of laws and result in punishment for us . . . Some cadres complain: it is possible that we, "in serving the party, will violate the law laid down by the party and be imprisoned by the party."[88]

Peasants have little sympathy for these risks run by cadres, as they are the perpetual target of the unlawful force. From their perspective the cadres are the villains who take their money and impose unpopular programs, even though the same cadres will be protected by their superiors when they have an unplanned child or fail to meet a target or quota.[89] It is this sense of unfairness and injustice that has provoked so many to violence.

Although these cadre and peasant concerns are not new, their extremity is the direct result of party policy over the last decade—what it has been willing or unwilling to do. The Deng regime was willing to loosen central planning in the rural economic sector, giving peasants greater autonomy and control. At the same time, it proved unwilling to loosen its political equivalent, the centralized party administration that kept local cadres under strict authority. As a result, peasants have been allowed to grow up, to make more decisions for themselves, whereas cadres, despite their control over local economic resources, remain bound to obey party orders (or give the appearance of doing so). Under these circumstances cadres have sometimes been forced to use a heavy hand against recalcitrant, resentful, and rebellious villagers.[90]

The question is, how long will they labor in this climate before they rethink their obligation to the party? While politics was in remission and profit easily come by, these burdens were onerous but worth the effort, especially to a younger, better educated cadre force with a bright future. How they will respond to renewed political fervor and economic retrenchment, however, must be cause for worry in Beijing.

The Politics of Migration in a Market Town

Helen F. Siu

When the mobility of Chinese rural residents was severely restricted in 1958, the nonagricultural sector in market towns and small cities developed for the next three decades as an exclusive enclave closed to new migrants. The worlds of villagers and town residents remained separate and unequal despite Maoist rhetoric about narrowing the distances.[1] Even at the lowest end of the urban hierarchy, in market towns, the status of town resident (*jumin*) with a nonagricultural job continued to be sought after and jealously defended against rural intruders.[2]

The post-Mao reforms have endeavored to correct the frozen state of village-town interaction by promoting agricultural specialization and rural marketing and by allowing labor mobility. To coordinate these changes, a series of party directives from 1983 on aimed at liberalizing the economy in the towns. These policies have apparently triggered tremendous energies and fluidities. The Yangzi River and Pearl River deltas have received the most attention in the official press as national success stories.[3]

This chapter focuses on the population movements in an area covered by a market town and its rural hinterland in the heart of the Pearl River Delta.[4] It considers how much the previously frozen political economy has thawed and examines the ways in which social groups are breaking out of an inherited pattern of immobility and are repositioning themselves through migration.[5]

At this moment, as in other areas of the reforms, the results are mixed. Some state goals have been achieved, but there are also local distortions of government policies as well as unintended outcomes. It is now possible to differentiate the bottlenecks from the breakthroughs, to examine the causes for the variations, and to refine our understanding of the links between changes in economic performance and changes in social institutions. The findings lead us to consider the ways the socialist state had previously penetrated subcounty society and then retreated. They will also illustrate how social hierarchies along the village-town nexus are being redefined and what cultural changes can be highlighted in the process.

NANXI TOWN AND VICINITY: A HISTORY

In 1986 I spent almost a year in Nanxi Town in the Pearl River Delta. I was struck by the vitality of the economic activities in and around the town. State commerce, town industries, private business, and village enterprises had been juxtaposed since the town was incorporated in 1952; since then competition has been minimized by a pecking order based on institutional links to the state sector. There had been few migrants in town. However, the order appears to have been rapidly redefined in the 1980s. Construction was everywhere, especially for private houses in the villages bordering the town. During the day, small boats transporting vegetables, fish, and poultry jammed the narrow waterways leading to the two regional markets on the outskirts of the town. The state-run department store on the main street was upgrading its appearance and aggressively offering discounts in face of the challenges from the shopping arcades newly established by the town government. At night the street bazaar next to the cinema house was packed with small peddlers offering an unusual range of goods, from food and imported clothing to prescriptions that treat cancer and schizophrenia. They nonetheless kept a respectful distance from the end of the main street where the town offices were located. The tall government building, guarded by iron railings around spacious courtyards, had stamped its towering presence on the lives of the residents. At the administrative merging of the town with the surrounding rural district in 1987, however, the building too succumbed to the forces of the reforms. It was converted to a factory. The government offices were moved to the western edge of town.

Among the faces in the crowd were those one would not have expected to see a few years ago—migrant laborers from the surrounding villages and from outside the province. They stood out from the town residents because of their weather-beaten complexions. Their clothes were often less "fashionable," indicating that they had not caught up with the Hong Kong television programs that every town resident watched. They spoke different dialects and hung together. "Shoe-repair women" from a rural county of Zhejiang lined the main street year round, and itinerant jugglers from Hunan descended upon the town in winter. Older residents recalled how their starving sisters and daughters had reluctantly been led away by "marriage brokers," who transported them up the West River to Guangxi during the Japanese occupation. Today they saw gangs of young women organized by labor recruiters coming down the same river to offer services. Human affairs in the market town had made a full circle back, they said. But had traditional strategies of making a living only been kept dormant for decades and were now being revived? Or had subcounty society been transformed in the socialist period to the extent that what we were observing bore the definitive stamp of that administrative history?

One must go back to the history of the area to differentiate some of its traditional institutions from features introduced after 1949. The division between the surrounding villages and Nanxi Town did not start with the Maoist revolution. Nanxi had been a sizable market town for a few centuries. In 1923 a town government was established within the third district, a subcounty division in the republican era.[6] By the late 1940s Nanxi Town and its suburban neighborhoods had over twenty thousand residents, consisting of numerous landlord and merchant families who lived off the rent and the grain trade from the surrounding sands,[7] river marshes reclaimed through the centuries under the auspices of ancestral trusts. The land was farmed by tenants from a stratum of boat people *(Dan)* whose ecological niches had been shrunk by the expansion of delta land. The sands were vast, but the villages in them were small. The straw huts of the tenants strung out on the dikes contrasted sharply with the wealth and cultural activities in town, as indicated by the rows of gray-brick mansions, the genealogies of the major lineages displaying an array of degreeholders, the 393 ancestral halls they built, and the 139 temples and monasteries, among which were two for the city god (Chenghuang).

The tenants had traditionally been treated as outcasts. They were considered poor, rural, and "Dan." They seldom maintained direct contact with their landlords in town, who relied on a stratum of functionaries to act as second-level landlords and set up what was known locally as the weiguan (enclosed compounds) on the dikes. The weiguan were equipped with an armed crop-watching force, a granary, a fleet of boats for grain transportation, and houses for the overseers. Social contacts were limited to the out-migration of poor males from the town, who joined the ranks of tenant farmers and semibandits, and to the in-migration of women from the upwardly mobile rural households, who became second wives, concubines, and maids in the rich households in town. Occasionally laborers in the weiguan hired themselves out in town as coffin bearers and grave diggers, occupations regarded as unclean.

The rise of local bosses in the rural fringes during the republican era changed the power relationship between town and village somewhat, but these military adventurers enjoyed little legitimate authority. Even today older town residents easily recite popular rhymes that ridicule their "pretentious" acts. A most frequently mentioned example is that of the leaders of Jiuji, a township three kilometers west of town, where local bosses who rose precipitously during the Japanese occupation decided to stage a jiao. Traditionally this religious ceremony took place in the seventh month of the lunar calendar. A large-scale exorcism ritual was staged to rid the community of unclean spirits. It involved services conducted by monks and priests, the parade of statuettes of local deities, and the feasting of the organizers. The residents in Nanxi were delighted that a storm flooded out the festivities, as they claimed "heaven knew when people acted out of their depths, and it spoiled their fun."

The local bosses were powerful, but their wealth was not entrenched enough to create alternative networks and to pose a legitimate threat to the elites in Nanxi Town. The land reform to an extent confirmed such a point, because in the villages the landlords singled out to be struggled against had little more than tiled roofs over their straw houses. Local cadres recalled also that it was not until the 1970s that they were able to make the rural settlers build brick houses. The social distance between the town and the villages has endured to the extent that today the villagers are still referred to as "the peasants out in the sands."

As one would expect, this distance, which embodies economic, social, and cultural exclusions of the rural residents by the town dwellers, narrowed after the revolution. The market town was incorporated in 1952 to govern an area of about four square kilometers. Its administrative superiors were in the Dagang county government some thirty kilometers away. Former tenants in the sands were able to retrieve the rent collected by the ancestral trusts based in town. They were also given land confiscated from these trusts. Land left over from the division was made into a farm administered by the town government. Town residents who wanted land to farm, and former landlords and rich peasants who were left with little to support themselves after the land reform, were assigned to it. Some of the boat people who moored at the confluence of the major waterways at the eastern edge of town were grouped into a boat brigade (*shuishang dadui*), which transported agricultural products for state corporations. Commercial wealth not categorized as "feudal exploitation" was retained in the town. Trading enterprises, light industries, handicraft workshops, and guilds were gradually collectivized, employing the bulk of the town residents.

The introduction of unified purchase of grain in 1953 and planned purchase of cash crops in 1955, together with the buildup of state and cooperative commerce, gave the town government and party committee a more central role in shaping people's livelihoods. The relationship of the town to the surrounding rural area was restructured. Vegetables and poultry became the only products still sold by individual farm families to town residents in the two daily markets. The two regional markets at the eastern and western edges of town that specialized in the trading of mulberry leaves, fruits, and aquatic products came to be dominated by agents from the town's collectivized enterprises as well as by state agents who were buyers for export corporations in the county government. Workshops for mat weaving, bamboo processing, and wood- and irontool making continued to serve rural clients, but the majority of the urban enterprises began to subcontract for the tiny orders from county-level factories higher up in the urban hierarchy. Nanxi Town gradually became a center of ancillary factories producing small metal products.[8]

Despite periodic campaigns that transported the town's resources (ranging from bricks and trees to youths and cadres) to the villages in

FIGURE 1   Administrative Structure, 1963–1987

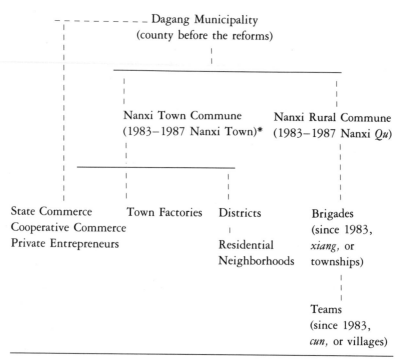

Dagang Municipality
(county before the reforms)

Nanxi Town Commune   Nanxi Rural Commune
(1983–1987 Nanxi Town)*   (1983–1987 Nanxi *Qu*)

State Commerce   Town Factories   Districts   Brigades
Cooperative Commerce   (since 1983,
Private Entrepreneurs   Residential   *xiang,* or
                                       Neighborhoods   townships)

                                                       Teams
                                                       (since 1983,
                                                       cun, or villages)

* In December 1987 Nanxi Town Commune and Nanxi Rural Commune were merged to form Nanxi Zhen. To avoid confusion, I use Nanxi Town to refer to the town proper, and Nanxi Zhen for the large unit after the merger.

the sands, town residents held on to their nonagricultural jobs. Although their livelihoods were increasingly managed and controlled by the town government, few wanted to be peasants, who, since 1958, were kept increasingly immobile. When a rule in the early 1960s stipulated that children must be registered under their mother's household status *(hukou)*, it created unexpected distances even within families. Some people with town residency status because they had been registered earlier under the household status of their fathers had younger siblings with peasant status who had to stay in the villages with their mothers. The administrative separation of the town and its rural vicinity was complete in 1963, when an urban commune, the Nanxi Town Commune, was established for the administration of nonagricultural residents (see Figure 1).

The residents worked in the factories and bought their quota of commodity grain at the grain stations. They had access to such amenities of town living as electricity and tap water and were able to use the county-run hospital, to send their children to the schools that had been supported by ancestral trusts but administered by the town government since the 1950s, and to patronize the area's large teahouses and shops.

Encircling the town was the Nanxi Rural Commune. It was made up of twenty-four townships, renamed brigades, covering seventy-two square kilometers. The brigades could be categorized into three zones. The zone adjacent to Nanxi Town encompassed six brigades, each with a large nonagricultural population employed in handicrafts and various enterprises.[9] Their members also grew vegetables, sugar cane, and mulberry on the dikes and raised fish in the ponds. They were obliged to contract with state agents under the planned-purchase schemes and were given a quota of commodity grain at a price slightly higher than the state price. The next zone was in an area of the sands rapidly developed after the socialist revolution. It consisted of brigades that grew cash crops as well as grain, both contracted with state agents. They too were given a quota of the higher-priced commodity grain. The zone farthest away from the town was purely grain growing. It was in the less developed part of the sands and reachable by road only in the last few years. Not only were the members of these brigades made responsible for their own grain rations, but also a large procurement quota was imposed. Without any large village, market, or school, this zone was considered poor and remote. Its residents were referred to as "peasants," a term that, because of the official policies, had combined with traditional prejudices to become most unflattering.

Town residents did not want to be peasants. Apart from the differences in provisions, the disparities in income were substantial. In town industries the average annual income per person in 1978 was 518 yuan, but the annual agricultural income in Nanxi Rural Commune was only 171 yuan. Commune officials blamed this on the low grain-procurement prices and the high quota.[10] Not until 1984–85, when the quotas were removed and prices were negotiated, did grain production become mildly profitable. One might argue that if one separated the agricultural income of the rural commune from that of its nonagricultural enterprises, the wages were not low. The commune operated small-scale industries at two levels, commune and brigade. In 1978 the average per capita income was 660 yuan at commune-level enterprises and 446 yuan at brigade-level enterprises. Workers and managers, however, generally regarded employment in the rural commune as insecure because its cadres were constantly pressured by county authorities to divert the profits to agriculture. In fact Yongding, a brigade within Nanxi Rural Commune, had been a target of criticism by the Maoists throughout the 1970s for "having derailed from the tasks of aiding agriculture."

Only at times of political pressure did some town residents wish they had a rural status. In the wake of the Cultural Revolution, when the town's educated youths were forcibly sent down to the sands, they envied their counterparts across the narrow waterway in the rural commune who were spared. The latest administrative maneuver involved the one-child campaign: villagers were allowed two children, whereas each couple in town was allowed only one.

Even without considering the quotas, it was generally agreed that enforcing the law was more difficult in the villages than in town. In Nanxi Town, cadres had many levers for conducting disciplined birth control campaigns. The first peak was in the fall of 1980, when pregnant women without quotas were rounded up and "convinced" to undergo abortion. Another campaign was conducted in 1984. In the fall of 1986 I watched neighborhood directors organize to cut off the electricity supplies of households that had exceeded birth quotas. In November 1987 violators again were rounded up and kept in the town guest houses at their own expense until they agreed to abortions. The paid workers were most vulnerable. Violators had their wages reduced 10 percent for ten years, their bonuses and work seniority eliminated. Most felt they had little choice but to quit and work in village enterprises instead. In the countryside the cadres had no such levers. The introduction of the production responsibility system made the campaign next to impossible. A woman cadre complained that, since the reforms extended the contracting of production resources to individual households to fifteen or more years, the peasants chose to ignore the official threats.

Personal maneuvering aside, the cadres of the two communes were locked into a relationship they sarcastically termed *nanjie nanfen* (too drawn together to be disentangled). The fact that their headquarters were within a stone's throw of each other, and that Nanxi Rural Commune had over ten thousand nonagricultural residents living in the neighborhoods that encircled the town, created constant conflicts over administrative rights and duties. On top of that, the decade of reforms that gave rural enterprises tax exemptions made the town cadres extremely anxious about competition. In 1985 Nanxi Town had a population of 32,000, of which

9,117 were employed in its 52 enterprises and produced an annual output of 138,249,000 yuan. The Nanxi Rural Commune (renamed *qu,* or rural district, in 1983) administered a population of 111,313, which produced an annual output of 301,097,000 yuan, out of which 142,507,000 yuan came from its 47 district-level and 275 township- and village-level enterprises hiring a total of 15,247 workers. [11]

But when the municipal government in 1985 proposed to reduce the competition by merging the two units, the idea was violently opposed by both sides. The cadres in town loudly reminded themselves of the lessons of history, when political campaigns had rechanneled the resources of the town to the poor fringes of the rural commune. On the other hand, the cadres in Nanxi Rural Commune were afraid that by merging, the subsequent acquisition of town status would subject their industries to the priorities of the state industrial sector and to stricter supervision by the tax offices.

Nevertheless, the new administrative unit, named Nanxi Zhen, was officially established in January 1987. Town residents generally watched the merger with some anxiety. Competition between the two communes had given them room for maneuver. In the decade of reforms, those who incurred official wrath had sought shelter in the rural commune. After the merger, however, the two governments became one, resulting in a more unified bureaucracy with a wider administrative net. [12]

In sum, the town and the villages had been linked by a structure of power traditionally based on social differentiation and cultural exclusion. After the revolution, administrative prerogatives further locked the rural and town residents into distinct categories that increasingly defined people's life chances and shaped their political strategies. The question is, has the recent decade of reforms dissolved, continued, or reproduced under different guises this village-town division?

POPULATION MOVEMENTS IN NANXI TOWN

The freezing and thawing of the worlds of the peasants and workers are illustrated by the area's population movements in terms of marketing activities as well as migration and settlement. In the past the more conventional marketing activities were conducted in the townships bordering Nanxi Town, where rich peasants owned grain fields and mulberry dikes. They used the grain for wine making and pig rearing, and the mulberry for rearing silkworms to produce cocoons for the specialized markets in

Shunde, twenty-five kilometers away. Mulberry was also sold in the two regional markets in Nanxi.

In the sands, where contact between tenants and their landlords in town was minimal, power relationships were fluid. It was not uncommon for tenants to foil their landlords by harvesting before the grain was fully ripe and then fleeing on their boats, an act locally known as *geqinghe*. By the early twentieth century armed local bosses competed successfully for a large share of the harvests. Poor males continued to migrate to the sands, and rural women moved to the town as second wives, concubines, and maids.

Corresponding to the shrinking of peasant marketing in the 1950s were restrictions on migration. By the late 1950s it became increasingly difficult for peasants to migrate to town outside of the officially approved channels. With strict supervision by the public security office in cooperation with the town's fifteen neighborhood committees and the grain stations, illegal migrants found it hard to maintain their stay for extended periods.

From 1963 to 1978 the population of Nanxi Town increased more by natural growth than by in-migration (see Table 1). In fact since 1968 many families in town dreaded the footsteps of the neighborhood-committee directors, who pressured educated youths to settle in the outlying villages and state farms in the sands.

Political pressure was intense, especially for families with "bad class statuses." In 1986 I was told the sad story of the family who used to own the town's largest teahouse. The eldest daughter was married and living in another county, and the second daughter was killed in an industrial accident. The neighborhood committee did not spare the youngest son, who had been admitted to a postsecondary school. On the other hand, the family of a cadre who had several sons was able to keep all of them in town. One of his sons became a leader in the party youth league in a town enterprise and was later selected to the town's party committee. "What could one do?" an elderly resident recalled. "The word *official* has two mouths (*guanzi liangge kou*), and these mouths are bigger than ours."

The first peak of out-migration from town was in 1968, though large in-migration reflected the general fluidity of population movements in the midst of the Cultural Revolution. The next peak came in 1972, and the third in 1976 (see Tables 1 and 2). It was not until 1978 that youths who had been sent away returned in large numbers, some illegally. In

TABLE 1 Population Statistics in Nanxi Town, 1963–1985

Year	Births	Deaths	In-migration	Out-migration	Year-end Total	Unregistered Residents[a]
1950[b]					27,044	
1953					19,522	
1963	375	95	394	394	24,138[c]	175
1964	416	104	215	313	24,352	62
1965	724	191	420	596	24,709	58
1966	557	164	539	515	25,126	55
1967	557	158	298	368	25,455	134
1968	693	173	1,611	1,782	25,804	182
1969	601	193	221	785	25,648	190
1970	509	154	251	415	25,839	147
1971	514	191	376	411	26,127	144
1972	499	183	1,321	1,499	26,265	198
1973	—	—	—	—	26,660	—
1974	493	190	542	578	26,927	—
1975	404	196	624	695	27,064	—
1976	347	182	811	1,090	26,950	—
1977	318	185	626	835	26,874	170
1978	348	165	1,122	764	27,415	—
1979	453	180	1,734	974	28,448	—
1980	436	166	1,059	878	28,899	—
1981	520	201	1,104	872	29,450	—
1982	421	205	1,266	1,036	29,896	—
1983	394	228	1,428	1,296	30,194	—
1984	331	221	1,535	1,198	30,641	—
1985	483	199	2,265	912	32,278	—

Source: Records of Nanxi Town government and neighborhood committees.

a. Unregistered residents are not included in the population figures.

b. Total population for 1950 and 1953 included for comparative purposes. The 1950 figure probably includes the nonagricultural population in the town and the periurban villages. The 1953 figure is the number of residents registered as town residents when Nanxi was incorporated.

c. The total population number for 1963 is problematic: from the records, it is listed as 23,323, that is, 815 persons fewer than my own calculations. The large discrepancy may be due to the initial formation of the urban commune when the status of many households was undetermined. Discrepancies in other years are all under 100.

TABLE 2 Educated Youths Sent to the Countryside,
1968–1972

		Distribution			
Year	Total	Guangzhou Military Construction Corps	Nanxi Rural Commune	Other Communes	State Farm
1968–1971	1,043	232	268	467	76
1972	191	1	a	a	0

Source: Records of Nanxi Town government.

a. The three major district committees reported that 187 youths were sent to rural communes in 1972 but did not specify which ones; 3 of the total of 191 youths were unaccounted for.

the 1980s, in response to national directives, the town government lifted the restrictions on labor mobility step by step. Local cadres interpreted party documents in the following sequence: Party Document No. 1 in 1982 confirmed the commitment of the state to respect production responsibilities *(bao);* the one in 1983 emphasized the notion of decollectivization *(fen);* and the one in 1984 highlighted the idea of enduring change by extending some production contracts to fifteen years or more. When the increase in agricultural production seemed assured by a revival of peasant incentives, Party Document No. 1 in 1985 introduced the notion of mobility or letting go *(fang)* by allowing peasants to live, to work, and to operate individual enterprises in the towns.[13] Moreover, the development of subcounty-level towns and their enterprises became an important item on the political agenda.

Viewing Nanxi Town's accessibility and its tradition of commercial activities, one might have expected an influx of rural migrants who would engage in marketing and in construction work, or who would join town enterprises. The town government, however, restricted migration. It stipulated that only rural residents who had immediate families in town, who had obtained housing, and who could provide for their own grain were to be registered. Once registered, they became "households who take care of their own grain" *(zililiang hu)* and were allowed to seek work in the factories.[14] But the historical separation of the town from the villages meant that few passed the first condition. This was a good example of local cadres using the unique history of the area to continue the power of exclusion without breaking official guidelines. An influx occurred only in a short period, in 1985, as shown in the aggregate data from the fifteen neighborhoods (see Table 3).

TABLE 3 Households Taking Care of Their Own Grain
Rations

Year	A	B	C	D	E	F	G	H	I	J	K	L	M	N	O	Total Households in Town
1984	9	5	0	6	2	20	1	0	2	0	4	1	0	2	1	53
1985	13	29	33	27	17	23	13	19	13	22	34	26	13	28	12	322
1986	2	1	2	4	1	0	0	1	5	1	0	0	0	0	2	19

(Columns A–O are grouped under the heading *Neighborhoods*.)

Source: Records of the fifteen neighborhood committees in Nanxi Town.

By 1986 this category of migrants had dropped to a trickle.[15] The enterprises in Nanxi Town seemed relatively untouched by the limited migration. Except for shoe and handbag factories, whose contracts with overseas Chinese merchants varied seasonally, there was little movement of workers in and out of the town's major enterprises. The total number of migrant laborers who registered with the town government in 1986 was 800, but the number included employment in state-run teahouses and in private enterprises. Interviews with the managers of the largest factories in town reveal that, except for those with seasonal overseas contracts, the percentage of rural migrants in their work force was extremely low (see Table 4).

If the enterprises were not hiring rural migrants, one might still expect rural entrepreneurs who sought private licenses to tap the town market and to settle in town for that purpose. From 1979 to 1985, 821 private-enterprise licenses were issued, but the head of the Office for the Administration of Industry and Commerce assured me in 1986 that

TABLE 4 Rural Migrants in Selected Town Enterprises, 1986

Factory	Total Number of Workers	Number of Rural Migrant Workers
Electronic factory	550	15
Number-one lock factory	415	16
Door hinges and chains factory	400	8
Printing factory	250	10
Handbag and hats factory	400	100 + [a]

Source: Interviews in 1986, 1987, and 1988.

a. Seasonal employment.

TABLE 5 Distribution of Private Licenses in Nanxi Town,
1985

Trades	Total Number	Number of Entrepreneurs	Previous Occupations		
			Retiree	Job Awaiter	Unemployed
Industry and handicraft	218	592	5	319	268
Construction	1	1	0	0	1
Commerce	413	584	5	241	338
Food	88	125	1	55	69
Services	57	70	0	32	38
Repair	43	52	0	28	24
Others	1	1	0	0	1
Total	821	1,425	11	675	739

Source: Records of Office for the Administration of Industry and Commerce.

the licenses were issued only to legitimate residents in the town (see Table 5).

He was in fact extremely annoyed that his counterpart in Nanxi Rural Commune at the time issued licenses for rural entrepreneurs who frequented the markets but evaded the fees and other restrictions of the town government. It seems that the most popular strategy for them was to acquire the style of "guerrilla warfare" *(da youji)*. They would move around instead of getting long-term, officially approved livelihoods.

Compared with the rigidities in Nanxi Town, the adjacent townships thrived with the relaxing of market restrictions and with increased labor mobility. Land was scarce.[16] Households kept small plots to grow vegetables for their own consumption and sold the surplus in the town market. In 1988 a woman in Yongding estimated for me that a crop of vegetables in her family plot could be sold for forty to fifty yuan, and six to eight crops were harvested in a year. Although vegetable growing could be profitable, young people sought work in nonagricultural enterprises. They joined the local factories or took construction and hauling jobs.

In 1987 factories in these suburban townships engaged in massive hiring of unskilled laborers. Yongding, the largest and already the most industrialized of the townships, rapidly developed its industries. Of the ten thousand migrant laborers who registered with the Nanxi Zhen government in January 1988, three thousand worked in Yongding's factories. Residents in Yongding constantly complained about "traffic jams." On the road leading to Yongding's industrial area, thousands of cyclists moved in one direction every morning and in the reverse in the evenings. The bulk of the migrants came from Guangxi, Hunan, and Jiangxi provinces. They were recruited by the factories through the county labor bureaus, and they settled in makeshift dormitories.[17] Yongding's factories also hired laborers from other villages in Nanxi Rural Commune and from neighboring communes, which were also undergoing rapid transformation.

These communities diversified their sources of livelihood. In Zhixi Xiang, for example, villagers continued to grow rice for their own consumption, but they converted part of their land into fish ponds and salable lawn squares. Some contracted vast areas from the village office and hired seasonal migrant laborers from Guangxi and Hunan, paying them a monthly wage of 80 to 100 yuan.[18] Young local laborers were notably absent because they had joined the factories in the townships surrounding Nanxi Town and only returned in the evening to help with the family plots. When I visited these communities in early 1988, it was not uncommon to find old men and women in the fields with grandchildren on their backs.

In the more remote part of the sands, structural transformations were also rapid. Minlong Rural Commune to the southeast of Nanxi Rural Commune had a dramatic increase in annual per capita income, from 90 yuan in 1978 to 1,000 yuan in 1985. The vast sands allowed each of its 17,300 members 5 *mu* of land for rice, 3 *mu* for sugar cane, and over 10 *mu* for orchards, an area larger than an average-sized household could handle. The number of workers in Minlong's newly established enterprises increased from 440 in 1978 to 1,990 in 1985. There were five small enterprises that did additional processing work in plastic products, handbags, knitting, costume jewelery, and molding, and depended on seasonal employees. Local youths, however, shunned seasonal employment; instead, 1,150 laborers migrated out of the community in 1985 for contract work. By 1986 the enterprises had to hire 50 migrant laborers from Yangjiang County to the southwest and pay each person up to 80 yuan a month. The connection with Yangjiang County is interesting. Minlong had been settled by *Dan* fishermen, some of whom moored along the coast in the poorer Yangjiang areas. In a sense, traditional cultural networks have worked into the contemporary economic strategies in which *Dan* migrant laborers continue to fill the community's less desirable livelihoods.

Therefore, although agriculture yields high income, rural communities have viewed nonagricultural employment as more desirable. This, combined with the traditional social networks and postrevolutionary administrative boundaries, has resulted in a tiered migration pattern, with young laborers moving from the more remote areas of the sands to the townships adjacent to Nanxi Town.

The difference in the experiences of Nanxi Town and Nanxi Rural Commune is not unique; an analysis of Hunan Province points to similar problems. The loosening up takes place mostly in the agricultural sector and in small market towns that are the headquarters of former rural communes and brigades, but not in the incorporated market towns.[19]

INVISIBLE BOUNDARIES

If the area surrounding Nanxi Town is booming with movements of people and goods, what inhibits rural migrants from working and settling in the town itself? One may suggest that reforms in agriculture are so successful that villagers continue to farm instead of committing themselves full time to industrial work. Evidence from Nanxi and Minlong rural communes shows that agricultural income increased severalfold after the reforms and at times might have surpassed wages in the factories. But young peasants are leaving the villages at an alarming rate. Moreover, it is interesting to note that even among the rural laborers who have settled in Yongding, few attempt to cross the street to join the enterprises in Nanxi Town. They are generally content with Yongding's enterprises, which offer good wages and are not rigid about enforcing official rules. When asked whether they would be interested in employment in the enterprises in Nanxi Town, they quite uniformly say they regard such employment as "unreachable." To them, the town economy belongs to a different "system" *(xitong)* not yet ready to include them.[20]

The fence seems to have been erected by both sides. Although migrants have become consumers in the town's shops and street bazaars, a majority of town industries have continued as before, hiring few migrants. The comparatively static picture may lead one to suggest that town enterprises are losing out to the competitive energies in the townships and that it would be difficult to absorb extra laborers, even if managers intend to do so. The problems for town enterprises have been real, as I have tried to show in two previous papers that describe Nanxi's competition with the rural enterprises.

The general insecurity of the town cadres and workers in this period of competition has in fact been reflected in prejudice against migrants.[21] Factory managers insist that migrants from outside the province are not used to the labor discipline, are slow to pick up technical skills, and are therefore undesirable. But in factories under contract to overseas merchants, which require labor with little technical skill in such jobs as clothes and shoe making, managers are obliged to hire cheaper migrants from outside the province.[22] Those from the nearby villages are shunned. It is believed that they demand higher wages and will "steal" the skills and contracts before leaving for better pay elsewhere. They are avoided as potential competitors. There are also numerous cases in which prized technicians are prevented by the town government from leaving the collective enterprises to start enterprises of their own. The significant point here is that threatened local cadres still have the power to stall market competition and labor mobility and to preserve the enclaves they have carved out for themselves.

The general attitudes of town residents are also loaded with prejudice. Migrants working in the adjacent townships are blamed for the increased crime and disorder in town. Neighborhood directors are told to step up their vigilance in cooperation with public security to spot unregistered residents. The popular night market along the town's main street is no longer patronized by the "locals." They show their disdain by staying home to watch Hong Kong programs on their color televisions and letting the migrants roam the streets. "We hardly mix with them," they emphasize. In their minds the "peasants" from the sands are bad enough, and the "outsiders" *(waidi ren)* worse still. It is clear that many town residents feel besieged and threatened; but, to an extent, they have managed to keep their work and social life separate from those of the migrants.

What is significant here is that, despite relative stagnation in the town economy, residents have held on to town enterprises. Few look for alternative livelihoods except for some technicians, who have been lured away by the extremely high wages offered by some rural enterprises, and those at the bottom of the town economy, who feel they have nothing to lose. Immobility seems to be partly self-imposed. The story of a 36-year-old woman worker reveals the typical concerns and dilemmas of this "silent majority." Ah Cai's grandfather owned a large bakery in Nanxi before the revolution. After private enterprises were collectivized in the 1950s, both her grandfather and her father worked for the town's biscuit factory. When her grandfather retired in 1968, she took his place. It was not what she, a junior-secondary-school graduate, had wanted to do, but she was already grateful that the job allowed her to remain in town.

After twenty years she found herself in the same biscuit factory, earning 70 yuan a month and a bonus of around 25 yuan. She paid 10 yuan toward her retirement funds and found her meager salary insufficient to keep up with the inflation in recent years.[23] Unmarried and living at home, she was embarrassed that she could give only 30 to 40 yuan a month to her mother for expenses, when a meal in the town's Hong Kong–style restaurants easily cost twice as much. Fortunately her father was still working, the family owned their home, and her mother, who was able to earn some supplementary income by helping out in weddings, never asked her for support. In fact Ah Cai felt that she remained a burden to her parents. On top of that, she had a younger brother who was still in junior-secondary school and a retarded 24-year-old sister.

She assured me that her work unit was not doing badly, but the performance of the workshops was uneven. Bonuses could differ 200 percent. Nonetheless, she thought that the factory management "swallowed up all the profits." She was tempted to leave the factory to join the enterprises in Yongding, because she figured that, if the peasants from Guangxi and Hunan could earn 150 yuan a month, a skilled town worker like herself could easily make 200 to 300 yuan.[24] In fact some of the young workers in her factory had done just that. Their rationale was: "So what if these factories do not give any fringe benefits; after all, what does Ah Cai have after twenty years? If things do not work out, we shall find other alternatives."

It was easy for them to leave, according to Ah Cai, because they had not accumulated job seniority. They had also joined the work force after the reforms had loosened up the rural economy and popularized the hiring of contract labor. None of them had lived under the threat of "being sent to the sands for life because they had no town employment."

She was envious of the individual entrepreneurs, the nouveaux riches who hired her mother for their weddings and grossly flaunted their wealth. Her mother was sympathetic but was worried that, once Ah Cai joined the enterprises in Yongding, she would be entirely in the company of migrant laborers. Her chance of finding a spouse, small to start with, would be next to impossible. After a year of agonizing over her future, Ah Cai finally decided to remain in the biscuit factory because, according to her, the Yongding factories across the street "are just too far away."

If we are to address the question of which sector of the subcounty economy has thawed in the late 1980s, Nanxi Zhen presents an incongruent picture. The booming economy and the fluidity of the labor movements in the villages of the former Nanxi Rural Commune are in striking contrast to the general stagnation and immobility in Nanxi Town. The fact that the two communes are so closely juxtaposed obliges one to look for explanations beyond locational advantages.

To look at the problem historically, traditional economic inequality and social distance between town residents and those in the sands were reinforced, if not reified, by administrative measures after the revolution. It is true that the nature of that division has changed substantially in the decade of reforms. In economic terms, peasants in the sands are no longer poor and immobile. The fact that enterprises in the periurban area have recruited thousands of them and that an increasing number of women are marrying into the area indicates that traditional social and cultural barriers are breaking down within the rural district.[25] On the other hand, from the restrained movements of the rural migrants, the barriers put up by the town managers, and the dilemmas of the town workers, it seems that the boundaries erected after the revolution that isolated the town from the surrounding villages continue to define mobility strategies and entrepreneurial energies.

Why is it that these divisions are so recalcitrant despite administrative intentions to narrow them? I would suggest that one needs to examine how economic and social life in the two communes has been penetrated in different ways by the bureaucratic structures developed after the revolution, and how the consequent structure of power has created entrenched interests and shaped perceptions. These interests linger to distort the very policies intended to remove them.

When rural migrants say that livelihoods in the town belong to a different system, they clearly depict the predicament of Nanxi Town. Unlike individual farms that cadres in the rural commune minimally oversee, and unlike the village and township enterprises that have only recently sprung up on the landscape under a liberalized atmosphere, industrial production in town has been more institutionalized. It is managed by a large corps of cadres whose careers are tied to the party organization and subjected to pressures exerted by the municipal bureaucracies, if not directly by the central government. The fifty-odd enterprises in Nanxi Town are dependent on state enterprises for contracts, raw materials, and technical expertise. At times they are given subsidies, but they are also subjected to the eight-grade tax schedule, as state enterprises are. The accounts of the largest factories are closely audited by the municipal tax bureau. In a word, the collective economy of Nanxi is heavily shaped by the privileges and the inconveniences of the state sector. The local town government may have its own grievances against the central government, but they are different levels of a monopolizing state machinery, which exerts tremendous control over every aspect of people's lives in Nanxi.

In the previous paper I have argued that the recent decade of reforms put the town cadres in untenable positions.[26] They are held responsible for the performance of the entire collective economy and have tried to sustain it by administrative means. Yet, at the lowest end of the urban industrial hierarchy, the town enterprises are most threatened by the market competition that the cadres are politically obliged to promote. Within their means, the cadres have managed to protect themselves by continuing to exclude rural migrants as well as to prevent their skilled workers from leaving.

As for the ordinary workers, many are reluctant to leave the town enterprises not only because they have twenty years of security tied up with it, but also because they are not convinced that market competition would have the lasting power to fight an all-encompassing party bureaucracy. Coping with such power has become a prevalent feature of the political culture of this silent majority. Joining the rank of peasants, even if it means securing a higher income, is not an attractive option. As long as economic strategies are shaped by these perceptions, the lure and the power of an urban state sector continue to be reinforced, although its administrative hardware is being eroded.

On the other hand, the shrewd use of market competition and administrative advantages by the leaders of the former Nanxi Rural Commune triggered unprecedented dynamism.[27] The township enterprises on the outskirts of Nanxi Town are the nerve center of this dynamism, which leads to transformations in other parts of the region. The tiered migration of the rural population toward these townships and the recruitment of laborers from outside the province are breaking century-old social and cultural barriers and reactivating traditional networks beyond the region.

As long as the suburban townships maintain the lead in industrial development, the hierarchy between them and the villages in the more remote areas of the sands will probably continue.

The movements, however, have created unprecedented tension for the residents of Nanxi Town. At this historical juncture, the lingering lure of the urban state sector may continue to dominate the decisions of people like Ah Cai. But her coworkers, less entrenched in the old, politically defined social hierarchy, are heading for new opportunities.

Will the logic of operation of the emerging economic structures, fueled by these energies, gain ground to the point of no return? I would predict only that it is not entirely up to the residents nor to the cadres to decide. A recent change in the ideological line of the party central committee has made local cadres nervous and cautious about the reforms. In fact after the 4 June incident in Beijing I revisited the town. Cadres reassured me that business was as usual and that overseas investors should not worry about an ideological shift. But I sensed that they were concerned about the situation, especially when Ye Xuanping, the provincial governor of Guangdong and a leading reformer, was rumored to be assigned to a position in Beijing. It was clear to them that, although the new national leaders continued to talk about economic liberalization, ideological tightening was on the agenda. This has already driven away some sensitive overseas investors whose capital is much needed.

Since the beginning of 1989, state banks have tightened the supply of money and are creating a minirecession in the delta. In an area where there has been an acute labor shortage since the reforms, factory managers are alarmed that an increasing number of their local workers do not have enough to do.[28] Everyone seems aware that a further tightening would hit Nanxi at a most vulnerable time. But if the cadres ignore the changing ideological signals and continue to push for an open economy for pragmatic reasons, they might become a political scapegoat. They find themselves in a no-win situation.

The dilemma of the cadres ripples outward to affect the livelihood of ordinary workers and entrepreneurs. The migrant laborers are the first targets. Anticipating a worsening recession after the June events, cadres in Nanxi have started to discourage migrants from staying in town. Those whose employment papers have not been approved by 1 June are systematically sent away.[29] Small private entrepreneurs are also bracing themselves for a storm. They cannot rely on state banks to supply credit. Relatives from Hong Kong and Macao are unsure of investment because they expect a shrinking market. The enterprises are already securing raw materials through nonstate channels at a higher price. The uncontrolled inflation adds to the difficulties. Their worst fear is not the market but the town government, which has considered them a competitive nuisance hampering its own enterprises and is waiting for an excuse to eliminate them. The workers who have quit the collective economy to join these enterprises are undergoing their own soul-searching. They have traded security for an economic adventure. Now they feel they have everything to lose. As for the rural migrants, they will hold on to their factory employment until driven away. Unlike the town residents, they have land to fall back on. Most will return to their farms and wait for the next cycle of political relaxation.

Few governments have so successfully shaped the pattern of migration between village and town as the Chinese socialist regime. Also, few have been able to maintain such a powerful distance between the populations in the two sectors. But as this case study shows, perception of the sheer weight of state priorities does not necessarily smother analytical attention to local choices.[30] By focusing on the differing degrees to which the cadres and workers in Nanxi Zhen have internalized the weight of the state sector and on how the process defines boundaries in migration strategies, one sees the presence of the macroconstraints and opportunities played out at the microlevel of subjective choices. By taking into account how local social groups maneuver within political institutions, no matter whether their actions reproduce old structures of power or create new superlocal networks, one also gives local initiative and human agency an analytical place they deserve.[31]

PART TWO

Urban Reforms and Urban Workers

Urban Job Mobility

Deborah Davis

In the 1980s rural Chinese were on the move. Between 1980 and 1987 thirty-five million left their villages to work in factories, join rural construction teams, or travel daily as itinerant peddlers in city markets.[1] Numerically the largest flow of migrants was to small towns, but the influx to large cities was so great that by 1986 in several of China's largest cities recent rural migrants constituted 20 percent of the work force.[2] Rural to urban migration appears to have begun as an ad hoc decision in the early 1980s to facilitate urban construction and improve the supply of fresh produce in urban markets. Subsequently it became formal policy when, in 1983, the central government changed the registration process to encourage "temporary" urban residents to invest and settle in small and medium-sized towns.[3] And by 1987 long-distance migration was explicitly endorsed as an essential strategy to remedy hardcore rural poverty.[4]

TABLE 1 Composition of Urban Work Force,
1952–1987

Year	State	Collective	Private/Other
1952	62.5%	0.8%	36.6%
1957	76.5	20.0	3.0
1965	72.9	23.7	3.6
1975	78.0	22.0	0.01
1978	78.5	21.4	0.1
1980	76.1	23.0	0.7
1982	75.5	23.2	1.2
1984	70.6	26.2	3.0
1985	70.5	25.8	3.5
1986	70.2	26.2	3.6
1987	70.0	25.3	4.6

Source: ZGTJNJ 1988, p. 153.

By contrast, Chinese citizens who were legally registered as "permanent" urban residents continued after 1980 to be highly immobile, both residentially and occupationally. Long-distance moves between cities were rare; particularly for the 70 percent who worked in state-owned enterprises (quanmin suoyouzhi) (see Table 1), the reforms only slightly increased the frequency of job changes. Switching employers within the same city or even within the same residential district continued to be a difficult experience that required lengthy bureaucratic bargaining on the part of the individual and the prospective employer.

In urban China the post-Mao critique of the "iron rice bowl" explicitly identified lifetime employment and low levels of job turnover as prime targets of reform. Yet a decade after policy shifts legitimated out-migration from the villages and created buyers' markets for a range of industrial inputs, there was no comparable shift to permit a labor market among urban employees of state enterprises.[5] Among technical and professional staff, annual turnover from 1982 to 1987 averaged less than 3 percent.[6] Moreover, by the end of the decade the rate of turnover among skilled staff in the state sector appeared to be declining even as it was increasing among those in small urban collectives and private enterprises.[7]

If one were to draw on studies of labor turnover in advanced capitalist societies, it would appear that the Chinese confront a classic case of internal labor markets, where those working in the most-organized, high-wage, and high-technology units prefer procedures that discourage interfirm transfers.[8] If this were true, then the failure of the Deng reformers to increase job mobility in the state sector would testify to the ability of current arrangements to satisfy preferences for security among firm managers and long-time employees. But in the urban state sector what we find are extremely high levels of *immobility* that are unsatisfactory to both managers and workers. In short, Chinese state employees are "stuck," and they feel frustrated by their inability to take advantage of the reform leadership's stated goal of reducing bureaucratic controls over employment practices.

By examining policy shifts between 1978 and 1987 and using a survey I conducted in Shanghai in 1987, I shall argue here that the keys to the persistently low rates of job mobility among urban state workers are both ideologically and structurally specific to contemporary China. Among the highest levels of CCP leadership, there is a fundamental hostility to labor markets that is more extreme than in any other socialist economy. And within each metropolitan region there is a level of territorial autarky that originated in the reforms of the 1950s but has been greatly exacerbated by the decentralization of the Deng era. Thus although employment patterns in state enterprises may superficially seem to resemble those in internal labor markets of Western capitalist economies, the underlying supports are fundamentally different.

Unlike Russian or Eastern European Marxists, leaders of the Chinese Communist party have refused to accept any labor market for state employees.[9] Instead, in both principle and practice, the post-Mao leaders have upheld the Maoist heterodoxy that jobs in the state sector are "assignments," and therefore they have continued to treat urban employment more as a question of social welfare than as a problem of efficient use of labor inputs.[10] One consequence of this perspective for state employees is that individuals have had almost no opportunity to decide on where to use their training. Rather, it has been the enterprise to which the individual is assigned by state planners that has formal, and final, control over every job change.

Migration and registration restrictions such as those discussed by Helen Siu (Chapter 3) have bound rural workers to home villages and severely constrained the horizon of each rural resident's job choices, but the ideological justifications by which assignments to state jobs were controlled were grounded in assumptions about the superiority of a planned socialist economy and the urban proletariat that were absent in the consideration of agricultural labor. Thus when the reformers reduced control over rural marketing and migration, rural residents were able immediately to seize the opportunity to change jobs and take up new occupations. In the urban state sector there was no parallel relaxation of control and no subsequent upsurge in voluntary job changes.

After 1979, but particularly after 1984, the Deng reformers adopted several policies that ostensibly were to increase job mobility in the urban state sector. In theory, the reformers' efforts to decentralize managerial decision making, to separate political and economic leadership at the factory level, and to increase monetary incentives for individual workers should have encouraged higher rates of job turnover. But in practice, the reforms adopted between 1980 and 1987 did little to increase the flexibility of hiring practices. Enterprises that wanted new workers still had to apply to higher-level supervisors to get hiring quotas; new graduates of colleges and technical high schools were still given an assignment (*fenpei*) according to annual quotas; and state employees wishing to quit a firm had to use special connections or argue for "release" on grounds of extraordinary personal hardship.

Unwilling to grant ideological legitimacy to a labor market for state enterprises, the architects of the post-Mao reform instead settled for incremental change of existing bureaucratic procedures. For example, between 1983 and 1987 leaders experimented with a variety of administrative changes such as citywide "centers for the exchanges of talent" (*rencai jiaoliu zhongxin*),[11] temporary transfers "without loss of salary or seniority" (*tingxin liuzhi*),[12] and limited amounts of direct hiring when units met certain productivity ratios.[13] However, because decentralization of authority—a primary principle of the Deng reforms—greatly increased the power of entrenched local-level administrators and politicians, even these incremental adjustments failed to increase job turnover. In fact, in areas where there had been some movement toward higher mobility in the early 1980s, the trend seemed to reverse itself after 1984.[14]

Because of its immense size and poor transportation, China has had a long tradition of strong regional economies that bound people and goods to distinct geographic areas. But in contrast to many agrarian nations, preindustrial, precommunist China also was characterized by interregional trade and long-distance migration. Therefore centralization of political and economic power by the CCP after 1949 and extremely restrictive controls over internal migration in the mid-1950s encouraged provincial and metropolitan autarky in a nation long accustomed to regional specialization and long-distance migration.

Although determined to break with the Maoist philosophy of local self-sufficiency, Deng's reliance on administrative decentralization as a primary reform policy further strengthened the autonomy of municipal authorities and state enterprise leaders. In the area of employment practice, most reforms of hiring and transfer procedures were city-specific experiments that other urban centers followed only if their municipal leadership adopted them. Moreover, the efforts to increase financial accountability at the city and enterprise levels made local-level leaders even more protective of "their" labor supply and their human capital. Thus in examining job mobility between 1980 and 1987, I have observed the same tendency toward hoarding of labor (especially skilled labor) that the economists Christine Wong and Barry Naughton found when they examined the self-interested behavior of managers in local governments and enterprises in 1982–1984.[15] In an unforeseen and somewhat counterintuitive way, the ideal of decentralization, which was to have encouraged increased flexibility for enterprises and workers alike, in practice often served to maintain and even intensify the very rigidities that the reforms had been designed to eliminate.

REFORM OF URBAN EMPLOYMENT PRACTICES

The essence of the Maoist "iron rice bowl" for urban state workers was bureaucratic allocation of undifferentiated labor within administratively defined enclaves. With few exceptions, priorities of planners and administrators—not the talents or preferences of workers—determined job placement and turnover. Factories, stores, and government offices were assigned a labor quota; individuals did not seek jobs or plan careers.

Overall the situation resembled the manpower policy of an army.[16] As in wartime, young people upon completion of school were "deployed"; once conscripted, the worker/soldier moved through the ranks with his or her entering cohort. Training was done on the job, and skills were acquired not for the advancement of an individual career but for the improved performance of the organization or the fulfillment of political objectives of the central or local party leaders. New graduates of the city secondary schools and universities did not choose a job but registered for an assignment. Job changes were "transfers" *(diaodong)* of labor between units, and promotions followed schedules of planners (often those outside the enterprise) rather than improvements in an individual's performance or skill level.[17]

By 1978 virtually every segment of the state work force was dissatisfied with these practices. Central and municipal planners criticized the system as irrational and inefficient because assignment through yearly quotas did not allow rapid transfer of skilled labor to areas of greatest need or highest return. Enterprise-level managers could neither fire incompetent workers nor resign themselves. Employees were also dissatisfied. If they hated their job, they could not quit, and if they wanted to upgrade their skills, their supervisor had to approve the upgrading and their enterprise finance the retraining. Moreover, once an individual had a new skill, the employer—not the individual—had almost total discretion as to where to allocate the new "capability."

Innovations of the early 1980s, particularly in the months immediately before and after the October 1984 Plenum of the Twelfth Party Congress, explicitly attempted to reduce this monopolistic control over labor. Defining the problem as "ownership by the bureau" (*bumen suoyouzhi*) and "ownership by the unit" *(danwei suoyouzhi)*,[18] innovations of these early years attempted to help individuals (particularly technicians and engineers) break free from their current employers and find jobs on their own initiative. Typical experiments were "talent centers" where engineers and technicians could register for new jobs, and a leave policy *(tingxin liuzhi)* that allowed workers to take an unpaid leave if they moved from a state to a collective job.[19]

As reflected in this list of reforms, the thrust of the Deng critique of *danwei suoyouzhi* did not initiate fundamental changes equal to those unleashed by the decollectivization of agriculture or the revival of rural trade and marketing. A brief overview of how reforms of employment practices evolved in the years after 1984 and an analysis of the many ways local interest constrained labor illustrate why decentralization—either to the enterprise or to the municipality—served to block job mobility among state employees.

Reform of Transfer Procedures

The talent exchange centers *(rencai jiaoliu zhongxin)* first set up in Shenyang in 1983 promised increased rates of turnover and a more individual choice of jobs for engineers, economists, statisticians, and other technically skilled staff in state industry.[20] Those wishing to switch jobs registered at the center for a job transfer. State and collective enterprises in need of technical staff could then use this center to identify good prospects and initiate a transfer of staff for their unit. Subsequently other cities followed the lead of Shenyang, and by 1985 there were exchange centers throughout urban China. Overall rates of turnover, however, remained low, and an individual wishing to transfer often had to fight prolonged battles to secure a "release" from the original employer. During the first two years of operation, less than 2 percent of those who had registered succeeded in changing jobs.[21] Moreover, the longer the centers were open, the lower the overall rate of mobility among technical applicants.[22]

The major reason the talent centers failed to fulfill their initial promise was that job changes continued to be treated as "transfers." Just as before 1978, there were at least four basic stages for a successful move.[23] In the first stage the worker approached the prospective employer. Introductions usually were arranged through a spouse, a former classmate, a neighbor, or another kinsman rather than through a talent center or a published advertisement. Once the new unit agreed to take on the person, the employee approached the immediate supervisor with an explanation of why the transfer was necessary. The most common reasons were poor health, a long commute, or heavy obligations in the home; virtually never could one emphasize a desire to use one's training more efficiently or to have new experiences. If the supervisor endorsed the request, the worker then made a formal application to the labor office (*laodong gongzike*) of the current unit. The final round of negotiations was between cadres in the labor office of the worker's current unit (or personnel department *{renshike}* if the person was of cadre rank) and the *laodong gongzi ke* of their supervising company or bureau. If the latter approved the move, they would contact their counterparts in the supervisory unit of the new employer, and the two units were then empowered to finalize the job change by authorizing the transfer of the worker—and almost as critical, the transfer of the worker's personnel dossier (*dang'an*). If the individual seeking a transfer occupied a leadership position in either the party or the enterprise, there was an additional step whereby the party committee at the next higher administrative level that supervised the hiring unit also had to grant approval.[24]

In addition to this hierarchical chain of command that constrained transfers, administrative guidelines—some newly drafted after 1978— further restricted the range of movement. For example, as early as 1983 technical cadres were not permitted to be recruited from units that were subordinate to the new employer or were in a smaller city,[25] and in 1984 new testing procedures were introduced to limit the number of job applicants.[26] Moreover, after 1987, when factories were allowed to redistribute wages of workers who had transferred among the remaining workers, units became even less willing to accept transfers unless the previous employer of that new worker was willing to allow the worker to "bring his wage" with him, a condition that virtually no unit "releasing" a worker was willing to do.

As is evident from this brief overview, transfers in the post-Mao era were subject to a multitude of vetoes and involved frequent administrative interventions. As a result, transfers were easiest for low-profile workers whom units did not strongly desire to retain, and were most difficult for the best trained and ambitious, who were in short supply.

There was variation over time, however, and also among different types of units. Turnover was highest in the very first years of the Deng era, when heavily overstaffed units could not imagine any cost of reduced payrolls and when many people first hired during the Cultural Revolution willing to accept any state job jumped at the first opportunity to move to a job closer to their own choice. The highest degree of turnover reported by the press was in rural schools and hospitals and in urban factories with shift work. During the Cultural Revolution most graduates of medical colleges and teaching courses had been sent to the countryside; even some senior staff were sent to rural areas on long rotations from which they "never returned." In the early 1980s, when urban hospitals were once again expanding and research institutes and government offices were seeking college-educated cadres, many rural hospitals and schools were threatened with the loss of almost all skilled staff under the age of forty. Some rural and suburban secondary schools reported the departure of as many as 80 percent of their university graduates.[27] In addition, there was a general trend to move from "front-line" production jobs in industry into office jobs in adminstrative agencies (jiguan), a trend that threatened manufacturing units in large as well as small cities.[28]

Units threatened by a massive outflow of skilled personnel quickly devised a variety of means to prevent individuals from transferring. Unable to raise salaries or significantly increase the quality of their work environment, they clamped down on the one input that they could control: personnel. Supervisors prevented staff from taking exams for further education either by refusing to sign the permission letter needed to sit for an exam or by denying them a day off to take the test. They refused to promote or release those who had obtained diplomas from secondary technical schools *(zhongzhuan)* or postsecondary institutes *(dazhuan)*, even when the newly earned degree verified expertise in a technical area for which the unit had no use and another unit was willing to employ the person. Factory heads or labor office cadres set quotas on the number of workers who could leave the "first line" of work, refused to allow resignations, and requested that units which had "borrowed" technical staff return them.[29] A 1987 piece in *People's Daily* summarized the situation in this eight-character phrase: "If I can't use it, I won't let you use it" *(wo bu yong, ye bu gei ni yong)*.[30] But in fact restrictions appeared at this time because many units that had been hurt by the initial increases in job turnover really were threatened with a shortage of skilled staff and workers; without any labor market or the ability to offer more attractive benefits, they resorted to defensive (and negative) strategies to stem further loss of essential staff.

Sometimes the restrictions used to control personnel were specific to a unit, at other times to a sector *(xitong)*, a municipality, or a province. In every case, however, the ability of these local-level administrators to frustrate the larger goals of the reform graphically illustrates how the essential territoriality and autarky of the urban opportunity structure reduced job turnover in the state sector even after the October 1984 party congress explicitly endorsed further restructuring of the urban economy.[31]

Reform of Hiring Procedures

Theoretically, reforms aimed at changing the general transfer process for urban residents in all occupations and of every age group should have had greater potential quickly to increase job mobility than more limited reforms aimed solely at new entrants to the labor force. In practice, however, efforts to reform "first hires" in the state sector initially appeared of greater consequence. In 1978 the primary innovation was the use of retirements to provide jobs in state units by allowing each retiree to have a child "substitute" *(dingti)* for the parent in the parent's former place of work. In 1980 the leadership moved to diversify placement procedures and increase the range of jobs available to urban secondary-school graduates. Responsibility for job assignments shifted from schools to district labor bureaus, thereby theoretically increasing the range of job choices.[32]

TABLE 2 Enrollment in Secondary Vocational
Schools, 1970–1987 (in millions)

Year	Total Enrollment	Entrants	Graduates
1970	0.064	0.054	0.028
1976	0.690	0.348	0.339
1978	0.889	0.447	0.232
1980	1.243	0.468	0.410
1982	1.039	0.419	0.446
1984	1.322	0.546	0.376
1987	1.874	0.715	0.578

Source: ZGTJNJ 1988, pp. 877, 878, 884.

Subsequently there was sustained growth in secondary vocational education (see Table 2) and rapid expansion of private-sector jobs (see Tables 1 and 3), which promised increased opportunities for young urban residents to enter skilled jobs outside their residential district and in a different trade from that of their parents.

In 1986 the third and potentially most radical shift came when the State Council announced that as of 1 October all new state workers, but not cadre or technical staff, would be hired on time-specific contracts.[33] Henceforth all urban residents seeking jobs, except those recently demobilized from the military or graduating from a specialized secondary school, a college, or a university, were to register for job placement by the labor bureau of their street committee. If they were first-time applicants who had not taken the college entrance exam, they would also take

TABLE 3 Job Destinations of New Entrants, 1978–1987

Job	1978 (N = 5.4)[a]	1980 (N = 9.0)	1982 (N = 6.6)	1984 (N = 7.2)	1986 (N = 7.9)	1987 (N = 7.9)
State	72.0%	63.5%	61.5%	57.5%	67.6%	62.4%
Collective	28.0	31.0	33.0	27.0	28.0	26.7
Private	0	5.5	6.5	15.0	4.0	10.6

Sources: For 1978–1985, Zhongguo laodong gongzi tongji ziliao 1949–1985 (Statistical materials on Chinese labor and wages 1949–1985), p. 110; for 1986 and 1987, ZGTJNJ 1988, p. 175.

a. N figures are in millions.

a test to rate their skills in Chinese and mathematics. With these test results in hand, the cadres of the labor bureaus would then try to match the individual with a unit seeking contract workers. Although in theory jobs could be anywhere in the city, in fact they were most often found within the district where the labor bureau was located.[34] Once both sides had agreed to the placement, the employing unit and the labor bureau drew up a contract that specified the length of time for probation (usually one to three months) and for the full contract (usually three years). If during this interval the worker proved unsatisfactory or the unit needed to drop surplus labor, the contract worker was to be sent back to the labor bureau for a new assignment. For those who were dismissed through no fault of their own, unemployment insurance—in part financed through contributions by the worker to an unemployment insurance fund—would provide basic subsistence until the labor bureau could arrange another job.[35]

To explain how decentralized decision making and increased accountability at the enterprise level affected these several hiring reforms, let me examine in more detail the three most important innovations after 1978: (1) the introduction and subsequent phaseout of *dingti,* (2) the limited reform of *fenpei,* and (3) the early efforts to universalize contract labor.

PENSION REFORM AND THE DINGTI OPTION. Chinese state workers and staff have been guaranteed lifetime pensions since 1951.[36] A youthful labor force, however, held down the numbers eligible to retire, and political attacks on retirement as antisocialist during the Cultural Revolution prevented full implementation through the late 1970s. Therefore the July 1978 revision of the retirement regulations that encouraged retirement and guaranteed improved benefit levels signaled a radical departure from the practices of the previous three decades.

According to *Guofa* (National law) No. 104 (1978), pensions of 60 percent of the last wage would be awarded to any state employee with ten (instead of twenty) years of continuous employment, and retirement would be mandatory for women at age fifty (fifty-five if cadre) and men at sixty. Equally important, and most relevant to the reform of employment procedures, all retirees would be able to use the "substitution" *(dingti)* option to designate one of their children as a "successor" in their old unit. Any child in good health who did not already hold a state job and was between the ages of sixteen and twenty-nine would qualify. Suddenly, in one stroke of an administrative pen in Beijing, every urban

TABLE 4 Growth of Pension Program,
1978–1987

Year	Number of Retirees (in millions)	Pension Expenditures (in billion yuan)
1978	3.14	1.73
1979	5.96	3.25
1980	8.16	5.04
1981	9.50	6.23
1982	11.13	7.31
1983	12.92	8.73
1984	14.78	10.61
1985	16.37	14.98
1986	18.05	19.47
1987	19.68	23.84

Source: ZGTJNJ 1988, p. 203.

parent near retirement age could control the job placement of one child who met these minimal criteria of eligibility.

The response was immediate and extraordinary. Between December 1978 and December 1981 the number of retirees trebled from 3.1 million to 9.5 million, and between 1981 and 1987 it doubled again (see Table 4).

I do not yet have any nationwide figures on the percentage of retirees who used *dingti* to secure a child a state job, but unit- and city-specific data suggest that the heaviest use occurred in 1979 and 1980,[37] when parents seized the appearance of *dingti* as an opportunity to solve the employment problems of the sons and daughters who had been sent to work in the countryside between 1969 and 1978 (see Table 5). Moreover, even when parents were too young to retire or had more than one child needing a job, the new pension regulations changed procedures for job placements. Parents now felt entitled to request temporary assignments for their children from their employer, and enterprise heads felt greater responsibility for providing jobs for staff children.[38]

In September 1983, *Guofa* No. 137 officially repealed the universal application of *dingti*. Many had concluded that *dingti* had wreaked havoc with personnel assignments within units and directly conflicted with the new requirements that each enterprise be accountable for its own profits and losses. In addition, by 1983 the majority of youth sent to the coun-

TABLE 5 Number of Urban Youths
Sent to Countryside,
1969–1979

Year	Total (in millions)	% Sent to State Farms
1969	2.673	17.5%
1970	1.064	29.5
1971	0.748	32.9
1972	0.673	25.4
1973	0.896	10.0
1974	1.724	10.8
1975	2.368	10.0
1976	1.880	12.5
1977	1.716	9.3
1978	0.480	6.2
1979	0.247	4.1

Source: *Zhongguo laodong gongzi tongji ziliao 1949–1985;*
p. 110.

tryside had been reabsorbed into the urban labor force,[39] and increased opportunities for postsecondary education reduced the number of unskilled secondary-school graduates seeking permanent employment.[40] Nevertheless, in many units personnel officers interpreted the 1983 restrictions to apply only to children of cadres, and the practice of *dingti* continued until September 1986, when new regulations on contract labor explicitly eliminated the provision.

Eight years of *dingti* had a major impact on patterns of employment. Before 1978 urban secondary-school graduates rarely moved voluntarily from the city of their birth, and many worked in or near their parents' place of employment. But it was only with the popularization of *dingti* that jobs in the state sector became nearly hereditary. Designed to solve a crisis of unemployment among urban youth, the pension reform accentuated preexisting tendencies to tether adult children to their parents' employers and thereby directly increased the overall immobility of young urban residents.[41]

NEW PROCEDURES FOR EMPLOYING UNIVERSITY GRADUATES. Reform of employment procedures for university graduates involved only a minority of those entering the urban labor force each year (see Table 6). Nevertheless,

TABLE 6   University Graduates as Percentage of
All New Entrants to Urban Work Force,
1982–1987

Year	Graduates (in millions)	New Entrants (in millions)	Percentage
1982[a]	.457	6.650	6.8%
1983	.335	6.283	5.3
1984	.287	7.215	3.9
1985	.316	8.136	3.8
1986	.393	7.931	5.1
1987	.532	7.991	6.6

Source: ZGTJNJ 1988, pp. 175, 878.
a. Figures for 1982 include those who entered in 1977 and 1978.

because the reforms in this sector have attracted much attention and generated rather high expectations of fundamental change, I would like to address their outcomes. They provide another illustration of the ideological hostility of national-level leaders to labor markets and of their preference for planned allocation when dealing with an elite minority.

Conclusions that the Deng reform substantially reduced reliance on yearly *fenpei* are primarily supported from accounts of experiments conducted first by colleges in the Shenzhen economic zone and a few municipal "branch universities" (*fenxiao*) and later by four or five of the most elite national universities.[42] Shenzhen University and Shanghai University (previously the *fenxiao* of Fudan University in Shanghai) eliminated guaranteed job assignments for students entering in 1983. The elite universities began in 1985 by allowing approximately 5 percent of the "top" students to choose among three or four units that had been invited by the university to hire directly on campus. Thus, as with changes in transfer procedures, reform was aimed at those on the margins, and especially at those with technical skills. As a result, the only noticeable departure from earlier practice for the majority of students was some relaxation of political screening and an increased emphasis on professional competence. Thus whether we look at *Guofa* No. 91 (1985), *Guofa* No. 34 (1986), Hu Qili's speech in September 1986 at the Sixth Plenum of the Twelfth Congress, or at concrete examples of reform, placement of new college graduates between 1984 and 1987 adhered to yearly quotas and the principle of labor allocation within administratively defined catchment areas.[43]

Moreover, even the highest-level support for the ideal of increased individual choice and reduced administrative controls, such as that articulated in *Guofa* No. 91 (1985), reaffirmed that the goal was "to rationalize, not eliminate, *fenpei*" and that there would be no "retreat from planned allocation" of university graduates.[44]

EXPANDED USE OF CONTRACT LABOR IN STATE INDUSTRY. The potentially most fundamental attack on administrative allocation of labor began on 1 October 1986, when a State Council decision to phase out permanent (*guding*) job assignments in state factories (*qiye*) went into effect.[45] Henceforth all new workers would be hired for a fixed number of months. Ideally, by eliminating lifetime employment enterprises could raise productivity because the disgruntled would quit and the inefficient would be fired. Because few of those hired under these new conditions had fulfilled their contracts at the time this chapter went to press, I was unable to accumulate sufficient data to know whether this reform had succeeded in its stated aim of increasing labor turnover. Information on the treatment of contract workers during 1987 and 1988, however, suggests that expanded use of contract labor within state enterprises did not immediately have a strong impact.

Contract labor is not an innovation of the post-Mao era. Throughout the 1950s and 1960s state enterprises had a mixed labor force of permanent and nonpermanent staff. The nonpermanent workers performed a variety of tasks and came from rural and urban areas. Some were essentially seasonal labor, others had contracts for specific auxiliary work, and some were hired on multiyear contracts to supplement the permanent labor force.[46] The terms of the contracts varied, but in every case contract workers had fewer benefits and less security than those not on contracts. During the Cultural Revolution the practice came under attack as inegalitarian and discriminatory, and it fell into disuse. By 1981, however, sectors that had relied heavily on contract workers before the Cultural Revolution—hauling, construction, and mining—resumed the practice under the rubric of raising efficiency and rationalizing labor allocations.[47] Thus even before the formal abolition of *dingti* in 1983, the total number of contract workers hovered around 0.5 million. By December 1983 it had risen to 3.15 million, and after October 1986 the total again rose rapidly, reaching 5.71 million in July 1987 and 7.26 million by December of that same year.[48]

The numerical increase is significant. The number of contract workers soon exceeded the number of urban private entrepreneurs *(geti hu)*, and for the year ending December 1987, 60 percent of all the newly hired urban residents joined units as contract workers.[49] Yet treatment of contract workers in the units I visited in Shanghai and Wuhan in 1987 and 1988 indicated that in the initial phase of implementation, introduction of time-specific contracts had done little to weaken the power of "ownership by the unit" *(danwei suoyouzhi)*. On the contrary, most of the material gathered in 1987 and 1988 suggests that initially the reform strengthened managerial control of labor and did little to encourage higher rates of turnover.

When cadres from a Shanghai street committee and union officials from three industrial enterprises explained their experiences in the first ten months of implementation, they described contract laborers *(hetong gong)* as young people who had been unemployed for several years or had failed to enter any type of postsecondary school or training course. As might be expected, young people with this background were treated as substandard employees and given short-term assignments in sanitation work, road repair, and old textile factories. During this same period new hiring for more desirable jobs continued to be done through assignments from vocational classes of the *xitong*. Factories hired on the basis of labor quotas *(dingyun ding'e)* set by supervisory units, and at least through July 1987 unit-level leaders assumed that those who entered from the vocational classes could still be treated as permanent staff. Furthermore, managers in these factories explicitly told me they would not use contract labor sent by the labor bureaus for any type of technical or even skilled assembly work, because they did not want to lose their investment in workers who would leave after only three or four years.[50]

In addition to the distinction between long-term unemployed and new vocational graduates among newly hired contract workers, there were also three other categories of contract workers already in the factories prior to 1987. One group of contract workers included those who had been hired outside the plan by the unit itself before 1985; another included short-term *(linshi gong)* workers sent by the street committees; and the third, peasants hired by the units directly from the countryside. Workers in the first group were relatively well treated and in some cases had been promised that they would be switched over to the ranks of permanent workers after completion of their first contract. They were also often allowed to receive technical training and generally were indistinguishable from the general work force. Those in the second and third groups, by contrast, were essentially the same as the temporary workers who had been used by state enterprises in the 1950s and 1960s. They could be, and were, dismissed because of either poor performance or slack demand. In general they functioned as a labor reserve to whom the usual perquisites of permanent employment were denied. Their increased mobility reflected insecurity and a generally disadvantaged position in the hierarchy of urban jobs; it did not signal greater flexibility and vitality in job-seeking and recruiting behaviors.

In my 1987 and 1988 visits to Shanghai and Wuhan, it became clear that in the first years of implementation the contract system functioned primarily to maximize managerial control. For example, in textile mills that had been plagued by labor shortages after 1985, managers used contracts to keep the most-skilled manual laborers from leaving the mill.[51] In enterprises and research units that had spent company funds to provide advance training to an employee, three-year (and in some cases five-year) contracts were forced on those who had received training at the unit's expense in order to prevent the unit from losing its investment.[52] If the individual insisted on leaving before the end of the contract, the next employer (or the individual) was required to pay the original employer the cost of the training course before the first employer would release the personal dossier. Thus in general it appeared that through 1988 expanded use of labor contracts reinforced bureaucratically controlled employment procedures and did little to facilitate job mobility for either blue-collar or white-collar workers.

PERSONAL EXPERIENCE OF 100 SHANGHAI FAMILIES

In June 1987 I interviewed 100 Shanghai women born between 1925 and 1935 about their own work histories and those of their family members.[53] By comparing the experiences of these women, 97 of their husbands, and 171 of their first-born sons and daughters,[54] we can assess the impact of the post-Mao labor reform on different generations of urban employees and also identify some individual characteristics that seem to afford higher levels of job mobility to some urban citizens than to others.

The families in my survey represent Shanghai's middle-class and labor elite. One-third of the fathers are well-paid blue-collar workers in state enterprises, one-third are low-level cadres doing routine white-collar work, and one-third are professionals or administrators at the factory or company level.[55] Thirty-six percent of the fathers and 19 percent of the mothers are members of the CCP. Thus as a group they enjoy high levels of job security, slightly above-average salaries, and a modicum of influence within their workplace and neighborhoods as members of the party.

Both males and females in this parent generation have experienced significant geographic and social mobility during their adult lives. Seventy-eight percent of the men and 68 percent of the women were born outside Shanghai. A minority of these came to the city with their parents; the vast majority came on their own initiative as teenagers or young adults.[56] After the early 1950s, however, very few had enjoyed geographic or job mobility comparable to their pre-1949 experiences.[57] Furthermore, when they did change employers, it was overwhelmingly at the discretion of government planners. Individuals changed employer when the supervising bureau decided to close the factory, merge small units, or reassign workers to factories in frontier areas. Few ever moved voluntarily to develop a new skill or enter a new line of work.[58]

Within this overall pattern of immobility, however, some individuals had moved more frequently than others. Most conspicuous among this minority of "movers" (that is, those who had worked in four or more enterprises prior to retirement) were male party members; most conspicuous among the "stayers" (that is, those who worked in only one enterprise for all their preretirement careers) were female textile workers (see Table 7). Altogether, it appears that employment in textile work is associated with higher than average levels of *immobility,* whereas party membership for men and advanced education for women is associated with higher than average mobility.

In a study of Chinese job mobility it is important to note that job mobility rarely is the result of individual ambition and that job changes often bring more losses than gains. As noted above, most job changes were transfers dictated by higher levels of the *xitong,* or party organization departments. Transfers did not increase salaries (these came with the time-specific wage increases for the workers' cohort), and they frequently meant longer commutes from home or extended absences from Shanghai. They also meant the loss of valuable support networks and the necessity to rebuild the informal reciprocities that characterize security in most Chinese workplaces.[59]

Among my respondents transfers went most often to CCP members in key leadership positions whom upper-level party leaders had decided to move in order to handle some new problem or to escape political vendettas. The careers of my respondents therefore did not reveal an or-

TABLE 7 Characteristics of Those Staying in One Unit and
Those Moving Four or More Times

Workers	Senior-High Education	CCP Member	Shanghai Born	Employed in Textiles
Men				
All men	52%	36%	22%	10%
"Movers"	55	72	27	0
(N = 18)				
"Stayers"	52	19	35	16
(N = 31)				
Women				
All women	26%	19%	32%	39%
"Movers"	34	19	36	23
(N = 11)				
"Stayers"	13	19	24	49
(N = 37)				

derly sequence of moves or a clear ladder of ranks to indicate upward mobility and occupational success. Frequently a party cadre would spend eight or nine years in one factory or enterprise, rising to be head or vice-head of the unit or party committee. Then a nationwide campaign would blast through the unit, and the cadre would find herself being transferred twice in eighteen months.

A comparison of parent-child job mobility following the imposition of new restraints on interunit transfers after 1984 indicates a similar connection between party affiliation and higher mobility. However, in the reform era, which has been noticeably undisturbed by extensive or intensive political mobilizations, it appears that the higher mobility of CCP members and their children is the result of the parent's past mobility, and not more frequent reassignments by higher-level supervisory groups. Because CCP members often have worked in more units than most of their peers, they have a wider network of contacts, and through this network they have been in an especially good position to know about some of the special opportunities that exist outside their own neighborhood or place of employment: openings in joint-venture hotels, creation of new collective restaurants, or citywide entrance exams to take courses in computer science or Japanese. One consequence appears to be that party members were twice as likely to have found new jobs in these four

TABLE 8 Party Connections among Transfers, 1984–1987

Workers	Males	Females
Parents		
% of CCP in sample	36	19
% of CCP among transfers	60	33
Children		
% with CCP parent in sample	42	44
% with CCP parent among those transferring	60	66

years than nonparty members, and children of party members were 50 percent more likely to have moved than children without a party parent (see Table 8).

CCP connections, however, were by no means the only route to new jobs among the parent generation. At least as important for those in their fifties and sixties was the structurally advantaged position of those who had retired after the 1978 pension reform and subsequently were permitted to take on postretirement employment. Thus if we include postretirement employment outside the original unit, then we find that parents were twice as likely to transfer as their adult children (see Table 9).

In sum, what the results of the Shanghai survey indicate is that after 1984, transfers averaged about 3 percent per year, but party membership and pensioner status doubled the likelihood of a successful move. Recent retirees have been permitted, primarily by the implementation of the *dingti* option, to leave the work force in their late forties and early fifties with pensions equal to 85 percent of their last pay. In addition, they continue to receive both pension and special subsidies even when they

TABLE 9 Percentage of Workers Moving to New Units, 1984–1987

Workers	Excluding Retirement Shifts		Including Postretirement Shifts	
	Males	Females	Males	Females
Parents	11.7	1.0	20.2	24.4
	(N = 11)	(N = 1)	(N = 20)	(N = 24)
Adult children	11.7	11.5	11.7	11.5
	(N = 10)	(N = 9)	(N = 10)	(N = 9)

hold a full-time job as a *geti hu,* a free-lance technical adviser, or an employee in a collective enterprise or in a state unit hiring "outside the plan." Unlike their children, they can move into these new units without traversing the bureaucratic labyrinth that blocks the road of those still in the work force. As pensioners they also do not threaten their employer with the loss of a valuable investment or property. In short, by virtue of their age, or more precisely their membership in the particular birth cohort that entered the urban labor force in the 1950s and qualified for retirement in the late 1970s and early 1980s, these retirees have been some of the most mobile members of the urban labor force since 1978.[60]

CAUSES AND CONSEQUENCES OF PARTIAL REFORM

After 1980 the CCP leadership renounced many of the tenets of their original formulas for economic growth. In rural areas they initiated the destruction of the people's communes, and farming became essentially a family enterprise. Households were encouraged to diversify their economic activity, and individual entrepreneurs were permitted to dominate local trading. In urban areas there was no parallel structural transformation, but there were equally radical departures in ideology. Mobilization by class struggle was rejected in favor of material incentives, and efficiency rather than equality became the criterion by which to measure the success of socialism. The Deng leadership repeatedly endorsed the economic benefits of privatization and commodification; the commitment to the virtues of collective ownership that had dominated policies and politics throughout the previous decade quickly disappeared. But in urban state enterprises, where the material rewards of Chinese socialism had been most fully realized before 1978, the leadership found it more difficult to renounce basic tenets of a command economy than they did for agriculture and petty trade. In particular they refused to legitimate a buyers' market for labor, insisting that without planned allocation of workers there would be waste and exploitation.

A second constraint on increasing job mobility for state employees was Deng's reliance on decentralization as a primary strategy of reform. Decentralization of authority and accountability was originally heralded as a means to make leaders at the enterprise level more cost conscious and to reduce the burdens of lifetime employment. But decentralization to the municipal or enterprise level sabotaged these goals because decentralization within the autarkical, cellular urban economy empowered local leaders to protect their short-term self-interests; it did not motivate them to maximize efficiency or encourage labor turnover.[61]

Reinforcing these two major impediments to higher rates of job turnover were two other characteristics of the state work force in the 1980s: antipathy to radical departures from current reward structures among the rank and file and persistence of "negative decision making" among managerial staff. Between 1978 and 1987 state enterprises continued to supply workers and staff with goods and services that were either not for sale or available only at very high prices. As a result, any state employee contemplating a job change had to consider whether the new employer would be able to match the quality of noncash supports provided by the current unit. Loss of housing built or purchased by an enterprise as "dormitories" for staff members and their families was the most powerful material disincentive to those considering a transfer, but the possibility that a move would result in loss of day care or in poorer-quality medical facilities also could dissuade even the most dissatisfied or ambitious from making a move.[62]

In 1978 Western economists estimated that subsidies to urban state workers doubled the value of cash incomes.[63] In 1987 unit-level subsidies to state workers averaged 85 percent of the monthly pay,[64] and subsidies (*jintie*) as a percentage of the wage bill had trebled over their 1978 levels.[65] Thus even as the structural reform of the economy attempted to raise unit-level efficiency and increase sensitivity to prices, "hidden" subsidies to state workers remained an essential (even growing) component of urban labor costs. State workers were well aware of the role of enterprise-level subsidies in maintaining their privileged position in relation to employees in the collective or agricultural sectors, and they were wary of changes in migration laws and employment policies that would reduce their benefits and create a "true" labor market such as existed before 1949. Therefore, although often dissatisfied with the continued restrictions on their job choices, most sought only to improve their individual situation, and virtually none actively supported an overhaul of hiring and firing procedures.

Negative decision making, or what I term "decision making through a hierarchy of vetoes," also reinforced the immobility of state workers. In this study one of the clearest examples was found in the discussion of the several stages of bureaucratic approval needed for a job transfer. At each step the individual who wished to move could be defeated through a committee or staff member who could veto the request or simply refuse to take action. Successful at one level of approval, the individual became vulnerable to rejection by the next level, and thus advancement was always the result of having avoided negative decisions rather than actively seeking specific rewards and career goals.

Negative decision making and strategies of avoidance also constrain individual mobility in noncommunist, market economies. But in market economies people have alternatives to jobs in the civil service, the military, or large corporations where such procedures prevail. In command economies individuals have fewer choices. And even in the context of socialist planned economies, Chinese state workers have had especially few alternatives because China did not develop as lively a "second economy" as did the Soviet Union or Eastern Europe. To the extent that the post-Mao reforms did not alter decision-making procedures, state employees continued to traverse a bureaucratic labyrinth whenever they, rather than a party or an enterprise bureaucrat, wanted to initiate new employment.

The post-Mao era now has a longer history than that of the Cultural Revolution. In rural China the reorganization and depoliticization of work has profoundly altered the structure and fabric of village life. In urban China the changes have been less dramatic. This is not to say that the post-Mao reforms have had no effect on urban residents. Urban families greatly improved their material standard of living between 1977 and 1987, and the range of opinions they heard and articulated was more diverse and less proscribed by state or party censorship than at any time after 1949. Yet in the area of job choice, the rules and precedents typical of the bureaucratic command economy established in the 1950s, and in particular the procedures necessary for entry into or exit from a state enterprise, did not significantly change.

The post-Mao reforms reduced the penetration of state supervision into everyday life. But in the case of labor practices applied to state workers, the strategy of decentralization was problematic and the consequences sometimes contradictory. For urban workers and staff, the contradiction was not simply between themselves and the state. For these individuals the reforms also created conflicting self-interests because they, unlike peasants and workers in small collectives, were relatively advantaged under the Maoist terms of exchange between rural and urban workers, and state and collective employees. Therefore sanctioning a buyers' market for labor posed risks as well as benefits. Cognizant of the enormous rural population that would eagerly flood the urban labor market, state workers reluctantly accommodated themselves to the status quo. The consequence for individuals was persistent immobility, and for Chinese society it was deep dissatisfaction among the most-advantaged stratum of the urban working class.

Micropolitics and the Factory Director Responsibility System, 1984–1987

YVES CHEVRIER

Chinese state enterprises have gained economic autonomy during the past ten years, but they are still far from achieving the management independence to which they are formally entitled. One important factor is that the failure to complete key reforms like price, tax, wage, and labor has created a dual, distorted mixture of planned and market economies, while freezing the labor force in overmanned economic units that must still perform costly social functions as mini-welfare-states. Yet the greatest obstacle is perhaps not the remains of the high-level command structure but the lingering power of party organs and the growing power of local administrative bureaus over microeconomic management.

In China, links between the local community and the outside have been perennially weak, a weakness that Maoism reinforced.[1] Economic decentralization, by putting state enterprises under municipal control, has in fact strengthened the "thousand hands" of local bureaucrats, whose weak links to the outside allow them considerable independence from external authorities. The strong local horizontal networks under these bureaucrats have blunted the impact of financial and market measures designed to increase economic efficiency, enterprise profitability, and competitive management. While state enterprises are subject to "soft budgetary constraints,"[2] competition on the still imperfect market involves not so much economic units and actors as communal interests dominated by local bureaucratic organs and party members. Reform-minded economists and some high officials made it clear as early as 1979–80 that these informal ties to local officials were depriving enterprises of their new "rights" and tapping their new resources, creating, among other problems, runaway investments and fueling inflation.[3]

It was precisely in a novel effort to break up these formal and informal patterns of local communal solidarities and interests structuring China's bureaucratic establishment that the factory director responsibility system (*changzhang fuzezhi;* FDRS) was launched experimentally in May 1984. The FDRS shifted the emphasis of reforms from organizations (that is, from the rights of state enterprises to be independent of the lines of authority of the command economy) to individuals (that is, to factory managers in their relations to the party-state bureaucratic environment). It did so by formally granting the power to manage state enterprises economically to professionals individually hired under contracts.

By 1986–87 it was quite clear that the FDRS had failed to improve significantly management in the state sector: the factory managers were overtaken by the very system they were supposed to reform. One major factor in this erosion was party resistance, first locally as long as central party authorities supported the reform, then centrally after the shift in national policies of the spring of 1985 allowed conservative elements in the party to reassert the right of "supervision" of party committees over microeconomic management. Even before the tide of macropolitics turned, however, the FDRS had been eroded as it was integrated into its local bureaucratic environment. The new managers confronted stubborn party secretaries in the enterprise and shifting party policies nationally, but the mesh of local interests and conflicts is clearest at the level of municipal government bureaus and party committees, where interpersonal and factional solidarities are knit informally together, and corruption, power, protection, and economic advantage are all traded informally. At local levels party members and party organs are but one thread in the "tight, complex, and interdependent bureaucratic relationships" that encompass state enterprises.[4] In the locality, horizontal communal solidarities often prevail against vertical loyalty to national party policies, but the overall privilege of the party is used by its members to buttress their local influence. Indeed, while a compromise over party involvement in state enterprises was sought in 1986–87 (and reached with the Enterprise Law of April 1988), further steps were taken (from legal and fiscal measures to social and political means) to strengthen the independence of management—not so much against the party per se as against local bureaucratic encroachment as a whole.

The FDRS appears, therefore, as part of the more general system of administrative and political reforms aimed both at separating and rebalancing party-state functions and at restructuring the bureaucratic apparatus to provide an adequate institutional framework for the individualized and contractualized economic and social setting developed by Deng's modernization.

But we should bear in mind that this new economic and social setting is itself in a state of transition and that the FDRS and similar or related reforms did not create overnight a full-fledged new social stratum alongside the bureaucratic structure. Rather, the social consequences of Deng's economic reforms bear the imprint of their environment, that is, of the party power structure and ideology, as well as of the bureaucratic and communal order of power and society inherited from China's traditional and Maoist past.[5] As a result, while a new generation of younger and better-trained professionals has started to take over management duties in the state industrial sector since 1984, it is still necessary to describe the managers in Chinese state enterprises both from the vantage point of the established power structure and as an emerging "interest group" belonging to the incipient social elites whom the economic reforms tend to foster outside preexisting structures. The fate of the FDRS reflects the difficulties encountered by this process of modernization and shows that the obstacles to individualization and to the expansion of contractual links in economic and social life stem not only from party organization and ideology but also from the bureaucratic and communal way in which power and society are interrelated in China.

It follows that this chapter is not a study of Chinese managers as a social group nor of the institutional and ideological environment of Chinese state enterprises.[6] It is a case study of the statecraft of modernization in Deng Xiaoping's China, that is, of the interactions of ideological rigidities, bureaucratic vested interests, emerging state-building policies, and new social pluralism in the political and social flux carried by Deng's economic reforms.

Because the institutionalization of management as an independent power upset the status quo ante before it was absorbed into the system, the study of the FDRS provides a good understanding of the interactions among party, state, and society at central and local levels in post-Mao China. In this light, the bulk of the chapter analyzes the fate of the FDRS—its introduction and erosion—at two levels. We consider first the level of *macropolitics,* where the FDRS was officially endorsed and where formal party resistance was strongest owing to ideological rigidities and to the retreat in central policies from support of urban reforms to retrenchment in the spring of 1985. At the level of *micropolitics,* the introduction of new contenders for local power and wealth created disturbances and factional feuds leading to the dismissal of outspoken managers and to the integration of the others into the existing structures. The confrontation between the new formal power in state enterprises (institutionalized under the FDRS) and the party structures and informal power networks that dominate them clearly ended to the advantage of the latter. Finally we look at the reforms that were initiated or suggested in 1986–87 so as to institutionalize further the new social setting required by economic modernization, that is, state-building policies in their relations to enterprise management in the state sector.

The social consequences of Deng's economic reforms cannot be properly assessed if we do not elaborate our vision of the resistance to social change in Deng's China. For the present topic, this requires that we introduce into the standard description of the relations between party and management[7] the multifaceted prism of local, decentralized micropolitics[8] in their relations to macropolitical events and state-building policies.

THE SPRING OF THE FDRS (1984–85): THE RISE OF THE MANAGER OR THE UPSWING OF AN OLD-STYLE CAMPAIGN?

The FDRS was introduced on an experimental basis in six cities (Beijing, Tianjin, Shenyang, Dalian, Shanghai, and Changzhou) in May 1984 and implemented on a large scale the following year in connection with the *zhengdang* (party rectification) campaign. By then it was already entangled in local micropolitics, and by 1986 it came under sharp criticism. Like other "movements" and reforms in China, however, the FDRS expanded in a gradual and piecemeal fashion. Thus in 1986 some units and provinces were still reporting enthusiastic implementation when the time had come for criticism and adjustment.[9]

The origins of the FDRS can be seen as a confluence of two different sets of reformist preoccupations. One stems from the effort to achieve a new balance between concentration and deconcentration of party power within state enterprises. The other evolves from the doctrine of contractual responsibility. These two concerns came together in 1984 to create a new perspective for organizational restructuring. The new leadership in state enterprises under the FDRS was to be collective, with a "management team" composed of vice directors, chief engineers, and accountants all appointed by the director. But replacing the rule of a single party secretary with collective management was not the most important departure from previous patterns of deconcentration. The real innovation in state enterprises was the separation of the realm of economic decision making from the party committees.[10]

The general trend of reforms since 1978 has not been for the ruling party elite to share political power, but rather for the elite to divide their economic and social monopolies by increasing functional specialization, professionalization, and individualization. In other words, while pre-1978 reforms had tried to reorganize power collegially within a monistic social system under tight party control over the economy and society, Deng's New Deal aimed at institutionalizing a pluralistic society resting on specialization and competence. By keeping the party committee in state enterprises in an advisory and supervisory capacity while promoting one responsible leader in the economic sphere, FDRS experiments separated and specialized functions in line with the new trend.

This strategy has become quite explicit since 1986, but in 1984 and 1985 it was still couched in the language of party rectification and "responsibility systems." The idea of responsibility was not only an organizational effort to clarify, quantify, and reward contractual obligations between state organs and economic units—be they farms or enterprises—by specifying the division of authority between higher and lower units.[11] The goal was also to further divide functions and contractualize individual social relations in many domains. The underlying vision was to create individually responsible persons in the chain of command out of irresponsible and inefficient collective-communal structures. This strategy was clearly argued in May 1984 at a conference on the implementation of the individual responsibility system in party and state organs held under the aegis of the Chinese Communist party's central organization and personnel departments.[12] The argument was pressed even more forcefully in newspaper articles commenting on the application of individual responsibility to decision making in state enterprises. One writer clearly stated that the functional specialization, individualization, and contractualization of social relations embodied in the FDRS required an ad hoc legal framework in order to protect responsible individuals against collective irresponsibility.[13]

These issues, along with the question of the manager's special interests within the new fabric of a pluralistic society, became topics of debate as a result of disillusionment and frustration in 1985–86 (discussed further below). In 1984 the ideal of the new rational manager was accompanied by visions of rejuvenation and individual ownership of expertise, as well as by the growing influence of new marketing and managerial techniques imported from Japan and the West.[14] While the FDRS was being officially launched in 1984 and early 1985, the party gave full support to these images, at least at national and provincial levels, where macropolitics are decided and implemented.

These developments coincided with the CCP Central Committee decision of October 1984 that the party must reform itself for the reform of the economic structure to succeed.[15] Although not pinpointed in other studies, by early 1985 the implementation of the FDRS became part and parcel of the party rectification in which party secretaries were to draw back to the restricted domain of their new functions, and "intellectuals" (meaning primarily "technical intelligentsia") were to be integrated into the party rank and file. Following standard campaign practices, models were widely publicized, model party units opened their doors to intellectuals,[16] and "enlightened party secretaries" shared power with their new functional "bosses."[17] Since persuasion by "enlightened" secretaries was not always as smooth as in the model sugar plant in Huhehot,[18] rectification teams were sent into enterprises following standard campaign practice. Support of the FDRS by party rectification (zhengdang) became a major area of party activity and propaganda during the first months of 1985, and amounted by then to the climax of an old-style campaign.[19]

As one might expect, the emergence of a new managerial group was exaggerated by official sources, which wanted to report successes in realizing party intentions. These "successes" do not so much indicate actual organizational and social change as they betray the archaic way in which the new policies of modernization were implemented. In fact the 1984–

early 1985 tremor was already being absorbed into the "soft rigidities" of China's industrial society and local bureaucratic establishment even before the official line turned from support of the FDRS to retrenchment in the spring of 1985.

EROSION OF THE FDRS (1985–86): CENTRAL RETRENCHMENT AND LOCAL INTEGRATION

Formal Party Resistance

Although officially proclaimed in written enterprise charters,[20] the plan of the party to withdraw into more specialized functions and to relinquish power over economic matters, personnel recruitment, and management was never, even for a brief moment, efficiently implemented. The overall formal organizational superiority of the party, its moral and political rights, and its ideological and propaganda roles enabled party committees in each enterprise to maintain a convenient beachhead for protecting their influence over enterprise management. Some reports show that even the shifts in the technical and managerial staff to implement the FDRS was an occasion for the party to assert its authority, for the directors themselves were in fact mostly party members.[21] The party's right of control has been periodically reasserted since 1985.[22]

The fact that enterprise managers are overwhelmingly party members and formally bound by party discipline and loyalty limits their power as managers and puts them in a vulnerable position in the event of a conflict with party officials or a shift in party line away from support for the reform. As early as January 1985 FDRS proponents had realized, with some anguish, that the fate of this reform was tied to the general political situation.[23] By spring their position had dramatically weakened. Faced with economic difficulties and spreading "evil tendencies" in economic-administrative management, party leaders redirected the rectification target from reluctant party secretaries to "selfish individuals looking after their own interests,"[24] namely, officials and managers found to be corrupt profiteers.[25]

As the targets of rectification shifted, the distribution of power established under the FDRS was formally challenged. Factory directors were now to consult with party committees whenever important *economic* decisions were to be made, said *Gongren ribao*.[26] Greater priority was given

to noneconomic matters—the political background of cadres, the ideological training of personnel—which could only increase the status and
role of the party. In July 1985 the organization department of the Central Committee explicitly called for a strengthening of party leadership
in enterprises.[27]

With this change, "good" directors were identified with communist
values, "bad" ones with "bourgeois individualism" and "selfishness" (*si*
as opposed to *gong*). In line with the new reformist principles, the Central Committee "Decision on Reform of the Economic Structure" in October 1984 had defined state enterprises as "economic operators" em-
bodying the "legal personality" (*faren*) of enterprises.[28] *Zhongguo fazhibao*
almost immediately elaborated by stating that this legal person was represented by the director.[29] But even then, good directors were more commonly depicted as men endowed not only with the technical qualities to
"raise the level of management" (*tigao guanli shuiping*) but also with the
moral and collective virtues found in model workers and "good" party
secretaries.[30] The best manager has the characteristics of the Communist,
and in fact he *is* one.[31] With the shift in the campaign, legal definitions
were all but forgotten. The good manager must put the "interests of the
people" not only before his own but also before those of the enterprise,
said the party committee of the Shenyang Bureau of Metal Industries in
a report on ideological work.[32] In June 1985 Deng Liqun bluntly declared that factory directors "represent the interest of the whole people
and of the Socialist state."[33] In compliance with the established rules of
party campaigns, managers displayed their loyalty by affirming these political images. They declared their determination to avoid any contradiction between enterprise and state. Failing this, state and collective interests were to be placed first; no single enterprise should grow wealthy at
the expense of the whole.[34]

These, of course, were prompted utterances, needed to demonstrate
that the manager was a politically responsible leader as the FDRS campaign underwent retrenchment. Some managers did not accept these images and even publicly argued that the new discourse of the party was
contradictory to the goal of improving economic management.[35] But they
were fighting a losing battle. Not only was the new policy managed
through an archaic political system, but it also antagonized the bureaucratic and communal order of power and society that dominates Chinese
state enterprises at grass-roots levels. And the central government's stress
on the illegitimacy of wealth and individual power as the campaign for

the FDRS waned provided local bureaucrats with fresh weapons in their protracted struggle against the new leaders of the economic sphere who had risen under the FDRS.

Informal Resistance and Micropolitics

"Exit, voice, and loyalty" are, according to A. O. Hirschman, the three options available to decisionmakers in "declining" complex organizations.[36] Factory managers found their new authority eroded and submerged into existing power networks, often after bitter conflicts that led to firing, forced resignation, and even jailing.[37] More frequently, following negotiation and compromise, they "loyally" submitted to the established, formal and informal, powerholders. Because some of these managers and some other vocal sectors such as the legal profession and large newspapers chose the "voice" option, as did some of my confidential informants, we may have some basis for understanding how formal party privilege and informal micropolitics were articulated to subordinate the managers.

At first sight, the disturbances created by the introduction of the FDRS seem to boil down to the crude reassertion of party power over state enterprises. Local party officials almost always occupied center stage in these acute power struggles. And when exposure in the provincial or national media triggered the redress of abuses, the decision whether to reverse sanctions against managers who were forced to "exit" or to act against the party officials who had abused them was the prerogative of party organs at the provincial level or below. The prevalence of party members in Chinese officialdom makes it natural that they should prevail wherever power is wielded and money circulates. Moreover, local politics share one common feature with national party rule: factory directors were ousted, jailed, or reinstated by party organs and fiat without any concern for due process of law. Law professionals can only complain that state legal channels were not properly respected.[38] In these as in other matters, local party organs, by the very definition of "privilege," *leges privatae,* are above and beyond the law. It is not surprising, then, that those who voiced their complaints about factory management located the vortex of local influence and "pull" in local party organs and officials.[39]

The absence of an independent civil service and the weak legitimacy of the legal apparatus allow central political hegemony to be translated into local bureaucratic privilege. But from the conflicts triggered by the implementation of the FDRS, we can see that the intricacies of local micropolitics go beyond the mere expression of party supremacy. These conflicts exhibit the basic features of China's political and industrial society and show how the FDRS failed to modernize these features. Although institutionalized as independent individuals, the managers never appear as individuals but always as participants in local networks and groups, just like party and state cadres. Within party and state organizations at the municipal and district levels, as well as within enterprises, there are often several conflicting groups, each dominated by active, sometimes "activist," individual leaders.[40] In several instances these conflicts amounted to genuine factional strife. As few managers hired under the FDRS were actual outsiders on the local scene, in some cases old factional feuds found new expression over the FDRS issue.[41] Members of the "enemy" faction were accused of moral and sexual "deviation" and of constituting a "power" clique that must be broken up.[42] Clearly the new managers were part of preexisting interpersonal networks (*guanxi wang*) and factions so characteristic of Maoist China. Furthermore, neither they, nor their allies, nor their opponents in the local party and state organs seemed to perform on the local political stage in their functional capacity. Rather, in order to exercise their power, management specialists had to participate in the endless cycle of political bargaining alongside party politicians and state administrators who were directly, and often personally, involved in economic affairs.

The bureaucratic milieu in which managers must operate does not function according to the organizational blueprints devised by higher levels. In the absence of a strong and legitimate state in which higher levels provide legal ("vertical") protection to particular interests, the local level is characterized by a communal mode of economic and social control in which power, protection, and money are exchanged horizontally. Competing individuals and groups must enter the system by using *guanxi* networks not only to gain access to opportunities but also to protect their economic advantages and resources. These networks thus allow newcomers to share the profits as long as they comply with the informal rules of the game. Corruption is the direct consequence of the margin separating informal patterns from formal ones or, to put it differently, it is the unavoidable cost not only of party privilege but also of the deficiency of the central state as a legal and economic regulator. Although banned formally, corruption is such a "normal" outgrowth of the system that it acquires an informal legitimacy. Extortion is also a "normal" extra price paid by the weak to the strong, unless the weak have an equally strong protector.

In spite of their new rights under the FDRS, managers were unable to challenge the standard practice of squeeze. Their enterprises had to submit to local bureaus and party committees following the established pattern of horizontal enterprise dependency, compounded by the fiscal chaos as well as by the legal void and by urban China's neocommunal organization, whereby enterprises are called on to fund community projects. Weak and rich enterprises alike are exposed to these pressures, which easily take the form of outright bullying and squeeze.[43] Factory executives and enterprises constantly complain about abusive bureaucratic "mothers-in-law." In January 1985 twelve "angry directors" in Zhengzhou described the burden of "contributions" as "unbearable" and bluntly said that while enterprises had been weaned from the "common big pot," their place had been taken by "society," namely, the local bureaucracy that feeds on enterprises.[44] Some analysts have shown how the pattern of bureaucratic interference survived the deconstruction of the command economy.[45]

Local bureaucrats can also, informally and illicitly, use their privilege and the resources it makes available to launch private business operations. As decentralization and market reforms provided new opportunities, corruption and other "economic crimes" grew in volume and scale. As money circulated more widely, it became an important criterion for status; local powerholders raised not only their economic expectations but the price of protection and made it more explicitly commercial.[46] Since these developments were perceived as a threat not only to the center's control of the economy but also to the identity of the party and the state's vertical structures, they were priority targets in the sharp ideological turn in the spring of 1985. But whereas the official rectification campaign attributed the rise in economic crimes to a sudden collapse of moral standards, some analysts, especially in the legal field, tried to explain it by citing structural factors, namely, the predominance of informal solidarities.[47] Although some of these structural explanations reflected the one-sided official line that criticized the "selfish" appetite of corrupt enterprises and managers for easy profits,[48] they also showed that these "evil tendencies" relied on appropriate protection and *guanxi* channels.

As they had to integrate existing lobbies, the new managers formally working under the FDRS were vulnerable to criticism for corruption, squeeze, and taking advantage of business opportunities. But those who were not flexible enough were also charged with "economic crime," the most frequent accusation leveled against factory directors by party officials in the power struggles triggered by the FDRS.[49] Being weak and highly dependent on the outside bureaucracies, managers tried to gain some support within their enterprise by turning a blind eye to excessive pay hikes and to the egalitarian distribution of bonuses without regard to merit.[50] As a result, since there were no independent audits to prove their success or innocence, these dependent, poorly supported professionals were vulnerable on the very ground of economic efficiency and economic abuses. It was all too easy to accuse them not only of economic corruption and abuse of power but also of "technical" mismanagement.

While enterprise management under the FDRS was embedded in myriad local economic deals and politics, the rhetoric remained remarkably personal and moralistic. The "enlightened secretary" or the "loyal director" remained a deus ex machina, capable of reconciling the interests of enterprises, state, and workers thanks to his or her charismatic virtue. They were fighting the villains, the "bad" party officials and the "selfish" managers seeking personal profit or treating their offices or enterprises as their own "kingdoms."[51]

In sum, although managers reached an individual status in the official discourse, the FDRS failed actually to individualize and emancipate management in state enterprises. The failure of the FDRS helps us to understand the real status of Chinese managers in state enterprises as members of the local power elite, that is, as *community leaders* who share in the informal decision-making process of the local community and who bestow protection and leadership on the enterprise, which is also a communal structure. If they are powerful and enjoy good connections, they can shelter their enterprise from squeeze and help it gain access to the profits from speculation, legal or illicit.[52]

Within the enterprise, directors also perform as *moral community leaders*. Their broad responsibilities in the *danwei* (the local unit, such as the state enterprise) allow them—and in fact require them—to control and influence the private and family lives of their employees through the control they exert on areas such as housing and leisure activities. This lets them build up strong personal bonds with reciprocal obligations that interfere with the maximization of economic rationality and nurture factional strife.[53] A few managers, like the one who resigned in Hubei (see note 37), have sought a narrower technical role, refusing both to cultivate personal contacts and to manage community affairs.

Finally, the real role of the manager in his bureaucratic and communal environment is reminiscent of the precarious status of wealth and private entrepreneurs in premodern China. Just like salt merchants or *guandu shangban* entrepreneurs (private merchants under state supervision) in late Imperial China seeking bureaucratic protection, enterprise directors are junior partners in local informal power groups. In other words, the attempt to formalize a new local power structure in relation to the rise of the market economy has thus far failed. By 1986 many enterprises had "turned back the clock" to the system of "factory director responsibility under party committee leadership" or had a director who served concurrently as party secretary, thus embedding the FDRS in existing structures.[54] The media continued to give directors publicity, but more became disillusioned and openly contemplated resignation.[55] The "management contracts" that had spread to most large and medium-sized state enterprises by 1987,[56] while in principle consolidating the rights of enterprises and management in the spirit of the FDRS, in fact strengthened the grip of local bureaucrats. Many Chinese observers acknowledged as much: the contracts merely formalized the dependency of state enterprises and managers.[57]

But while the FDRS failed to reach its stated goal, its erosion and integration underlined what has to be changed in the political and social organization of China if modernization is to succeed. Indeed, several steps taken in 1986–87 to strengthen the independence of management focused on the weaknesses that had been detrimental to the FDRS, namely, the weakness of the state versus the party and of the central state as economic, fiscal, and legal regulator versus local bureaucratic power. Owing to these initiatives which reflected a growing political stalemate preventing the policy reversal of mid-1985 of phasing out all reforms, the declining phase of the FDRS displayed an ambivalent character, with ideological and organizational retrenchment on the one hand, but also state-building policies designed to reinforce and regulate a new economic and social pluralism on the other hand.

COMPROMISE AND CONSOLIDATION (1986–87)

Formalizing and Protecting New "Interests"

In macropolitics the debate on who should lead state enterprises was ongoing in October 1986[58] when new regulations were issued by the central government making a revised FDRS a crucial step in the reform of the urban economy.[59] The enterprise and bankruptcy laws which had been delayed at that time were finally passed by the Seventh National People's Congress in April 1988. Besides restating the formal factory director rights under the FDRS, the enterprise law put managers in charge of the ideological and political work in the enterprise, giving them power over the functional domain of party committees. Party organs, however, were to continue supervising the overall leadership of the managers and to share with managers the responsibility for administrative organs, trade unions, and Youth League committees. Thus the macropolitical equilibrium—or stalemate—was embodied in the new law, "a sure recipe for confusion."[60] Such a law, in fact, would have been a mere macropolitical event if it had not been paralleled by significant micropolitical developments.

During a symposium on management modernization in state enterprise held in Wuhan in July 1986, a new demand emerged for a strict evaluation of the director's performance at intervals during his term and before he could leave the enterprise or be promoted or demoted.[61] Actually, *Zhongguo fazhibao* had already lent its voice to the new trend by reporting a campaign that had begun locally in early 1986 and then moved to the provincial level in the northeast before becoming a countrywide movement that received central government approbation in October. It was natural enough for managers to seek protection from accusations of mismanagement and profiteering and for central authorities to use this strategy to try to regain some actual control over the economy. This new development overshadowed the more conventional argument over local administrative coordination and the longer duration of the director's term.[62]

However, a new perception and definition of the power to evaluate emerged in the evaluation efforts of 1986. Evaluation was to be made in technical terms only, involving accounting and financial variables, by independent bodies whose audits could be formalized in written, even notarized, documents.[63] Such procedures, of course, can easily be controlled and contrived by the local and provincial state or party authorities who initiate them. But some reports were initiated by directors who requested an independent audit because they were faced with accusations of profiteering and mismanagement or because they feared taking over a troubled enterprise whose difficulties might later be attributed to them.[64] In such cases the directors relied on new forces in the state and on new sources of legitimacy to gain protection through legal means and with quantifiable data.

This use of evaluation is just one prominent example of the effort by managers to seek protection for their specific interests through legal structures and procedures rather than rely on the "morality" of officials.[65] The new wave of reforms since 1984 has prompted the growth of legal and auditing services, within and outside large state enterprises, including legal counsels for negotiating and implementing contracts and fiscal and accounting experts working either as independent consultants or within bureaucratic structures.[66] These and other related facts in 1986 point to a fundamental evolution of modernization strategies in China and to a crucial political debate centered on the issue of state building.

State Building

Initially the FDRS was launched by reformers attempting to break China's pattern of collection irresponsibility in decision making. But as it formalized and promoted individual interests without actually protecting them against bureaucratic interests vested in party privilege and local power networks, the FDRS found itself at the center of the overall problems of social and institutional modernization raised by the economic reforms. While the reforms initially benefited from the low integration of the Chinese state and from the pervasive communal social patterns, the continuing protracted negotiations and compromises have become so counterproductive that state building is now the great challenge for Chinese modernization.[67]

The example of the FDRS shows that China's archaic political structures and social organizations make central power too strong where it should give more leeway to autonomous social forces, and too weak locally where it should be strong enough to use other forms of intervention to support a modern market economy and, specifically, to protect economic operators against local power holders. The development of legal practices and the legal professions may provide a new framework for the exchange of protection, which in any society must parallel the exchange of goods and services and the accumulation of wealth and power. The state, after relinquishing its monopoly over economic life and social organization, should tighten its monopoly on the circulation of protection by adopting the rule of law necessary to a modern contractual economy and society.

The growing legal protection of individual economic operators such as independent managers is part of the progressive strategy to create a modern state-society complex regulated by law. This strategy has other facets. State building requires that from the archaic and bureaucratic command structure a new civil service be created, separate from the party. Other reforms must aim at producing an ad hoc, individualized society out of the communal mold. New market factors created by the reduction of the command economy and the progressive commercialization of land, housing, and employment will help generate new social actors, such as managers, job seekers, and house renters, who are elements of a "commodity society" (shangpin shehui). Such a commodity society moderated by a rationalized state appears now to be a prerequisite for supporting the rational development of the new "commodity economy" (shangpin jingji). The political articulation of this scheme was more controversial. Some claimed that a strongly authoritarian and nationalist ideology is to be developed for welding together this new atomistic grid and for easing social tensions, while others insisted on the political translation of the resulting social pluralism. At any rate, these debates indicated that democracy alone is not a panacea in the light of state building.[68] Of special relevance is the fact that contractual economic activities tend to provide fertile ground for legal professions and procedures, whereas private conflicts seem to be settled out of court or through mediation.[69] In other words, the modernization drive on the eve of Tiananmen seemed to foster the individualized and guaranteed contractual links that were so instrumental in the rise of modern economies in the West and Japan but that have thus far not predominated in China, while communal relations and values are retained by the government in order to pave the transition to individualization and urbanization.[70]

With the debate on "political reforms" in 1986 and the call for a working legal framework, state building became the focal point of the reform program. However, with the leadership split sharply over the implications of pluralism in the aftermath of Hu Yaobang's dismissal (in January 1987) and paralyzed by inflation fears (which climaxed in the summer of 1988), practical measures remained painfully inadequate while two opposite strategies of state building for modernization became political antagonists. One was the redistribution of power and functions between the party and the state apparatus in the authoritarian fashion favored by Zhao Ziyang's think tank and officialized at the Thirteenth Party Congress in October 1987.[71] The other one, which can be traced to Hu Yaobang's circle, acknowledged that such a redistribution cannot be implemented by administrative fiat and requires a rearticulation of state-society relations, that is, a working, if limited, pluralism channeling the various interests of a diversified society and thus providing the necessary checks and counterweights to party power. This option, which was not unlike the one M. S. Gorbachev was to spread later in the Soviet Union and Eastern Europe, was defeated by early 1987.

Instead of a controlled modernization process, the years 1987 and 1988 saw a mounting crisis of social disintegration and frustration, while the government's continued inability to control microlevel units and investment fueled economic overheating and inflation.[72] In the hope of controlling a runaway growth, the ambitious economic reforms proposed by Zhao Ziyang in lieu of Hu Yaobang's political program had to be shelved by the summer of 1988 and replaced by a drastic program of austerity launched under the leadership of Li Peng. The authoritarian strategy was plainly unable to prevent a growing political paralysis and the worsening of the social crisis, a situation that directly generated the wave of urban protest in the spring of 1989.

In the light of state-building policies, the fate of enterprise management from 1986 to 1988 reflected the contradictions and the limits entailed by the political divisions of the leadership. Yet the fact that deep structural reforms (for example, of prices and labor allocation) were considered until mid-1988 allowed discussion and some local experiments to reach toward the goal of a "commodity society" made possible by a better macroeconomic regulation and working legal framework. But no general breakthrough was achieved. We have already noted how, ideologically and organizationally, the year 1987 saw the widespread diffusion of management contracts that cut the wind out of the sails of the FDRS. For ideological, financial, and institutional reasons, the reforms leading to a market allocation of employment, housing, and health continued to depend on whether a state-run welfare system could break the hold of the *danwei* on their individual members and free state enterprises from noneconomic duties.

Perhaps the best examples of the ambiguous situation of the managers in a period of uneasy transition and political uncertainty were the contradictory signals sent from the legal "front." In actual daily life, China's individualized contractual relations guaranteed by law lagged far behind Japan's or Hong Kong's. Enterprise directors remained vulnerable to local pressures and official hostility that took the form of broken employment contracts.[73] As before, these embattled professionals who, according to an acute observer, hold "one of the toughest jobs in China today,"[74] could not rely on the courts to defend their rights, as most cases were decided within local power networks.[75] The courts, however, did intervene[76] or, failing this, higher state authorities sometimes superseded "abusive" party organs.[77] Legal professionals explicitly stated that one of their goals must be to break *guanxi* networks.[78] But their local representatives, like managers and bankers, are not impervious to the still dominant power relations at local levels.[79] And what can be the real independence of lawyers who are state agents and supposed to reconcile their clients' interests with those of the community?

The plight of the managers and, above all, the negative economic consequences of local bureaucratic interference with management and investment highlighted the necessity of strengthening the state as a legal regulator that both strategies for building a modern Chinese state acknowledged as a top priority. Yet the political conflict over these strategies and the victory in 1987 of the advocates of authoritarianism resulted in the fact that managers and other economic operators had to depend on central administrative and legal reforms and could not rely on a fully pluralist system to articulate and defend their interests. They had and still have to make do with the limited social pluralism and counterweights working locally that Deng's economic reforms generated from the outset; before their development had to be contained for the sake of preserving the political status quo.

Social Pluralism and Social Counterweights

Managers have not been the sole focus of this limited strategy, but they stand as an important element in the evolution away from the Maoist dialectics of social classification and conflicts. The integration of the Chinese intellectuals into the working class was a significant step in this evolution. The new professionals, such as managers, who are the new "technical intelligentsia," were accordingly coopted as "intellectuals" into the party in 1985.[80] They are now recognized as so many "interest groups." This notion of interest groups has allowed the achievement of some progress in making the idea of class struggle peripheral to current Chinese sociology.[81]

The Chinese notion of interest groups points toward that of "civil society" in Eastern Europe and the Soviet Union, but it does not actually cover the same ground.[82] The political purpose of Chinese interest groups is to allow a limited social pluralism and to show that the party can become the ultimate repository of diverse but well-tuned interests. Some progress in this direction occurred at the Thirteenth Party Congress in October 1987 when private entrepreneurs and managers were given as much publicity as party members and delegates.[83]

Some of the "democratic parties," which until now have been used more to control their members than to represent their interests, clearly intend to contribute to this task of fine-tuning by providing a forum for higher intellectuals and other experts.[84] Much like the local and professional semiautonomous bodies through which the state exerted indirect control over the private sector in the Qing dynasty, the professional associations of managers that emerged in 1985 are semiofficial organizations relaying the official line while they provide a regular framework for consultation and action outside, and sometimes against, party and state structures.[85] Many associations do include lawyers among their membership[86] and have been instrumental in relaying the chains of protest against bureaucratic fiat that lead sometimes to debates in the local representative bodies[87] but more often to the vast inertia of the party, which may or may not move control organs into action.

These chains of protest often start in newspapers, which, for want of an independent stage where private interests could be expressed independently, are currently the most efficient regulators of China's nonpolitical social pluralism. We have seen in several instances that the Chinese national or provincial media have "voiced" the interests of management and supported individual managers against bureaucratic abuses. Some professional periodicals, especially economic and legal ones, in indicting bureaucratic abuses have published penetrating analyses of the institutional weaknesses stifling modern state-economic management.[88] And some large newspapers have developed investigation and legal teams that aggressively report public scandals.[89] The "tigers"—as *Yangcheng wanbao* calls the party and state officials who abuse their official functions, in contrast to the "flies," those who lack official power to receive large shares—are favorite targets.[90]

The "chain reactions," however, are carefully self-controlled. Mainland news reporters cannot trace bureaucratic-economic networks all the way to the top, as their Hong Kong colleagues freely do.[91] Short of official campaigns organized and controlled by the party, which insulate and sacrifice a few symbolic targets, denunciations are confined to narrow geographic and sectoral compartments. What we see is an array of secondary loci of power exerting a delegated tribunal authority whenever the established powers breach certain limits within specific domains.

The conclusion is that the trends of social change have widened and specialized the practice of social contest in the new context of modernization. Although it is difficult to assess whether and how these new attitudes relate to the kernels of bold reformism consolidated in the party and state apparatus under the patronage of prominent leaders, it seems that the evolution in China is not unlike the process of incremental change described by Moshe Lewin as one important factor leading to the emergence of Gorbachevism.[92] But the numerous difficulties in defending the independence of enterprise management also make it clear that China's evolution is still far from maturity.

Economic Levers

Because of this lack of social maturity, and because bold new economic reforms were kept on the official agenda until the fall of 1988, whereas political reforms had been frozen since early 1987, economic forces were expected to help a weak society break the bureaucratic yoke without raising directly the delicate issue of political change. In fact, even before some grand schemes of economic pluralism were suggested in 1987–88, the economic option had been widely practiced at microlevels. Many managers have sought to escape from their local bureaucratic predicament by establishing "freer" economic structures.[93] But it is questionable whether they can really escape this predicament. The new *gongsi* (companies) still need bureaucratic protection. And many are set up by bureaucratic entrepreneurs who "project" their wealth and power. These new companies represent more the economic rise of the informal networks of bureaucratic power than the emergence of sheltered business areas reserved for managers per se. The latter do not receive more independence from the continuing transformation of bureaus and "industrial companies" (*gongye gongsi*) into "economic entities."[94]

Some new management formulas that began in 1987 tried to circumvent these difficulties. Some localities tried stocks and stock markets. Li Yining, the famous Beijing University economist, sparked the experiment of granting managers property rights (*jus utendi*) through leases, paralleling more closely the leasing of land to rural households with production responsibility, to enhance the economic power of managers.[95] By codifying ownership, that is, by separating (public) ownership from (private) management and grinding the latter into a de facto privatized property system these leases aim to guarantee freedom of state enterprises from communal power relations. Yet we know that even farmers with contractual rights are not entirely immune from the squeeze. Despite giving managers ultimate responsibility for the enterprise, profit-sharing stipulations in leasing contracts provide ample ground for informal negotiation after the contract is signed, for outside intervention, and for disguised extortion. Economic levers are not therefore a panacea dispensing with legal, administrative, and political reforms. They cannot do more than tactically circumvent political obstacles, and for a while only, since they are bound to accelerate social change and to increase the pressure for political reforms in the long run. Therefore, because the new leasing contracts could create not just a specialized technostructure but a potentially alien and competing economic elite at the heart of the urban-industrial establishment, the new system is guarded very closely. To date, local governments have tried the system only in small state enterprises, and official pronouncements list it as one formula among many and as a means for further implementing the harmless economic-legal pluralism called for in the October 1984 "Decision on Reform of the Economic Structure."[96]

CONCLUSION: MICROECONOMIC MANAGEMENT AND THE STATECRAFT OF MODERNIZATION

As far as the history of the FDRS from 1984 to 1987 is concerned, we may safely conclude that this formal attempt to introduce professional management in the state sector was more changed than it changed. In the end, although the new system opened new windows of power and new accesses to wealth, a strong party at the top and established party elites at the local level defended existing power and gained control over new wealth. Perhaps because the new system directly confronted the privilege of ruling elites, the fate of the new managing elite called for by the urban economic reforms was sealed almost from the outset, well before the Tiananmen crisis froze other urban reforms. The effort to create management with independent power within state enterprises did not even significantly alter the patterns of structural dependency, solidarity, protection, conflict, and profiteering established through interpersonal and functional bureaucratic networks that had undermined the autonomous "rights" granted to enterprises after 1978. Factory directors were compelled to enter these networks to fulfill their assignment and to achieve protection. The emergence of new persons and interests often led to factional conflicts as factory directors were forced to align with one local group or microfaction in a conflict-ridden local scene. Steering a difficult course among local micropolitics, that is, managing power relations at the local level, is still one important, if not the most important, dimension of enterprise management in the PRC. Conversely, state enterprises are not merely economic units accumulating capital or profits. They are, essentially, a nexus of power.

Thus the FDRS was one test among many others of the necessity and the difficulty of reshaping not only party power but also the fundamental order of society inherited from history and from Maoism. The difficulties in modernizing the institutions of Chinese industrial management that the FDRS was meant to solve, and its failure, underline the basic flaw of the Chinese reforms resulting from their deficient treatment of the inherited political and social setting.

The formal retreat of the central command system since the early 1980s created the illusion that social and economic actors are now individualized and emancipated in a mixed market and planned economy. In fact the evolution has mainly strengthened the domination of intermediate bureaucratic structures operating at the local level. New opportunities have created new centers of bureaucratic interest and therefore strengthened bureaucratic pluralism and widened the multiple gaps between bureaucracies. These conditions have weakened central authority and national integration while fueling unregulated economic growth and accelerating social disintegration.[97] The illusion was held not only by many Western observers who freely spoke of a Chinese capitalism, as if socioeconomic forces had been emancipated. It was also shared by many Chinese who thought they could manage their farms or businesses without paying much attention to the world of politics, by arranging practical deals with local powerholders through *guanxi* networks and corruption. The managers in state enterprises found soon enough they could not entertain that illusion.

The discrepancy between the incipient socioeconomic forces of modernization and the archaic power structure that has been maintained under Deng Xiaoping's rule is a crippling factor in view of the modernization goals of the leadership, amounting to a virtual collapse of the ancient command structure as an economic and social regulator. It is also a source of the social tensions and political paralysis that reached a climax from the inflation crisis in the summer of 1988 to the generalization of social and political protest in urban China in the spring of 1989.

Before the crisis erupted, that is, from 1985 to 1987, a new strategy emerged for controlling economic growth, checking bureaucratic power, and preserving the new professional and economic interests. The effort through the FDRS and subsequent measures to redistribute power within state enterprises reflected this broader approach to the modernization of Chinese society at large. The strategy called for responsible professionals, responding to indirect macroeconomic controls, protected by law, to help create a "commodity society" resting on individuals responsible to the state and to markets rather than on old personal networks and factions. The growing awareness that the Chinese leaders would have to reform the economy while simultaneously creating a legal framework, social pluralism, and a commodity society was progressively centered on the need to build a modern state performing as a macroeconomic and legal regulator over an individualized society.

In principle, state building should not have been a divisive issue. While the scope of the ancient command structure would decrease, the reach of the modernized state would increase as it extended to individuals, breaking up ancient communal structures, and articulated the nationalist ideology mobilizing individual citizens, as analyzed by Vivienne Shue of Cornell University. And yet no agreement could be found. The neoauthoritarian school, whose models were Japan and Taiwan, envisioned a careful tutoring of social forces and a progressive restructuring of the party, which would have to withdraw from state functions and recruit among the new social elites. It was believed that an incremental process of social and even some institutional change, including the modification of certain traditional values and the recruiting of managerial professionals and other experts into party ranks and decision-making bodies, could slowly tilt the balance in favor of the new legal-state framework and gradually redistribute interests among party bureaucratic constituencies.

The weakness of the authoritarian scheme was that the existing power structure would have to find enough internal strength to reform itself while reforming the economy and the society. This is precisely where it was challenged by the "pluralist" school among party members and intellectuals, who claimed it would be necessary to reach beyond the party to build the modern state and carry out modernization policies. At the same time, the traditional patriarchal culture was viewed not as a possible asset in the hands of a strong state but as a formidable dead weight, and the contrast between tradition and modernity as a matter of essence rather than of balance.

As reflected by the embattled status of managers, the choice for authoritarian policies in 1987 was not followed by any decisive breakthrough in state-building achievements. And the subsequent crisis of 1988–89 has shown that authoritarianism works only if the state works, that is, if it performs its regulating duties by providing a suitable macroeconomic environment and a working legal framework. Authoritarianism alone cannot build a modern state, and the mainland cannot be another Taiwan. The necessary rearticulation of the power structure on a changing society and changing mentalities is bound to involve a process of political change. The oligarchs representing local power and vested interests, who backed Deng's new economic deal inasmuch as they gained new benefits, have much to lose in a real modernization and in the emergence of a new citizenry. But they will remain in power, blocking any real microstructural adjustment of informal and formal institutions and attitudes, until such change occurs.[98] The reorganization of the economy, of the state, and of Chinese society will have to be supported and tested by forces from below, but the go signal will have to come from a political breakthrough at the top.

The political dimension will be all the more decisive and unavoidable in the long run as the spring crisis in 1989 made clear that radical students and intellectuals are no longer isolated in their demand for bolder reforms. And yet China is far from the clear-cut confrontations between the communist power structure and active civil societies that are tilting the balance in Eastern Europe. The prospects for management in China, and the possible attitudes of management professionals, have to be assessed against this multifaceted background. We cannot take for granted that the new professional elites, and the managers among them, will remain good-willed under CCP domination and join the ruling elites as junior partners if they cannot count on the economic, social, and legal compensations and protection enjoyed by their Taiwanese counterparts, who obtained these benefits in exchange for long-term acceptance of authoritarian politics. Will they rather follow the tradition of mainland intellectuals and articulate their interests more forcefully, as have done those who joined reformist "salons" in the large cities or who demonstrated on Tiananmen Square, together with *geti hu* (individual) entrepreneurs and CITIC executives? But at the same time we should not ignore the vast number of those who submit to the tradition of compliance with the dead weight of the bureaucratic establishment.

These questions belong to the more general problem of a nascent civil society not yet fully shaped. Time and further studies will provide some answers. But it is clear that sooner or later the problems created and exemplified by the rise of autonomous management, which are political in essence, will move from the relatively safe arena of micropolitics to the more destabilizing level of macropolitics.[99]

CHAPTER SIX

Economic Reform and Income Distribution in Tianjin, 1976–1986

ANDREW G. WALDER

China's economic reforms, it is commonly presumed, have ushered in an era of heightened social inequality. This presumption is not unwarranted: Maoist egalitarianism has been officially, and loudly, repudiated. Open commodity markets, petty private enterprise, profit motives, and large cash bonuses—all ruthlessly suppressed in the past—are now commonplace. Some of China's leaders have argued openly that increased inequalities will hasten economic prosperity, long delayed by misguided efforts to level incomes. The publicity lent to rich peasant entrepreneurs, the promise of high incomes in the urban private sector, the spread of large bonuses in industry, and the constant calls to differentiate the bonuses sharply by individual and enterprise productivity, all create the expectation that China will experience a decisive trend toward greater inequality and perhaps a polarization between rich and poor. [1]

In striking contrast to these presumptions about China, similar reforms in Hungary are commonly perceived to have led to, or to promise, a reduction of the inequalities of the past. Surveys of housing quality, earnings, and standard of living have shown that bureaucratic methods of distribution systematically favor the well educated, the administratively powerful, and the higher paid, whereas the lower paid and less well educated, who presumably were to benefit from bureaucratic redistribution, are systematically neglected.[2] Aware that the less privileged were already turning to a private "second economy" to satisfy their needs, many came to view the expansion of the market economy as a force for enhanced needs satisfaction for the less privileged.[3] One exhaustive comparison of Hungary and Poland shows no necessary connection between reform and increased income inequality.[4]

Is China's experience really so different from that of countries like Hungary? One possible difference is that, unlike its Eastern European counterparts, China's reform followed an era of celebrated income leveling. Within rural and urban communities, China's income distribution was highly egalitarian compared with that of other developing countries, and near the bottom of the range of socialist countries (see Table 1).[5] It is no doubt the widespread knowledge about past intracommunity leveling that leads students of China to view subsequent reforms as inegalitarian in their consequences.

There were, however, pronounced forms of inequality introduced inadvertently by the Maoist model of development. At the same time that incomes within villages and cities were being leveled, the gap between city and countryside, and between rich and poor rural regions, was growing to a degree that surpassed other developing and developed countries. The urban-rural income gap, the most striking example, grew from 2 : 1 in the 1950s to 3 : 1 by the 1970s (or to 5 or 6 : 1 if one counts state subsidies of urban living standards).[6] Moreover, differences between rural regions were exacerbated as autarky prevailed, rural sidelines were suppressed, and all regions were forced into a grain subsistence agriculture for which many areas were geographically ill suited.[7] Inequality is therefore a multifaceted concept, often elusive in eras of change because there is no necessary connection between change in one facet and change in another.

Several scholars have suggested that China's reforms are not necessarily inegalitarian in their implications, and in fact may be an equalizing force in some respects. As China's reforms began, William Parish noted that

TABLE 1 Gini Coefficients for Urban Income, Selected Socialist and Developing Countries

Country and Date	*Gini Coefficient*
Socialist economies	
USSR, 1979	
Individual wages in public sector	.25
Including private income	.30
Per capita household income	.37
Poland, 1965	.26[a]
Yugoslavia, 1965	.24[a]
Hungary, 1965	.21[a]
China, mid-1970s	.20[a]
Czechoslovakia, 1965	.19[a]
Developing economies in Asia	
India, 1975–76	.42[b]
Indonesia, 1976	.43[c]
Pakistan, 1970–71	.36[c]
Thailand, 1975–76	.40[b]

Sources: For income in the USSR, Aaron Vinokur and Gur Ofer, "Inequality of Earnings, Household Income, and Wealth in the Soviet Union in the 1970s," in James R. Millar, ed., *Politics, Work, and Daily Life in the USSR: A Survey of Former Citizens* (Cambridge, Cambridge University Press, 1987), pp. 176, 187, 193.

    For income in Poland, Yugoslavia, Hungary, and Czechoslovakia, Shail Jain, *Size Distribution of Income* (Washington, D.C., International Bank for Reconstruction and Development, 1975), as presented in William L. Parish, "Destratification in China," in J. L. Watson, ed., *Class and Social Stratification in Post-Revolution China* (Cambridge, Cambridge University Press, 1984), p. 90.

    For income in China, Parish, p. 88.

    For income in developing economies in Asia, World Bank, *China: Socialist Economic Development* (Washington, D.C., 1983), I, 89, as presented in Carl Riskin, *China's Political Economy: The Quest for Development since 1949* (New York, Oxford University Press, 1987), p. 249.

a. Based on individual income.
b. Based on per capita household income.
c. Based on total household income.

several socialist countries had already implemented similar incentive mechanisms and had only slightly more unequal income distributions than China's of the mid-1970s. He suggested, and Martin Whyte subsequently cited official data to illustrate, that rural reforms will lessen the income gap between countryside and city.[8] Whyte also reasoned that some aspects of urban wage reform, like large production bonuses, might favor lower-paid manual workers and therefore serve to reduce income differences.[9] Victor Nee has shown that the income advantages of cadres over peasant producers in the hinterland of Xiamen have steadily diminished in the 1980s.[10] Other analysts have also documented a lessening of certain income inequalities in rural areas, even as new inequalities arise.[11]

To these discussions we bring a clear finding about the cash incomes of urban wage earners in Tianjin Municipality. Despite the fact that the distribution of money incomes in Tianjin, as in the rest of urban China in the mid-1970s, was already highly egalitarian, there has been a *marked further equalization* of incomes in the ensuing decade. With survey data gathered in the city in 1986, we shall document the extent of this equalization and examine the ways that the allocation of salary raises, the distribution of bonuses, and the new opportunities for earning second incomes have contributed to the overall trend toward greater equality in earnings.[12] After presenting our evidence on the narrowly quantitative question of the amount of inequality, we shall analyze briefly the ways that reform has affected income differences by age, gender, education, rank, and other individual characteristics, and by selected characteristics of workplaces.

THE SURVEY

Our 1986 survey sampled randomly 1,011 households in the nine urban districts of Tianjin.[13] We selected the wage earner in the household whose date of birth was closest to 1 October and asked a long series of questions, two of which were about the individual's current monthly wage, bonus, and other income and, if he or she had worked in 1976 (815 had), the same data for that year.[14]

Our sample limits the conclusions that we may properly draw, and we should specify these limitations at the outset. Our survey unfortunately excludes individuals employed in the "individual" *(geti)* sector of the economy. These people earn incomes that reputedly surpass those of state- and collective-sector wage earners. Only one respondent worked in the individual sector, and that person's reported income was 30 percent above the city average. Our sample, however, does include many individuals employed in small collective enterprises and in "new collectives" *(xin jiti),* many of which are effectively outside the planning system and which also enjoy relatively high incomes.[15] In Tianjin in 1986, according to official statistics, only 1.5 percent of the urban population was employed in the individual sector.[16] This figure probably underreports the extent of private activity, especially among those not officially registered as Tianjin residents (but that raises the conceptual question of whether these people should be considered urban or rural residents). Even if the real figure is several times the percentage reported officially, it is not certain that the presumed high incomes in this sector would greatly affect overall measures of wage inequality for a city where the numbers of privately employed are so small.

While excluding the individual sector prevents us from measuring the presumably greater income variations introduced by that sector, *this exclusion cannot logically account for the marked equalization of earnings among the vast majority who work in the state and collective sectors.* It is possible that the individual sector, if fully represented in our sample, would partially offset the trend toward equality in the rest of the labor force. But even so, we still need to account for this important equalizing trend in the dominant state and collective sectors.

Since bonuses may affect the degree of wage inequality, we should be concerned that respondents might underreport this aspect of their income. There is little indication of such underreporting in our survey. Our respondents reported an average monthly bonus that equaled 24 percent of their total income (see Table 2), virtually the same as the official figure of 23 percent.[17]

"Other" income earned outside of one's primary job is another important part of the new wage trends, and we should consider possible underreporting here as well. One could easily imagine that respondents would hesitate to reveal large incomes from after-work activities. Our respondents reported an average of only 4.10 yuan of outside income per month, less than 5 percent of their average income. Yet closer examination shows the distribution of "other" income to be highly skewed: 70 percent reported no "other" income. But 22 percent reported that they earned between 1 and 19 yuan per month; 6.5 percent reported incomes that were between 20 and 49 yuan; and the top 1 percent earned second incomes that ranged from 50 to 149 yuan. Since we have at best anecdotal evidence about these incomes in previous studies, we have no way to judge whether these figures should be considered low or high. We shall analyze the distribution of outside income and offer some preliminary ideas about how this category of income, as reported by our respondents, affects the overall distribution of income in our sample.

Finally, there are conceptual limits to this study. The most important

TABLE 2 Summary of Income Trends, 1976–1986

Item	1976	1986[a]	% Change
Average monthly incomes[b]			
Respondent salary	49.72	75.98	+53
Respondent bonus	4.47	25.45	+469
Respondent "other income"	1.09	4.10	+276
Total for respondent	55.28	105.54	+91
Per capita family	28.81	62.65	+117
Coefficients of variation ($s/\overline{X}$)			
Monthly salary	.38	.31	−18
Monthly bonus[c]	1.99	.75	−62
Total monthly income[d]	.42	.29	−31
Per capita family income	.43	.34	−21
Gini coefficients			
Monthly salary	.197	.165	−16
Monthly bonus[c]	.729	.359	−51
Total monthly income[d]	.213	.157	−26
Per capita family income	.219	.171	−22

a. 1986 incomes are in nominal terms.
b. Retirees are excluded from all calculations, except family income.
c. Of the respondents who worked in 1976, over half received no bonuses, greatly inflating the measures of inequality (only 4 percent received no bonus in 1986).
d. "Total monthly income" is for the individual respondent and includes monthly salary, monthly bonus, and "other" income.

has to do with the definition of *reform*. Except for the small minority who earn large incomes outside, our respondents do not earn their incomes directly in markets for their labor or products. Therefore the subject of this study is conceptually distinct from questions about incomes in the market economy of rural China. Our urban respondents, except as consumers, have not been profoundly affected by the workings of market mechanisms.

Instead, urban citizens have experienced such new organizational mechanisms as regular pay raises, enterprise profit retention, and greatly expanded incentive pay. These have been the norm in the urban state and collective sector throughout the 1980s. As a proportion of the total national wage bill, bonuses grew from 3 to 23 percent between 1978 and 1986.[18] In a 1986 survey, factories were found to retain an average of 22 percent of their profits and to distribute 37 percent of this amount as bonuses.[19] Bonuses are certainly large enough for them to have inegalitarian implications, if that is indeed their effect. But we should note that the first several rounds of post-Mao wage raises were in fact "readjustments" designed primarily to supplement the pay of those whose wages had been frozen for long periods at low levels.[20] Chinese analysts have also complained consistently in the 1980s that bonuses have not been differentiated sufficiently.[21] We observe here the effects of urban wage reform as actually implemented, not as a pure expression of the economic principles championed by reform economists.

Money earnings are not, of course, the sole measure of inequality in China, today or in the past. We would like to be able to measure, for both the 1970s and 1980s, the considerable nonmonetary aspects of "income" (various state and workplace subsidies, housing, privileges of rank, and services and other goods delivered at the workplace). It is entirely possible that other kinds of inequalities are being introduced, especially as social services decline in the countryside and as a larger transient labor force is attracted to cities.[22]

Within these conceptual and sampling limits, our data permit strong preliminary conclusions about changes in urban wage inequality from the 1970s to the 1980s. We analyze the effects both of wage reform as actually implemented (more frequent wage raises and larger monetary bonuses) and of opportunities for outside income on the distribution of cash wages among urban employees of state and collective enterprises—still (officially) over 96 percent of the urban work force nationwide.

THE CHANGING PATTERN OF INCOME INEQUALITY, 1976–1986

The *nominal* monthly income of our respondents almost doubled between 1976 and 1986: basic salaries increased by 53 percent, while bonuses grew more than fourfold (see Table 2). All of this nominal increase, however, was nullified by inflation, which according to official indices totaled 49 percent over the decade. In real terms total incomes decreased by 2 percent. Interestingly, real incomes were maintained only because of large increases in bonuses and other incomes: basic salaries dropped by 22 percent, whereas bonuses increased by 187 percent.[23] Despite the fact that bonuses grew to a large percentage of income, and despite the fact that the measures of inequality for bonuses are more than double those for the basic salary, variation in total incomes declined strikingly. The coefficient of variation $(s/\bar{X})$ of monthly incomes (a measure of dispersion around the mean) declined by 31 percent. The Gini coefficient, a measure of the deviation of successive strata from a theoretical "equal-share" line, decreased by 26 percent.[24] The same trend is evident in per capita family income: the coefficient of variation and Gini coefficient declined by 21 and 22 percent, respectively (see Table 2).

Note the agreement between our measures of income inequality and those reported in other studies of urban incomes. In their analysis of urban incomes in the mid-1970s, Whyte and Parish reported a Gini coefficient for income of .20, compared with our 1976 figure of .21; their estimate of the percentage of income received by the top 10 percent of the population was .21, ours .22 (see Table 3).[25] In their analysis of 1984 Tianjin data collected by the Tianjin Statistical Bureau, Hu Teh-wei, Ming Li, and Shuzhong Shi reported a Gini coefficient for basic salary of .168, compared with our 1986 figure of .165; .414 for bonuses, compared with ours of .359; and .211 for total income, compared with ours of .157 (in their study total income did not include "other" incomes) (Table 3).[26] Finally, our figures correspond closely to those derived from Wen Xie's 1984 survey of Beijing residents.[27] While his data yield coefficients for salary closer to ours for 1976, the Beijing figure for total income (.171) is close to our 1986 Tianjin figure (.157).

Cross-tabulations of income by years of work, party membership, and gender (summarized in Table 4) show a consistent pattern. The income gaps between the oldest and youngest, men and women, and party members and nonmembers all declined considerably.[28] The greatest wage inequalities in the 1970s, according to prior studies of urban workers, were those by age. The wage freeze from the early 1960s through the late 1970s froze preexisting inequalities in place and led to the accumulation of two generations of workers at the lowest rungs of the wage ladder.[29] Table 4 bears this out: the greatest differences in wages according to individual characteristics in our sample by far were (and still are) those due to age. The oldest and highest paid made more than triple the incomes of the youngest in 1976. By 1986 the gap was reduced by more than a third. Rank and gender differences, at least in terms of income, also appear to have been reduced significantly. The significant income advantages enjoyed by party members and men appear to have been reduced by half (Table 4).[30]

The only exception to this pattern of leveling between groups is by educational level. Because of the long denigration of intellectuals, the

TABLE 3 Indices for Urban Income Inequality in China,
Various Studies, 1970s and 1980s

Sample	Salary	Bonus	Total Income	Household Income
Urban China, mid-1970s			.20	.25 [a]
Tianjin, 1976	.197	.729	.213	.219 [b]
Urban China, 1981				.16 [b]
Tianjin, 1984	.168	.414	.211	—
Beijing, 1984	.193	.402	.171	—
Tianjin, 1986	.165	.359	.157	.171 [b]

Sources: For urban China, mid-1970s, William L. Parish, "Destratification in China," in J. L. Watson, ed., *Class and Social Stratification in Post-Revolution China* (Cambridge, Cambridge University Press, 1984), p. 88, and Martin K. Whyte and William L. Parish, *Urban Life in Contemporary China* (Chicago, University of Chicago Press, 1984), p. 44, based on a Hong Kong survey administered to 133 emigrés, who reported on 899 economically active individuals from 305 households.

For Tianjin, 1976, Table 1 of this chapter.

For urban China, 1981, Carl Riskin, *China's Political Economy: The Quest for Development since 1949* (New York, Oxford University Press, 1987), p. 249. Estimate is based on a national urban survey reported in State Statistical Bureau, *Statistical Yearbook of China 1981,* p. 438. The statistic was based on six categories, but the categories did not have equal numbers of cases.

For Tianjin, 1984, Teh-wei Hu, Ming Li, and Shuzhong Shi, "Analysis of Wages and Bonus Payments among Tianjin Urban Workers," *CQ* 113:77–93 (1988), p. 92, based on a Bureau of Statistics survey of 1,116 individuals in 500 households. However, statistics for bonus and total income are based on 300 individuals.

For Beijing, 1984, calculations based on survey data gathered by Wen Xie from 1,639 individuals; he kindly made these available to me. See Nan Lin and Wen Xie, "Occupational Prestige in Urban China," *American Journal of Sociology* 93:793–832 (1988).

For Tianjin, 1986, Table 1 of this chapter.

a. Household income is total for the household.
b. Household income is per capita.

high representation of poorly educated individuals from the revolutionary generation in prestigious jobs, and the disruption of the educational system in the Cultural Revolution era, there was a negative relationship between number of years of education and income in 1976.[31] The highest paid—university graduates—made 35 percent more than the lowest paid— the middle school graduates. But the university graduates made only 16 percent more than those with no formal schooling. The low pay of middle school graduates unable to continue their education is not surprising: since the early 1960s they were overrepresented among the unemployed and delinquent and were the main target of the rustication programs of the 1960s and 1970s.[32]

TABLE 4 Comparison of Total Incomes of Highest- and
Lowest-Paid Groups, Various Individual
Characteristics, 1976 and 1986

| | % Difference | | % Change of |
Grouping	1976	1986	Difference
Age (over 60/under 20)	214	135	−37
Party membership (member/nonmember)	44	19	−57
Gender (men/women)	33	18	−45
Education (university/middle school)[a]	35	38	+9
Education (university/no school)	16	8	−50

Notes: Retirees were excluded from all calculations. 1986 incomes are in nominal terms.

a. The lowest-paid educational group in both 1976 and 1986 was the graduates of academic middle schools.

Given the government's consistent stress on educational qualifications in promotions over the ensuing decade, one would expect increased income differences by 1986. Surprisingly, to the extent that we can see significant change, it has been toward greater equality. The gap between the university educated and those with no formal schooling has been reduced by half, but there has been only the slightest increase in the much larger gap between the university and middle-school graduates. The poorly educated still hold relatively high-paying positions, and middle-school graduates still have the lowest incomes. Despite the consistent stress on educational standards for the past decade, there is still a negative relationship between years of education and monthly income.[33]

THE SOURCES OF INCOME LEVELING

Since reported "other" incomes are on average too small greatly to affect overall income distributions, there are two possible sources of income leveling: wage raises and bonuses. We have already noted that in the first years of reform, wage raises (or "readjustments") were given preferentially to the lower paid as a matter of policy. Is this primarily responsible for the equalizing trend? We have also noted the common criticism inside China that bonuses have been distributed too nearly equally to have an incentive effect—but this, even if true, does not appear to explain wage equalization in our sample, since in Table 2 we have already seen that 1986 bonuses were in fact distributed much more unequally than sala-

TABLE 5 Determinants of Proportional Increase in
Total Income

| | Regression Coefficients | |
Variable	b	Beta
Increase in bonus pay, 1976–1986	.021***	.470***
Increase in salary, 1976–1986	.027***	.654***
Salary in 1976	−.0002	−.006***
Bonus in 1976	.008***	.141***
Adjusted multiple R^2	.647	
N	739	

Notes: Retirees in 1986 are excluded. Incomes for 1986 are in real terms. The dependent variable is defined as 1986 total real income minus 1976 total income, divided by total income in 1976. Increases in bonus pay and in salary are defined as real 1986 levels minus 1976 levels.

*** Significant at $p < .001$.

ries. If bonuses have contributed to wage equalization, it has been because higher bonuses have gone to people with lower salaries. What is the importance of bonuses relative to salary raises?

To answer this question, we estimated the effects of absolute increase in bonus and salary on proportional increase in total income, controlling for salary and bonus levels in 1976 (see Table 5). The coefficients for increase in salary and increase in bonus are virtually the same. This suggests that bonuses and wage raises contributed equally to the trend; it is not the result primarily of early wage readjustments that favored those with low salaries.

A NOTE ON OUTSIDE INCOME

We have already noted that substantial outside incomes were too rare in our sample for them greatly to affect income trends, but can the distribution of these incomes tell us anything about their future effect, if outside incomes were to expand greatly? In our data there is no significant correlation between "other" incomes and income in 1976, or with salary in 1986. Other incomes appear to be distributed randomly with regard to salaries and bonuses.

What kinds of people are earning high outside incomes? In Table 6

TABLE 6 Characteristics of Respondents Earning Significant
Other Incomes

Characteristic	Mean Income (nominal)	N	N in Sample	N as % N in Sample
Monthly salary				
Up to 60 yuan	15.39	44	231	19
61 to 75	16.83	75	285	26
76 to 90	17.29	65	291	22
91 to 105	15.00	23	120	19
106 and more	13.72	18	84	21
Age				
Up to 29	14.72	47	199	24
30 to 39	18.60	92	358	26
40 to 49	14.70	63	264	24
50 to 59	14.18	22	145	15
60 and older	14.00	1	45	2
Education				
Below primary	18.25	12	102	12
Primary	16.69	13	92	14
Lower middle	15.64	109	396	28
Upper middle	14.67	30	172	17
Technical middle	16.73	45	150	30
College	20.06	16	98	16
Type of work unit				
New collective	20.50	4	25	16
Collective	17.63	36	190	19
State enterprise	16.26	139	588	24
State institution	15.72	32	150	21
Government office	12.50	14	57	25
Rank of work unit				
Street	22.67	3	26	12
Company under district	15.50	20	107	19
Company under city	17.10	106	446	24
District	15.46	72	297	24
City	15.24	17	62	27
Ministry	12.60	5	67	7
Occupation				
Unskilled worker	16.98	44	220	20
Skilled worker	15.61	75	322	23
Sales and services	17.56	27	135	20
Clerical	17.23	31	124	25
Professional	16.42	31	126	25
Administrative cadre	12.94	17	83	21

we report breakdowns by various social characteristics. In the column labeled "Mean Income", we exclude all individuals who earned less than 5 yuan per month in other incomes, and report the average of all those who had incomes of 5 yuan or more. In the next column we report the number of people in each category who had high outside incomes, compare it in the next column with the total number of people in that category, and in the right-hand column report the percentage of people in the category who earn high outside incomes.

There are few clear patterns. If we look at salary groups, the only conclusion we can draw is that those with the highest salaries make somewhat lower outside incomes, but all groups appear to have a roughly equal opportunity to earn high outside incomes. If we look at age groups, we find that older respondents reported high outside incomes much less frequently than others. If we look at educational groups, the best and worst educated make the highest incomes when they find outside jobs, but they are less likely to find them. People who work in small collectives make larger outside incomes than others, and government office workers make less, but they are less likely to find outside jobs. There are no apparent differences by occupation except that administrative cadres earn lower incomes. The only clear relationships are those by type and rank of work unit: the higher the rank or the greater the prestige of the unit, the lower the outside income.

We must await further studies before we shall know whether we have underestimated the amounts of outside incomes, so our conclusions here are tentative. From this evidence we detect no incipient trends that allow us to predict whether outside earnings, if they expand greatly in the future, will come to benefit preferentially the working class, the middle class, or the marginal poor. But it does appear that outside incomes are not becoming a vehicle for the highly salaried and privileged to enrich themselves further (we are naturally forced to exclude corruption from our definition of outside income). At least at this stage in their growth in Tianjin, outside incomes appear to be distributed very unequally among individuals, but randomly across social groups.

THE CHANGING SOCIAL DETERMINANTS OF INCOME INEQUALITY

So far we have considered only the *degree* of inequality. We have documented an overall decline in income differences, and we have examined the role of salary raises, bonuses, and outside income in contributing to this leveling trend. We have also looked at wage differences between the highest- and the lowest-paid groups, defined by certain social characteristics, and have found that, generally speaking, these social differences have declined. But global measures of inequality tell us little of interest about changes in inequality. What social changes lie behind these statistics? After all, it is possible for measures of inequality to grow, while the formerly poor are becoming the newly rich, or while old patterns of advantage and privilege disappear. In such cases what meaningful conclusions can we draw about inequality?

Here we turn away from the question of the *amount* of income inequality and turn to the *social determinants* of inequality. Changes in the social determinants of inequality are just as important, and arguably more interesting, than changes in amounts. For they tell us about qualitative changes in Chinese society. Are certain social privileges and disadvantages of the past disappearing? Are new privileges and disadvantages emerging?

We anticipated this discussion in Table 2, when we examined changes in the gap between the richest and the poorest groups defined by age, gender, party membership, and education. But that approach was too simple to capture the complex changes in which we are interested. We need to take into account the fact that these variables are also correlated with one another and with other variables that we have not yet considered. It may well be the case that the reduction of wage differences by party membership simply reflects a decline in wage differences by age, not a systematic reduction in advantages of rank. It may also be the case that the lack of a zero-order relationship between income and education in 1986 might be due to a negative relationship between age and years of education. We need to sort out these quantitative complexities before we can come to a qualitative assessment of the social changes wrought by ten years of reform.

To control for the relationships of these variables with one another, and to estimate their relative impact on income before and after the reforms, we need to place them in regression equations for income in 1976 and 1986. If we compare the equations for the two years, we may be able to detect significant changes over time: some variables may have a significant relationship with income in one period but not in the other.

Table 7 summarizes the results of the regression analyses of income, using the four variables for which we have information for both 1976

TABLE 7 Selected Individual Determinants of Total Monthly
Income, Simplified Model, 1976 and 1986

Variable	1976		1986	
	b	Beta	b	Beta
Years of work	.029***	.620***	.018***	.590***
Gender (male)	.135***	.169***	.105***	.179***
Party membership	.079*	.061*	.045*	.054*
Years of education	.002	.019	.010***	.104***
Adjusted multiple R^2		.481		.406
N		801		932

Notes: The dependent variable is the natural logarithm of total income. Retirees are excluded.
Nominal 1986 incomes are used.
***Significant at $p < .001$.
*Significant at $p < .05$.

and 1986: age (measured here as years of work), gender (entered here as a dummy variable, "male"), party membership (entered here as a dummy variable, "member"), and years of education (measured here as total years of formal education before the first job).

If we examine the standardized regression coefficients (Beta) for 1976, we find that the results confirm what we might have expected based on our earlier comparisons of means, though we can for the first time sort out the relative importance of these four factors. In 1976 years of work was far and away the most important determinant of wage differences, once the effects of the other variables are taken into account. Gender was also a strong predictor of income. Party membership had a significant, though less pronounced, effect on income than did gender. Years of education, not surprisingly, was unrelated to income. In sum, of the four variables we have examined for 1976, years of work, gender, and party membership, in descending order of importance, were the significant determinants of income.

If we compare these results with the equation for 1986, however, we can see some things that were not at all apparent earlier. Years of work is still by far the most important determinant of income, gender holds its position as the second most important of the four variables, and party membership is still significant. The major revelation of this comparison is the clearly enhanced importance of education—something we would not have expected given our earlier bivariate analysis. Now that we have

TABLE 8 Selected Individual Determinants of Monthly Salary, Simplified Model, 1976 and 1986

Variable	1976		1986	
	b	Beta	b	Beta
Years of work	.029***	.689***	.024***	.747***
Gender (male)	.104***	.140***	.075***	.119***
Party membership	.092**	.076**	.087***	.097***
Years of education	.005	.043	.016***	.145***
Adjusted multiple R^2	.559		.601	
N	801		932	

Notes: The dependent variable is the natural logarithm of total salary. Retirees are excluded. Nominal 1986 incomes are used.
***Significant at $p<.001$.
**Significant at $p<.01$.

controlled for the effects of age, gender, and party membership, years of education, insignificant in 1976, is about as important as gender and more important than party membership.

What lies behind these changes? Were they due to changes in the criteria that determined the basic salary, or to the fact that the greatly expanded bonuses and new opportunities for outside income offset the principles enshrined in national wage scales? In Table 8 we exclude bonus and "other" income and look at changes in the importance of these four variables in determining the basic salary. Note that for 1976 the picture is about the same (not surprisingly, since bonuses and other income were so small). In 1986, however, we find that the effect of education is now somewhat stronger than that of gender, and that party membership is more strongly related to salary than to total income.

We can draw from Tables 7 and 8 two sets of conclusions about changes in income inequality. We have already seen that income inequality has declined. Here, keep in mind, we are talking not about the amount of inequality but about the social factors that contribute to it. The first set of conclusions involves changes from 1976 to 1986. Years of work and gender are strong predictors of total income in both years. Education, however, has grown in both absolute and relative importance. Party membership continues to be an important determinant of salary and total income, though by 1986 it was less important than education.

We draw the second set of conclusions from comparisons of salary and total income in 1986. This comparison can be thought of as an effort to assess the effect of bonus and other income on the principles of income determination enshrined in the salary structure. Note that our four variables explain much more of the variation in basic salary than total income (compare the "adjusted multiple R^2" in Tables 7 and 8 for 1986)—about 50 percent more by 1986. This indicates something very important about the effects of the new sources of income ushered in by the reforms: they have reduced the extent to which one's income would be otherwise determined by these four variables. Therefore despite the fact, as we saw in Table 2, that bonuses are distributed much more unequally than basic salary, the principles that determine this variation are probably unrelated, or negatively related, to years of work, party membership, and years of education.

AN EXPANDED MODEL OF INCOMES IN 1986

So far our analysis has been based on the simplest of models, forced on us by the fact that there are only a handful of variables for which we have information for both 1976 and 1986. But if we employ the same logic as in our comparisons of Tables 7 and 8, we can observe the effect of a larger list of factors on salary, bonuses, and total income in 1986. This will allow us to include a larger number of variables that might affect incomes and to come to a fuller assessment of the impact of bonuses on income differences.

In Table 9 we report an analysis of salaries, bonuses, and total incomes that includes an expanded number of variables. To the original four we have added the rank of the work unit in the hierarchy of government "systems" *(xitong)*, whether or not the work unit is in the state (as opposed to the collective) sector, the respondent's rank in the workplace, and whether or not the respondent is a manual worker in an economic enterprise. In addition to the original four, we therefore add variables that attempt to measure, respectively, sectoral inequalities by the bureaucratic status of the workplace, sectoral inequalities by state versus collective ownership, individual inequalities by one's rank on the job, and the advantages (or disadvantages) of being a manual worker.

Once we add these new variables, we find four things of note (see Table 9, column headed "Total Income"). First, the effects of some of the original variables are reduced significantly once the new variables are taken into account, and three of the new variables are important predic-

TABLE 9 Determinants of Income, Expanded Model, 1986

Variable	Regression Coefficients[a] (Beta/b)		
	Salary	Bonus	Total Income
Years of work	.699***	.002	.552***
	.023	.0002	.017
Rank of work unit[b]	.108***	.022	.110***
	.033	.017	.031
Gender (male)	.104***	.123***	.158***
	.066	.201	.093
Years of education	.087***	.007	.067*
	.009	.002	.007
Worker in enterprise	−.078**	.110**	.022
	−.054	.196	.014
State-owned work unit	.060**	.075*	.091***
	.047	.152	.066
Job rank in work unit[c]	.050*	.062	.079**
	.018	.057	.026
Party membership	.049*	−.048	.027
	.044	−.112	.022
Adjusted multiple R^2	.625	.023	.427
N	925	925	925

Note: Nominal incomes are used.

a. The dependent variables are the natural logarithms of salary, of 1 + bonus income, and of total income. Retirees are excluded.

b. Rank of work unit has the following values: 6 = ministry, 5 = city government bureau, 4 = district government bureau, 3 = company under city bureau, 2 = company under district bureau, 1 = street committee.

c. Job rank refers to the number of levels of leadership between the respondent and the top leader of the work unit. The lowest recorded value was 0, coded as 7, and the highest recorded value was 6, coded as 1.

***Significant at $p<.001$.
**Significant at $p<.01$.
*Significant at $p<.05$.

tors of total income. Years of work and gender are still the two strongest predictors of total income, and their coefficients are not reduced appreciably when the new variables are taken into account. Some of the advantage of higher education, however, is apparently due to the fact that the highly educated tend to be concentrated in higher-ranking work units, in the state sector, and in higher-ranking positions (see the significant positive correlations in Table 10). These variables reduce the effect of education, though it is still significant. The same can be said for the impact of party membership, once the effect of party membership per se is separated from the effects of job rank, state-sector employment, and the rank of the work unit (it is correlated with all three of these variables—see Table 10). Party membership has no direct effect on total income once these new variables are taken into account.

Some of the new variables are strongly related to high total income. The rank of the work unit, state-sector employment, and job rank within the work unit are all significant determinants of income; compared with the other variables in the equation, they rank in importance behind years of work and gender, but ahead of education (compare the Betas). In light of the importance of these variables, we find noteworthy the resilience of years of work and gender as predictors of income. Their strong effects are not changed by taking into account the new variables.

Second, all eight of our variables are significant predictors of basic salary. The coefficient for party membership was smaller compared with the equation reported in Table 8, but it is still significant. Note that the rank of the work unit is the second most important of the variables. It is now roughly equal in importance to gender, which is more weakly related to salary than to total income. Note also the significant negative impact on the basic salary of being a worker in an enterprise, a variable that had no significant positive or negative effect on total income. The total amount of variance explained by these variables is still about 50 percent higher for basic salary than for total income (compare the figures for R^2), indicating that salary differences are more closely attuned to these individual and sectoral factors than is total income.

Third, our equation for bonus income shows that it is unrelated to most of these variables. Note that these variables explain only 2 percent of the variation in bonus income (compared with 63 percent for salaries and 43 percent for total income). While, as we saw earlier, there is more variation in bonuses than in salaries and total incomes, bonuses are distributed according to a logic very different from that of salaries. Only three of our variables are significantly related to bonus income. Males get significantly higher bonuses than females; workers in enterprises get significantly higher bonuses than everyone else; and employees in the state sector get significantly higher bonuses than those in the collective sector.

Finally, if we compare each row across all three columns of Table 9, we can more fully appreciate the effect of bonuses and other income on the overall distribution of income. Since bonuses and other income are

TABLE 10 Correlation Matrix, Variables in Table 9

Variable	(2)	(3)	(4)	(5)	(6)	(7)	(8)	(9)	(10)	(11)
(1) Years of work	.105***	.166***	−.305***	−.176***	.179***	.182***	.245***	.756***	.021	.581***
(2) Rank of work unit	—	.119***	.106***	−.156***	.281***	−.110***	.121***	.242***	.042	.195***
(3) Gender (male)		—	−.019	−.079**	.139***	.090**	.172***	.275***	.139***	.287***
(4) Years of education			—	−.261***	.129***	.070*	−.007	−.115***	−.026	−.101***
(5) Worker				—	−.200***	−.436***	−.337***	−.310***	.094**	−.116***
(6) State sector					—	.005	.133***	.246***	.049	.218***
(7) Job rank in work unit						—	.317***	.247***	.089	.191***
(8) Party membership							—	.332***	−.023	.226***
(9) Salary 1986								—	−.036	.771***
(10) Bonus 1986									—	.607***
(11) Total income 1986										—

***Significant at $p < .001$, one-tailed.
**Significant at $p < .01$, one-tailed.
*Significant at $p < .05$, one-tailed.

the components that have increased greatly in recent years, we can view their effects as one way of representing the impact of reform on income inequality. What has been their effect?

First, these new forms of income tend to reduce the salary advantages of education and party membership, while they offset completely the disadvantages of manual workers. However, they add to the advantages of those in the state sector, those with higher ranking positions, and especially those of the male gender. In other words, they appear to reduce certain dimensions of income inequality: educational, political, and occupational. But they appear to strengthen certain other sources of inequality: economic sector, job rank, and gender.

We draw three conclusions from the observations made in this chapter. First, despite the real possibility of increased wage inequality, there has been a decisive equalizing trend among urban residents working in the state and collective sectors. It is unlikely that such a trend will continue, since the current measures of inequality are extraordinarily low. And it is possible that further reform will reverse this trend in the future. We do not know whether the (presumably) greater inequalities introduced by private employment have offset the trend toward equality among the salaried wage earners. We still know very little about income distribution in the private sector in Tianjin; only that the sector is tiny according to official statistics, and that it is small in Tianjin relative to most other parts of China. Future research in Tianjin and elsewhere, in addition to testing our findings about the state and collective sectors, should try to devise accurate ways of sampling the privately employed and measuring reliably their income (this will be no easy task, given the transient nature of much of this population and the tax implications of income reports).

Second, if we turn from quantitative questions about the extent of inequality to qualitative ones about its social determinants, the reforms have not had clear-cut consequences. If we are speaking of total income, important age and gender inequalities have not measurably changed. The privileges of party members remain, but they are now less important than education, which has increased dramatically as a predictor of income. This overall trend, however, masks two separate ones involving the basic salary and bonuses, and these trends often work in contradictory directions. Higher education is a bigger advantage in obtaining large salaries than large total incomes. Males reap significantly larger bonuses than women, and bonuses also enhance the advantage of those working in the state sector. On the other hand, bonuses offset the lower salaries of manual workers.

Finally, this study implies, as Carl Riskin has already argued, that the leading politicians of the Mao era did not fully understand the causes of the inequalities they sought to eradicate, and were often blinded to varieties unrelated to their political agenda.[34] It is ironic to find that the very material incentives earlier banned as inegalitarian—regular salary raises and large cash bonuses—have in the short run served instead *further* to *reduce* income disparities. Linking salaries more closely to education has not broadened income gaps, though it certainly has done nothing to help the poorly educated who have risen through party service and political loyalty. This is doubly ironic, because egalitarian urban income distributions are commonly considered one of the few positive accomplishments of the Mao era.

Urban Private Business and Social Change

THOMAS B. GOLD

An urban private-business class has emerged as a direct consequence of China's economic reforms. China's reformers encouraged its establishment virtually from scratch in order to help solve some serious social and economic problems. It evolved and expanded as the reform program progressed, with further consequences for Chinese society. This chapter first explains why China's reformers decided to create a private-business class. It then looks at the policies adopted to establish an environment conducive to urban private business and describes the growth of this class and the changing social background of its members. The final section explores linkages between urban private business and more general social changes in China since the economic reforms began. I argue that the class itself evolved in a way unanticipated by its creators—in particular, with respect to the types of people it began to attract. It was integrated with other social changes occurring in China, especially social diversity, corruption, and privatization. As the post–4 June 1989 leadership cracked down on those trends, it used the private sector as a scapegoat and also took the opportunity to try to redirect its activities into more easily regulated channels.

WHY CREATE A PRIVATE-BUSINESS CLASS IN THE URBAN AREAS?

The post-Mao elite created a new class of private-business people in China's cities in order to help solve some of the severe economic and social problems it had inherited. Several problems dated back to the establishment of the People's Republic of China in 1949; some were endemic to socialism as actually practiced, others derived from China's particular circumstances. Most of the problems emerged from the decade of the Cultural Revolution (CR), 1966–1976. The reformers decided that only a fundamental structural reform could solve these matters. This involved reconceptualizing the very essence of socialism, at least as practiced in China. One component of this reformist redefinition of Chinese socialism has been the encouragement of small-scale private business in China's urban areas.

Whereas economic problems prompted the decollectivization of agriculture and its replacement with a production responsibility system, the reformers saw urban private business as a way to ameliorate social as well as economic difficulties. The definitive statement proclaimed that "reviving and developing the nonagricultural individual economy in cities and towns has important significance for developing production, enlivening the market, satisfying the needs of people's lives, and expanding employment." [1]

The primary social problem that urban private business could address was the critical need to expand employment opportunities. Since completing the socialist transformation of capitalist industry and commerce in the late 1950s, the state had monopolized urban employment. After eliminating the labor market, the state stepped in to allocate jobs to qualified urban residents. [2] It assigned school-leavers to state or collective enterprises; the elimination of the private sector meant that setting up one's own enterprise was not an option for jobseekers. If no jobs were available, jobseekers had to wait until the state found something for them to do. Because it was extremely difficult to be dismissed from one's state or collective enterprise, China until 1978 claimed to have no "unem-

TABLE 1 Number of Persons Awaiting Jobs in Cities
and Towns, 1978–1987

Year	Total Persons Awaiting Jobs (in millions)	Youths Awaiting Jobs	
		N (in millions)	As % of Total Number
1978	5.30	2.49	47.0%
1980	5.41	3.82	70.6
1981	4.39	3.43	78.0
1982	3.79	2.93	77.4
1983	2.71	2.22	81.8
1984	2.35	1.95	83.1
1985	2.38	1.96	82.6
1986	2.64	2.09	79.2
1987	2.76	2.35	85.0

Source: State Statistical Bureau, *Statistical Yearbook of China 1988* (Beijing, 1988), p. 145.

ployment" problem. It did, however, admit to having large numbers of people "waiting for employment." By the late 1970s members of this category came from several sources.

First were the recent school-leavers not going for higher education, into the army, or to the countryside, who had to wait for the state to assign them jobs *(daiye qingnian)*. They numbered 3 to 5 million a year between 1977 and 1980.[3] With the urban economy in severe straits and already suffering from overstaffing, enterprises were loathe to accept new employees. In 1978 there were 5.3 million urban people awaiting jobs, of whom 47 percent were youths (2.49 million). As Table 1 indicates, the proportion of youths jumped to more than 80 percent of the total during the 1980s. These youths, having no legally permitted outlets to earn money on their own, became a burden on their parents. To compound the problem, the government began to increase production of consumer goods. Adolescents with time on their hands began to covet the new clothes, tape recorders, and other commodities appearing on store shelves. Many turned to crime as a way to get them, thereby threatening social order.

A second group of jobless urbanites grew more directly out of CR policies. At certain periods the state encouraged or even compelled urban dwellers to move to the countryside, temporarily or permanently. This policy intensified during the CR decade when approximately 17 million urban-educated youths were "sent down."[4] Ostensibly the purpose was to recruit their skills in the development of rural and mountainous areas or to help them learn about peasant life, but certainly the latent function was to delay their entrance into the labor force.[5]

In late 1978, after the overthrow of the Gang of Four in 1976 and with impending criticism of the CR, many of the "youths," now in their thirties, who had settled in the countryside for life, claimed that the rustication policy was incorrect and that they had a right to return to their homes. The cities consequently sustained a massive influx of former residents. Many of them had been Red Guards, and they utilized disruptive CR tactics to draw attention to their cause. They had formally, if not completely voluntarily, relinquished their urban residence permits, so the state had no legal obligation to accede to their demands. But given the anti-CR mood and the desire for stability and economic growth, the authorities did not send them back. They made it clear, however, that the state had no obligation to find jobs for them.[6]

In addition to the returned youths and those waiting for jobs was another group of unemployed, the so-called socially idle persons (shehui xiansan renyuan). This residual category comprised people released from prison and reform-through-labor and education programs; the disabled; senior citizens, mostly women, who had never entered the labor force and thus did not qualify for a pension; workers let go from their jobs either because of malfeasance on their part or because the enterprise, now compelled to be responsible for its own profits and losses, had trimmed its work force; and peasants who had entered the cities over the years and never left.

Finally, the unemployed included retirees, among whom were trained workers and professionals who had quit their posts so their children could fill their slots, if not their exact jobs (dingti), in their work units. Many retired below the formal retirement age of sixty for men and fifty-five for women. Not only were they idle, but their valuable skills (for example, traditional handicrafts, preparation of special foods) were being wasted, as their often untrained children staffed many units.

The total number of urban unemployed can only be estimated, ranging between 10 and 25 million, or 8.5 to 18 percent of the nonagricultural labor force.[7] These people strained urban resources and, since many of them had actually served time in detention, they were believed to be especially prone to engaging in crime or other disruptive activities.

Another social problem confronting the elite in the late 1970s was the people's unhappiness with the quality of life, which easily translated into disaffection toward the regime. The poor quality of life stemmed from such conditions as worsening diet, frozen wages, and terribly crowded and dilapidated housing. Urban life was generally unpleasant and difficult. During a year's residence in Shanghai in 1979–80 I, like the Chinese, frequently experienced problems in going to a restaurant, getting around town, having clothes made, and getting things repaired. Not only were supplies and personnel inadequate, but the quality of goods and services was appalling.

For example, to ensure a seat for dinner at a popular restaurant such as the Minjiang, one had to occupy a chair at 4:30, well before dinner was served. The menu was limited, the service surly and unhelpful (customers had to go to a counter to order and pay, risking loss of their seat), the food unappetizingly presented, the ambiance repellent, and the sanitation shocking. To make matters worse, late arrivals lined up behind those who were eating, impatiently waiting to pounce on their seats the second they showed signs of leaving.

Shopping and services were equally disagreeable, with crowds, long waits, and service that assaulted one's dignity. One reason for the poisonous service was that many of the employees, the young ones in particular, had been assigned jobs almost randomly, regardless of their training or personal aspirations. Although lucky to have jobs at all, they conveyed with little subtlety their dissatisfaction with their personal lot, including the virtual impossibility of job transfers.

How could permitting private business in urban areas help to alleviate some of these social problems? Clearly the state could disclaim responsibility for finding everyone a job and could tell those without an assignment to become private entrepreneurs. This would dramatically reduce unemployment. Involving social marginals in jobs working for themselves could keep them out of mischief. Private businesses could improve urban life by providing more services and goods. Allowing dissatisfied employees to start enterprises that would better utilize their talents could lessen the surliness of service and improve morale. Recruiting skilled workers and professionals back into service could extend the useful life of their talents.

Economic problems also drew the reformers' attention to private business for a partial solution. Under both the Stalinist and the Maoist models, China had emphasized heavy industry, neglecting both light industry and "nonproductive" investments such as housing, schools, and recreation. As in other socialist economies, China eschewed hard budget constraints. The soft budget constraints for industry resulted in inefficiency, low productivity, waste, and chronic shortages, especially of consumer goods and food.[8] All of this cost the state a great deal of money.

Private business could help in several ways. Private enterprises set up with private capital would not draw down state reserves. Through taxation, private businesses could enhance state revenues. Their small size and flexibility would enable them to move quickly into areas where they were needed. They could supplement the state and collective sectors and produce and supply goods and services neglected by the heavily bureaucratized sectors. This would improve the circulation of commodities and help achieve the reform goal of "enlivening the domestic economy" (gaohuo jingji). Through head-on competition in selected sectors against state and collective enterprises that had to assume responsibility for their own profit and loss as part of the reforms, the challenge from private business could improve efficiency and introduce hard budget constraints. All told, it could facilitate achievement of the broader underlying objective of the Four Modernizations program, raising the level of productive forces.

In sum, urban private business offered one way to help the newly established reform elite solve inherited problems and thereby stabilize society and stimulate the economy while consolidating its own power.[9] The Chinese Communists had only to look elsewhere in Asia for examples of the positive role that small private business had played in economic development and social-political stability. Chinese entrepreneurial prowess had brought about rapid economic growth in Chinese societies such as Taiwan and Singapore, and Chinese emigrés dominated the economies throughout Southeast Asia. Their companies were primarily small-scale family operations, and the business class generally avoided politics.[10] Urban private business in the PRC was integrated into a broader reform program designed to readjust the economy and stimulate development while tapping human resources.

CREATING A SUITABLE BUSINESS ENVIRONMENT

Deciding that urban private business could help solve some critical problems was one thing; translating that decision into policies and then implementing them was another. Permitting, even encouraging, private business represented a tremendous about-face for the Chinese Communists after several decades both of intense criticism of private business as

a "tail of capitalism" and of policies aimed at eliminating it and preventing its reemergence. Subsequent actions reflected this underlying
ambivalence: [11] passing laws to protect private business and encourage the
targeted social groups to start up enterprises, while simultaneously reas-
suring party members and supporters that this initiative could be handily
controlled and was not tantamount to reviving capitalism.

The first step in creating an urban private business class was formally
to legitimize it in an officially socialist society. The First Session of the
Fifth National People's Congress, meeting in March 1978, reaffirmed the
right of individual enterprises to exist, as did the Third Plenum of the
Eleventh Central Committee of the Chinese Communist party in December of that year.

The first major formal statement explicitly codifying the parameters
for urban private business was the State Council's "Some Policy Regulations Concerning the Urban and Township Nonagricultural Individual
Economy," dated 7 July 1981. [12] This important document legitimated
"the coexistence of diverse economic components and diverse operating
styles . . . for a relatively long historical period" and granted legal protection to those engaging in individual business. It specified the types of
support government departments should provide and prohibited discrimination against the individual economy *(geti jingying hu)*. Those undertaking individual business enjoyed the status of laborers; however, they could
hire *(qing, dai)* up to seven assistants or apprentices *(bangshou, xuetu)*.

"Supplementary Regulations to 'Policy Regulations Concerning the
Urban and Township Nonagricultural Individual Economy,' " promulgated on 13 April 1983, formalized a number of practices apparently
already commonplace among private operators, practices that exceeded
the limits stipulated in 1981. [13] In particular, the state permitted individual enterprises to use power tools, motorized vehicles, and boats and
to engage in the long-distance transport of goods and the wholesaling of
certain commodities. The document warned officials again about infring-
ing on the legal rights of private business.

In December 1982, between the promulgation of the 1981 regulations
and the 1983 supplementary regulations, the National People's Congress
passed a new state constitution. Article 11, concerning private business,
states: "The individual economy of urban and rural working people, operated within the limits prescribed by law, is a complement to the socialist public economy. The state protects the lawful rights and interests
of the individual economy. The state guides, helps, and supervises the

individual economy by exercising administrative control." Unlike the preceding 1978 constitution with its CR overtones, this one says nothing about eventual socialist collectivization, while it goes on explicitly to protect the right to own and inherit property.

During 1983 there were many local efforts to crack down on private business. At year's end the drive to clean up spiritual pollution, supposed to focus on pornography, provided many officials with the opportunity they had been waiting for to go after individual businessmen, by accusing them of purveying pornography and engaging in a host of other unhealthy activities.[14] This campaign fizzled out early in 1984.

The Third Plenum of the Twelfth Central Committee promulgated a "Decision on Reform of the Economic Structure" in October 1984. Clearly reflecting the reform position of Premier Zhao Ziyang, it called for numerous institutional reforms with positive implications for the further development of the urban individual economy. These centered on enterprise autonomy, revamping the labor system, more closely tying reward to effort, "smashing the iron rice bowl," and generally compelling individuals to take more personal responsibility for their own economic well-being.[15] The tentative introduction of a stock market also began to redefine the idea of public ownership of economic enterprises.

Party leaders provided theoretical justification both for the decision to encourage and protect private business and for some of the anticipated social consequences. In his definitive June 1984 statement, "Build Socialism with Chinese Characteristics," Deng Xiaoping asserted: "Pauperism is not socialism, still less communism. The superiority of the socialist system lies above all in its ability to increasingly develop the productive forces and to improve the people's material and cultural life . . . The socialist principle of distribution to each according to his work will not create an excessive gap in wealth. Consequently, no polarization will occur as our productive forces become developed in 20 to 30 years from now."[16] Zhao Ziyang's 1987 declaration that China was in the "primary (chuji) stage of socialism" granted additional legitimacy to experimentation with a mixed economy.[17]

The popular media and the official press gave prominent coverage to positive role models among private entrepreneurs. Zhao Ziyang, Hu Yaobang, and other leaders received them, and some of their numbers were recruited into the CCP, the Communist Youth League, and people's congresses at various levels.

These formulations reflected the reform elite's confidence that the overwhelming dominance of the state economic sector and the bureaucracy could guarantee that the private sector could be rather handily restricted and its development effectively guided. Although the evolution of official pronouncements shows a steady retreat of the state in the face of expanded private activity, the reformers nevertheless confidently disputed Lenin's prediction that "petty production will engender capitalism and the bourgeoisie daily and hourly, spontaneously in a big way." It could be restricted "at any time" *(suishi)*.[18]

GROWTH OF THE URBAN INDIVIDUAL ECONOMY

Between 1979 and 1989, especially from 1984 to 1988, regular visitors to China's cities could easily gauge the rapid expansion of private business.[19] From a handful of glum bicycle and shoe repairmen scattered around the cities, the individual economy exploded into large and vibrant permanent and temporary markets, itinerant entrepreneurs calling out their trade, private transport of all kinds jockeying for position on the increasingly crowded thoroughfares, and a broad range of new service establishments in fixed street frontages. A subsidiary sector to serve the free-spending individual entrepreneurs *(geti hu)* also grew up, and a distinctive life style took shape.

Table 2 provides official figures for the growth of the individual sector in the urban areas from 1978 through 1987.[20] This table demonstrates the tremendous growth of the urban individual economy from a minuscule base. The dramatic positive effect of the 1983 supplementary regulations, and especially the Third Plenum of October 1984, is evident in the high growth rates for 1983–84, in spite of the anti-spiritual pollution campaign. In 1986, however, there was a crackdown on private business, which frightened some people away, as did the campaign against bourgeois liberalization at the end of the year. But the growth rate picked up in 1987 as the campaign flopped, and the urban individual sector exceeded 1 percent of the national labor force, 4 percent of the urban labor force.

There is great regional variation in the relative size of the individual sector compared with the total labor force. At the end of 1987 urban individual laborers made up a mere 0.7 percent of Beijing's work force, 1 percent of Shanghai's, and 3.4 percent of Zhejiang's, but constituted 6.6 percent of Fujian's, 5.9 percent of Guangdong's, and 12.1 percent

TABLE 2 Urban Individual Laborers in Labor Force, 1978–
1987 (in millions)

Year	Total Labor Force (1)	Urban Labor Force (2)	Individual Labor Force (3)	(3) as % of (1) (4)	(3) as % of (2) (5)
1978	401.52	95.14	0.15	0.03	0.15
1979	410.24	99.99	0.32	0.07	0.32
1980	423.61	105.25	0.81	0.02	0.77
1981	437.25	110.53	1.13	0.03	1.02
1982	452.95	114.28	1.47	0.32	1.29
1983	464.36	117.46	2.31	0.49	1.97
1984	481.97	122.29	3.39	0.70	2.77
1985	498.73	128.08	4.50	0.90	3.51
1986	512.82	132.92	4.83	0.94	3.63
1987	527.83	137.83	5.69	1.08	4.13

Source: State Statistical Bureau, Statistical Yearbook of China (Beijing, 1988), p. 123. Columns 4 and 5 calculated from table.

of Tibet's, where the authorities had dramatically freed up the economy.[21]

The figures in Table 2 must be approached with some caution: they greatly understate the scale of involvement in the private sector. At any given time the people actually working in an enterprise are likely to be the parents, siblings, spouse, friends, and relatives of the person whose picture is on the license. They help out after their own work, often without remuneration, which is permitted. They do not appear in the individual-sector employment figures. This reveals the extent to which the individual economy is family based, with start-up capital commonly accumulated from the kin network, and family members assisting in the endeavor while maintaining their jobs and benefits in the state or collective sector.[22]

There are also many entrepreneurs who do not have a license. Farmers who come to the city to do business on a temporary basis do not need a license, and many other business people simply evade the authorities. In addition, moonlighters, such as off-shift factory and office workers and consultants, do not all have licenses. This practice became a controversial subject in the second half of 1989.[23] One study estimated that 4.6 percent of Beijing's private individual enterprises were unlicensed in 1987.[24] In a 100-day campaign to clamp down on illegal businesses in Beijing in the fall of 1989, authorities turned up 62,000 unlicensed enterprises.[25] There is also a sizable floating population of licensed and unlicensed individual businessmen. In Lhasa, for instance, an official in the Individual Laborer Section said that 30 percent of the private entrepreneurs in Tibet came from outside the region. They are supposed to get a license at home, which is switched once they reach Tibet.[26] I interviewed a middle-aged female Han merchant from Sichuan who came up seasonally to sell goods made from canvas; a young Hui man from Gansu who came to sell sheepskin; a young Han from Yangzhou who ran a barbershop in the new western part of town, primarily to cater to other Hans; and a Han farmer from Sichuan who drove a pedicab he leased from the government from May through November. There are also the ubiquitous Tibetan women, bedecked in jewelry, who materialize wherever tourists are to sell handicrafts. According to the official, they are unlicensed and "a big problem for us."

Among the most peripatetic entrepreneurs are those from Wenzhou. The city itself was first held up as a model, then downgraded simply to an "experience" of market-driven modernization.[27] With their licenses, Wenzhou entrepreneurs travel nationwide, buying and selling goods and setting up operations. An example is the Wenzhou tailor in Jinan. According to an informant from Wenzhou, however, such people receive only a little training in Wenzhou, where they could never succeed, then set themselves up outside Wenzhou, playing on the famous name.[28] In addition many private businesses in Wenzhou and elsewhere attach themselves to *(guakao)* collective enterprises for better tax rates and higher political and social status.

The figures in Table 2 also do not provide information on business closings. We can get some sense of the situation from a study done in Yueyang, Hunan Province, in 1988. The authors discovered that fully 65 percent of individual operators who closed business did so for "unnatural reasons," that is, for reasons other than finding other work, joining the army, or general business failure. Some of them closed owing to political, economic, or social discrimination, but many gave up because of excessive "fees" collected by the multitude of officials claiming to have jurisdiction over them. In addition to the Industrial and Commercial Bureau, these "mothers-in-law" *(popo)* included cadres from taxation, urban construction, city management, environmental protection, epidemic control, sanitation, price, measurement, public security, transport, civic affairs, water, electricity, and neighborhood agencies. Former business-

TABLE 3 Sectoral Breakdown of Urban Individual Laborers,
1978–1987 (in millions)

Year	Total	Farming, Forestry, Animal Husbandry, Fishing	Industry	Construction	Transport, Telecommunications
1978	0.15	—	.03	.01	.01
1979	0.32	—	.06	.01	.01
1980	0.81	—	.10	—	.01
1981	1.13	—	.11	.01	.02
1982	1.47	—	.16	.01	.02
1983	2.31	—	.24	.01	.04
1984	3.39	.01	.38	.04	.12
1985	4.50	.02	.51	.05	.22
1986	4.83	.02	.60	.05	.24
1987	5.69	.02	.74	.06	.31

Year	Commerce, Catering	Real Estate Administration, Residential Services	Public Health, Sports, Welfare	Education, Culture, Arts, Broadcasting
1978	0.09	.01	—	—
1979	0.18	.06	—	—
1980	0.57	.13	—	—
1981	0.79	.20	—	—
1982	1.05	.22	.01	—
1983	1.72	.29	.01	—
1984	2.42	.40	.01	.01
1985	3.25	.41	.03	.01
1986	3.37	.51	.03	.01
1987	3.91	.59	.04	.02

Source: State Statistical Bureau, *Statistical Yearbook of China 1988* (Beijing, 1988), p. 140.

men complained that cadres infected with remnant "leftist thinking" employed various forms of "negative restrictions," making it impossible to carry on a trade.[29]

Table 3 presents figures on the sectoral breakdown of individual laborers from 1978 through 1987. The data indicate the concentration of entrepreneurs in commerce and catering—hovering around 70 percent most years. This categorization masks further sectoral breakdown. According to another set of figures from the State Administration for Industry and Commerce, at the end of 1986, 53.1 percent of the laborers were in commerce; 12 percent in industry; 10.3 percent in catering; 8 percent in transport; 7.2 percent in repairs; 6 percent in sideline industries; and 0.4 percent in construction.[30]

In Beijing, for mid-1987, the breakdown for 31,219 enterprises with 56,686 workers (6,823 of these enterprises hired a total of 15,206 workers) was 48.2 percent in commerce; 12.7 percent in repairs; 12.6 percent in catering; 7.3 percent in services; 6 percent in clothes making; 5.8 percent in transportation; 5.2 percent in handicrafts; and 2.2 percent in house repairs.[31] For Shanghai, the 1985 figures for 84,008 enterprises with 113,937 workers were 52.76 percent (all figures are for enterprises) in commerce; 14.04 percent in services; 10.37 percent in catering; 10.34 percent in industry and handicrafts; 7.66 percent in repairs; 2.12 percent in house repairs; and 1.46 percent in transport.[32] If nothing else, these figures demonstrate how unstandardized research into this subject is.

The high proportion of individual operators in commerce translates into a significant percentage of the nation's total retail trade. In 1978 they accounted for 0.1 percent of commodity retail trade. This leaped dramatically from 2.9 percent in 1982 to 6.5 percent a year later. In 1985 it reached 15.4 percent and in 1987, 17.4 percent.[33]

The average income of individual operators is much higher than that of workers in state or collective units. According to the State Statistical Bureau, the average annual income for a state worker in 1987 was 1,546 yuan, and for a collective worker, 1,207 yuan.[34] In 1985 a sample of individual laborers pegged the average annual income at 3,063 yuan. While 28.2 percent of the sample earned less than 1,000, 31.1 percent made more than 3,000, and 5.7 percent topped 10,000 yuan annually.[35] Because private entrepreneurs are notorious for underreporting income, these figures are probably low. State workers and some collective workers enjoy a package of benefits that private workers do not have. This enhances the value, if not the cash flow, of employees in the state and collective sectors but still leaves them below the average of private entrepreneurs. With the 20–30 percent inflation of 1988–89, this disparity in cash holdings made a critical difference to one's standard of living and perceptions of equity and fairness.

As we have seen, the "individual economy" is not really "individual" but has a strong family component and involves the hiring of wage labor by private investors. The logic of capital is to expand, and some enterprises exceeded the limit of seven salaried employees. After much debate, in April 1988 the National People's Congress amended the 1982 constitution to permit private companies to hire more than seven workers. On 1 July 1988 the Temporary Provisions for Private Business went into effect. This legislation defined a new category, "private business" *(siying qiye)*, for those profit-oriented enterprises with privately owned capital that employ eight or more workers. They may have a single investor or several partners, or they may be limited-liability companies. In 1988 there were 225,000 such enterprises, 51 percent of which had a single investor. They employed 3.6 million workers, and their output accounted for 10 percent of national production.[36]

Individual entrepreneurs have their own organization, the Self-Employed Laborers Association (*geti laodongzhe xiehui;* SELA). The inaugural one was established in Jilin in 1981, and a national body was formed in 1986. Its first national congress in December of that year was visited by Zhao Ziyang, Hu Qili, Tian Jiyun, and Yang Jingren. In point of fact, the SELA is set up by the Industry and Commerce Bureau at each level, which appoints members to the board. Individual laborers are to use SELA to teach one another about law, taxation, and morality; to manage their affairs; and to serve and protect their members.[37] Because individual operators do not have a "unit" and their licenses enable them to travel freely around the country, they pose a difficult control problem. SELA is supposed to be one means of keeping tabs on their movements and activities, but many entrepreneurs ignore it as much as possible, perceiving it quite correctly as an agent of control, not of interest articulation.

SOCIAL BACKGROUND OF INDIVIDUAL OPERATORS

The party-state established the legal, institutional, ideological, and social conditions for an urban individual sector to emerge, and, as described earlier, it had specific types of social groups in mind to form this new class, namely, youth waiting for employment, socially idle persons, and retirees with skills. It assumed that a combination of incentives, legal protection, and lack of alternatives would induce these social types into private business. The first requirement to qualify for a license is urban residence; the second is not having a job; and the third is demonstrating some skill or possessing capital and a place to do business. It is fair to assume that the authorities believed the private-business option was fine for such decidedly marginal groups who could meet these requirements, and it would have little appeal for urban citizens already integrated into the better-paid, benefits-rich, high-social-and-political-prestige sectors. It would keep marginal groups occupied and out of trouble. Their activities could be easily supervised and regulated.

In the initial stages after 1978, things generally proceeded in the anticipated fashion. In a Beijing survey, socially idle persons and retirees constituted the bulk of individual operators in 1980: 42.7 and 53 percent, respectively. School-leavers waiting for work were loathe to join, even though the government promised that they would not lose their qualification for a state or collective job when one became available. In the same survey they constituted only 4.2 percent of individual operators in 1980.[38] Some went to labor-service companies for a short time, but the pay was quite low. Young entrepreneurs I interviewed up through 1982 had very low self-esteem. One observer noted that young people even in Guangzhou were embarrassed about having to operate private enterprises, as it showed they had failed the test for higher education or a job and that they did not have connections to get a job. This interviewee also said that licenses were very difficult to get, as the state wanted to restrict the number of people entering private business.[39]

For ex-prisoners, on the other hand, becoming an entrepreneur gave them a fixed status in society and a chance to start over again.[40] The media played up this aspect of private business. The Beijing restaurateur Gong Chong is an example. He served two and a half years in jail for robbery and, upon release, became an entrepreneur to earn a living. He became quite successful and then realized that, besides making a living, he was creating social wealth. In 1985, with more than thirty other entrepreneurs, he established a "Fund to Save Youths Who Lost Their Way" to provide books and other materials for youth in prison. He gave 5 percent of his monthly profits to the Beijing Children's Welfare Fund and, under pressure from the Chongwenmen District, contributed 1,000 yuan to build a playground.[41] Parenthetically, this sort of philanthropy has roots in Chinese traditional practice, whereby merchants, always socially marginal, would build schools partially as a way to win social prestige and acceptance.

The social background of individual entrepreneurs began to change— in particular as more and more job-waiting youths opened businesses.

Nationally they constituted 25 to 28 percent of urban operators from 1982 to 1985.[42] For Beijing the proportions ranged as high as 45 percent in 1983, dropping back into the 30 percent range in 1984,[43] whereas for Shanghai—in 1986 at least—these young people accounted for only 16 percent of the total.[44] In 1980, 6.1 percent of job-waiting youths became individual laborers, but from 1983 to 1985 the figures ranged between 10 and 11 percent, dropping back to 7 percent in 1986.[45]

As the acceptability of becoming an individual laborer increased and the government seemed sincere in its pledges that it was a long-term strategy and not an expedient tactic,[46] the private sector began to attract people who were not marginal to Chinese society but in fact were in the mainstream. In my research in 1985 I began to turn up several individual entrepreneurs who had jobs in the state sector, but through an arrangement called "stop salary, keep position" (tingxin liuzhi), they paid a fixed amount to their unit to maintain benefits and seniority. For example, a taxi driver in Changsha paid 40 yuan monthly to his unit. He had received a bank loan of 10,000 yuan at 5–6 percent interest to buy a broken-down Russian car for 17,000 yuan. His main motivation was the desire to earn enough money to support his blind mother, three children, and wife, who earned only 40 yuan a month plus a small bonus as a store clerk.[47]

Another attraction of private business is the "freedom" it provides. Two sisters in Kunming took leave from their jobs, paid in less than 20 yuan a month for benefits, and opened a clothing stall with their parents. They went to Hunan to buy straw hats and Shanghai to buy shirts. The state did not object to their taking leave and in fact encouraged it.[48] Freedom includes travel and keeping one's own hours, as well as liberation from the stifling control of the unit (danwei), which involves not only a job but a total environment, including housing, schooling, medical care, and constant supervision. A related motive is the desire to "bring one's talents into full play" (fahui caineng). Since many job assignments appeared random and arbitrary, Chinese youth in particular felt they had no chance to utilize what they saw as their real talents, and so opening a restaurant, making clothes, styling hair, and so on, offered this opportunity.

A further pull factor is the obligation to join a family business. In Guiyang children of the proprietors of a certain restaurant never took job assignments, so that they could help their parents. In Quanzhou a barber in a state barbershop quit his job to start his own barbershop. His brothers and one of their wives all worked in it. The wife never took a job assignment. Although the salaries were about the same as those of a state job, they claimed, they were more conscientious and hard working in their own company.[49]

Many individual operators maintain other ties to the security of the state sector. For instance, the 30-year-old proprietor of a new "hot-pot" restaurant in Chengdu completely quit his job as a bus driver, investing 500,000 yuan with a partner. This sum included a loan from the Industrial and Commercial Bank ("I had a friend in there") to buy a three-story building, with the intention of renting out the two upstairs floors. His wife, however, kept her job with the bus company to maintain the childless couple's benefits. She helped out, as did seven other employees, all of whom were relatives ("you cannot trust nonfamily").[50]

In the mid-1980s people who voluntarily embarked on the private road exuded confidence and optimism, emphasizing that there was no social stigma to this choice. They cited the documents of the 1984 Third Plenum as protecting their rights and guaranteeing that the private sector would have a positive role to play for a long time. Still facing severe underemployment problems, the state acquiesced in letting people give up their jobs to make their own way.

An unexpected trend started in the mid-1980s and gathered steam later in the decade: university graduates began to forsake secure jobs in the state sector to go into private business. The best-known example is the Beijing Stone Group, the self-styled "IBM of China." It was founded in 1984 by Wan Runnan and six fellow computer technician-researchers at the Chinese Academy of Sciences. The company had backing at the highest levels of the party. It scored an early success by developing software and a new technical design for Mitsui. Stone expanded into hardware and had a sales network throughout China and abroad. It anchored "Beijing's Silicon Valley."[51]

Stone's success has motivated other university graduates to start up private companies or to take jobs in the private sector.[52] They cite a freer work environment, better wages, and a chance to utilize their skills as reasons for this choice. In particular, by 1988—as the salaries and living standards of intellectuals did not keep pace with inflation, to say nothing of those of private entrepreneurs, and intellectuals still had to contend with political supervision and interference—private business presented an attractive alternative. The state originally announced that it would terminate the job assignment system for the class matriculating in 1989, meaning that graduates would be responsible for finding their own jobs anyway.

Private activity begins while students are still in school, because they need money to cover expenses, as the former stipend system has been terminated. In 1988 at the Hengyang Medical College, for instance, more than two thousand students had formed over twenty different commercial entities. They engaged in tutoring, organizing social activities, teaching skills such as *qigong* (breathing exercises), selling goods on commission, and providing a variety of services such as ironing clothes and repairing electrical appliances.[53] This does not mean that they will necessarily become private workers after graduation, but it represents a significant shift in thinking about the types of activities suitable for intellectuals in China. On a university campus in Xian, a junior Chinese literature major operates a store in a building owned by the Communist Youth League, renting books and cameras, selling film, and sending film out to be developed. He hires fellow students to work, paying them 2 yuan for a five-hour shift. He himself nets between 500 and 600 yuan a month, considerably more than a full professor. He laughed out loud at the suggestion that he would become a Chinese teacher after graduation, as expected.[54] Other university graduates have begun consulting firms, translation firms, publishing houses, research institutes, and so on.[55]

The fact that trained talent is abandoning state jobs has stimulated controversy, but a more disturbing trend is the rapid rise in the dropout rate from schools. In an environment where many believe "studying is useful but does not bring money," a decreasing percentage of the cohort bothers to take the exams for the next level. In Jinhua County, Zhejiang, where formerly nearly all junior-middle-school students took exams for senior high, only 52.5 percent sat for them in 1988.[56]

THE PRIVATE-BUSINESS CLASS AND SOCIAL CHANGE

The emergence and evolution of the urban private-business class is closely linked to some of the other social changes brought about by China's post-Mao economic reforms. The complaints raised by demonstrators around the country in the spring of 1989 touched on some of these changes, setting private entrepreneurs up for potential retribution.

It is a genuine class, in terms of relation to the means of production, in a Marxist sense, and by its position in the market, in the Weberian concept. When added to the corps of rural private entrepreneurs, this class's numbers as well as economic significance are evident.

Andrew Walder has argued that "China's industrial labor force, reflecting a pattern of stratification characteristic of society as a whole, is divided into several status groups, each of which has its own publicly defined rights to income, job tenure, social security, labor insurance, and housing and residence—each of which, in other words, is legally entitled to a distinctive style of life."[57] Private entrepreneurs enjoy none of this as a right; rather, their social position is achieved by success in the market, making them a unique social force in urban China. As the government moved to commoditize things such as housing, education, insurance, and health care, quite clearly wealthy private entrepreneurs would have access to benefits formerly allocated bureaucratically. This would give them certain status in society as well as threaten a key source of cadre power: the ability to allocate scarce goods. As money assumed new importance in Chinese society and citizens were compelled to assume more responsibility for their personal economic situation, individual laborers held many advantages.

The success of many private entrepreneurs has spawned various reactions. A common one is "red-eye disease" *(hongyanbing),* that is, jealousy, on the part of those in the state system who enjoy benefits as a right but not the access to unlimited income as do private entrepreneurs. Some citizens have turned their jealousy into vandalism and other acts of violence. Others have engaged in moonlighting to supplement their fixed wages in their spare time.

Many officials have used their political power to reap the best of both worlds: the benefits accruing to their status and the income from private business. At one level, officials involved with individual operators, such as tax collectors, extort all sorts of fees that go unreported. At another level, commonly in the countryside, officials abandon their posts and become private entrepreneurs themselves. With the personal networks built up over the years, they have a great advantage over farmers who must start from scratch.[58]

In another variation, officials engage in private business indirectly through their spouses, children, and other kin. An example might be the children of officials establishing a "briefcase company" *(pibao gongsi)* with no more assets than a business card and powerful connections that can facilitate a deal. But until recently, much more ominous was the establishment of several "companies" by powerful people who became important players in the international aspects of China's economy. Civil-service profiteers *(guandao)* utilized both connections and positions in enterprises to broker scarce commodities. They easily took advantage of the dual-price system, buying goods at the lower fixed state price, then re-selling them at a market price. One of the most notorious companies was Kanghua Development Corporation, a firm oriented to the domestic economy with ties to Deng Xiaoping's son, Deng Pufang.[59]

Public disgust with this activity boiled to the surface during the demonstrations of April–June 1989. One of the first actions taken by the new leadership after the crackdown was to pass a decision to "do seven things the masses are concerned with." The first was to clean up these companies, and the second was to terminate the commercial activities of the high-cadre children *(gaogan zidi)* in business.[60] The Central Committee and State Council followed quickly with another decision to intensify this cleanup, and by late August Ren Zhonglin, director of the State Administration of Industry and Commerce, reported that thousands of such companies had been closed or merged and the incumbent cadres working in them compelled to choose the civil service or business.[61]

Urban individual operators, the young ones in particular, have developed a distinctive life style. It is characterized above all by conspicuous consumption.[62] They can be easily spotted in garish and tight-fitting clothes, riding motorcycles, going to discotheques, and hanging out in expensive restaurants. A subsector of coffee shops, restaurants, bars, and hair salons has emerged as places where they congregate to enjoy each other's company. Many of them have little faith in the longevity of the private sector and believe they should consume their earnings quickly, with little concern for what will happen to them if there is a political change. Since many of the younger ones were marginal to society in the first place, termination of private business would not be their first setback. They are singled out in the periodic campaigns against pornography and general spiritual pollution.

Their distinctive life style is part of the trend toward diversity and pluralism in Chinese society that took hold in the 1980s. It can be seen in one light in the emerging income inequality discussed above. This inequality, tied to uncontrolled inflation, was another major complaint expressed in the spring of 1989. Even before becoming general secretary of the CCP, Jiang Zemin wrote an essay entitled "Conscientiously Eliminate Unfair Phenomena in Social Distribution" in the party's new theoretical journal, *Qiushi* (Seeking truth).[63] In this essay Jiang tried to strike a balance by criticizing both egalitarianism, which stifled initiative, and inequality caused by the ability of only a select part of the population to earn high incomes, legally or illegally. It is no coincidence that another of the post–June 1989 regime's first actions to win public support was to initiate a campaign to collect taxes from individual entrepreneurs as a sign of its determination to deal with income inequality. The director of the State Taxation Bureau announced that although rural and urban individual businesses had paid 9.2 billion yuan in taxes for 1988, they had evaded another 70 to 80 percent of what they owed! He fixed a goal of 12 billion yuan in tax revenues from the private sector for all of 1989 and compelled individual entrepreneurs to keep written accounts.[64]

Another indication of pluralism was the revelation by scholars that a great diversity of opinion and values existed in China. Numerous public opinion polls demonstrated this, and scholars urged leaders to find new ways to balance the relations among people and between the individual and the collective.[65] In a pioneering effort to tie private business to social change, the Stone Corporation established a think tank, the Social Development Research Institute. Individuals involved in Stone and its institute participated actively in support of student demonstrators in the spring of 1989 and suffered a severe attack after 4 June.[66] China's hard-line leaders tried to "unify" thinking about what had happened and especially began to "reeducate" students and rectify the social sciences. These actions suggest an effort to reject the legitimacy of diversity as well as to prevent the transfer of economic wealth to political activity.

A final general trend linking individual entrepreneurs to the reforms is privatization. In the rural areas in particular, as the private economy expanded, entrepreneurs established their own far-flung wholesale and retail trading networks.[67] The 1983 supplementary regulations legalized what was obviously already in practice. This meant that large amounts of key commodities were in private hands. In the urban economy the state sector had more control, but there too, individual operators often had to use private networks to obtain capital and materials.

Some scholars began to advocate expanded economic privatization. Many of them wrote for the *World Economic Herald* of Shanghai,[68] and after the June 1989 crackdown, they were criticized for using the privatization argument as a means of spreading bourgeois liberalization throughout Chinese society.[69] At the end of 1989 the economic signals indicated that the private sector faced a period of very tight restrictions and supervision.

√ This discussion suggests that the social effects of the private-business class, urban and rural, have extended well beyond the boundaries the reform elite had anticipated when it established the foundations for private business and channeled certain social groups into it. Three trends with direct ties to private business have been singled out for rectification: corruption, income inequality, and privatization. Private business did not cause them, but it exacerbated contradictions latent in Chinese society and serves as a useful scapegoat for a regime frantic to consolidate power.

PART THREE

Urban Society

Changes in Mate Choice in Chengdu

MARTIN KING WHYTE

The family is the basic unit of social organization in any society, and in Chinese culture the centrality of family organization has been explicitly acknowledged for centuries. Efforts to change society must deal with the family as an institution, and since the process of mate choice is a central defining element of family organization, changes in the nature of the mate-choice process will be an important aspect of such efforts. In this chapter I wish to consider how the nature of the mate-choice process has changed over time in urban China. I am concerned here with both long-term and short-term changes. In the long term I want to examine how much the process of mate choice has changed in general since 1949 in the PRC. In the short term I want to know how much this process has been changed in the post-Mao or reform period.

In discussing changes in the process of mate choice in urban China, I shall rely primarily on data from a survey of mate choice and marriage relations in Chengdu on which I have been collaborating over the last several years. The survey data from Chengdu were collected from a representative sample of 586 ever-married women between the ages of 20 and 70 residing in the two main urban districts of Chengdu. These women were interviewed during May 1987. Since the year of first marriage of these women ranged from 1933 to 1987, it is possible to use these data to make both longer-term and shorter-term comparisons of the nature of mate choice.[1]

CHANGING CHINESE MATE CHOICE: A BRIEF OVERVIEW

The process of mate choice has been an arena of contention for Chinese reformers and revolutionaries for much of the twentieth century. The main features of the "traditional" system of mate choice in China are familiar. Most marriages were arranged, and in many cases these were "blind marriages," with the bride and groom not even meeting until the day of the wedding. Not only was consent of the principals not required, but ages and relative ages could be suited to family concerns rather than to individual preferences, resulting in such phenomena as "adopted little daughters-in-law," child betrothals, and wide age disparities between spouses in either direction. Partly to ensure their control over the mate-choice process, parents restricted the social interactions of young people, and particularly of daughters, for they wanted to preserve female virginity. No laws regulated age at marriage, and since there was no direct governmental control through licenses or registration, the couple was considered married with the holding of the wedding feast (usually by the groom's family) and associated ritual activities. Negotiations between the families produced marriage-finance transactions that varied by class, region, and other factors. Commonly the bride's family made demands of the groom's family for various gifts in cash and kind and then expended some of these and perhaps additional funds of their own to equip their daughter with a dowry, which was transported with her into her new home, usually in the groom's family.[2]

These "traditional" marriage customs, under attack from the early decades of the twentieth century, had changed gradually even before 1949. The most spirited attacks of the May Fourth reformers focused on the system of arranged marriage, but lavish wedding feasts, patrilocal postmarital residence, and even the stress on female virginity were also criticized. Industrialization and increasing wage labor helped alter mate-choice customs, but probably the main impetus for change was Westernization. Through increasing exposure to Western ideals of freedom of mate choice, romantic love, and neolocal postmarital residence, some Chinese came to see changed marriage customs as a requirement for modernity. Still, even on the eve of the Communist victory in 1949, changes in the direction of such western-style mate-choice customs were mainly confined to a portion of the well-educated urban elite and had little impact on less-educated urbanites or rural residents.[3]

When the Chinese Communists came to power, they were determined to foster systematic and rapid family change. They wanted to induce the population to replace old "feudal" or "bourgeois" marriage customs with "socialist" practices. The desired socialist marriage practices included freedom of mate choice, marriage only in adulthood, the absence of marriage-finance demands and transactions, mate selection based on compatibility and political and moral criteria rather than on such factors as wealth or attractiveness, and simple and frugal wedding celebrations without elaborate feasts or traditional ritual activities.[4] Some traditional marriage customs, however, were permitted to remain. For example, virginity was stressed by the new order if anything more than by the old, although after 1949 it was to apply to males as well as to females. Also, patrilocal residence after marriage was never the object of concerted criticism.[5]

After 1949 the party-state in the PRC purposefully used laws, regulations, propaganda campaigns, and other mechanisms to get people to alter their marriage customs in the manner just described. The pressure for such changes, however, has not been uniform. As in other realms, there have been "high tides" of family-change efforts interspersed with periods in which other goals have had much higher priority. Generally speaking, the periods when official family-change efforts reached peaks were in 1950–1953, during the campaign to implement the 1950 Marriage Law, in 1958–1960 during the Great Leap Forward, and during the Cultural Revolution decade (1966–1976). The last period witnessed the most pervasive and sustained hostility to "nonsocialist" marriage customs. Since Mao's death (September 1976), official efforts to foster family change have been relaxed, although the commitment to fostering socialist marriage patterns has not been formally abandoned.[6]

In examining the results of the Chengdu survey, I want to see what aspects of marriage customs have changed most and least, and also which time periods experienced the most dramatic changes in these customs.

My assumption is that both the differential nature of changes and their timing provide clues to the nature of the forces producing the changes. If the governmental family-change efforts in the PRC were the major force affecting marriage customs, we might expect to see popular customs in this realm conforming more and more to the officially prescribed socialist customs, but through a process of lurches forward in this direction, followed by backsliding toward traditional marriage customs, in response to varying governmental pressure for family change. To anticipate my conclusion, the actual pattern of change in marriage customs in Chengdu does not conform to this expectation. Rather, in many but not all realms, what the survey data show is that marriage customs had experienced major changes by the mid-1950s but have not altered nearly as much in more recent periods, in spite of the ebb and flow of campaigns and political lines. This dominant pattern of change I shall refer to as "stalled convergence," since it suggests that Chinese marriage customs had begun to change in the direction of patterns familiar in more modern societies, but then became "stuck" and did not continue to converge toward such patterns.[7] But the reasons for this terminology, and how I would explain the actual patterns, will not become clear until I have presented the results of the Chengdu interviews.

TRENDS IN MARRIAGE CUSTOMS IN CHENGDU, 1933–1987

Table 1 presents the results of several different questions aimed at assessing the degree to which a marriage was arranged by parents and the amount of freedom of mate choice that was involved.[8] Several observations can be made about these results. First, and not surprisingly, it is apparent that a major shift away from the traditional pattern of parentally arranged marriages has occurred, with the instances in which parents dominate the proceedings declining from 60–70 percent among the pre-1949 marriage to under 10 percent today. Those who met their husbands directly rather than through an introduction, those whose introductions came from peers rather than from parents, and those who feel that they played the dominant role in the mate-choice decision all have increased sharply in comparison with the pre-1949 era.[9]

The figures in Table 1 also make it clear that, even though progress has been made toward increasing freedom of mate choice, in at least a good share of even recent marriages (say, 11–43 percent, depending on which measure is used), parents still continue to have some important

TABLE 1 Changes in Aspects of Freedom of Mate Choice

| | *Year First Married* | | | | |
Mate-Choice Pattern	1933–1948 (N=71)	1949–1957 (N=107)	1958–1965 (N=82)	1966–1976 (N=116)	1977–1987 (N=210)
Traditional arranged marriage	69%	22%	1%	0%	0%
Type of marriage					
Arranged	68	27	0	1	2
Intermediate	15	33	45	40	41
Individual choice	17	40	55	59	57
Dominant rule in mate choice					
Parents	56	30	7	8	5
Mixed	15	11	6	3	6
Respondent	28	59	87	89	89
Introduced to husband	91	76	54	59	60
Provider of introduction					
Own generation	38	43	75	75	74
Other	8	17	7	6	9
Parents' generation	53	40	18	19	17

influence on whom their daughters marry.[10] Finally, the most important pattern visible in these figures, and the one most relevant to the present discussion, is that the major changes involved seem to have been consolidated by the end of the 1950s, with little sign of further change toward increasing freedom of mate choice since then (as shown by columns 3–5 in the table). The Cultural Revolution period, for example, is not characterized by a lesser parental role or by greater freedom of choice than the preceding period, and the reform era gives no evidence of either "backsliding" toward arranged marriages or changing incrementally toward greater freedom of choice.[11]

In order for freedom of mate choice to operate, individual young people must have opportunities to meet potential marital prospects and to explore their feelings for them. In the modern West these goals are served by our "dating culture," which enables young people to link up romantically without adult supervision in a setting that is not defined as leading to marriage. This "decoupling" of dating from marriage makes it possible to "try out" various partners without the immediate pressure of making a lifetime commitment.[12] In our survey we were interested in the extent to which various elements of such a dating culture were visible in urban China. The results of the relevant questions are displayed in Table 2.

The patterns in Table 2 closely parallel those in Table 1. It is clear that major changes have occurred in comparison with the prerevolutionary years, with many more women in recent marriage cohorts having had dating and romantic experiences prior to marriage. These figures, however, also make clear that there is not yet much of a dating culture in Chengdu. Large proportions of women in recent times rarely or never dated their eventual husbands, few women had more than one romantic relationship, and even fewer had a relationship with more than one man they seriously considered marrying. For most women, it would appear, dating is still something that happens after the matter of whom one will marry has been settled, rather than serving as a practice that helps one select among alternatives. The vast majority of women still marry the first person they seriously consider.[13] Again we lack data on how men would respond to such questions, but on an anecdotal level, Chinese often feel that the sort of changing of dates and boyfriends implied by a fully developed dating culture would be particularly problematic for women, since "fickleness" prior to marriage is popularly assumed to warn of the wife's unfaithfulness after marriage. Such assumptions do not hold

TABLE 2 Aspects of Dating

	Year First Married					
Dating Pattern	1933–1948 (N = 71)	1949–1957 (N = 107)	1958–1965 (N = 82)	1966–1976 (N = 116)	1977–1987 (N = 210)	
Dated husband prior to marriage						
Often	12%	17%	24%	40%	48%	
Sometimes	6	18	27	13	21	
Rarely	23	22	30	31	24	
Never	59	44	18	16	7	
Number of romances						
None	73	29	9	5	5	
One (the husband)	24	63	74	66	67	
More than one	3	8	18	29	28	
Had other marital prospects	4	5	2	6	9	
How much in love when married						
1. Completely	17	38	63	61	67	
2.	26	29	22	26	19	
3.	35	20	9	11	10	
4.	9	4	4	1	3	
5. Not at all	13	9	2	1	0	

with the same strength for men.[14] In these figures we see modest indications that matters have changed since the end of the 1950s. Some increase has occurred in the last couple of marriage cohorts in the percentage of women who dated their eventual husbands often and who had more than one romance, and perhaps also in those having more than one marital prospect, but still the dominant pattern is of dramatic changes in earlier periods followed by rough stability in marriage customs since the 1960s. The reform era has not produced much further change in these realms.

Could the crudeness of the division into five marriage cohorts in these tables obscure important fluctuations in the freedom of mate choice over time? In order to investigate this question, I constructed a summary scale from six of the measures included in Tables 1 and 2.[15] I then computed a three-year moving average of the resulting summary freedom-of-mate-choice scale scores and graphed this against the years in which the respondents got married.[16]

Several things are apparent from examining Figure 1. First, the graph reveals that the trend toward greater freedom of mate choice was already well under way prior to 1949, and that women who married during the 1940s were enjoying somewhat more freedom in picking a mate than their elder sisters, aunts, and mothers had earlier. This finding should not be entirely surprising, since it confirms the "family revolution" that Marion Levy, Olga Lang, and others argued was under way in Republican China, at least in urban areas. Second, the graph confirms the most important conclusion reached above: there has been little change in the overall degree of freedom of mate choice within the sample since about 1957. Neither the Great Leap Forward, the Cultural Revolution, nor the reform era has produced clear trends toward a further increase (or for that matter a reduction) in the trend away from arranged marriages. It is the pattern of this curve that gives most dramatic testimony to the stalled-convergence pattern mentioned briefly earlier. The dominant pattern in mate choice has shifted away from strictly arranged marriages to one in which youth initiative is predominant, but parents still play a significant role. As already noted, the dominant pattern contains no more than the rudiments of a dating culture, and most women marry their first real "boyfriends" and begin to date only after their relationship has become "fixed" (kending guanxi), which is tantamount to engagement. Again, this pattern of change over time does not suggest that the pressure of official directed-change efforts is the major factor at work, but exactly

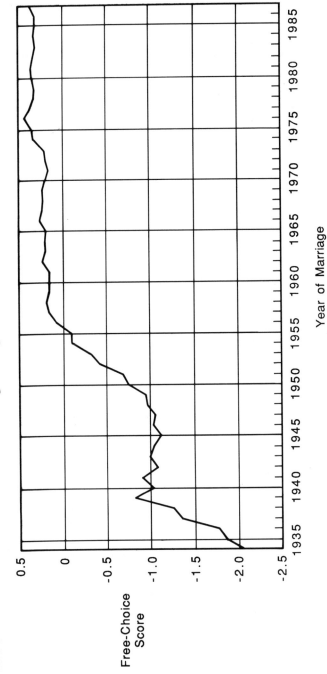

FIGURE 1 Freedom of Mate Choice Moving Average

what alternative explanation might account for such an arrested change pattern I defer until after other aspects of the process of mate choice have been examined.

Table 3 displays a variety of indicators of the life situation and aspirations of our Chengdu respondents at the time that they married. The indicators in this table do not relate directly to important official family-change goals, nor to alternative marriage customs that individuals have to choose among, but they nonetheless reveal interesting patterns about the changing circumstances women faced when they got married. The items about whether the parents were together and whether the husband had been married before testify to the increased "regularization" of family life produced mainly by longer life spans, with marriage increasingly occurring to never-married men and taking place while both parents are still alive (and together). This latter feature is particularly important since, other things being equal, one would expect parental influence on mate choice to be more of a factor when both parents are still around and able to exert such influence. But other things are not equal in this case, and we have already seen that in spite of the increased longevity of parents, they have had less ability in recent times to control the pattern of mate choice.

In the final two rows of the table we can see that already by the end of the 1950s respondents had adapted to the new reality of working more or less constantly outside the home, and that the great majority of them were already at work at the time they married (although the percentage at work increases further across the post-1957 cohorts).[17] Although the changes in regard to women working at the time of marriage may reflect official policy, which stressed the importance of paid employment for both sexes, this trend may also be influenced by changing ages of marriage, since if women are marrying later and later, they are more likely to be at work already by the time they do marry. Trends in marriage ages bring us back into a realm that official policy has attempted directly to influence.

Table 4 displays items dealing both with premarital sexual experience and with marriage ages of brides and grooms. Two of the three measures dealing with premarital sexual experience (items 1 and 3) are indirect estimates, so the results should be interpreted with caution. The estimate of premarital conceptions and births (item 1) shows only modest hints of any increase in these experiences in recent cohorts.[18]

In the second item of the table we see some evidence of an aspect of

TABLE 3 Changes in Life Circumstances at Marriage

			Year First Married		
Life Circumstance	*1933–1948* (N = 71)	*1949–1957* (N = 107)	*1958–1965* (N = 82)	*1966–1976* (N = 116)	*1977–1987* (N = 210)
Parents together when re- spondent wed	56%	57%	51%	65%	79%
Husband married before	15	15	5	6	3
Premarital employment	18	27	83	86	98
Premarital work plans					
Be a housewife	36	9	1	2	5
Work some of the time	8	9	3	2	2
Have a lifelong career	56	81	96	96	94

TABLE 4 Maturity and Sexuality prior to Marriage

Premarital Pattern	Year First Married				
	1933–1948 (N=71)	1949–1957 (N=107)	1958–1965 (N=82)	1966–1976 (N=116)	1977–1987 (N=210)
1. Timing of First Birth					
Before marriage	2%	3%	3%	3%	1%
Within 8 months	7	4	5	4	9
Later	92	93	93	93	90
2. Premarital cohabitation	6	3	5	5	12
3. First sex before marriage	4	15	15	19	18
a. Premarital sex (max%)	12	21	24	25	30
4. Knew husband before marriage	1.2 yr	1.2 yr	2.4 yr	2.2 yr	2.4 yr
5. Bride's age at first marriage	18.1 yr	19.9 yr	22.5 yr	23.7 yr	25.1 yr
6. Groom's age at first marriage	25.3 yr	25.9 yr	26.5 yr	27.1 yr	27.7 yr

the mate-choice process that may have changed in the reform era. Even though the figures are still modest in size, when directly asked whether they had lived together with their husbands prior to marriage, a slightly higher proportion of women marrying recently admitted to having done so. At first I wondered whether this sign of an increase in cohabitation might be a "fluke" due to some misunderstanding of our question. Certainly the general presence of grass-roots moral "enforcers" in Chinese urban neighborhoods and work units would seem to make such cohabitation hard to conceal. However, the existence of Chinese press accounts describing an emerging trend toward premarital cohabitation suggests that the findings of our survey are not a fluke.[19] Apparently popular concerns about difficulties young people have in regard to employment, housing, and mate choice, in the context of the official late-marriage policy, lead some parents to accept or even encourage their children to enter such cohabitation arrangements. Apparently not all neighborhood enforcers are so offended and vigilant that such couples risk public criticism for their actions.

Two separate estimates of premarital sexual experience are presented in row 3 of the table. The first is based simply on comparisons of the age a woman was when she first married and the age she said she was (in a separate part of the questionnaire) when she had her first sexual experience. Simple subtraction allows me to compute the conservative estimate given in row 3.[20] The second estimate makes use of information from rows 1 and 2 as well—women who either cohabited or were estimated to be premaritally pregnant, as well as women who were younger when they had their first sexual experience than when they married, are grouped together and considered sexually active prior to marriage (in row 3a). From these figures a couple of conclusions can be drawn. First, even in recent years the great majority of Chengdu women appear to be virgins at marriage.[21] Second, there has been some increase in premarital sexual experience, and the major change in this regard seems to have occurred by the 1950s, but with some modest further increases recently. If, however, these modest increases are viewed in the context of the substantial increases in age at marriage (reported in rows 4 and 5) and of the increases in premarital dating noted earlier, still on balance the ability to "hold the line" against premarital sex appears impressive. Finally, these figures give at least qualified support to the pattern of stalled convergence noted earlier in discussing freedom of mate choice. Although there are modest signs of increasing premarital sexual experience in the reform era, on balance the most important change occurred earlier, by the 1950s.

The final rows in Table 4 indicate trends in ages at first marriage and in the length of time couples were acquainted prior to marriage. The length-of-acquaintance figures in row 6 form a by now familiar "plateau" pattern. As we might expect from the increases in youth initiative and premarital dating reported in the first two tables, as well as from the official late-marriage policy, couples appear to have roughly doubled the average period of acquaintance prior to marriage. But again the major change in this regard was consolidated by the end of the 1950s, with little further change since then.

The figures on ages at first marriage show a quite different pattern. From the figures given, it appears that there has been a more or less constant increase across time in mean age at first marriage for both males and females, with the increase for females being considerably larger. (Or, looked at in another way, the average age gap between brides and grooms appears to have shrunk markedly.) In this instance, however, it turns out that the rough grouping of respondents into marriage cohorts conceals as much as it reveals. Figure 2 displays the three-year moving average of the mean age of first marriage of women in our sample, and this graph reveals several additional features of the pattern of changes.

The first obvious feature in Figure 2 is that, as in Figure 1, changes were already under way prior to 1949, by which time the average female age at first marriage had already increased from about 17 to around 19.[22] Second, the dominant trend already commented on is still visible: throughout most of the years since 1949 the age of first marriage has continued to rise. This gradual rise cannot be explained simply by the official late-marriage policy, since that policy has been systematically stressed only since about 1970, by which time the major part of the increase in marriage age had already occurred. Most likely factors such as rising education for women (as well as men), the decreasing availability of housing, and growing employment and income-earning opportunities for women prior to marriage (see Table 3, row 3) lie behind this long-term trend.

The graph reveals that within this longer-term pattern, however, there have been a number of interesting reversals. There are temporary "peaks" in female marriage age in 1959, 1966, and 1979, and these are followed by reductions in the next few years. These secondary trends are more readily interpretable in terms of the variable strength of the directed-

FIGURE 2 Bride Age at Marriage Moving Average

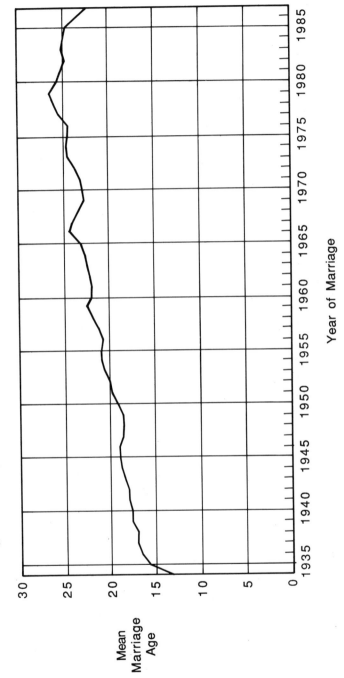

change efforts of the government. The first "relapse" occurred in the wake of the Great Leap Forward and its ensuing famine, when concern about feeding the population superseded any efforts to enforce family-change goals. The second instance corresponds to the latter stages of the Cultural Revolution, a time during which political chaos again made concerted governmental pressure for late marriage impossible.

The third reduction in the average female marriage age is the most striking. According to these figures, the average female marriage age in Chengdu has declined by about three years (from about 26 to roughly 23) in the years since 1979.[23] As noted earlier, it was at the start of this period that the new marriage law, with its de facto reduction of minimum marriage ages, was promulgated. It is hard to avoid the conclusion that the 1980 law, by proclaiming legal minimum marriage ages of 20 for females and 22 for males, and thus undermining official efforts to enforce ever later marriage ages, was a primary contributor to this startling drop. Other factors may have contributed as well. The policy of sending massive numbers of urban youth to the countryside may have contributed to the pre-1979 increase by leading many to postpone marriage until they could return to the cities, when they would have to begin the mate-selection process relatively late. The discontinuation of this program at the end of the 1970s eliminated one important source of delay in marriage. In addition, perhaps the modest increases in dating and premarital intimacy discussed earlier have helped to encourage some-what earlier marriage, as has rising prosperity.[24] In any case, the graph shows the clearest sign of any of the indicators looked at so far of an important change in the reform era—in this case, a shift toward earlier marriage.

The final measures I want to examine concern the nature of wedding celebrations. Table 5 displays a variety of such measures. The pattern shown in these data is strikingly different from that seen in earlier tables, and we see here dramatic evidence of new trends in the reform era, not a pattern of stalled convergence. In all respects, the simplification that had occurred in earlier periods, and that for the most part appeared to have been consolidated by the end of the 1950s, has been dramatically reversed. Elaborate and expensive weddings are once again "in" in the reform era, and if respondent memories are accurate, in some respects the average wedding today is more elaborate than was the case prior to 1949. In terms of specifics, in the reform-era marriage cohort (column 5) we can see that wedding celebrations and wedding banquets were more

TABLE 5 Changes in Wedding Behavior

				Year First Married			
Wedding Behavior	1933–1948 (N=71)	1949–1957 (N=107)	1958–1965 (N=82)	1966–1976 (N=116)	1977–1987 (N=210)		
1. Wedding ceremony held (%)	85	74	66	74	89		
2. Attendance at wedding (mean N)	60	55	66	66	102		
3. Wedding banquet held (%)	75	46	20	28	68		
4. Banquet attendance (mean N)	60	49	49	51	85		
5. Location of banquet (%)							
a. At home	72	78	69	76	33		
b. Other	28	22	31	24	67		
6. Mode of delivery to wedding (%)							
a. Sedan chair	55	22	0	0	0		
b. Bicycle	1	1	1	11	20		
c. Automobile	8	0	0	1	9		
d. On foot	24	50	67	71	50		
e. Other	11	27	32	17	21		
7. Honeymoon trip taken (%)	1	3	2	14	21		
8. Postmarital residence (%)							
a. With bride's family	10	7	4	7	12		
b. With groom's family	45	25	13	16	28		
c. In own place	39	64	71	68	51		
d. Other	6	4	12	9	9		

TABLE 5 Changes in Wedding Behavior (continued)

Wedding Behavior	Year First Married				
	1933–1948 (N=71)	1949–1957 (N=107)	1958–1965 (N=82)	1966–1976 (N=116)	1977–1987 (N=210)
9. Gifts from husband to bride (% giving)	34	18	21	22	31
10. Mean value of gifts to bride (in yuan)	198.6	204.9	52.4	105.8	200.2
11. Bride price (% giving)	18	9	5	6	9
12. Mean value of bride price (in yuan)	35.9	158.9	23.3	49.7	61.9
13. Dowry to bride (% giving)	56	36	26	32	71
14. Mean value of dowry (in yuan)	228.7	167.3	139.2	128.1	343.4
15. Total spent on wedding (%)					
a. Under 500 yuan	82	89	94	80	15
b. 500–999 yuan	10	8	6	13	32
c. 1000+ yuan	7	3	0	7	53

often held than for previous cohorts, that banquets more often took place in restaurants (the primary subcategory within "other" in item 5), that gifts of various kinds increased in frequency and expense, and that the total expenditure on weddings also rose.[25]

Several other features of this main trend should also be noted. First, it would appear that the era of the most frugal and ritually simple weddings was not, in fact, the Cultural Revolution but the years from 1958 to 1965.[26] A more fine-grained analysis of the time trend will be presented shortly, but this initial observation reinforces the claim that something more than varying official pressure affects wedding behavior.

It is also interesting to note that of the various kinds of gift presentations that may occur in a wedding, the dowry appears to be the most common and the most expensive. This finding is somewhat of a surprise, since press critiques of wedding expenses mostly focus on exorbitant demands made for gifts from the husband-to-be and his family to the bride-to-be.[27] Our figures show that, although there are modest increases in the frequency and cost of such male gifts (see items 9 and 10) as well as in bride prices (see items 11 and 12),[28] these are dwarfed by the reported dowry transactions (see items 13 and 14). On reflection, perhaps this finding should not be so surprising. Bride-price payments tend to be large when rights in the fertility and earning power of women are being transferred from their natal family to their husband's family, as still tends to occur in much of rural China, and lavish gifts from the male to the bride-to-be tend to occur when women occupy a stronger position than men in the marriage market, permitting them to be very choosy. Neither condition, however, accords with the dominant reality of urban China today. Most newly married couples do not live with the husband's family (see item 8), and even if they do, the pattern of external employment for wages means that the husband's family does not have automatic or total control over the new wife's earnings.[29] And in the current highly competitive urban marriage market, particular anxiety is expressed about the problem of "overage maidens" *(daling guniang)*. In this context heavy demands for gifts from male suitors would be a risky strategy. Other aspects of the current scene make dowry exchanges likely. Although a variety of theories and explanations have been proposed cross-culturally to explain dowry exchanges, one common element is that dowries are a mechanism for status competition between families in a stratified society.[30] The official efforts to encourage consumerism and status competition in the reform period may inadvertently be contributing to the revival of substantial dowry payments.[31]

We can also use the figures in Table 5 to consider whether the increasing elaborateness of weddings in the reform era should be seen as a return to traditions or instead as representing the impact of new and perhaps Western influences from the "open-door" policy. The evidence on this point is mixed. We do not see, for example, any taking of sedan chairs out of mothballs, while the use of bicycles and even automobiles to deliver the bride to the celebration is becoming more common (see item 6). In addition, wedding feasts in restaurants and honeymoon trips after the celebration are becoming increasingly popular, just as happened earlier in Hong Kong and Taipei. Also, most of the gifts exchanged are modern consumer durables and furniture, rather than items that would have gone into a traditional set of wedding gifts.[32] And from anecdotal information not dealt with in our questionnaire, we know of even clearer instances of Western influence being reflected in wedding customs. For example, in recent years it has become more and more common for urban couples to go to a photographer to have a formal wedding portrait taken, and for this portrait the bride wears a rented Western-style white wedding gown. Even though the gown is generally worn only in the photographer's studio, and not during the wedding celebrations themselves, it will be this photo that will be hung on a wall in memory of the occasion.

The increasingly elaborate wedding feasts, however, are obviously not simply or even primarily a reflection of Western influence. The feast, as noted earlier, was the central event in the traditional wedding, and the evidence from our survey points to a very significant revival in this realm, even if the venues in which such feasts are held are now modernized or even Westernized. Indeed, it could be argued that, in the reform era, the need to cultivate personal connections *(guanxi)* in order to cope with the complexities of life in a partially reformed but still heavily bureaucratized urban social landscape provides an important and quite traditional motivation for large guest lists and elaborate wedding feasts. In sum, we may conclude that the increasing elaborateness of weddings shown in Table 5 is fueled by both Western and traditional Chinese influences, and that both are working together to undermine popular support for frugal official wedding norms.

The figures in Table 5 reveal other ways in which Chinese traditions are resurfacing in the reform era. In particular, I note in item 8 that in recent times it has become *less* common rather than more, for the bride and groom to start out married life in their own apartment. Neolocal residence was most common in the period from 1958 to 1965, and since then starting out "in their own place" has decreased markedly, with both residence with the bride's parents and residence with the groom's becoming increasingly common. (The latter is still more than twice as likely as the former.) The most obvious explanation for this reversal of trends is the severe housing shortage in urban China generally, which even the extensive residential construction of the post-Mao era has not fully relieved. But whatever the cause, these results show that, even though young people now pick their spouses in a nontraditional way, an increasing share of them have to start out married life living in a traditional family structure.[33] This trend is occurring despite signs in recent public opinion polls that there is an increasing preference, by young people and even some old people, for nuclear family living.

The familial interdependence expressed in these housing arrangements is also revealed in data about the pattern of payment for weddings (not displayed in Table 5). As the expenditure on weddings has increased, the proportion of brides and grooms who pay for everything themselves has dropped from a high of 79 percent for Great Leap era marriages to only 28 percent among reform-era couples. Increasingly, the resources of a diverse family network must be pooled to meet the expenditures required, and even grandparents and others are likely to chip in.[34] So although I again stress that this extended-family interdependence does not indicate a return to a pattern of arranged marriages, still in certain respects the reform-era trends in family life seem quite contrary to the move toward the more competitive and even individualistic society that China's reformers are trying to foster. Indeed, although I have noted that the figures in Table 5 are strikingly different from those in earlier tables and give strong evidence of accelerating change in the reform era, in these specific respects these new trends actually are compatible with, and perhaps reinforce, the pattern of stalled convergence I noted in those earlier tables. The process of mate choice has moved part of the way from being a transaction between families to becoming a decision of individuals, but only part of the way, and family influence and contributions are still centrally involved. The increasing dependence on families in urban China to provide financing for the wedding and housing afterward stands in the way of mate choice becoming more of a purely personal decision.

As was the case earlier in examining trends in freedom of mate choice and ages of marriage, one may ask whether the crude marriage cohort categories used might obscure the details of the change process. In order to confront this possibility, I constructed a seven-item mean scale of wedding elaborateness and expenditures from items 1, 2, 3, 4, 13, 14, and 15 in Table 5.[35] The three-year moving average of this wedding-elaborateness scale is graphed across various years of marriage in Figure 3. For the most part the form of the graph simply reinforces the conclusions drawn from Table 5. An initial sharp decline in wedding elaborateness and expenditures, followed by their more recent revival, produces the U-shaped-curve pattern visible in Figure 3. In this case, as with earlier figures, it now becomes apparent that changes were under way even before 1949. During the depression and the early years of World War II, wedding expenditures declined, with a partial revival that peaked in 1946, during the brief interlude between the anti-Japanese and civil wars. Then the simplification trend resumed and continued after 1949. In general, weddings were held to a fairly constant and spartan level throughout the period between 1953 and 1970. Within this period the most spartan levels were reached during the post–Great Leap Forward crisis and in the early years of the Cultural Revolution, presumably owing mainly to economic restraints in the first period and political restraints in the second.

The most striking new feature revealed by the graph is that the shift back toward more elaborate and expensive weddings began as early as 1970, six years prior to the death of Mao and eight years before the launching of the current reform program. So even though this trend has continued and been accelerated during the reform era, it cannot be explained solely in terms of new policies and influences that have affected Chinese urbanites since 1978. Factors that may have contributed to this revival include the return to some degree of political and economic normalcy following the most chaotic years of the Cultural Revolution, as well as the heightened anxiety about attracting a desirable mate that was produced by the program of sending youth to the countryside and by urban unemployment. Perhaps the damage done to the party's authority by the Cultural Revolution turmoil also prompted increasing numbers of families to turn deaf ears to the calls for frugal nuptials.[36] In any case, families were more willing and able to celebrate weddings with some fanfare in the final years of Mao's life, even before the reformers mounted the stage and made conspicuous consumption officially fashionable again.

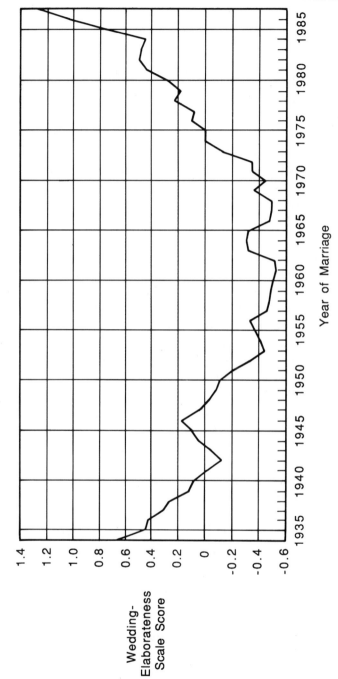

FIGURE 3 Wedding Elaborateness Moving Average

INTERPRETING THE TRENDS

Relying on data from the Chengdu survey, I have reviewed a wide range of features of the mate-choice process and how these have changed over time. The patterns reviewed are quite diverse, including aspects of freedom of mate choice that increased markedly through the 1950s but then have stalled since then; premarital sexuality increasing only slightly after 1949 and perhaps a bit more during the reform era; marriage age rising more or less continuously until the late 1970s but then dropping noticeably in the 1980s; and wedding celebrations that declined sharply in elaborateness and expenditures in the earlier years, remained at very low levels through the 1950s and 1960s, and have been increasing markedly in the 1970s and 1980s. It seems most unlikely that a single explanation or source of change could account for such diverse results. But one thing that should be apparent from the previous discussion is that most of the trends observed cannot be interpreted simply as responses to changing official policies in the PRC. The timing and direction of changes are in too many instances different from what a prediction based on changing official policies would lead us to expect to enable us to rely on this simple explanation. Perhaps by considering changing official policies in the context of other influences, I can arrive at persuasive interpretations of the trends observed.[37]

The key to understanding the variety of change patterns observed is recognizing that different aspects of the mate-choice process respond to different influences. Freedom of mate choice, to get specific, requires a number of complex conditions in order to be fully realized: that the idea of individual choice of mates on the basis of personal attraction be popularized and accepted; that young people be relieved of dependence on parental resources (for example, inherited property and occupational skills) in becoming adults; that young people have ample opportunities to meet and get to know potential partners outside the range of strict adult supervision; that parents increasingly come to feel that their long-term interests (and particularly their security in old age) are not threatened by the autonomy of their offspring; and that the young people involved can autonomously acquire the resources needed for full adulthood (for example, education, employment, housing).

When economic development takes place in a capitalist mode, these conditions are increasingly brought into being, but in a gradual and incremental way, and some before others. For example, young people may begin to rely more on schooling and a growing non-kin-based job market and less on parental training and property, and they may begin to accept romantic love and individual choice of a mate as ideals, even when they still confront a social world that gives them few opportunities to meet and become romantically involved with potential partners.[38] The crucial mechanism involved in this change is the loosening of the inter-dependence between generations that occurs gradually with economic de-velopment, as a result of the growth of formal schooling, bureaucratic employment, and labor markets; the decline of families as production units; and the spread of pensions and old-age welfare provisions.

The circumstances surrounding the transition to free mate choice un-der Chinese socialism were in key respects different. To begin with, there was an activist government that attempted to accelerate the ideological acceptance of freedom of mate choice.[39] Furthermore, the socialist trans-formation of the economy accomplished in a short period of time (basi-cally 1955–1957) what in a capitalist society takes generations—the vir-tual elimination of family production units and the reduction in importance of family-controlled property as the key resource needed for adult status (and the creation instead of a bureaucratic system of employment). Fur-thermore, the majority of Chinese urbanites who worked in state enter-prises became eligible for a variety of fringe benefits, including retire-ment pensions, which potentially made them less dependent on grown children than is generally the case in capitalist societies at the same level of economic development. These important changes in the structure of social life provided the context for the increases in freedom of mate choice through the 1950s that are visible in Table 1 and Figure 1.

The urban social structure, however, has not changed substantially in subsequent years in ways that would have altered the conditions fostering freedom of mate choice. For example, even though the authorities advo-cated that young people be allowed to choose their own mates, they took vigorous action to inhibit the development of a dating culture to facili-tate that freedom. A variety of recreational and leisure-time facilities that existed in urban areas prior to 1949 were closed or revamped to fit the spartan atmosphere desired by the CCP, reducing the venues available for informal socializing between the sexes. The growth of coeducational schooling promoted contacts between the sexes, but formal bans on dat-ing ("talking romance"—*tan lian'ai*) in all schools up through the university level, reinforced by criticism and even expulsion of students revealed to be romantically involved, helped to maintain a wary distance between the sexes within such schools.[40]

Other developments during the post-1958 years also helped to inhibit the development of opportunities for the young to experiment romantically or to become more autonomous. For example, the curtailing of housing construction in the wake of the Great Leap Forward made it increasingly necessary for young people to move in with parents upon marriage, and the assistance of parents in infant care and performance of other domestic chores was also crucial in coping with the growing pressures and shortages of urban life through the 1970s.[41] The millions of urban youths sent to the countryside after 1968 were discouraged from pairing off and getting married for fear of being stuck forever in their places of rural exile, and even when romances did develop between two such young people, often reassignment to urban areas at different times and even to different locales tended to destroy the romantic bond that had been established, making youths returning to the city more susceptible to parentally inspired marriage arrangements.[42] Furthermore, even those young people who avoided rural relocation and were assigned urban jobs could hardly feel very autonomous. Typically their lives and activities were tightly supervised by their work units, and in addition they might feel they owed their exemption from rural exile and even their employment to their parents.[43] Even if they lived separately from parents in a work-unit dormitory, usually they were expected to contribute some of their earnings to their parents, and they might also anticipate having to move back in with their parents in order to marry, in view of the growing shortage of urban housing.

In the reform period these circumstances have changed in some respects, but not in others. There has been a modest relaxation in the degree to which school and work-unit authorities scrutinize the daily lives of their charges and enforce a spartan atmosphere, and there has also been a modest increase in the availability of youth-oriented recreational facilities (coffee shops, discos, amusement parks, and so forth). The program of sending urban youths to the countryside, which disrupted so many young people's lives, has also been discontinued. On the cultural level the theme that romantic love (rather than simply compatibility on political or other grounds) is the most suitable way to select a marital partner has received increasing prominence in the mass media, with the popularity of this theme fueled in part by the increasing availability of

Western novels and movies and popular songs from Hong Kong and Taiwan that deal with romance.

In other respects, the situation young people face has not changed very much in ways that would affect the degree of freedom of mate choice. The venues in which young people can congregate and experiment romantically are still relatively scarce and subject to official harassment (with discos closed down, parks shut or patrolled at night, and so forth). The proportion of urban families, and of young people, who have disengaged from state employment and now rely on private-enterprise activities and market exchanges is still quite small, and for most young urbanites life still means movement from the home through school and into a bureaucratic work organization, with little autonomy or opportunity along the way to escape the watchful eyes of parents and bureaucratic superiors. As noted earlier (in Table 5), the dependence of young people on their families to provide both housing and financing in order to marry has actually increased during the reform era. In summary, the reason why freedom of mate choice has not progressed beyond a moderate level is because the declining direct economic control that parents have over their offspring has not resulted in substantial youth autonomy, but rather in youth subordination to a combination of parental and bureaucratic authority. Chinese socialism perhaps accelerated the process already under way of undermining the strictly arranged marriage system, but then it inhibited the development of youth autonomy in mate choice beyond the level I have referred to as stalled convergence. The reforms of the Deng Xiaoping era, by introducing only modest and partial changes in urban social structure, have not "unstalled" this convergence trend to any great degree.

With regard to premarital intimacy, many of the same constraints operate that affect the degree of freedom of mate choice, but with some important differences. Premarital sexuality is most likely to be promoted when sexual maturity occurs early and marriage late, when there are ample opportunities for young people to experiment romantically prior to marriage and ample privacy within which to do so, when there is no popular view that premarital sexuality is inherently immoral and sinful, when there is popular acceptance of the idea that sexual relations are both a suitable way to demonstrate love and commitment and an important means to judge the suitability of a potential marriage partner, and when premarital sex or even pregnancy does not pose serious risk to one's future career opportunities and prospects for marriage.

Chinese culture may well lack a strong sense that premarital sex is inherently sinful, at least in comparison with the Christian West. And over the years the average marriage age has increased substantially (see Figure 2), while we may presume that with improved health and nutrition the average age of sexual maturation has declined, thus increasing the number of years "at risk" of premarital intimacy. But most of the other conditions specified are decidedly not present or conducive to premarital intimacy in the PRC, and this situation has changed only marginally in the reform era.

In this realm, as in regard to freedom of mate choice, the role of parents in inhibiting sexual intimacy has diminished, but the role of bureaucratic institutions (schools, work units, and neighborhood organizations) has increased.[44] The state's decidedly puritanical attitudes (as transmitted and enforced through those institutions) have reinforced popular feelings that premarital sexuality represents evidence of a character defect and, particularly for a woman, is a predictor of unfaithfulness as a marital partner. As a result, premarital sexuality has remained not only difficult to engage in in terms of opportunity and privacy, but also potentially dangerous. To be known to be engaging in sexual relations prior to marriage has meant risking public criticism at least, with resulting damage to educational and career opportunities, and in some cases even risking being ostracized from the marriage market or being confined to a youth reformatory (again, more so for women than for men).[45] In this sort of hostile environment, generally only in cases of a firm commitment to marry do some women consider the risk of premarital sex worth taking.

It was not simply the case that official policy pronouncements discouraged premarital sexuality. The social structural changes that occurred in the 1950s created substantially increased bureaucratic surveillance over the lives of all urbanites, and this capacity was used in part to inhibit the development of premarital intimacy, even as the age of marriage was getting later and later. In the reform era this situation has changed only at the margins. On the one hand, more novels, movies, and mass media articles are available that treat premarital sexuality in a nonjudgmental way; modest increases in youth recreational facilities and dating activities prior to marriage may increase the temptations and opportunities for intimacy; and perhaps the wide publicity given to difficulties of finding a mate in urban areas may induce some parents to be more tolerant of sexual involvement and even cohabitation by their offspring. On the other hand, the decline in the female age at marriage (seen in Figure 2) should work in the other direction by decreasing the time period prior to marriage during which sexual relations might begin. On balance the result is still stalled convergence in this realm as well. Premarital intimacy is somewhat more likely than was the case prior to 1949, but it is still not as common as we might expect, given the late ages at which urban Chinese get married.[46]

As in the case of freedom of mate choice, I argue that the primary explanation for this continued inhibition of premarital sexuality is that declining parental controls do not produce much genuine youth autonomy. Instead, control is partially shifted to the bureaucratic structures of China's socialist state. In spite of the popular impression that there is a dramatic upsurge in premarital sex in the reform era, we find in the Chengdu data only modest indications that the inhibitions against premarital sex have eased.

The age at which people first marry is also influenced by a complex of factors. A number of circumstances may foster late marriage for women: a ceding of initiative in mate choice to the younger generation;[47] increased reliance of parents on the earnings of daughters; lengthened years spent in schooling and other preparation for adulthood; heightened expectations about how economically established individuals need to be before they can start a family; increased difficulties in reaching the desired economic levels; increased difficulties in finding suitable marital partners; lengthened time needed to gain access to housing or to save the funds needed for a wedding; and greater official efforts to dissuade individuals from marrying at young ages.

In general a number of these constraints operated during most of the history of the PRC to delay marriage, and the pattern we observe as a result is not one of stalled convergence. The socialist bureaucratic structures established during the 1950s did not inhibit further change beyond a certain level, as was the case with freedom of mate choice and premarital intimacy. Rather, this social structure contained elements with a built-in tendency to delay marriage—the expansion of schooling, the growing housing shortage, and the development of mechanisms of enforcement of the government's late-marriage policy, in particular.[48] When, after the onset of the Cultural Revolution, the length of time spent in school actually became shorter, new elements of uncertainty faced by young people—the disruptions of lives produced by sending urban youths to the countryside and rising urban unemployment—more than compensated for the effect of shortened schooling and sent marriage ages upward again.

By the late 1970s young people were often marrying later than would be necessitated by problems in the search for a mate or in getting established in a job. Primary factors were the obstruction of bureaucratic authorities and the difficulties caused by the severe housing shortage. In the 1980s both factors lost much of their influence. As noted earlier, the adoption of the new marriage law, with its stipulation of age 20 as the female minimum, undercut the ability of local bureaucrats to dissuade determined young people and their families from getting married at ages younger than 25 or 26. And new housing construction made it possible for some families to acquire quarters large enough to accommodate a married child and family.[49] In addition, the reduction in urban unemployment and the reintegration of returning "sent-down" youths reduced the number of people in urban areas who were still having trouble getting established in adult careers. In this instance the effect of the changes in the reform era was substantial, and it involved a weakening of some of the "escalator" factors that tended to drive marriage ages up in earlier years.

Finally, it is necessary to explain the U-shaped-curve pattern that wedding elaborateness has taken over time, as seen in Table 5 and Figure 3. Again, the elaborateness and expenditures involved in a wedding can be affected by a variety of influences: the prosperity of individuals and families and the range of alternative things they can spend their funds on; the availability of locales where elaborate celebrations can be held and the acceptability of holding such celebrations; the influence of parents in the mate-choice process and the extent to which a wedding is seen as a family and not simply an individual matter; the extensiveness of social ties with kin, friends, workmates, and others and the extent of social obligations that can be reciprocated through a wedding invitation; and the acceptability of the social-status competition between families of the sort that elaborate weddings entail.

In the 1950s income levels and economic security were generally increasing, but most of the other conditions specified were changing to make elaborate weddings less likely. Parents were losing some of their control over the mate-choice process, many of the restaurants and shops that had catered to the wedding trade were converted to more spartan uses, and the status competition and displays of prosperity involved in lavish weddings had become less acceptable, if not downright dangerous.

It is in this context that the sharp declines in wedding elaborateness and expenditures documented in Table 5 and Figure 3 can be understood. After 1958 the economic hardships caused by the Great Leap and frozen wage levels and then the increased political risks of engaging in "feudal" ceremonials during the Cultural Revolution combined to keep most weddings very simple. This was not a case of stalled convergence, however, since wedding expenditures might be expected to go up over the course of development, rather than down.[50] So in this realm, unlike the others considered in this chapter, the influence of socialist developments was to produce an initial trend quite different from that visible in other societies. As the economic and political disruptions of the period 1958–1969 receded into the background, as restaurants and other facilities catering to the wedding trade reemerged, and then as official policy in the reform era switched from condemning displays of wealth to encouraging them and as extended families got more involved in providing housing and in financing weddings, the grounds were prepared for the revival of wedding elaborateness and expenditures that was described earlier.[51]

CONCLUSIONS

Several primary conclusions emerge from considering changes in the process of mate choice in Chengdu. First and most obvious, the nature of mate choice and weddings has changed substantially since 1949, even though many of the changes were already under way in the Republican period. The reform era has seen further, dramatic changes in some aspects of the mate-choice process (wedding elaborateness, age at first marriage), but other aspects appear to have changed only modestly or not at all (freedom of mate choice, premarital intimacy). Even in those realms that have changed markedly in the reform era, it is not obvious that the reforms per se have been the primary force at work. The reduction in marriage age seems to have occurred primarily because of a relaxation of bureaucratic efforts to foster late marriage, a relaxation that has no direct connection with reform policies.[52] Even the trend toward increasingly elaborate weddings, while clearly fostered by the rising income levels and the "rehabilitation" of a conspicuous-consumption ethic produced by the reforms, began prior to Mao's death. A primary lesson here is that the reforms have not produced an across-the-board or uniform impact on the social realm we have considered (transition to marriage in urban China) and should not be expected to have done so on other realms.

The tracing of the pattern of continuity and change in urban mate choice also yields clues about the nature of the underlying social structure and whether that has changed. The central claim here is that a substantially transformed and bureaucratized social structure had been set in place by the mid-1950s. In that transformed social structure, the main "players" in mate-choice matters were not simply parents and their offspring, but parents, their offspring, and bureaucratic controllers of access to scarce resources and opportunities. The new actors involved—the local bureaucratic agents of the state in schools, work units, and neighborhoods—acted to inhibit some further changes in mate choice (for example, by stifling the emergence of a dating culture) even as they tended to foster continued change in other realms (for example, through delayed marriages). Furthermore, when state policies were altered, such alterations contributed in some cases to reinforcement of previous trends (as when the program of sending urban youths to the countryside delayed marriages further) and in others to a reversal of previous trends (as in the declining marriage ages and rising wedding expenditures of the 1980s). But state policies and their bureaucratic enforcement were only one element in the urban social structure that individuals and families faced, and in some instances the impact of state actions in this realm was indirect and led to outcomes that were unintended and disliked by the authorities. Much of the discussion earlier in this chapter was devoted to showing how the actual trends in the process of mate choice could not be interpreted simply as a response to changing official policies.

At the same time, it is also clear that we cannot simply leave the nature of the urban bureaucratic system out of the picture in interpreting and explaining trends in mate-choice behavior. Modernization theory, despite the criticisms it has received in recent years, has remained a powerful device for interpreting and even predicting changes in family life in the process of development. If one utilizes a modernization framework, one would anticipate that as a society develops, arranged marriage will increasingly give way to free-choice marriage, some sort of dating culture will emerge, postmarital residence will increasingly tend to be neolocal rather than, say, patrilocal, and premarital sexuality will become increasingly common.[53] Modernization theory, however, is based fundamentally on the idea that young people become increasingly "liberated" from parental controls and reliant on formal schooling, external labor markets, and non-kin employment, with the controllers of access to such external opportunities essentially indifferent to the private lives and marital choices of the young. That sort of conception does not describe the social structure of urban China after 1949 accurately. The bureaucratic structures of state socialism are definitely not indifferent to the marital and family lives of citizens, and the complex trends we observe in mate-choice behavior cannot be interpreted simply in terms of a constant increase in youth autonomy. Youth autonomy was promoted up to a certain point and then prevented from developing much further. The reform era has not changed this situation in fundamental ways, and the bureaucratic gatekeepers in China's cities continue to loom large in the calculations that both parents and their offspring make in this realm. Even if we suspect that the eventual direction of changes in the process of mate choice is predictable from modernization theory, as described above, whether in the near term changes of the sort experienced by other developing countries will be accelerated, stalled, or even reversed can only be understood by examining closely the concrete structures of Chinese urban society and how these affect different aspects of the mate-choice process.

New Options for the Urban Elderly

CHARLOTTE IKELS

"OLD PEOPLE—A NEW PROBLEM FOR SOCIETY" [1]

It is 9:50 A.M., and the dance floor on the balcony of the Xinhua movie theater is alive with fast-moving couples. Thanks to the air-conditioning, they waltz and tango their way across the darkened room, oblivious to the heat and humidity of a typical July day in Guangzhou. The dancers are all retired workers, mostly in their fifties and early sixties, and predominantly women. They pay 80 fen each time they attend. Across town stands the six-story Guangzhou City Old Cadres' Activity Center, built at a cost of 14 million yuan and officially opened in July 1986. Dancing is also a regular morning activity here, and in addition formal classes in ballroom dancing and disco are available for those lacking confidence in their skills. An annual membership fee of 50 yuan entitles the retired cadre to access to the full range of the center's facilities: restaurant, shop, game rooms, tennis court, swimming pool, library, a daily movie, exercise machines, and the like.

In official circles *activity* is the buzz word now when talking about retired people. It is no longer enough, I was told, for society to be satisfied when it can meet the material needs of the elderly through pensions and health-care plans. Today's elderly have other needs as well: the need to study, the need to contribute, the need for sociability. And—perhaps most important of all but seldom directly stated—the need to avoid causing problems for the rest of us. Keeping active in retirement helps the elderly in two ways: (1) It stimulates their bodies, keeping them healthy and even restoring to health those suffering from lethargy and a host of other physical maladies. (2) It stimulates their minds by bringing them into contact with others and keeping them engaged in local and national affairs where their (voluntary) contributions toward the Four Modernizations are welcome.

The elderly are perceived as a "new problem" by the state primarily because of their rapidly increasing numbers and because of their entitlements to pensions and medical coverage, the financing of which competes with investments considered desirable for economic growth. The elderly are also viewed as potential liabilities to families who may find themselves overwhelmed by their efforts to meet the long-term needs of the ill or disabled elderly. My purpose here is to examine the actual circumstances of the elderly in the city of Guangzhou (Canton), the capital of Guangdong Province, and to determine the magnitude of this "new problem" for the state and for families by paying particular attention to how cost-consciousness brought about by the post-1977 reforms has affected their situation.

Although I use some national-level data to illustrate points and to place Guangzhou in perspective, my focus is on the urban elderly. The circumstances of the rural elderly, whose income and medical resources are quite different from and generally inferior to those of the urban elderly, will not be discussed.[2] Moreover, economic reform in Guangdong has been allowed to proceed further than in most other provinces;[3] therefore local enterprises and government organs became aware quite early of the difficulties inherent in trying simultaneously to increase wages and to meet financial obligations to retirees. Also important to note is that Guangdong has had much greater access than other provinces to ideas and investments from abroad. The vast majority of Hong Kong residents and overseas Chinese have their origins in Guangdong and maintain contact with their local relatives. Consequently Guangdong residents may be exceptionally open in their willingness to experiment with novel solutions to the "new problem" of old people.

THE IMPACT OF AN AGING POPULATION
ON THE ECONOMY

The early 1980s witnessed a surge in local and national attention to the new problem of the elderly because of increased awareness of the actual aging of the population and concern that this aging population would place enormous fiscal demands on the state—possibly undermining China's efforts at economic development. Numerous writers have pointed out how improvements in life expectancy (from 35 in pre-1949 China to nearly 70 by the mid-1980s) have contributed to the growth of the aged population, but they emphasize that the major reason for this rapid growth is the success of the family-planning program.[4] Over the short span of twenty-three years the proportion of the population under the age of 15 dropped dramatically from 40.5 percent to 28.8 percent whereas the proportion of those aged 65 or older increased from 3.6 percent to 5.5 percent (see Table 1).

These percentages, however, seriously understate the magnitude of the problem. Over the same twenty-three-year period the actual number of people in the oldest age category rose from 24.7 million to nearly 59 million, with major implications for the dependency ratio.[5] In addition, as a result of the 1978 reforms a substantial number of workers were encouraged to take *early* retirement resulting in rapid increases in the worker-to-retiree ratio. As Deborah Davis points out, in 1978 this ratio was 33 : 1, but by the end of 1985 it had fallen to 13 : 1, and in some of the oldest industries to 5 : 1.[6]

Pensions are not the only financial drain faced by enterprises with a large number of retirees. Because illness and disability are closely correlated with age, enterprises also have to expend large sums on health care for their elderly retirees. While it is difficult to obtain figures that break down medical costs by age of consumer, the fact that medical costs have escalated enormously poses serious problems for all work units. In Guangdong the annual costs of operating the state medical-coverage program (*gongfei yiliao*) soared from 41 million yuan in 1980 to 190 million in 1986, and provincial per capita expenditures rose from 49.72 to 147

TABLE 1 Changes in National Population Age Structure

Age (in years)	1953 N (in thousands)	1953 %	1964 N (in thousands)	1964 %	1982 N (in thousands)	1982 %	1987 N (in thousands)	1987 %
0–14	206,845	35.7	281,650	40.5	337,251	33.5	308,067	28.8
15–64	347,558	59.9	388,608	55.9	621,506	61.7	703,863	65.7
65 and older	25,401	4.4	24,687	3.6	49,366	4.9	58,700	5.5
(60 and older)[a]	(42,142)	(7.3)	(42,427)	(6.1)	(76,749)	(7.6)	—	—

Source: For 1953, 1964, and 1982, Jersey Liang, Edward Jow-Ching Tu, and Xiangming Chen, "Population Aging in the People's Republic of China," Social Science and Medicine 23:1354 (1986); for 1987, State Statistical Bureau, "China's Population Structure," Beijing Review, 5–11 December, 1988, p. 31.

a. Most references by the Chinese to the elderly population are to those 60 and older. Thus the perceived "problem" is greater than the 5.5 percent that is 65 and older.

yuan in the same period. Nationally the 1986 per capita state expenditure was 73 yuan.[7]

Additional post-Mao reforms affecting wages and prices also threatened to overwhelm state and provincial budgets and to erode the value of the pensions received by the elderly. From 1962 to 1978 workers' wages had been essentially frozen and ranged from a low of 32 yuan for those in grade 1 to a high of 104 yuan for those in grade 8.[8] Then in late 1977 Yu Qiuli, chairman of the State Planning Commission, announced that about 60 percent of the nonagricultural work force would be advanced one salary grade. At about the same time, bonus schemes were being introduced on a trial basis. The bonus system was rapidly expanded, and by 1985 urban state workers in Guangdong derived 22.4 percent of their monthly wage income from bonuses, 58.5 percent from their basic wage, 16.7 percent from subsidies, and 2.4 percent from other sources such as overtime. Similarly, urban workers in the collective sector in Guangdong derived 24.9 percent of their monthly wage from bonuses, 61 percent from their basic wage, 12.5 percent from subsidies, and 1.6 percent from other sources.[9] Pensions, however, continued to be based on the basic wage.

Yet decisions made in 1982 to begin releasing price controls meant that whatever wage gains workers made were endangered by inflation. Nationally consumer panic was already setting in in 1987 when, during the first six months of the year, the retail price index rose 11.1 percent and intensified one year later (July 1988), when it rose another 19.2 percent—the greatest increase since 1949. In some areas the inflation was in fact much worse. The indices in the urban areas of Guangdong and Fujian went up nearly 31 percent between mid-1987 and mid-1988.[10] Tables 2 and 3 demonstrate that per capita income has just managed to stay ahead of expenditures and that food continues to be the major expense facing urban families. On the other hand, the standard of living has been steadily rising, and nowhere is this better demonstrated than in the acquisition of household appliances and other durable goods (see Table 4).

By the mid-1980s the rapid growth in the absolute number of retired and/or dependent elderly was perceived as a major financial burden to the state and its enterprises. The expected growth in their health care needs was seen as an important contributor to the accelerating expenses encountered by the various medical benefits plans. Yet the overall value of the pension income of the elderly relative to the income of those still in

TABLE 2 Guangzhou City Proper,
Monthly per Capita
Income and Expenditure
(in yuan)

Year	Income[a]	Expenditure[b]
1977	32.89	—
1980	46.21	43.42
1981	51.68	47.93
1982	58.27	54.21
1983	61.16	59.56
1984	69.81	67.84
1985	87.21	84.29
1986	102.51	98.99
1987	117.95	114.56

Sources: For 1977–1986, *Guangzhou nianjian 1987*
(Guangzhou annual 1987), table on, p. 441;
for 1987, *Guangzhou tongji nianjian 1988*
(Guangzhou statistical annual 1988), pp. 366–
368.

a. Refers to living-expense income *(shenghuofei shouru)*,
including basic wage, bonus, subsidies, pensions,
and other employment-generated expendable income. Not included is income from remittances,
savings, or unreported private-economic activity.
b. Refers to living-expense outlay *(shenghuofei zhichu)*,
including items such as foodstuffs, clothing, daily
necessities, and durable consumer goods as well as
water, electricity, rental, transport, educational,
and recreational fees.

the labor force was decreasing, and the absolute value of pensions, particularly of those of the oldest elderly, was being eroded as the inflation
rate soared. The state faced two seemingly irreconcilable questions: How
could China's elderly enjoy their twilight years under the threat of financial hardship, and how could the state alleviate this financial insecurity
without threatening its own goals for economic development?

SHARING THE COSTS OF AN AGING POPULATION

The Chinese have a new catch phrase to describe their dilemma: "Unlike
the West, which developed first and then aged, China has aged first and
is still developing." This reversal has been interpreted to mean that China

TABLE 3 Guangzhou City Proper, Monthly per Capita
Expenditures (in yuan)

Type of Expenditure	1980	1985	1986	1987
Consumer goods	40.19	76.14	88.65	102.03
Food	30.81	53.13	61.22	70.18
Clothing	4.48	5.94	6.80	7.42
Daily necessities	4.90	17.07	20.63	24.43
Other expenses[a]	3.23	8.15	10.34	12.53
Total expenditures	43.42	84.29	98.99	114.56

Source: For 1980, 1985, and 1986, Guangzhou nianjian 1987, table on p. 443; for 1987, Guangzhou tongji nianjian 1988, pp. 368–371.
a. Includes water, electricity, rent, transport, education, recreation, repair, and service fees.

is not in a position to adopt the costly medical and social-service programs characteristic of some Western countries. Indeed, China sees Japan as the country whose experience most closely parallels its own, a relatively rapid aging of the population in the context of a rhetoric of filial piety. Accordingly the Chinese government has attempted to reduce the state's share of current and anticipated costs by spreading the burden more equitably—by addressing the issue of uneven pension burden, by introducing copayments into medical benefits programs, by targeting selected segments of the elderly population for special services, by reminding families of their filial obligations, and by encouraging the elderly

TABLE 4 Guangzhou City Proper, Number of Appliances per
100 Households

Appliance	1980	1982	1984	1986	1987
Bicycles	140.0	156.5	182.5	183.0	192.3
Electric fans	98.5	166.0	204.5	269.3	299.0
Washing machines	1.5	20.5	59.0	68.0	74.3
Refrigerators	0.0	4.0	28.0	52.0	59.3
Black-and-white TVs	49.5	79.5	83.5	67.0	62.0
Color TVs	1.5	4.0	19.5	46.0	57.0
Tape recorders	31.0	63.0	85.5	99.0	104.6

Source: For 1980–1986, Guangzhou nianjian 1987, table on p. 444; for 1987, Guangzhou tongji nianjian 1988, pp. 372–374.

themselves to be resources rather than liabilities to their families and communities.

Pension Reform

One way to reduce pension costs, of course, would be to retain the elderly in the state labor force by raising the age of retirement; but given current official concern with youth unemployment, it is highly unlikely that this option will be explored.[11] Furthermore, there are other reasons for removing the elderly from the state labor force. First, because of their lack of technical training and their presumed adherence to doing things the old way, the elderly cannot contribute as the young can to innovation. Of course, one cannot speak simply of "the elderly." As many writers point out, there are subcategories of the elderly who can play a significant role in the modernization process.[12] The highly educated can translate foreign works, cultivate ties with their former universities if they studied abroad, and train their own replacements. Only a small minority of the elderly are highly trained, however, and presumably most can best serve by creating openings for others or by engaging in private-household economic activity. Second, the elderly in high places are often perceived as both economic and political obstacles to modernization, and their acceptance of retirement has had to be carefully negotiated.[13]

Another possibility, already being tried out in many provinces, is to reduce the inequality of pension burdens borne by diverse state enterprises. The magnitude of this inequality is amply illustrated by Yuan Jihui, who pointed out that in the mid-1980s in the textile industry in Shanghai there were 0.45 million employees and 0.23 million retirees; the pension expenditure was equal to 34.5 percent of the total amount of salaries paid to the work force.[14] In the Second Silk Factory of Wuxi in Jiangsu Province there were 1,470 retirees but only 1,308 employees. The pension expenditure was equal to 89 percent of the salary expenditure for the work force. Newer industries understandably had a more favorable ratio. The pension expenditure in the electronics industry in Wuxi, for example, was equal to only 5 percent of total salaries.

Beginning in the early 1980s the national government endorsed a variety of experiments in shared funding to cope with this unequal distribution of burden. Funds were gradually set up to which all state enterprises within a particular jurisdiction, such as a city district, contribute and which disburse the funds to retirees of the participating enterprises.[15] Ideally the jurisdictions will eventually become more and more comprehensive. The basic aim is gradually to free the individual worker's pension from his specific enterprise and thus to facilitate labor mobility. Certain segments of the elderly population, however, are frequently not covered by pensions at all, as they retired before the maturing of the state and collective pension schemes or never worked in enterprises with pension benefits. Their circumstances will be discussed more fully below.

Health Care Financing

Although inflation was certainly a factor in the escalating costs of health care, Guangdong officials attributed the increase in costs to other unavoidable as well as avoidable causes. Unavoidable causes included the aging of the population as well as related changes in morbidity patterns, that is, a shift from acute infectious diseases requiring one-time medical interventions to chronic conditions, such as heart disease and cancer, requiring multiple interventions. Also unavoidable was the imbalance between the fees charged hospitals by suppliers and the fees charged consumers by hospitals; that is, as a result of price reforms hospitals were caught in the middle between flexible prices on many of the items they needed to purchase and fixed prices on the services they were expected to provide. Among the avoidable causes were unrealistic expectations on the part of consumers, who were said to seek treatment irresponsibly even for trivial ailments, and outright fraud, such as claiming illness when in fact the patient was seeking medications for an uninsured third party. State efforts to cope with these problems are discussed below.

In the fall of 1987 the Guangdong provincial government, following months of negotiations among the concerned government offices, finally introduced modifications in the health care program provided to workers in state offices, schools, hospitals, and the like. To reduce costs these workers now have a 10 percent copayment as outpatients and a 5 percent copayment as inpatients; that is, whereas previously all normal costs (except for a nominal registration fee and hospital meals) were completely covered, now they are only 90–95 percent covered. These rules also apply to retirees of these units except for those who left the work force with *lixiu* (retired party cadre) status,[16] who are to be charged only a 5 percent copayment as outpatients and no copayment as inpatients.[17] State and collective enterprises (above the level of the neighborhood) are also expected to implement these basic reforms.

Smaller collectives, dependent on their own resources for funding, have usually been responsible for setting up their own eligibility rules and benefits systems. Faced with rising costs and demands from workers for higher wages, some collectives have cut back on their health coverage by establishing monthly benefit maximums as low as 3 or 5 yuan, with the individual responsible for all costs above the set amount. Other collectives—and some state enterprises as well—have forbidden their workers and retirees to patronize the lowest-level health care facility, the neighborhood clinic, on the grounds that such facilities overprescribe medication, the sale of which constitutes one of their few sources of income.

Targeting Selected Segments of the Elderly Population

Another cost-cutting measure is to restrict eligibility for certain programs to selected segments of the elderly population. Accordingly the Chinese government has decided that since it cannot afford programs for everyone, political expedience will dictate which categories of elderly will receive special attention: namely, the politically powerful and the childless. Maintaining the good will of the powerful elderly is seen as essential to obtaining their cooperation in stepping back from the "front line" so that a more technically trained and development-oriented leadership can come to the fore. Assuring a minimum standard of living for the childless demonstrates that the state will not jeopardize the lives of those who have accepted the mandate of the One-Child-Family policy and thus presumably will reinforce compliance.

In order to ensure the good will of elderly cadres, the government has made it clear that their roles in the construction of the nation are not to be considered complete upon retirement.[18] Rather, they should view themselves as freed from onerous daily routines so that, with their knowledge and experience, they can make more appropriate contributions to the nation or to their former work units by offering their help when and where it is most needed. Generous pensions and special prerogatives protect them from economic insecurity, and old cadres' activity centers have been built to allow them to maintain their health and to cultivate their minds.

Meeting the needs of the childless elderly means being sure that they receive a certain minimum of food, clothing, shelter, and medical care. In the cities only a very small proportion of the elderly population—

those with no children *and* no responsible unit (former workplace)—qualifies for the designation of relief household. An official of the Guangzhou Civil Affairs Office estimated that there were somewhat over two thousand such old people in the entire city. Such individuals are entitled to 35 yuan a month from the government, but since this is clearly not enough to live on, each neighborhood automatically adds 10 yuan. From the figures in Tables 2 and 3, however, we can see that, while 45 yuan might have offered a decent living standard in the early 1980s, it was totally inadequate by the middle 1980s. On the other hand, relief households do not have to pay rent and receive all their medical care free. They are also eligible to live in a "home of respect for the aged."

Under a national policy dating back to 1983, every urban street committee is expected to provide such a facility for the well elderly if there is a need for it. In 1987 there were thirty-five neighborhood homes of respect for the aged in Guangzhou. Such homes are normally quite small, seldom exceeding ten residents. The three I visited had between three and eight occupants. Residents of neighborhoods lacking such a facility (or who for some reason do not wish to live in their neighborhood home) are eligible to live in the city-run home that opened in 1965 and is located forty kilometers from the city center. It was enlarged in 1985 to some five hundred beds and is clearly a model facility. Like the residents of neighborhood homes, individuals in the city home must be capable of self-care on admission; but unlike the former, should they subsequently require nursing care, three separate levels of care are provided: minimal, intermediate, and skilled. Admission to these nursing divisions is theoretically possible only for those already living in the home. Preference for admission to the city home is given to the relief elderly, but because a surplus of rooms existed in 1987, some 100 of the 430-odd residents were actually fee paying (either personally or via their units).

The vast majority of China's urban elderly fall into neither of these designated categories: they do not occupy high party or government positions nor are they childless. They are retired workers or homemakers with family members in their immediate environment. Policymakers seem to assume that elderly with families are nonproblematic with regard to care and that their families are happy to look after them.[19] In the remainder of this chapter I investigate these assumptions by examining the circumstances of typical urban elderly and their families, the problems they face with aging, and the solutions they manage to piece together.

THE ELDERLY IN A GUANGZHOU NEIGHBORHOOD

I gathered the data on which this section is based between June 1987 and January 1988. A random sample of 200 households containing at least one member 70 years of age or older was drawn from two Guangzhou neighborhoods. The minimum age of 70 was chosen in order to maximize the likelihood of encountering older people who were already experiencing health problems or other age-related difficulties. Each older person (or a proxy in the case of informants too disabled to participate) was interviewed between one and two hours at home. Immediately following the interview with the elder, a younger family member was also briefly interviewed. Although illustrative examples from other parts of Guangzhou are used, statistical data are drawn only from the first neighborhood whose residents were judged representative of the general elderly population. (The residents of the second neighborhood were disproportionately retired cadres and intellectuals.) Unless otherwise stated, the figures used in the tables are absolute numbers. Tables 5 and 6 provide basic sample descriptors.

TABLE 5   Age and Sex Composition

Age (in years)	Male (N = 44)	Female (N = 56)	Total (N = 100)
70–74	20	26	46
75–79	17	14	31
80–84	5	6	11
85 and older	2	10	12

Source: Neighborhood survey, 1987.

Income in Old Age

As these and subsequent tables will demonstrate, people enter old age with substantially different resources. The legacy of differential access to education means that older women are far more likely to be illiterate than older men and that their employment opportunities were thereby severely compromised (see Table 7). Women who had never been in the labor force, who had been petty traders and withdrew from the labor force before collectives were set up, or who had done agricultural work

TABLE 6 Educational Attainment

Level of education	Male (N = 44)	Female (N = 56)	Total (N = 100)
None or less than 4 yr	18	46	64
4 yr to completion of elementary school	14	6	20
Some adult education	1	0	1
Some middle school or equivalent	8	3	11
Completion of upper middle school	0	1	1
Post-secondary degree holder	3	0	3

Source: Neighborhood survey, 1987.

in the countryside before coming to Guangzhou in late middle age to look after grandchildren are not officially entitled to any pensions, as they have no responsible units and are not normally entitled to a share of their husband's pension after their husband's death, even had he been a state employee.

Even among elderly men and women who do have work units, substantial differences exist in pension income (see Table 8). These differences are a function of the nature of the unit from which the individual retired (government office, state enterprise, or collective), the number of years he or she worked for that unit, and the timing of retirement. Informants in their eighties, for example, who in some cases retired more than twenty years ago, were not in a position to acquire much seniority within units that were established only in the late 1950s. Consequently they are often eligible for only 60 percent of their previous wages. Fur-

TABLE 7 Previous Type of Work

Previous Work	Male (N = 44)	Female (N = 56)	Total (N = 100)
Not in labor force/at home	0	24	24
Production, transport, and related work	22	18	40
Service (servant, maintenance, restaurant)	8	8	16
Clerical work	3	1	4
Cadre	7	0	7
Specialist of technical work	4	2	6
Unknown	0	3	3

Source: Neighborhood survey, 1987.

TABLE 8 Monthly Income (Pension and Subsidies)

Income (in yuan)	Male (N = 44)	Female (N = 56)	Total (N = 100)
0	3	32	35
Less than 50	5	5	10
50–74	9	10	19
75–99	11	8	19
100–149	10	1	11
150–199	3	0	3
200 and more	3	0	3

Source: Neighborhood survey, 1987.

thermore, the wages of those who retired in the 1960s and 1970s were considerably lower than those who retired in the 1980s after wage reform. In 1983, to compensate for increases in the cost of living, the provincial government granted an increase of 10 yuan a month to all (state) pensioners, and in 1985 an increase of 17 yuan a month. Individual units also sometimes add subsidies to the monthly pension by providing a few yuan to help meet electricity, rent, or water fees. All these subsidies are included in the amounts listed in Table 8. Retired workers, however, are no longer eligible for the transport and clothing subsidies that those still employed may be receiving.

When the Chinese talk about pension burdens, it is not the population over 70 that is currently the problem but the population between 50 and 70. Similarly, when scholars point out that the income of some retirees is substantially greater than that of their adult children (largely because of seniority-based wages), they are also generally referring to the population between 50 and 70.[20] The few older exceptions to this age-based phenomenon are those individuals (mostly cadres) in their seventies and eighties who resisted retiring until Deng turned the pressure on in the early 1980s. As we saw above, this privileged cohort is beginning to lose its relative advantage over the young owing to the expansion of the bonus system.

Many of my noncadre informants resisted retiring also because they wanted to work until they were eligible for a higher percentage of their wages, because they still had dependent children, or because they wanted to wait until a child was able to replace them. Alternative sources of income are scarce for this age group. Although some did attempt to find new work after retirement, most did not, because they were already too worn out. Only a very few informants were working at the time of the interview, and most were not in highly sought-after positions. Typical postretirement positions included collecting fees at a bicycle parking lot, opening up the neighborhood market for early-morning produce deliveries, and supervising a collection depot for used household items.

Those elderly without pensions were usually entirely dependent financially on their children. A very small number owned the buildings in which they lived and were entitled to receive rents from other occupants of the structure. The rents they received were, however, very modest. At least one couple who had been banished to the countryside during the Cultural Revolution but had since had their rights restored banked the back wages they had been handed and were receiving some income in the form of interest.

Physical Status in Old Age

The elderly in Guangzhou die from much the same causes as the elderly in the United States. According to statistics from the provincial Public Health Department, in 1986 the leading causes of death for people of all ages in Guangzhou were, in rank order, cancer, heart diseases, respiratory diseases (emphysema, chronic bronchitis, and pneumonia), cerebrovascular diseases, digestive tract diseases, and tuberculosis. For those 75 years of age and older the order was somewhat different: cancer moved to fourth place behind heart, respiratory, and cerebrovascular diseases. Except for those individuals who die quickly from a first unexpected heart attack, most elderly will experience long periods of disability as they cope with heart, lung, or circulatory failure. Although they do not necessarily require hospitalization except during acute episodes, they do require substantial assistance in living in the community and meeting their daily needs.

Similarly, individuals with visual, mobility, or mental impairments also require major assistance from others. Tables 9, 10, and 11 show the reported prevalence of these conditions in the sample population. The figures reported in these tables, particularly with regard to vision and cognitive function, probably understate the actual magnitude of the impairments, as many older people have very modest standards for how well the body can be expected to function.

TABLE 9 Degree of Visual Impairment

| Age (in years) | Degree of Impairment | | | | No. of Informants |
	None	Minor	Moderate	Major	
70–74	36	6	3	1	46
75–79	17	6	7	1	31
80–84	7	0	1	1	9
85 and older	3	1	5	1	10
Total	66	12	14	4	96

Source: Neighborhood survey, 1987.
Note: Four of the sample of 100 cases could not be evaluated.

To assess visual functioning, I asked the informants general questions such as "How are your eyes?" and "Can you see television clearly?" These kinds of question generate subjective evaluations that are conditioned both by expectations of how well a person of 80 years could be expected to see and by how much poor vision actually interferes with the individual's daily life, that is, translates into disability.[21] Residents of Guangdong, along with residents of Tibet, have the highest prevalence of cataracts in all of China, and, indeed, many of my informants stated that they had cataracts and took eye drops because of them. Yet many of these same people maintained that their vision was fine. Similarly, many old people proudly noted that unlike others they could still thread a needle with no difficulty. Yet this ability could be a function of lifelong nearsightedness never diagnosed.

Mobility impairments—that is, impairments that affect a person's ability

TABLE 10 Degree of Mobility Impairment

| Age (in years) | Degree of Impairment | | | | No. of Informants |
	None	Minor	Moderate	Major	
70–74	29	10	4	3	46
75–79	13	10	4	4	31
80–84	4	0	1	6	11
85 and older	0	1	5	6	12
Total	46	21	14	19	100

Source: Neighborhood survey, 1987.

TABLE 11 Degree of Mental Impairment

Age (in years)	Degree of Impairment				No. of Informants
	None	Minor	Moderate	Major	
70–74	38	5	1	0	44
75–79	28	1	0	0	29
80–84	4	2	1	3	10
85 and older	2	1	3	2	8
Total	72	9	5	5	91

Source: Neighborhood survey, 1987.
Note: Nine of the sample of 100 cases could not be evaluated.

to get around—were the easiest to confirm. I could see that the informant could not get out of the chair without assistance or needed a cane to cross the room. Skeletal problems were the leading cause of mobility difficulties, but arteriosclerosis (resulting in extreme weakness in the legs), respiratory ailments (making it impossible to climb stairs), visual decrements, and the like were also contributing factors.

In the case of mental impairments, I relied on the ability of the person to recall recent events and long-past events and to participate in the interview itself. One part of the interview involved asking the informant to analyze a set of short stories about an older person with a problem and to propose a solution for each story. A number of individuals whose memories I could not independently verify by checking with family members were judged impaired on the basis of their performance on the stories (performance was essentially independent of level of education). In some cases estimation of visual or mental acuity was impossible because of the older person's deafness or illness. Several of the elderly were noticeably impaired, but since the degree of impairment could not easily be determined, they were not rated on this dimension.

Personnel from the residents committees who were helping to arrange the interviews sometimes forewarned me that certain interviews were likely to be unproductive, as the target older person was mentally deficient. Nevertheless, all such persons were contacted, though if unable to participate themselves, they were indirectly interviewed through a family member. At the grass-roots level there is ample familiarity with the phenomenon of dementia. *Biantai* (abnormal, anomalous), *chidun* (slow in thought or action), *hutu* (confused, bewildered), *lao mengdong* (muddled, ignorant), and *sha* (stupid, muddle-headed) were among the wide range of terms used to describe older people whose mental faculties or personalities had deteriorated. Cantonese terms for which no exact Mandarin equivalent could be found included *chijo sin* (to have become ridiculous or idiotic) and *leuhnjeuhn* (clumsy in physical or mental performance).

As can be clearly seen from these tables, the degree of impairment, particularly in terms of mobility and mental function, increases substantially with age, posing serious problems for the affected individuals as well as for their families. Of the 100 elderly residents in this ordinary urban neighborhood, 1 was completely bedridden and 18 more were housebound. Housebound in this context describes individuals who could not leave their homes without assistance or who ventured out on their own less than once a month. Without families, and in some cases even with them, such individuals lead extremely limited lives.

Health Care in Old Age

Despite the fact that work units are the usual source of health insurance, older people without their own work units may still be eligible for some health coverage via a child's work unit. Government offices and state enterprises, for example, allow an adult child to carry a parent as a dependent provided that the parent has no responsible unit. This type of coverage normally pays 50 percent of the dependent's medical expenses, but it is not available to a parent with a former work unit even if that unit is so impoverished that it does not offer medical coverage. Even under the state system, however, when the child retires, the parent's coverage is usually discontinued. Unfortunately, such parents are naturally among the oldest and presumably the most medically needy. Just when they need coverage the most—in their eighties—they become ineligible as all their children retire.

I encountered a few cases in which older people had indeed outlived their eligibility for medical coverage in just this way. One was able to transfer to a grandchild's plan. In another the informant's only daughter pleaded with the unit to retain her mother's coverage, as there was no other alternative, so the unit agreed. But some disenfranchised dependents and their families have no recourse but to assume responsibility for all costs. If the children are not employed in the state sector, their units usually do not allow them to include their parents as dependents at any point. Table 12 describes the kinds of coverage found among this sample.

TABLE 12 Amount of Medical Coverage

Coverage	Males (N = 44)	Females (N = 56)	Total (N = 100)
No coverage	3	11	14
Fixed monthly maximum	3	3	6
Sliding percentage	1	1	2
50% (Dependent coverage)	1	17	18
51%–89%	4	3	7
90%–100%	32	20	52
Unknown	0	1	1

Source: Neighborhood survey, 1987.

Among those with no coverage were two or three individuals who actually could have been included as dependents on their children's coverage. Because the children's units required the first visit for any medical problem to be made at the unit clinic far from the parental home, the parents had decided it was not worth the bother to seek coverage. They preferred to go to the local public health clinic or to a nearby hospital, even if they had to pay the fees themselves. For routine ailments these fees are very low. In fact hospitals have a two-tier payment scheme, with lower prices for some services and medications charged to patients with no coverage.

On the other hand, nonroutine events and services can be very expensive. For example, one 83-year-old woman suffered a stroke and was admitted to the Guangzhou No. 1 Hospital very near her home a year prior to the interview. She had never been employed, and all three of her children (one in his sixties and two in their fifties) were retired, so she had no medical coverage. During her slightly more than a month of hospitalization, her children chipped in to pay the hospital more than 1,000 yuan, but they did not feel they could pay much more. Consequently they carried her home on a stretcher, and her coresident retired daughter looked after her.

Hospitalization even when nearly completely covered can nevertheless constitute a major burden on a family, as the hospital assumes that a family member will be present throughout the day and, in the case of the severely ill, throughout the night to minister to the patient. I encountered several elderly women near exhaustion from providing care to hospitalized or at-home bedridden spouses. In theory if a family member is not available to provide 24-hour care in the hospital, a *baomu* (nurse-maid) can be hired as a replacement. According to the manager of the Home Labor Service Company of Liwan District, which recruits such workers, the wages vary by skill, but typically someone working a 12-hour shift would probably earn 8 yuan a day, and someone working a 24-hour shift would earn 15 yuan a day. Someone who had a long-term contract with a particular family would probably make about 200 yuan a month. Given that monthly per capita income in Guangzhou City proper was estimated to be 117.95 yuan in 1987 (see Table 2), these expenses, which are not normally covered by unit health plans, impose a serious financial burden on families who must provide long-term care, whether in the hospital or in their own homes, as the following two cases illustrate.

Following hospital discharge, most stroke victims continue to need a great deal of attention at home. One elderly woman, for example, required 24-hour care, and in the course of two years her relatives ran through seven *baomu*. The old woman was irascible and demanding—for example, she would send people out in the middle of the night to fetch a bowl of noodles and would accuse the *baomu* of stealing her things. Her daughters paid the *baomu* 50 yuan a month straight wage and an additional 25 yuan to cover the costs of partial night duty, and they provided food and shelter. Total monthly costs were around 100 yuan.

Not only are *baomu* expensive, but they are very difficult to obtain. Just about no one in Guangzhou, and recently—thanks to economic growth—just about no one in Guangdong Province, is interested in this type of work. Most *baomu* are recruited from Guangxi and Hunan, and even they switch to factory jobs as soon as they see a good opportunity. Another informant who had already run through three *baomu* whom he and his siblings had hired to look after their frail parents, both of whom were in their eighties, lamented that they do not make *baomu* like they used to:

The standards the *baomu* set are hard for most families to meet. First, you have to provide them with a place to live. Second, they want to eat the same things you do. Third, they are not content with 30 or 40 yuan as in the past but require a wage at least as high as 100 yuan a month. Fourth, they require you to spell out the number of hours a day they are actually supposed to be on duty.

All neighborhood clinics are supposed to operate a Home Sickbed program, and the elderly are the primary service beneficiaries. Each clinic normally assigns one physician for a several-month tour of duty about the neighborhood. Being elderly is not a sufficient condition to merit a visit. One must be unable to get to the clinic, before a physician will be sent. Such doctors tend to discharged hospital patients, acute cases, and emergency cases. A nurse assistant is more likely to be sent out to monitor the routinely chronically ill, though the physician will go if there is a complication. Some medical plans reimburse for home visits, others do not.

Family Life in Old Age

As with pensions and health coverage, there are gender differences in opportunities for family life in old age. As in most other countries, elderly men in China are far more likely to be living with wives than elderly women are to be living with husbands. Higher age-specific death rates for men, the tendency of women to marry men older than themselves, and the greater permission given to men to remarry all conspire to produce a surplus of widows in old age (see Table 13). Consequently, when caregiving involves old men, the caregivers are usually their wives, but when caregiving involves old women, the caregivers are usually their children. Thus, from the point of view of the younger generation, the problematic parent is most likely to be the mother.

TABLE 13 Marital Status

Marital Status	Male (N = 44)	Female (N = 56)	Total (N = 100)
Married	27	9	36
Married, living separately	9	4	9
Widowed (including 1 divorce)	12	43	55

Source: Neighborhood survey, 1987.
Note: The majority of the sample live with children or other relatives; 12 percent live alone; and 7 percent live as couples.

Coresidence with children is not a simple expression of the wish of parents to live with their children or vice versa. In many cases families must stay together because of the housing shortage. In some cases married children (who actually live elsewhere) have retained household registration with their parents in order to register their own children locally.

TABLE 14 Living Arrangements

Living Arrangement	Male (N=44)	Female (N=56)	Total (N=100)
Alone	7	5	12
Couple only	5	2	7
With unmarried child(ren)	6	4	11
With unmarried child(ren) and a married child	3	1	4
With a married child	12	30	42
With a married child but eating separately	2	1	3
With two married children	6	4	10
With a grandchild or other junior relative	3	8	11
With other relatives	0	1	1

Source: Neighborhood survey, 1987.

Local registration means that the child may attend the nearby grade school and stay with the grandparents once school gets out. In fact the provision of child care is a major benefit of continued coresidence with parents.

These high rates of coresidence with children and grandchildren contrast markedly with the situation in the United States and play a major role in reducing the impact of impairments on daily life. In the United States even modest levels of impairment in mobility or mental functioning may seriously compromise an older person's ability to maintain an independent household. A host of informal arrangements and formal programs have been developed in the United States in order to enable an impaired older person to continue "independent living." In China independent living for the elderly is seldom viewed as a desirable goal. As Table 14 points out, only 19 percent of the sample live in a household without younger people. Consequently, when an older person slows down, there are others who can gradually pick up the tasks he or she is no longer able to perform with minimal disruption to their own or the elder's routine.

The psychological concomitants of impairment are less devastating to the elderly in China than in the United States because the two societies value independent living differently and because the actual readjustments required are less drastic; for example, the Chinese elder resigns herself to giving up the daily marketing and cooking, whereas the American may have to consider giving up her home and moving many miles to join a child or entering an institution. Furthermore, family care in China usually can be provided—at least at the moment—at less cost to the family as a whole than in the United States. This is so primarily because those providing the care, women in their fifties, are highly likely to be already retired and receiving pensions and health coverage. In the United States, in contrast, unless they have been lifelong homemakers, women in their fifties are still employed. If they give up their jobs to look after a parent, they forfeit their current income, reduce their eligibility for future retirement income, and lose their employer-sponsored health coverage as well. If, in an effort to cut down on pension burdens, China raises the retirement age for women, family care giving will become a much more difficult undertaking.

For those currently in the labor force, this difficulty already exists. One 52-year-old kindergarten teacher, for example, has complete responsibility for her bedridden mother's daily care, including bathing and toileting. The mother spends day and night on her back in a room no larger than a queen-sized bed. She has no television and no view, but it scarcely matters, as she has cataracts in both eyes and can barely see anyway. She has no friends and no small grandchildren to keep her company. Thanks to the housing shortage, she does have an elderly cotenant who comes by in the afternoon to give her the medicine that her daughter set cooking during the lunch hour. No one is happy with this situation, but they can see no other solution.

New Options for the Elderly

It is too late for the kindergarten teacher's family, but Chinese policymakers have recently been wrestling with these problems. They have looked far down the road and seen the specter of one couple looking after four (or even more) old people and have realized that old people are themselves the solution. How can this be?

Although earlier I focused on physical impairments, I should point out that most of the elderly do not in fact perceive themselves as especially impaired. Of the 100 older people in this neighborhood, nearly one-third (31) claimed to have no impairments at all (not even impaired hearing, which I also investigated). Those in their sixties are presumably in even better shape. Such individuals can easily make major contributions to the household, and many were entirely responsible for the marketing, cooking, and management of the home, and, as already noted, elderly women are in fact the primary caregivers for elderly men. Clearly, then, remarriage is the solution of choice.

In publicizing this solution, of course, the caregiving element is not so baldly expressed: articles attempting to popularize remarriage of the elderly speak more of sentiment, common interests, and companionship.[22] In December 1985 the Beijing People's Art Theater staged a play by Li Wanfen entitled *The Morning Strollers,* dealing with elderly romance. A longtime widow is courted by a never-married gardner, but despite an unhappy home situation she is reluctant to marry him for fear that people will laugh at her. Eventually she is persuaded to marry him by her morning exercise companions (the "morning strollers" of the title). According to Lu Panqing and Li Ning, since 1984 matchmaking services exclusively for older people (presumably aged 50 and older) have been set up in thirteen Chinese cities, including Beijing, Tianjin, Xian, and Chengdu.[23] In the short span of three years the Xian service was utilized by four thousand clients.

Remarriage of the elderly has not been eagerly supported by everyone. Not only are many elderly afraid of being "laughed at," but their children frequently raise objections. In a 1981 article entitled "Children Should Not Interfere in the Marriage of Parents," Deng Weizhi set out the ground rules governing remarriage of the elderly:

Strictly speaking, middle-aged and the elderly in remarriage are the same as youth falling in love; it's normal. The marriage law only limits the minimum age, not the maximum. Consequently, as long as it is not a case of an old, useless man, who moves like a log, teasing a lass of eighteen, there should be no obstruction. Actually, even in the case of "a white-haired seeking one with ruddy complexion," it is not against the law. In such cases, one can only persuade but not obstruct . . . Even if suddenly one feels the arrival of a stranger in the house which breaks the equilibrium of the family situation, the sight of which one cannot stand, it is still for the sake of the happiness of the elders; one must strive to adjust to the new family environment.[24]

Children's opposition is usually laid to "feudal ideas" or to coveting a parent's property. Not mentioned, but certainly worth considering, are some children's fears about the long-term outcome of parental remarriage in old age. The logic might run something like this: "Right now I just have my parent to look after. If he/she marries this widow/widower, when my parent dies, I might still have to look after this stranger."

In order to discover the attitudes of both young and old Guangzhou

TABLE 15 Advice to a Widow about Remarrying

	Males		Females	
Advice	*Younger* (N/%)	*Older* (N/%)	*Younger* (N/%)	*Older* (N/%)
Need more information	0/0	1/1.6	0/0	0/0
Do not remarry	6/20	15/40	8/17	30/75
Persuade son to agree	4/13	5/13	7/15	3/7.5
Elderly are free to remarry	3/10	3/8	1/2	0/0
Weigh things carefully	9/30	8/21	19/40	4/10
Remarry	8/27	6/15.7	12/26	3/7.5
Total	30/100	38/100.3	47/100	40/100

Source: Neighborhood survey, 1987.

Note: Percentage errors are due to rounding.

residents on this issue, I presented my informants and a younger family member (separately) with a story in which a longtime widow had an opportunity to remarry but was encountering opposition from her son. Given these circumstances, I asked, what should the widow do? According to the findings shown in Table 15, the modal response for older informants was to yield to the son, whereas for younger informants it was to advise the widow to weigh all the alternatives and then make her own decision. Missing from this table is the intense emotion that accompanied some of the responses of the older people. More than one elderly female reacted with shock when I reached the point in the story where "in fact Mr. Lo wants to marry Mrs. Lee." Several older men reacted indignantly to the son's opposition.

The reluctance of the older women to encourage the widow to go forward stemmed from a variety of factors. Those who expressed shock at the very fact of the marriage proposal (even before the son's opposition was stated) were, indeed, victims of the "feudal mentality" that in theory at least forbade remarriage of widows. Most older women, however, had far more practical reasons for rejecting remarriage. "Why look for trouble?" they asked. One elderly woman demanded to know who was going to look after whom in such an arrangement. She had barely been able to manage her own now-deceased husband's hospitalization. Most elderly women wondered why anyone would risk what was clearly her most reliable resource in old age: her son's good will.

Unrelated older people, drawn together through formal organizations, are another potential source of companionship and help. Liu describes the Linghai Old People's Society of Guangzhou as the first citywide old people's organization in China.[25] It was founded in 1982 to give Guangzhou's elderly more opportunities for social contact, to safeguard their legal rights, and to offer advice on family and employment problems. In 1987 Linghai opened a new kind of facility for China—an eight-story building of which three serve as a retirement home for older people. Women aged 55 and older and men aged 60 and older who are capable of self-care but do not have children to look after them or whose children live elsewhere are eligible to become residents.

Unlike traditional homes of respect for the aged, this facility charges fees and does not cater to elderly on relief. Residents pay a one-time fee (4,000 yuan for a single person and 6,000 yuan for a couple) that entitles them to live in the facility for the rest of their lives, as well as a monthly service charge (28 yuan for a single person and 40 yuan for a couple). This charge covers maid service, the security guard in the main entrance, and maintenance services such as plumbing repairs. The facility can house between thirty and forty residents, depending on whether the rooms are occupied by couples or singles. Most of the residents I encountered were retired schoolteachers, cadres, and intellectuals. To subsidize its services, Linghai rents out two floors to other organizations and rents the rooms on one floor as hotel rooms.

A second innovative housing arrangement is the so-called elderly care center. In May 1987 the *Yangcheng wanbao* carried an article introducing the center to the public. The response was so overwhelming that two months later (13 July) the newspaper published another article, with the dramatic headline: "Why Do Three Hundred Old People Want to Enter an Elderly Care Center?" The center was the brainchild of one neighborhood committee which discovered, on the completion of its neighborhood home of respect for the aged, that there were not enough relief elderly to fill it. They decided to open it to other elderly who would pay a modest fee for a temporary stay. To their surprise they received a great many inquiries not only from the elderly but also from family members of the elderly who thought this was an idea whose time had come. The major reasons people gave for wishing to live in the home were loneliness, poor living conditions, and disturbed family relationships. As the requests to move into this home suggest, there is an unmet need for special living arrangements for the elderly. Residents of both this facility and the Linghai one were very positive about the benefits of living with their peers.

Conspicuously absent from these living arrangements are any for those incapable of self-care, that is, the seriously impaired. Whereas the acutely ill have hospitals all around the city, the nearest that the chronically ill or disabled have to a facility of their own is the Longevity Hospital, a private geriatric facility, which opened in July 1983. It is, however, widely regarded as a hospital for the terminally ill (it has beds explicitly reserved for advanced cancer patients) and therefore is not favored by those who do not perceive their conditions as terminal.

POLICY OPTIONS

The Chinese are currently developing a range of solutions to keep the rapid aging of the population from interfering with economic development. First and foremost, the elderly are encouraged to retire when they are perceived as hindering the achievement of national goals and encouraged to delay retirement or to seek reemployment when perceived as capable of contributing. Second, once retired, they are encouraged to remain physically fit as long as possible—thus the emphasis on activities such as dancing and sports. Third, they are encouraged to take some of the pressure for socialization off the younger generation by involving themselves heavily with their peers, either as spouses or as companions. Fourth, the younger generation is constantly reminded that filial care is the quintessence of Chinese culture and that the government cannot be expected to bear much of the financial burden of supporting the elderly beyond their pensions and acute-care costs.

Yet none of these recommendations can really help families with a severely impaired older member. Fortunately there are at least three low-cost ways of assisting families in this kind of situation. The first is to grant paid leaves of absence to family caregivers who are not yet eligible to retire. Should the Chinese government, in the interest of keeping down pension costs, decide to raise the age of retirement for women, a paid-leave policy for caregivers (not limited to women) would still allow for meeting the needs of the disabled elderly. In a family with several potential caregivers, paid leaves could be provided on a rotating basis so that no single work unit would have to incur all the costs and inconveniences of the temporary absence of a worker.

A second possibility is to take a lesson from the neighborhood committee that opened up its home of respect for the relief aged to other elderly. Although the elderly care center required its residents to be capable of self-care, there is no reason why this limitation could not be removed in some cases, provided that a family member continued to supply the bulk of the care. Alternatively the neighborhood committee could hire someone to look in on the impaired residents several times a day while their family members are at work. This type of arrangement has benefits for both the old person and the caregiver. The old person is not isolated during the day, and the caregiver is given respite by not having to be in attendance all day and all night.

Third, it seems reasonable to consider a service-credit-bank type of program. This concept is currently being tried out in some localities in the United States.[26] Basically, a volunteer contributes several hours of service monthly and earns credits to be redeemed when he or she needs them. Thus, for example, instead of dancing in ballrooms or sitting in the park, the healthy elderly could provide services to other elderly in the knowledge that they were protecting themselves and their families from the heavy burdens of their own eventual ill health. Variations on the service-credit theme could include having younger people, such as youth awaiting employment, provide services to the elderly with the option of transferring their hours of service entitlement to their own family elders. Under these sorts of arrangements the elderly can stay in their own neighborhoods and be looked after by people from their own families or from among their neighbors. Careful use of these diverse options could reduce the likelihood that providing care for China's elderly would come to be viewed primarily in terms of its possibly detrimental effects on economic development.

The Spiritual Crisis of China's Intellectuals

RICHARD MADSEN

The Maoists used to claim that the Cultural Revolution would change people in their very souls, would remake them into "new socialist persons." They failed to fulfill such grandiose ambitions, of course. The reformers of the post-Mao era do not talk much about changing souls, only about making the economy more productive and the nation more stable. Nevertheless, their reforms are changing souls; they are inevitably challenging the assumed meanings and motivations of Chinese culture. Economic reforms have stimulated desires for more individual self-expression through the acquisition of consumer goods. Political reforms have heightened the aspirations of many groups for more participation in the processes of government. The opening to the West in search of modern technology has made widely available liberal ideas about human rights.

These changes in China's cultural system have engendered profound political conflicts. The massive demonstrations for "science and democracy" of the 1989 Beijing spring and the brutal crackdown against protesting students and workers on 4 June 1989 were only the most convulsive phases in a series of cycles of change and reaction that marked the decade since the beginning of the reforms. Although the reformers do not claim to be engineers of souls, they do claim responsibility, in traditional Chinese fashion, for being guardians of souls. They feel impelled to do something to stop perceived "unhealthy tendencies" in their society's culture. What to do, however, is inherently ambiguous. When a culture's fundamental definitions of what is right and wrong are in flux, there can be no uncontroversial decisions about which changes are salutary and which unhealthy. And even if a consensus could be achieved, no one knows enough about what causes cultural change to offer any clear-cut remedies for cultural problems. Such ambiguity inevitably leads to controversy and makes the outcome of cultural politics unpredictable.

Thus, as the process of political and economic reform has unfolded, culture has, as the Chinese say, become "hot"—that is, it has become a topic ardently debated. The more difficulties encountered in implementing the reforms, the hotter the debates over the culture, especially among Chinese intellectuals. In an extensive series of interviews conducted in the fall of 1988, I heard many Chinese intellectuals give the following account of their current obsession with the problem of cultural reform: At the end of the seventies, we thought we could modernize by introducing advanced science and technology. That ran into difficulties. So we realized that to introduce modern science and technology, we needed to modernize the economy. But that ran into obstacles too. Then we realized we needed to reform the political system. But when our hopes for political reforms were frustrated, we realized that the fundamental problem was cultural, a matter of the basic values and psychological attitudes of our cultural traditions. The cultural "heat" began around 1983, it boiled over during the Beijing spring of 1989, and for now it certainly simmers underground beneath the weight of repression begun on 4 June.

The issues here are at least as old as the *ti-yong* ("Chinese culture as the essence"—*ti*—"Western culture for its utility"—*yong*) controversies of the late nineteenth century. What kinds of noneconomic ideas and practices should be imported from the West if the economic reforms are to enhance Chinese wealth and power? Which ideas and practices should be imported if China wants to complement the best in her cultural traditions? Which rejected? Such questions can never be resolved definitively, once and for all. They need to be continuously reanswered through dialogue. If such a dialogue is to be carried out constructively, intellectuals must be willing to play a creative role in it. Until the current repression lifts, they will have little chance to play such a role. But if the repression does lift, how will they behave, how will they define their social roles? To help answer this question, I shall describe how intellectuals conceived of their roles between the repression of 1986–87 and the tumultuous spring of 1989.

INTELLECTUALS AND "BOURGEOIS LIBERALISM"

I write not only as an observer but in some small way as a participant in the cultural controversies of that period. The previous wave of repression against critical intellectuals had extended from late 1986 to mid-1987. In March 1987, in the midst of this campaign against "bourgeois liberalism"—a set of cultural tendencies allegedly produced by "spiritual pollution" from Western ideas—the *People's Daily* published a long essay entitled "Some Thoughts on Certain Aspects of Modern Western Culture: Reading Notes," by Zhao Fusan, the Vice-President of the Chinese Academy of Social Sciences.[1] I was at first delighted to see that a large part of Zhao's essay was devoted to *Habits of the Heart*, the book on individualism and commitment in American life coauthored by Robert Bellah, William Sullivan, Ann Swidler, Steven Tipton, and myself—and then dismayed to see that the essay used our account of American culture to support the arguments against bourgeois liberalism.

The 1986–87 campaign against bourgeois liberalism had been sparked by massive student demonstrations throughout China in December 1986. A common theme in the demonstrations was a demand for democracy and political reform. The demonstrations had been preceded by a spring and summer of "blooming and contending" within the party. A major issue had been the increasingly blatant corruption that had accompanied the reforms: massive profiteering from bribery, embezzlement, and smuggling, usually involving high-ranking cadres and their children. Some intellectuals—most notably the physicist Fang Lizhi, the writer Wang Ruowang, and the journalist Liu Binyan—argued that the problem lay in a combination of China's Marxist-Leninist ideology and its feudal political traditions. Marxism, their writings suggested, had become an empty dogma, at least in the form in which it was promulgated by party officialdom. Moreover, in the name of "democratic centralism," Leninist political organization had allowed entrenched political officials to exercise authority in a self-interested way, like feudal overlords rather than public-spirited guardians of the people's interests. The solution was a fundamental reinterpretation of Marxism-Leninism, perhaps even a replacement of it by a system of government that emphasized checks and balances and widespread political representation. In opposition to these advocates of cultural and political reform, other political officials declared that the problem of corruption was caused by "spiritual pollution" from the West, the unfortunate result of China's opening to the outside world.

This debate culminated in the main resolution of the Sixth Plenum of the Eleventh Central Committee, which met in September 1986. The resolution concerned the "Guiding Principles for Building a Socialist Society with an Advanced Culture and Ideology." The product of bitter debate (it had been rewritten nine times), this document refused to blame feudalism for any of China's "unhealthy tendencies." The most serious problem, it warned, was "bourgeois liberalization," which it defined as "negating the socialist system and favoring the capitalist system." When the student demonstrations broke out in December (probably caused in part by frustration due to the political developments symbolized by the contents of the Sixth Plenum's resolution), the party leadership blamed the unrest on "bourgeois liberalism" and expelled from the party its three most prominent proponents, Fang Lizhi, Wang Ruowang, and Liu Binyan. Throughout the spring of 1987 various intellectuals were mobilized to write essays explaining the errors of bourgeois liberalism. One of these was Zhao Fusan.[2]

In his *People's Daily* essay, Zhao Fusan tried to demonstrate that even prominent Western intellectuals agree that the culture of Western capitalism is fatally flawed and neither can nor should be exported to countries like China. He began by discussing an article by Jacques Barzun which argued that Western democracy is so tied up with the particular histories and unique circumstances of Western societies that it cannot be exported to other societies. Then he undertook a long, critical discussion of Western individualism that at first closely paralleled and then directly referred to the arguments of *Habits of the Heart*.

Zhao agreed with *Habits* that the key cultural characteristic of American society is its individualism. Many sociologists who have studied America believe, he wrote, that the chief goal of most Americans—and for that matter of most people in other Western capitalist societies—is individual success. And most theorists who support capitalism believe that this is natural, realistic, and the best way of thinking about a good life. Other Western scholars, however, from Tocqueville to Daniel Bell and the authors of *Habits,* have seen this individualism as problematic. Zhao quoted the concern expressed in the preface to *Habits* that American "individualism may have grown cancerous—that it may be destroying those social integuments that Tocqueville saw as modifying its more destructive potentialities, that it may be threatening the survival of freedom itself." [3]

Individualism, said Zhao, leads Americans to replace objective standards of value with the individual's subjective feelings about what is right and wrong—"what feels good is good." Ultimately such a subjectivistic concept of value leads to the "hippie, drug-addiction, fanatical rock and roll" popular culture so common in America. Individualism, moreover, leads Americans to define *freedom* in a socially irresponsible way as meaning simply the lack of any constraint and to define *justice* purely in terms of equal opportunities to engage in market competitions, which the rich, with their greater resources, will inevitably win.

Perceptive American scholars, like the authors of *Habits,* thus themselves agree, said Zhao, that the culture of individualism is morally vacuous and socially irresponsible, that "the ideologies of Western capitalism are in a morbid state and have developed into a cancerous state." In China's cultural traditions, on the other hand, "individuals have always been closely linked with society. Individuals are allowed to have their individuality and the beliefs of individuals are always respected. However, individuals have never been placed above society, and the values of individuals have always been unified with the responsibilities of society. This is one of the important factors that have contributed to the continued powerful cohesion of the Chinese nation." As a consequence, Chinese should be wary of indiscriminately absorbing Western values. Recognizing that "modernization is not equal to Westernization," they should carry out economic reform and development in a manner appropriate to the Chinese context.

By 1988 the pressure of the anti-bourgeois-liberalism campaign had receded, and intellectuals were arguing more passionately and more urgently than ever before about the need to change Chinese culture in response to the exigencies of modernization. During a five-month research trip to China in the autumn and early winter of 1988, I carried out about fifty interviews with Chinese intellectuals about their understandings of the cultural challenges posed by the reforms and the opening to the outside world. I often made it a point to direct part of the discussion around *Habits of the Heart* and Zhao's use of it in his anti-bourgeois-liberalism essay. Partly because Zhao's use of *Habits* had made me a participant in controversies of profound significance to these intellectuals, their conversations with me were, perhaps, exceptionally lively, thoughtful, and candid. As such, these conversations provide an excellent vantage point for exploring how intellectuals understood their role in the period leading up to the Beijing spring of 1989.

INTELLECTUALS' IDENTITY CRISIS

Many of the intellectuals with whom I spoke said that they had been furious at Zhao for writing his essay. Others, though, were more sympathetic. Zhao had been, as one of the sympathetic ones put it, "under a lot of pressure" to publish something in support of the campaign against bourgeois liberalism. As in such campaigns in the past, the party strove to get control of the leadership of all major social institutions relevant to the purposes of the campaign. As a vice-president of China's major institution for social scientific research and as an intellectual with extensive Western ties who had written widely about Western ideas, Zhao was a key person to enlist in support of the campaign. Had he refused to go along, the consequences for himself and for his institution could have been serious.

Zhao's expression of support for the campaign was, moreover, much more subtle and ambiguous than most other articles published at the time. It was abstract in content and detached in tone. Criticizing no one in China by name, it for the most part merely summarized criticisms Western intellectuals were making of their own culture. It was not against the assimilation of Western ideas; it merely wanted that assimilation to be carried out in a thoughtful, discriminating manner. Zhao's main concrete recommendation was simply for more academic study of the West: "In order to acquire a better understanding of the four cardinal principles and the historical significance of the reform and the opening to the outside world, it is necessary for us to deepen our scientific understanding of modern western culture and conscientiously sum up the modern history of China's contacts with western culture."

Why should many Chinese intellectuals, then, be angry at Zhao for publishing his article? They were angry because, while writing as an intellectual, he was acting as an official. "He's not really an intellectual, he's simply an official," one well-known victim of the anti-bourgeois-liberalism campaign said scornfully to me. If Zhao's article had been written under different circumstances, it may indeed have been regarded as the work of an intellectual. It was a well-informed, fairly subtle exposition of current Western social philosophy, which sought to make a reasonable case against uncritical acceptance of Western ideas. As such, it could have formed the focus for a fruitful academic debate on this important topic. But the context of its publication clearly rendered it a political document. Obviously Zhao was adding his voice to those in the party who were denouncing "wholesale Westernization," although he was careful not to use those exact words. Moreover, his depiction of the socially destructive consequences of unconstrained self-expression, his account of the superficiality of the purely procedural approaches to justice common in the West, and his use of Jacques Barzun's doubts about the exportability of democratic institutions—all bolstered party criticisms of those who were advocating more personal freedom and more thoroughgoing democratic reform. In the context of its publication, the function of Zhao's article was not to open up debate but to close it off. As his essay was being published, other scholars in the Academy of Social Sciences, who had written articles advocating acceptance of Western values such as individualism, were being told that their papers could not be published, not because they lacked scholarly merit, but because their publication would cause political trouble for various institutes within the academy.

Those sympathetic toward Zhao could argue that he was in fact protecting them, buying time for them, cooperating with the party just enough to keep it from harsher attacks against academics, but cooperating with enough ambiguity to provide an intellectual basis for renewed exploration of democratic reforms once the pressure of the campaign was off. At issue in the discussion of Zhao Fusan among Chinese intellectuals was, in short, the proper role of intellectuals in a China undergoing reform. Was an intellectual to be independent from the state and dependent on nonofficial sources for his or her intellectual, moral, and even economic sustenance? Or was an intellectual basically to be an appendage of the state, an official-in-waiting? There were hundreds of years of imperial Chinese precedent—not to mention the consistent policy of the Chinese Communist party since 1949—for the idea that the intellectual was to be an appendage of the state. Zhao Fusan, it could be argued, was a capable, humane representative of this ancient tradition. But in the wake of the reforms, some intellectuals were demanding a new kind of role. They were beginning to aspire to professional autonomy and to define intellectual integrity as above all the willingness to defend such autonomy.

Partly, some intellectuals were being pulled to aspire to such autonomy by their perceptions of the status enjoyed by their Western colleagues. But largely they were pushed toward such aspirations by the bitterness of their own situation in the wake of the reforms. "Foreigners cannot comprehend the depths of our pain," lamented an active, widely respected young scholar of international relations at a conference in Beijing in late 1988. The present-day anguish was perhaps so deep because it had been preceded by such profound hope and joy. No part of Chinese society had greeted the reforms with more hope and joy than China's intellectuals. After being persecuted almost since the beginning of the People's Republic of China, in thought reform campaigns, in the anti-rightist movement, and finally, most brutally, during the Cultural Revolution, they were told at the end of the 1970s that they were the key to China's future, that it was their knowledge that was crucial to the fulfillment of the "Four Modernizations." Now, they thought, they might become leaders of a revitalized China. But although in the late 1980s their status was immeasurably better than during the Cultural Revolution, the profound hopes they had experienced in the initial stages of reform were being frustrated. A decade after the reforms were launched, it was apparent to many of them that most of the people who had gained real control over the Chinese government did not respect, value, trust, or listen to intellectuals. Although they did not see any danger in the foreseeable future of a return to Maoism, they worried that the kinds of social forces that led to the thought reform and antirightist movements were still embedded in the Chinese political system. All too often, campaigns like the anti-bourgeois-liberalism one proved this point.

But the campaigns, as they saw it, were only a dramatic manifestation of a deeper anti-intellectualism pervading the political center of China. This anti-intellectualism manifested itself in economic policies that, since the mid-1980s, allowed the salaries of intellectuals to become deeply eroded by inflation. The anger at the deterioration of their own salaries was compounded by a sense of injustice as they saw people they regarded as far less worthy than they—for instance, small-scale entrepreneurs—making far more money. "An independent barber can now make more money than a doctor!" was a statement often heard in China by the late 1980s. Intellectuals were especially bitter at the corruption among high officials that had accompanied the reforms. They might agree in principle with the slogan that in the reforms some people must get rich first; but, bluntly put, many of them believed that it was the wrong people who were getting rich.

In addition, intellectuals had been disappointed by the irrationality of the reform process. They tended, for instance, to think that national economic policies should be made on the basis of careful calculation and coordination of economic consequences. But they saw instead an increasingly anarchic decentralized policy process in which powerful units and regions throughout the country each grabbed as much short-term profit for themselves as they could, without any consideration of long-range national consequences. Intellectuals like to think of themselves as being fit to exercise authority by virtue of their competence and expertise. It galled them to see their advice largely ignored in a government run by people who in their view were incompetents.

Intellectuals were thus coming increasingly to demand political independence and efficacy. Such independence was their only protection from the campaigns that had so oppressed them in the past. And it was the only way for them to play the leadership role that was their due and their responsibility because of their scholarly accomplishments. As Fang Lizhi put it in one of the statements that brought him trouble during the 1987 anti-bourgeois-liberalism campaign:

Intellectuals in the western countries are different from us. They not only have a great deal of specialized knowledge, they are also concerned about the larger society. If they were not, they wouldn't even be qualified to call themselves intellectuals. In China, with its poorly developed scientific culture, intellectuals do not exert significant influence on society. This is a sign of backwardness. The progress of a "spiritual culture" requires the contributions of intellectuals. In August [1986] I was invited to attend a convention of scientists from around the world. The subject was disarmament. The involvement of scientists in an issue like disarmament makes no sense to our government: it is a subtlety beyond their understanding. Not only do they fail to understand, they don't even want scientists thinking about matters like this. And this is exactly the same attitude regarding China's internal problems. But an intellectual has a responsibility to his society. We have to keep that in mind.[4]

Words like those of Fang Lizhi's resonated powerfully among the ranks of China's intellectuals. Not all intellectuals, of course, thought it possible or, at present, desirable to seek such an independent role. Some of the intellectuals I interviewed in China were more willing than Fang to compromise with rather than to confront the established political order. (Often these were scholars with strong personal connections with high officials. It was my impression, indeed, that the key difference between intellectuals like Fang who uncompromisingly demand autonomy from the state and those who were willing to compromise to various degrees in the name of an "ethic of responsibility" was not a difference in age, ideology, or party affiliation but a difference in the extent of personal ties one had, either through kinship or long-term association, with China's ruling aristocracy.) But the words and example of intellectuals like Fang Lizhi exerted an enormous appeal, my interviews made apparent, among all sorts of intellectuals, even those who for their own personal reasons were willing and able to blend the role of intellectual with that of official.

POLITICAL-ECONOMIC DISORGANIZATION AND INTELLECTUAL CONFUSION

To the extent, though, that intellectuals began to realize a measure of autonomy, they began to encounter a widespread, fundamental challenge: the need to develop a positive, realistic vision about the future of their country. This was proving extremely difficult. "The problem with intellectuals nowadays," one prominent senior scholar in the Academy of Social Sciences told me, "is not that they have no ideas—everybody has plenty of ideas—but that they have no common ideas." Thus, in the humanities and social sciences, one could find advocates of practically every new intellectual trend under the sun, from systems theory, cybernetics, and econometrics to existentialism and Jungian psychology, to mention only a few sets of ideas whose proponents I personally know. As during the May Fourth movement, these new ideas tended to be enthusiastically adopted by small groups of scholars and often quickly discarded before their proponents could fully master their vocabulary or fathom their implications. It was common to hear intellectuals say that the root of this May Fourth style of eclecticism was a profound lack of self-confidence.

Besides commonly manifesting itself in a floundering eclecticism, this lack of self-confidence also appeared in the guise of a virulent iconoclasm. Not only must every new idea be accepted, but, because the Chinese tradition was fundamentally closed, static, oppressive, and unscientific, every old idea had to be rejected. None of this boded well for hopes of moderate, balanced solutions to the economic and political difficulties encountered by China's attempts at reform.

If it had not been so heavily politicized by its use during the anti-bourgeois-liberalism campaign, Zhao Fusan's essay might have provided a valuable source of perspective for intellectuals drifting in a sea of confusion about how to confront China's cultural predicaments. In his essay Zhao did not deny the importance of learning from Western culture or the importance of reforming Chinese culture. But he counseled discrimination in the adoption of Western values, especially the value of individualism; and he warned against wholesale rejection of Chinese cultural traditions. In short, he counseled a measured, balanced approach to the transformation of China's culture. Unfortunately the sociological conditions for such a prudential balance have not been present.

The sense of desperate spiritual crisis experienced by Chinese intellectuals mirrored, and at the same time contributed to, the economic and political dilemmas engendered by the reforms. There was a new liveliness to the political economy as Chinese society broke free of the fetters of a rigid state, but it was an aimless, fragmented liveliness with little coherent direction or public purpose. By the late 1980s the reforms had led to a devolution of power. The central government had lost the ability to control the management practices and investment decisions of enterprises, work units, and administrative systems throughout China. The various sectors of Chinese society were thus vigorously asserting newfound independence even when this went against evident national interests. Regional banks, for instance, were defying central government regulations restricting the issuance of excessive credit and in the process were helping to cause severe inflation in the economy. Several regions had set up protectionist barriers against trade with other regions, frustrating attempts at wider economic coordination. Lacking centralized institutions for effective public coordination, the Chinese political economy appeared, by the late 1980s, to be aimlessly drifting. Lacking an effective institutional basis for professional cooperation, China's intellectuals seemed to be aimlessly drifting also.

Another important result of the reforms was that the party had been losing the ability to control Chinese intellectuals through political means. The opening to the outside world had given intellectuals the opportunity to participate actively in international associations of scholars. There were new opportunities for Chinese academics to study abroad, to participate in international conferences, to publish in international journals, and to compete for financial support from internationally oriented foundations. Even those who had not yet had the opportunity to participate in such international associations could realistically aspire to it. Chinese intellectuals' scholarly reputations were thus not so completely dependent on the judgments of their Chinese peers. Significant amounts of their research support came from abroad. They received moral support from colleagues abroad. Success in their careers was no longer so tightly controlled by political superiors. To gain a favorable academic reputation and economic support from abroad, it might indeed be helpful for them to demonstrate some independence from political control in China.

Furthermore, in line with the economic reforms, the Chinese government had encouraged its scholars and research units to be entrepreneurial, to seek research support from nongovernmental sources, including foreign sources. At the same time, it had depressed their salaries and harassed them through campaigns like that against bourgeois liberalism. While losing political control over them, it had failed to win the allegiance of their hearts and minds. Such a situation understandably stimulated intellectual ferment while discouraging calm, balanced reflection on China's future.

By January 1989 it was becoming very apparent to well-informed intellectuals (though not to foreign observers of China) that a major, probably disastrous confrontation would likely occur between dissastisfied intellectuals and the leaders of the Communist party. In late December, soon before I left Beijing, I had a long, exceptionally candid talk with a scholar who took unusual precautions to ensure that our conversation would take place at a site where it would not be electronically bugged. Stagflation in the economy, out-of-control corruption in the government, and a general loss of faith by intellectuals in the legitimacy of Marxism-Leninism were leading to an explosive situation, he said. The year 1989 would be one of important anniversaries, he noted: the seventieth anniversary of the May Fourth movement, the fortieth anniversary of the founding of the People's Republic of China, the two hundredth anniversary of the French Revolution. Trouble might well break out around the occasion of one of these anniversaries. If turmoil occurred, the party would probably impose martial law. There were those in the party who would push for a restoration of the economic and political policies of the 1950s. Ultimately, he predicted, this attempt to roll the clock back would fail, because the world environment was fundamentally different from that of the fifties. But in the meantime, there might be a lot of suffering. Six months later his predictions proved tragically accurate.

In restrospect, what he predicted so bluntly was consonant with what many other scholars I had gotten to know were predicting more implicitly. Perhaps, though, one could take heart from the positive predictions that some intellectuals made privately at the beginning of 1989. Short of a radical repudiation of the reforms and a total closing of the country, they thought, the party would not be able to regain firm political control over Chinese intellectuals. "There was a fundamental difference between the campaign against bourgeois liberalism and earlier campaigns like the antirightist campaign of 1957," one intellectual, who after 4 June had to flee into exile, told me. "In the antirightist campaign, many intellectuals united with the party to attack their colleagues who were targets of the campaign. But in the anti-bourgeois-liberalism campaign, there was no such cooperation." Perhaps because of the guilt that many middle-aged intellectuals felt for not having spoken out as boldly as they should have in the fifties and sixties, and because of their rueful recognition that they had gained nothing from having thus compromised themselves, many intellectuals were determined not to give in now. Under such circumstances, punitive campaigns like that carried out in the wake of the 4 June crackdown may only in the long run make intellectuals bolder, more defiant, more estranged from the Communist party—and more motivated to offer radical proposals for solving the social problems unleashed by China's modernization.

INTELLECTUALS AND THE FUTURE OF CHINA

Intellectuals in China like to boast of their "spirit of distress" (*youhuan yishi*) over the fate of their country, a phrase that connotes a duty to criticize social problems daringly out of a profound sense of moral responsibility for their society. Although the bitterness and gloom attached to their concern bespeak a deep sense of frustration in fulfilling that responsibility, the sense of responsibility nonetheless remains. Although it is impossible to predict exactly how they will be able to exercise that responsibility in the future, I can offer some speculations based on my earlier descriptions.

The reaction of Chinese intellectuals to the repression that followed the 1986–87 campaign against bourgeois liberalism suggests that, once the repression lifts slightly, intellectuals may emerge more courageously creative than ever before. Within months after the conclusion of that earlier campaign, Fang Lizhi, Wang Ruowang, and Liu Binyan, joined by other prominent dissidents like Wang Ruoshui and Su Shaozhi, were again publishing essays more sharply critical of the government than ever. Although expelled from the party, they had become international celebrities, and their writings gained widening audiences not only at home but also abroad.

A particularly interesting example of the creativity prodded into being by the government's clumsy repression was the immensely popular television series *River Elegy (He shang)*, broadcast in the summer of 1988. With an extraordinarily sophisticated use of video images to convey a sweeping historical and philosophical argument about the state of Chinese culture, the series achieved a level of rhetorical power and conceptual complexity rarely reached by television documentaries in the West. The message of the series was gloomy: China's civilization was in an ineluctable process of decline.[5] There was no hope of building on China's past, the announcer for the television series solemnly intoned. The only solution was to throw off all tradition and embrace the culture of the Western, industrial civilizations. If the content of the message reflected the despair of many Chinese intellectuals over their society's "feudalistic" culture, the sophistication of its presentation manifested their ability to master the possibilities of the new era of global telecommunication.

It was partly the possibilities opened up by global telecommunications that enabled the demonstrations of the 1989 Beijing spring to mushroom out of the control of the Chinese government. Thus, when the government forcibly suppressed the mass movements on 4 June, among those it immediately targeted for arrest were the authors of the *River Elegy*. Wang Luxian, one of the two chief writers of the TV series, was in fact arrested; but the other, Su Xiaokang, escaped to Hong Kong and from there to Paris, where he now belongs to a large, active international network of Chinese intellectuals who are striving to bring about a democratic China from exile. The future may well belong to them. In ways only dimly understood by communications theorists, the dynamics of this new communications age are making it possible for mass movements to engulf what a decade ago seemed to be impregnable socialist regimes throughout Eastern Europe. In spite of present hardships, those who know how to take full advantage of these modern dynamics may well triumph in China.

If they do triumph, the moral foundations of their victory will probably be an ability to blend Chinese traditions about the moral responsibilities of intellectuals with Western traditions about the social responsibilities of modern professionals. Although constantly in danger of being coopted by the state and corrupted by commercial interests, the learned professions in the West embody a set of universalistic ideals that motivates many "dedicated professionals" to worry about and to protest such cooptation and corruption. Thus the learned professions engage their members in practices of criticism and self-criticism aimed at seeking out objective truth. They profess to honor those persons who come closest to such truth. They punish members who blatantly twist the truth for reasons of political expediency. They sometimes defend members who are harassed by governments for daring to speak the truth. They resist efforts by governments and for that matter private corporations to determine standards for what constitutes truth.

Moreover, the professions legitimate their activities in terms of a quest for universal human welfare. They support research that exposes "social problems." They encourage a constant search for solutions to such problems. They profess to reward members whose primary commitment is to solutions to social problems rather than to the maximization of their personal wealth and power. They profess to accord the highest honors to comprehensive solutions rather than solutions that are only in the interests of particular groups, classes, or nations. They reward solutions that transcend conventional wisdom.

The search for expert knowledge from the outside world has led many Chinese scholars to become members of modern transnational professional institutions for research and the promotion of human welfare. (What is crucial here, of course, is not simply formal dues-paying membership in professional associations, but active participation in the scholarly conversation and cooperative practices of the professions.) This gives Chinese scholars both moral support and practical resources for seeking a truth that is relatively independent of the ideological interests of the Chinese state—and for that matter of the American state, whose geopoliticians sometimes worry about the destabilizing effects of too much agitation over issues like "human rights" in places like China. The transnational character of the modern professions and their possession of resources for research and publication derived from a multiplicity of sources—not just from a single nation state or from a single social class—provide an international social basis for Chinese scholars to realize moral aspirations that have long been a part of the Chinese cultural tradition.

What is important about this participation is not the nature of the specific ideas that Chinese scholars gain through it, but the forms of solidarity they acquire. "Woe betide any man," writes Michael Ignatieff, "who depends on the abstract humanity of another for his food and protection. Woe betide any person who has no state, no family, no neighborhood, no community that can stand behind to enforce his claim of need."[6] Participation in international professional institutions gives Chinese intellectuals a cosmopolitan community of colleagues who can stand behind them to enforce their need to say something significant about the direction their society is to take. If a Chinese scholar gets into trouble at home for advocating particular ideas, the scholar's international counterparts may come to his or her aid, not now because of some abstract commitment to human rights but because of personal and professional ties with that scholar. If the search for truth gets lonely, scholars know that they are in company with other people around the world who would approve of what they are doing. And if scholars are tempted to give up the search for truth, they might be deterred by the knowledge that they are abandoning ideals that honorable people around the world have fought for. And at the same time that the international professional community can support the highest moral aspirations of Chinese intellectuals, the courageous dedication of those intellectuals can remind the professions that what they have traditionally stood for is not merely the mastery of techniques but the application of those techniques to service of the public good.

Several prominent Chinese experts on American society, whom I interviewed in 1988, expressed admiration for the degree of consensus that they thought existed in American intellectual life. For an insider to American culture, there seems little such consensus here. *Habits of the Heart* indeed criticized the lack of coherence in our culture and thus could be used by Zhao Fusan to warn against the dangers of "wholesale Westernization." Yet compared with contemporary Chinese culture, American intellectuals, for all of their fractious individualism, adhere to a surprising degree to common norms of conduct, standards of excellence, and codes of professional responsibility. What fascinated the Chinese experts on American studies whom I interviewed was the ability of American professionals to cooperate voluntarily and in a responsible, disciplined way in the pursuit of larger national purposes. China needs, the experts thought, some such blend of freedom and responsibility to pursue national modernization in an orderly, effective way. Not a few intellectuals shared some of the fear of government officials that a radical quest for autonomy would lead to social anarchy. But they generally insisted that government coercion could not produce the requisite sense of social responsibility. Coercion would only destroy the intellectual creativity necessary for pursuing China's modernization.

Pushed to its radical limit, Western-style individualism can indeed become cancerous, as Zhao Fusan points out. It can atomize a society to such a degree that only a coercive state can maintain minimal order. But the antidote to such individualism is not more political coercion. Whether carried out in the name of social responsibility or of some pseudo patriotism, coercion only creates more individualism. It makes citizens cynical. It poisons the fund of social trust that is the matrix of any positive sense of social responsibility. It makes negation of the forces of social order the only route to a sense of individual efficacy. The only antidote to radical, socially irresponsible individualism—and this was the main message that *Habits of the Heart,* drawing on a Western "civic republican" intellectual tradition represented by figures like Montesquieu and Tocqueville, sought to convey—is free, honest debate about the responsibilities of citizens for one another on the basis of their common heritage and common destiny. The Confucian tradition in its own way recognized this when it made heroes of those scholars who sought the truth and spoke the truth in the face of political intimidation by emperors. Brave scholars like Liu Binyan, Fang Lizhi, Su Shaozhi, and Su Xiaokang have been drawing on this tradition even when some of them argue that China must shed itself of the ideas of Confucianism.

Undoubtedly, and understandably, many intellectuals will withdraw from Chinese public life in face of the brutality of the current regime. Zhao Fusan, for example, who happened to be in Paris when the 4 June crackdown occurred, resigned from his post at the Academy of Social Sciences and arranged to stay abroad, without, however, becoming involved with any groups of Chinese dissidents in France. Many like him in China, while going through the necessary motions of giving lip service to the crackdown, will avoid any active cooperation with the regime.

Others, inspired by the new heroes created by the democracy movement, will carry on a quiet defiance. Blending the best in Western ideals about the socially responsible independence of the professions with the best in traditional Chinese ideals about the moral responsibilities of scholars, they will in the long run serve their country well.

PART FOUR

National Trends

CHAPTER ELEVEN

Increased Inequality in Health Care

GAIL HENDERSON

Views differ about the impact of the reforms on health care. On the one hand, health status indicators reported in Chinese statistical publications show rapidly increasing longevity and declining mortality from acute infectious diseases. Major investments have been made in health services, particularly in the urban areas that were neglected during the Maoist era. Almost all regions of the country have spent more on health manpower training, construction of new facilities, and the purchase of sophisticated medical equipment. Biomedical science in China's research institutes has produced clinical applications ranging from the use of recombinant DNA technology in the production of a new hepatitis vaccine to experiments in Beijing and Shanghai with an artificial heart.[1]

On the other hand, a variety of new health problems have begun to emerge in the post-Mao era. Some are related to economic development. The increase in cigarette smoking, childhood obesity, occupational hazards, and environmental pollution is related to higher incomes and growth in rural industrial enterprises.

Other health problems may be related to the changes in the way health services are financed. In the countryside, for example, the weakening of collective organizations and the demise of most rural insurance programs[2] seem to be related to a decline in preventive services and a rise in the incidence of some infectious diseases.[3] In the cities, partly because of an irrational pricing system, the demand for more sophisticated hospital care far exceeds the supply. This creates inefficiencies and contradictions in the use of services and consequently in the delivery of adequate medical care.

With the declining role of the state in the development of health resources and with the rising cost of care, the market is playing an increasingly important role in the distribution of medical care. In some sectors distribution by the market may act as a counterbalance to earlier inequalities created by the state allocation system.[4] In medical care, however, the poorest members of society now have fewer community-based health benefits and insurance programs. Those most privileged under the Maoist system, cadres and industrial employees with medical insurance coverage, continue to enjoy the best access to care and to have the least worry about its cost.

It is not just the type and availability of health resources that have changed under the reforms. China's health problems have also changed considerably over time, and the relationship between health problems and the resources intended to address these problems has become more complex and ambiguous. The striking accomplishments of the Maoist era, of nearly doubling life expectancy and reducing mortality to rates close to those of the developed world, were achieved through political and organizational strategies, not by hospital-based, curative care. As a result, during the 1970s the leading causes of death changed from infectious diseases to heart disease, stroke, cancer, and chronic respiratory disease. These are long-term conditions that may require increasingly expensive, technically sophisticated resources, which are also more difficult to distribute widely.

Even in much wealthier countries, rationing of high-technology medicine has become a necessity.[5] Furthermore, contrary to the experience of the early years, when a small investment could make a significant impact on health status, the use of technology-based medicine to address China's current health problems may not have such a dramatic result. Recent studies in China have shown that greater health resources (such as hospital beds, medical personnel, and capital investments) are not correlated with decline in mortality.[6] Although access to medical facilities may affect health in more subtle ways than mortality statistics reveal, these findings clearly indicate that access to health care services cannot simply be equated with improved health status.

This chapter therefore examines health as a measure of equity in two respects: first, the changes in availability of and access to health resources; and second, the changes in health status that have occurred before and after the reforms. The thesis presented here is that, although the economic reforms of the post-Mao era have brought increased investment in health care services, they have resulted in an increased inequality in access to those services, as well as in a decreased investment in rural services in some areas. Health status has generally been improving as the reforms promote improvements in the standard of living; however, the decline in availability and equitable access to health resources may produce deteriorating health conditions in certain sectors of the population.[7]

FROM MAOIST HEALTH CARE TO MARKET HEALTH CARE

China's health care system under Mao reflected the economic and political decisions made during that era.[8] Its policies included a more equitable distribution of resources between urban and rural areas, restriction of foreign technology and hospital-based care, and emphasis on state-sponsored preventive health care. This entailed public health campaigns, mass-inoculation programs, environmental sanitation control, and the establishment of county- and township-level organizations that targeted epidemiology, infectious disease work, and the promotion of maternal and child health.

No unified hospital system developed. Rather, the Ministry of Health administered urban hospitals at the national, provincial, municipal, and county levels; large industrial enterprises, other ministries, and the army operated their own hospitals. In the countryside the rise of secondary and primary care facilities and the creation of the well-known three-tiered referral system depended mainly on local resources. In both urban and rural areas, referral cachement districts were established that required patients to visit basic-level clinics run by paramedics before possible referral to higher-level facilities.

Medical care was considered to be a public rather than private good.

Doctors were employees of the state; there was no private practice. Medical prices were set well below the cost, and income from patients covered less than half the actual costs of care. Hospitals and clinics operated as financial middlemen, with substantial subsidies from the state, from enterprises, or from the collective.[9] During the Cultural Revolution years, the number of rural hospital beds and medical personnel increased substantially. In urban areas, however, there was little investment in new equipment or facilities, and medical education and research were also curtailed.

In the early 1950s health insurance programs for state cadres (*gongfei yiliao*) and state-enterprise workers (*laodong baoxian*) were established, providing cost reimbursement for medical expenses to approximately 2 percent and 12 percent of the population, respectively. Cooperative insurance programs developed gradually in rural areas, reaching significant levels with the onset of the Cultural Revolution and the policy to "put stress on rural areas." Only in the wealthiest areas could coverage be as comprehensive as in the urban programs. Even at the height of the Cultural Revolution, however, it was estimated that 15 percent of the population was without medical insurance.[10]

The economic policies of the reform era have introduced remarkable changes in the Maoist medical system.[11] Major investments have been made in personnel, facilities, equipment, and medical research. Between 1978 and 1984, total health care expenditure increased by 115 percent, professional staff by 72 percent, all health personnel by 35 percent, hospital beds by 17 percent, number of medical research institutes by 47 percent, and capital construction expenditures by 250 percent.[12] According to the Ministry of Health, during this time increases in medical care expenditures rose twice as fast as overall government expenditures.[13]

The organization and management of medical practice have also changed. Medicine has been professionalized, with standardization of training and increased specialization of services. Technical experts rather than party leaders have been moved into leadership positions. The daily management of hospitals as well as policy and major investment decisions are dominated by professionals. New medical specialties have developed as China opened its doors to the radical advances that took place in medical technology and medical specialties in the West during the 1960s and 1970s. Intensive care and emergency medicine, for example, have been established in major cities.[14] Between 1978 and 1984 the number of radiologists in China increased by 106 percent.[15]

Changes in the criteria for medical diagnosis have resulted from new equipment, such as ultrasound, CT scanners, blood gas analyzers, and cardiac monitors. Furthermore, new technologies have changed the standards of medical treatment. For example, China recently purchased two lithotripter machines, costing $1 million each. This technology, which uses sound waves to break up kidney stones, could eliminate the need for surgery for this condition. If it becomes widely used, however, it would raise the cost of care dramatically. In a related example, during the Maoist era patients with chronic renal (kidney) failure (CRF) were considered terminal. Since 1979 a small number of CRF patients have been given maintenance dialysis at hemodialysis centers in over three hundred hospitals. Kidney and other organ transplantation is also being developed.[16] Many of the newest treatments are also the most expensive. Dialysis, an extreme example, costs 15,000–20,000 yuan ($4,000–$5,000) per year.

The reforms have emphasized decentralized authority. Hospitals have consequently become much more autonomous. Although the state continues to subsidize hospitals through salary and payments for other recurrent expenditures, hospitals are increasingly responsible for balancing their budgets beyond these subsidies. Each year the annual state deficit for hospital care is close to 1 billion yuan ($270 million),[17] and current policies aim to cut back these additional subsidies.

The pressure on hospitals to be more productive has generated various reforms, including improved efficiency in patient care management.[18] Continued state control over prices and distribution of some goods, however, have also resulted in serious inefficiencies in the entire system.[19] Chronic shortage of medicines, for example, has been attributed to inadequate supply of raw materials and to the unwillingness of factories to produce medicines that do not make big profits.[20] While requiring hospitals to balance their budgets, the state also continues to set prices for most treatments below actual costs. This has added incentive to the acquisition of new technology, one of the few categories for which local units may set their own prices.[21] A radiology center solely devoted to CT scanning opened in Hebei with a 24-hour-a-day service, examining over 3,500 patients in six months.[22] On the other hand, the difficulty in acquiring imported equipment has contributed to an increase in the production of domestic medical equipment. Between 1980 and 1985 medical equipment production rose 12 percent; in 1985–86 it rose 22 percent.[23] Chinese equipment is far cheaper than imported equipment, although maintenance and repair are often more difficult. For example, a locally made ECG monitor cost 1,000 yuan ($268), compared with a German-made Siemens monitor that sold for $25,000.[24]

With many more people paying for medical care themselves, the pressure on higher-level urban facilities has increased. Shortages in urban hospital beds, medical personnel (particularly nurses), medicines, and new technology are widely reported. The phrase *kanbing nan, zhuyuan nan* (hard to see a doctor, hard to get a hospital bed) is frequently used to describe the situation. The difficulty in finding a hospital bed has lead to irrational use of services. For example, visits to emergency rooms can become a strategy on the part of chronic patients to gain admission to the hospital. One report stated that 20 percent of emergency clinic patients were chronically ill individuals sent in for terminal care.[25] Pressure is so great that in many cases use of personal connections and even bribery are the only means by which admission is assured.[26] Access to very expensive treatments, such as kidney dialysis, often involves personal connections as well.[27] "Unhealthy tendencies in hospitals"[28] were not created by the reforms. Nevertheless, these tendencies are exacerbated by the introduction of expensive, scarce resources into a system that continues to be characterized by state control over the supply of personnel, facilities, and most prices and by poor coordination with other sectors.

Finally, these problems are accompanied by an overall loss of national-level planning ability. Redistributive capabilities have been sacrificed to encourage local initiative. With few exceptions, rationing of scarce resources now takes place at the local level. Purchasing decisions are made by hospitals; doctors decide which patients will receive scarce medical treatments.[29] Thus the health care "system" that has evolved under the reforms has concentrated more expensive resources in facilities to which a smaller number of people have access. And at the same time it has undercut the ability of the state to redirect these trends.

In the countryside the impact of the reforms has received considerable attention, since China's most serious health problems as well as most of its population are found there.[30] The decollectivization of agriculture in the late 1970s resulted in a restructuring of rural health services at the basic level. County hospitals continued to receive state funds and gradually updated personnel and facilities, but township (commune)-level hospitals did less well. More dependent on local community resources, they have been hard hit by decollectivization.

At the lowest level, the village paramedics received more standardized training, and many are now in private practice. By 1986 only 37 percent of the basic-level clinics were still collectively run; 11 percent were contracted out to local doctors; 45 percent were privately run; and 8 percent had other management forms.[31] This diversity in organization and financing created a wider variety of available services. Yet the profit-making incentives of prescription medicine and other curative services may well have contributed to a decline in community prevention services.[32]

Probably the most significant result of the reforms in rural areas was the demise of many cooperative insurance programs. In 1980, 68.8 percent of the villages were covered. This number fell to 5.4 percent in 1985, though it rose to almost 10 percent in 1987.[33] The consequence of this change was, first, that many farmers paid for curative (inpatient and outpatient) services themselves. Second, farmers, no longer constrained by the referral regulations of insurance programs, increasingly chose to go directly to higher-level urban facilities for their medical care. This placed additional strain on already overcrowded city hospitals and led to declining occupancy rates and incomes for rural hospitals. At present, lacking any single system of rural health care financing, local officials resort to a wide variety of management and financing strategies.

Urban-Rural Differences in Health Resources

The post-1949 period is well known for great improvements in the distribution of health resources to the Chinese countryside. Nevertheless, even during the Cultural Revolution substantial urban-rural differences persisted. According to a study by Nicholas Prescott and Dean Jamison, health resources in the 1970s were strongly related to income and urbanization. They found that a "1% increase in urban income was associated with: 1% increase in density of hospital beds and salaried health workers; 1.5% increase in the density of doctors; 2.5% increase in density of general hospital beds; and 3% increase in the levels of both recurrent and capital expenditure."[34] The authors conclude that "current trends in Chinese economic policy are likely to increase these inequalities."[35] In the post-Mao period, while investment in health resources has increased for all areas, it has also been shifting toward urban areas. In 1981 the urban-rural differential in recurrent health expenditure was more than 3:1.

Tables 1 and 2 document trends in the distribution of hospital beds between urban and rural areas over the period 1957–1986. The majority

TABLE 1 Percentage of Hospital Beds in Urban and Rural
Areas, 1957–1986

Hospital Beds	1957	1965	1975	1980	1984	1986
Urban	74.9	59.8	39.9	38.7	42.4	45.0
Rural[a]	25.1	40.2	60.1	61.3	57.6	55.0

Source: ZGWSNJ 1987, p. 493.
a. Rural refers to both county- and township-level hospitals.

of hospital beds were located in urban areas until the Cultural Revolution, which promoted the development of township- and county-level hospitals. During the 1980s the percentage of beds in rural areas has fallen slightly relative to urban areas. As Table 2 demonstrates, the number of beds per thousand persons went from a very skewed ratio favoring urban areas to one that stabilized at about 3:1 in 1975. It has remained fairly constant at 3:1 since then.[36]

Health care is improving in big cities faster than in small cities. According to a Ministry of Health report, between 1980 and 1985 health care expenditures in large cities (20 percent of China's cities) increased by 95.5 percent, while in medium and small cities the increases were only 62.3 percent and 61.5 percent, respectively.[37] The rise of high-technology medicine builds on and intensifies these differences among urban areas. Compared with inland city areas, coastal city hospitals and key medical institutions have larger budgets for foreign equipment, more access to foreign currency, and more staff members who have studied abroad. One-quarter of all CT scanners in China are located in four cities, with more than twenty in Beijing alone. Furthermore, hospitals run by the army or by powerful ministries generally have better facilities and access to imported equipment.

TABLE 2 Number of Beds per 1,000 Persons, 1957–1986

Hospital Beds	1957	1965	1975	1980	1984	1986
Urban	2.08	3.78	4.61	4.70	4.77	4.48
Rural	.14	.51	1.23	1.48	1.49	1.54
Total	.46	1.06	1.74	2.02	2.10	2.18

Source: ZGWSNJ 1987, p. 493.

In contrast to the expansion of urban facilities, the decollectivization of agriculture in the countryside has been accompanied by a decline in the number of village health clinics and the number of village paramedics. Between 1975 (the year with the highest number of "barefoot doctors") and 1986, the number of barefoot doctors, now called countryside doctors, declined 18 percent, while the total number of brigade health personnel declined by more than 50 percent.[38]

As noted above, the next level of referral, the township hospital, is also under considerable financial pressure. A study on urban-rural differences in government health expenditure between 1976 and 1983 showed that the proportion of state funding for provincial hospitals almost tripled, whereas that for township hospitals and disease prevention stations declined by about one-third.[39] The plight of township hospitals is reflected in the title of a recent article: "Township Hospitals are Unable to Make Ends Meet."[40] As Table 3 shows, whereas the number of county hospital beds in China has increased steadily, the number of township hospital beds has declined since 1980. Possibly too many beds were built at the township level. Given the very low number of beds per thousand persons in rural areas, however, it is more likely that the decline in township hospital beds is an unfortunate consequence of decollectivization.

TABLE 3 Development of County and Township Beds, 1957– 1986

Hospital Beds	1957	1965	1975	1980	1984	1986
County	69,545	175,409	262,598	326,335	361,343	375,308
Township	—	132,487	620,281	775,413	731,411	711,234

Source: ZGWSNJ 1987, p. 494.

Insurance and Access to Health Resources

Between 1980 and 1985 the charges for medical care doubled. This increase was caused by several factors. The state mandated rate increases for certain medical services so that hospital charges would more closely reflect actual costs. There was a general inflation in prices for various medical service inputs, such as pharmaceutical raw materials and heating fuels.

Medical personnel wages increased. A two-price system was introduced, enabling hospitals to charge higher prices to employees with cadre or worker insurance for certain services. Lastly, the acquisition of new technology was accompanied by new and usually higher charges. Income from medicines and new technology accounted for the greatest proportion of the increase in hospital income.

In urban areas the public insurance program for state cadres is funded by the state, and, despite calls for reform it continues to provide cost-reimbursement insurance to cadres. In 1981 this 2 percent of the population received 24 percent of the Ministry of Health's recurrent expenditures.[41] Between 1981 and 1985 public insurance and labor insurance expenditures doubled.[42] In Guangzhou between 1978 and 1983 the number of cadres increased by 37 percent, while public insurance expenditures for cadres more than tripled.[43] This increase can be explained by the implementation of the two-price system, the pressure to provide the best possible care to state cadres, and the lack of incentives to economize.[44]

Protection under the labor insurance programs for state workers is more variable. Unlike the cadre program, funds for worker insurance come from the welfare fund of each work unit. Large, wealthy enterprises are able to offer comprehensive coverage; increasingly, however, smaller enterprises find themselves unable to meet the costs of expensive care without turning to enterprise profits. Small factories may use all their medical funds on one very sick worker or be forced to deny coverage.[45] Insurance protection for temporary or contract workers in both urban and rural areas is much more limited in the type of care covered and the maximum amount of benefits.

Data from many sources, including the 1984 World Bank study, demonstrate that for farmers the breakdown of insurance programs has contributed to less equitable access to health services.[46] For example, a 1988 study of rural cooperative insurance found villages with no insurance had lower utilization of inpatient, outpatient, and maternal and child health services.[47] Another study of the health expenditures of farmers and town-enterprise workers in a Heilongjiang county found that town workers with employment-based insurance spent twice as much on medical care than did uninsured farmers and visited doctors more often.[48]

Many of the newest treatments are beyond the means of farmers. Research on kidney dialysis found that at some centers costs were so high that farmers were categorically denied treatment.[49] Many rural residents cannot afford some of the sophisticated prevention technology. Tuberculosis screening, for example, can cost as much as 125 yuan.[50] In one instance, cancer screening proved so expensive that it was limited to urban employees' work units rather than made available to the population groups with known risk factors for cancer.[51]

The urban-rural differential in health resources declined considerably during the Maoist era, stabilizing by the end of the Cultural Revolution at about 3:1. Access to those resources, particularly through insurance programs, was always related to income and occupation, but the Maoist policies fostered increasing equality in access. The modernization period has featured a reversal of this trend, with a rise in urban-rural resource differentials and less equitable access to care.

CHANGING HEALTH STATUS

A number of different measures are used to describe health status. The most common indicators are the leading causes of death, the infant mortality rate (IMR; number of deaths in the first year of life per 1,000 live births), and life expectancy. The populations of developing countries die mainly of infectious diseases. Their IMRs are high and life expectancy low. Developed nations, which have the capacity to prevent and treat major infectious diseases, have passed through what is called the epidemiologic transition. Chronic conditions replace acute infectious diseases as the leading cause of death. More infants survive, and populations live longer.

Morbidity (illness) is a more finely tuned indicator of health status. Disease incidence, and particularly the incidence of childhood diseases, reveals more about the conditions of a population and the relationship between health status and the use of health services. For example, whereas mortality figures may show a decline in infectious disease as a leading cause of death, morbidity statistics might demonstrate that acute infections continue to cause persisting and costly problems.

Mortality

The 1973–1975 Cancer Epidemiology Survey provided the first systematic estimates of death rates and causes of death in China. Prior to that, official statistics were based on small-scale surveys and an information system that reported only 54–60 percent of all deaths between 1953 and 1961, and 79–92 percent after 1961.[52] As a result, official statistics un-

TABLE 4 Crude Death Rate per 1,000 Persons,
1950–1986

Year	Official Chinese Statistics	World Bank Model	Banister's Estimates
1950	18.00	33.5	30.0+
1957	10.80	23.4	18.1
1960	25.42	36.0	44.6
1967	8.43	13.5	10.5
1970	7.60	10.1	9.5
1977	7.87	8.9	7.7
1980	6.34	7.8	7.7
1984	6.70	—	8.0
1986	6.69	—	—

Sources: Official Chinese Statistics from *ZGWSNJ 1985*, p. 53; *1987*, p. 504. World Bank model from Dean Jamison et al., *China: The Health Sector* (Washington, D.C., World Bank, 1984), pp. 122–123. Banister's estimates from Judith Banister, *China's Changing Population* (Stanford, Calif., Stanford University Press, 1987), p. 116.

derstated mortality rates throughout the period.[53] The 1981 census and the national retrospective fertility survey, in combination with the cancer survey, provide data to reconstruct more realistic mortality rates. In addition to the official Chinese statistics, at least two other models have been developed, one by the World Bank and the other, more recently, by Judith Banister. Tables 4 and 5 present crude mortality rates and infant mortality rates from these three sources.

These tables demonstrate the remarkable decline in mortality that took place between 1950 and 1975, with the exception of the increase during the Great Leap Forward period. By the mid-1970s the rate of decrease had slowed. After 1978–79 the rates began to increase somewhat for overall mortality. It is difficult to know whether or to what extent the infant-mortality rate increased during the 1980s. Earlier Chinese estimates were based on samples in which very poor, rural areas were underrepresented. A recent re-estimation of the 1986 rate is similar to World Bank and other estimates and reveals a large difference between urban and rural areas.[54]

Banister asserts there has been a significant increase in rates, beginning in 1978, was primarily caused by a rise in female infant mortality (see Table 6). She bases her projection on the difference between the

TABLE 5 Infant Mortality Rate per 1,000 Persons,
1950–1986

Year	Official Chinese Statistics	World Bank Model	Banister's Estimates
1950	200.0 (pre-1949)	252	200.0+
1954	138.5	225	164.3
1957	—	200	132.4
1958	50.8 (urban) 89.1 (rural)	214	146.3
1960	—	300	284.0
1965	—	165	84.4
1970	—	109	70.4
1975	13.1 (urban) 32.4 (rural)	84	48.6
1978	—	59	37.2
1980	13.0 (urban) 23.9 (rural)	53	41.6
1981	34.68 (census)	48	43.7
1983	13.6 (urban) 26.5 (rural)	—	50.1 (1984)
1986 (re-estimation)	51 20 (urban) 59.3 (rural)	—	—

Sources: Official Chinese statistics from *ZGWSNJ, 1985,* p. 54, and *1987,* p. 505. For 1986, Zhou Youshang et al., "Zhongguo ying'er siwanglü fenxi" (An analysis of infant-mortality rates in China), *Zhongguo renkou kexue* (China population science) 3: 35–46 (1 June 1989). World Bank model from Dean Jamison et al., *China: The Health Sector* (Washington, D.C., World Bank, 1984), p. 113. Banister's estimates from Judith Banister, *China's Changing Population* (Stanford, Calif., Stanford University Press, 1987), p. 116.

normal Chinese sex ratio at birth (SRB) of 106.0 and the reported SRB in 1981 of 108.47. She concludes that at least 230,000 female births in 1981 were unreported and asserts that most have died from infanticide or selective neglect. In contrast to Banister, Chinese demographers deny allegations of widespread female infanticide.[55] In fact, recent Chinese sources continue to show higher male infant mortality rates. The State Statistical Bureau's "In-depth Fertility Survey" of 1986 found higher male rates for Shanghai, Shaanxi, and Hebei (see Table 7).

More recent data from the 1987 "One Percent Population Survey,"

TABLE 6 Infant Mortality
Rates by Sex,
1953–1984

| Year | IMR | |
	Males	Females
1953	179.3	169.5
1960	283.2	284.9
1965	87.2	81.5
1970	70.3	70.4
1975	48.4	48.9
1978	36.8	37.7
1980	35.8	47.7
1984	33.9	67.2

Source: Judith Banister, *China's Changing Population* (Stanford, Calif., Stanford University Press, 1987), p. 116.

TABLE 7 Infant Mortality Rates in Shaanxi, Hebei, and
Shanghai, 1965–1984

| Year | Shaanxi | | Hebei | | Shanghai | |
	Male	Female	Male	Female	Male	Female
Pre-1965	108.6	91.8	91.4	68.1	64.8	45.1
1965–1969	84.4	67.8	58.5	39.9	25.9	18.0
1970–1974	69.2	52.1	41.1	34.8	20.3	17.1
1975–1979	54.8	41.2	38.2	27.1	24.8	13.0
1980–1984	40.0	27.8	41.0	26.1	—	—

Source: State Statistical Bureau, "China In-depth Fertility Survey," October 1986.

described by Terence Hull, indicate that the SRB in 1986 had risen to
110.94.[56] In other words, 595,400 female births in 1986 were apparently unreported. According to Hull, the three possible explanations for
the rising sex ratios between 1982 and 1987 all relate to pressures from
the family-planning program: (1) female births were concealed so the
parents could try again for a son; (2) sex-specific abortions were performed; (3) female infants were killed. The underreporting of infant deaths
will make the debate difficult to resolve. Even if most of the excess
female births were concealed, however, the agricultural reforms that fos-

ter the desire for male children may have had a profound effect on the health and health care of female infants in China.

Urban-Rural Mortality Differentials

Urban and wealthy rural areas passed through the epidemiologic transition more or less during the years of the Cultural Revolution. In 1956–1959 the leading causes of death in a Beijing district were respiratory diseases (28 percent) and infectious diseases (14 percent). By 1974–1978 they were heart diseases (28 percent), cerebrovascular diseases (23 percent), and cancer (16 percent).[57] In the earlier years infants, children, and young women were the population groups with the highest mortality. By the late 1970s they had been replaced by the middle-aged and the elderly.

The dramatic impact of the epidemiologic transition is demonstrated by a World Bank analysis of the 1973–1975 Cancer Epidemiology Survey. It showed that life expectancy in urban areas was twelve years higher than in average rural areas and seventeen years higher than in the poorest rural areas. Income was highly related to better health, such that a 10 percent increase in income was associated with about a seven- or eight-month increase in life expectancy.[58]

The substantial urban-rural variation in the leading causes of death has gradually narrowed as more rural areas experience the epidemiologic transition. By the mid-1980s the five leading causes of death were similar. Table 8 presents recent statistics, although they may not represent the poorest areas of the country.

Morbidity

An examination of the leading causes of morbidity reveals the particular diseases that continue to be problems for China, as well as the new health problems that have arisen during this period.

Several sources document a rise in childhood infectious diseases in the post-Mao era, particularly in rural areas. Table 9 shows, for example, a tripling of the incidence of measles between 1977 and 1980. In urban areas immunization for childhood infectious diseases was fairly complete after 1965, but in rural areas only half the population was covered during the 1970s and early 1980s.[59] The increase in disease incidence has been attributed, in part, to the breakdown of rural collectives that managed

TABLE 8 Leading Causes of Death in Urban and Rural
Areas, 1986

Disease	37 Cities (% total deaths)	81 Counties (% total deaths)
Heart diseases	23.03	24.49
Malignant tumors	21.15	15.18
Cerebrovascular diseases	21.11	15.65
Respiratory diseases	8.88	12.58
Digestive diseases	4.21	5.46
Trauma	4.11	3.62
Pulmonary TB	1.72	3.45
Urinary diseases	1.63	1.26
Toxicosis	1.62	3.86
Neonatal diseases	1.49	2.14
Total	88.95	87.69

Source: ZGWSNJ 1987, p. 505.

preventive services such as childhood immunization programs. In one 1988 study the incidence of childhood infectious disease was found to be twice as high in villages with no insurance programs than in villages that had maintained cooperative insurance.[60]

In response to this problem, UNICEF provided funds in the early

TABLE 9 Nationwide Incidence (per 100,000 persons) of
Infectious Diseases, 1974–1986

Disease	1974	1977	1980	1984	1986
Diphtheria	2.6	3.2	1.0	.3	.1
Measles	110.9	107.9	299.9	60.1	16.6
Pertussis	73.3	70.3	32.3	21.0	7.0
Polio	1.2	.8	.8	.2	.2
Dysentery	285.3	261.8	293.4	375.0	261.0
Viral hepatitis	26.5	27.9	48.4	67.6	84.9
Malaria	1,090.8	442.8	336.9	87.7	30.3
EHF	1.6	1.8	3.1	8.8	9.7
Typhoid, paratyphoid	.4	7.6	7.6	9.7	8.5

Source: For 1974–1980, Dean Jamison et al., China: The Health Sector (Washington, D.C., World Bank, 1984), p. 127. For 1984, ZGWSNJ 1985, p. 56. For 1986, ZGWSNJ 1987, p. 509.

1980s to implement national immunization programs. The goal was 85 percent coverage of all children by 1988. In one Shandong county that began the campaign at the end of 1984, immunization coverage for tuberculosis, polio, measles, diptheria, pertussis, and tetanus was raised from 50–60 percent to 79–87 percent by 1986.[61] By 1986 the mortality rate of these six childhood diseases in China reportedly dropped 40 percent.[62] If these statistics are reliable, the immunization effort will have a very significant impact on infant mortality and life expectancy in the countryside.

China's most serious infectious disease problems are hepatitis, tuberculosis, and dysentery. The financial and personal toll is substantial. One study of a county in Heilongjiang, where only half the population had been immunized, found that tuberculosis and hepatitis accounted for half the health care costs.[63] Although of less statistical importance, the rise of epidemic hemorrhagic fever (EHF) is also of concern (see Table 9). It is tempting to use the persistence of or rise in infectious disease as an indicator of negative consequences of the reform policies. The following discussion of hepatitis and EHF illustrates the complexity of factors involved in disease incidence and prevention.

HEPATITIS. The rising incidence of hepatitis is recognized to be one of the leading health problems in the Third World. As Table 9 shows, it is increasing in China,[64] although reports often fail to distinguish between hepatitis A and B. Hepatitis A is a mild form, passed in families and kindergartens through fecal contamination. Prevention efforts focus on improved hygiene. Hepatitis B is a much more serious disease. Because it is passed through blood and semen, it is transmitted from mothers to children and between spouses. China's incidence of active hepatitis B carriers is 8 percent, or about 100 million people.[65]

The solution to hepatitis B is vaccine production. Vaccination of newborns can prevent vertical transmission and essentially eradicate the disease in one generation. Each year 18–20 million babies are born in China, requiring 60 million doses of the vaccine. China has recently produced its own hepatitis B vaccine, using newly acquired recombinant DNA technology, which has made widespread distribution possible for the first time. In 1986 the production of the vaccine reached 9 million doses, enough for 3 million people.[66] Thus, although the reform period has witnessed an increase in hepatitis cases, it has also fostered the foreign aid that produced a vaccine and, it is hoped, an ultimate solution.

EPIDEMIC HEMORRHAGIC FEVER. EHF is caused by a virus carried by rodents. There is no vaccine for EHF. In earlier years the mortality rate for people who developed the disease was high, but since the 1970s, EHF patients have been hospitalized and provided with supportive therapy. In 1986 the death rate for EHF patients was 2 percent.[67] The incidence of EHF is related to work at construction sites and to other outdoor activities. Its rising incidence in the post-Mao period is probably due to decreased rat control efforts and an expansion of building construction. In one county with an outbreak of EHF in the mid-1980s, a new rat control campaign was launched by public health personnel at the county, township, and village levels, with a reported drop in incidence.[68] The breakdown in prevention efforts for rat control, as well as the childhood immunization work noted above, illustrates the negative impact of the reforms. Yet coordinated and effective efforts to reorganize public health programs, building on the health service infrastructure still in place in rural areas, also illustrate China's continued capacity to respond to health problems.

Chronic Health Conditions in the Post-Mao Era

In addition to persisting infectious disease problems, China must deal with the rising incidence of chronic health conditions. These are by no means "caused" by the reforms; rather, they are the result of success in treating infectious disease. Most common are cancer, heart disease, hypertension, cerebrovascular disease, and chronic respiratory disease. Treatment for most chronic conditions involves increasingly intensive hospital-based care. Cancer patients, for example, are treated with conventional therapy, including surgery, radiotherapy, and chemotherapy. China is experimenting with "home beds" for chronic patients and the use of traditional herbs to reduce costs. Nevertheless, the potential increase in demand for services to treat chronic conditions in the future is staggering.

Although the reforms have not directly caused chronic disease, they are associated with the rise in several risk factors for chronic illness and other health problems. These include increased smoking, particularly among males, which increases the risk for heart disease, stroke, and chronic respiratory diseases;[69] dietary factors, including childhood obesity and foods that have been linked to cancer and stroke;[70] environmental and industrial contamination;[71] and traffic and occupational accidents.[72]

In other nations these changes have been seen as inevitable results of economic development. Some are related to life-style changes and increased disposable income. Others involve economic or industrial changes that have taken place at a community or societal level. Whereas the case of EHF demonstrated that some of China's earlier public health efforts continue to be effective, many of the new health problems are more difficult to address. This is particularly true as the reforms are associated with a loosening of state control over Chinese society. The intense political mobilization strategies employed in the campaigns to eradicate venereal disease in the 1950s are not available for the 1980s efforts to reduce smoking. Environmental regulation of millions of small rural enterprises will be an administrative nightmare. The reform period thus offers new problems and a new environment. The challenge will be in devising inexpensive, prevention-oriented solutions.

INEQUALITY IN HEALTH

The technical level and professional standards of medical care in China have improved considerably during the past decade. The increased cost of care, the concentration of resources in urban centers, and the breakdown of rural insurance have adversely affected the ability of poorer rural residents to purchase the best medical services. Those with cadre or enterprise insurance continue to have easier access to the most expensive urban facilities. The urban-rural and coastal-inland gap in health resources is further exacerbated by the inefficient and partial implementation of the market reforms, creating shortages, poor planning, and persistence of the use of personal relationships to gain access to services.

On the other hand, many commentators in the fields of medicine and public health policy are beginning to ask whether increasing investment in modern medical care services really buys significantly better health outcomes. Furthermore, although distribution of health resources may be an indicator of equity, it is only one of several determinants of health outcomes.

For these reasons this chapter also looked directly at changes in health status as a way to evaluate the impact of the reform period. Poor health outcomes are associated with poverty and other aspects of social disadvantage in all nations, irrespective of insurance coverage or level of development.[73] If the economic reforms result in increased income inequality, as well as in weakening of government programs that attempt to counteract the health effects of social disadvantage, then the poor in China are at greater risk for health problems.

China's health care system was designed to function as an inexpensive, community-based welfare system. It is now required to manage much more sophisticated organizations with different rules and objectives. This transition phase is characterized by dynamism as well as by pressure on an increasingly dysfunctional financing system, planning decisions that are often propelled by short-term economic incentives, and a lack of central direction regarding the overall strategy for health care. The challenge that China faces as it attempts to promote health and prevent disease is not simply to acquire the information and technology to combat a new range of health problems. It is the reintegration of a decentralized and fragmented system. Without a strong central management and planning capability, the post-Mao economic reforms will indeed continue to produce increasing inequality in health.

The Impact of Reform Policies on Youth Attitudes

STANLEY ROSEN

China's reform process, initiated at the Third Plenum of the Eleventh Central Committee in December 1978, has undeniably altered the country's economic landscape over the past decade. This chapter focuses on the impact of China's reforms on one segment of Chinese society: youth. Because youth are making decisions affecting their future even into the twenty-first century, their views are particularly sensitive to the images people have for how society is evolving. Furthermore, since they will be the adults shaping the future, they are a particularly interesting group for considering long-term social trends. Much of the chapter will examine, directly and indirectly, the changing values and behavior of youth as the country seeks to build "Chinese-style socialism." In addition, the Chinese leadership's response to the challenge posed by the new "thinking generation" will be addressed. Under the inducements of a more open system, with increasing opportunities for wealth and mobility, new patterns of behavior have affected virtually every area of Chinese social life and created open conflict between divergent value systems.

My underlying argument is that the reform process, with its broad emphasis on the expansion of the market, has created an environment that promotes greater permissiveness in society and provides the freedom to pursue materialistic goals. As the state's ability to control social change has declined, the options available to young people have multiplied. Increasingly, it appears that upward mobility may be achieved without a job in a state enterprise, or a university education, or even party membership.

The state's loss of social control reached its zenith during the April–June 1989 demonstrations and occupation of Tiananmen Square. The nightly news broadcasts of tens of thousands of defiant students revealed, far more graphically than any public opinion poll, the failures of political-ideological education in China. In the aftermath of the military crackdown, China's aging orthodox Marxists introduced policies that would prevent a recurrence of the "turmoil" and "rebellion." The return to heavy-handed political indoctrination was part of a larger program seemingly designed more as a punishment and control mechanism than out of any strong conviction regarding its efficacy. The new policies toward students—cutting enrollments in sensitive social science fields, stepping up military training for freshmen, tightening controls on job assignments, and so forth—are intended to reverse the CCP's loss of authority over China's youth. Nevertheless, it is difficult to see how stepped-up ideological indoctrination at a time when the regime is most unpopular can be successful in reducing student alienation. If the new policy thrust is sustained and expanded, the mobility options for youth will probably be narrowed. The effect on attitudes and behavior could be substantial. It is too early, however, to assess the impact of the 1989 events, particularly in areas outside Beijing and on youth not in college. The arguments on youth attitudes made below are based on data gathered prior to the recent unrest and should be viewed in that light. At a minimum, the data show the difficulty the regime will have in reversing trends that have been developing for the past decade.

The areas documented in this chapter—value change among students, attitudes toward the party and the military, and schooling and the labor market—were selected because they are central issues of particular concern to Chinese social scientists and political leaders. Highly visible changes in each area have stimulated widespread debate. Authorities remain divided over three interrelated questions: (1) How much change in values has occurred? (2) Should the changes revealed by survey research be seen, on balance, as positive or negative? (3) What is the proper response in dealing with Chinese youth in the 1980s?

The discussion will introduce and draw heavily on survey research, which has become increasingly important as an analytical tool for Chinese social scientists. The growth of such surveys, sometimes reflecting highly negative attitudes, and the increasing willingness of respondents to answer questions about their personal beliefs and motivations are in themselves a major change in the past decade. Publication of these survey results and of detailed statistical data has given us a much more complete picture of Chinese society than at any time since 1949.

How reliable are Chinese surveys? [1] While a healthy skepticism toward survey data is appropriate anywhere, some surveys appear to be of superior quality. Moreover, Chinese surveys provide a great deal of information about Chinese society unavailable from other sources. Aware of certain pitfalls, one can judiciously select those that appear reasonably sound methodologically, as well as informative. There are also some obvious rules of thumb. For example, one almost always avoids surveys published in English for a foreign audience or in Chinese for large-circulation newspapers such as *Renmin ribao*. Publication in such forums is clearly intended for propaganda or indoctrination. Thus the method of dissemination tends to be an important indicator of a survey's purpose.

The surveys discussed below are drawn primarily from academic journals with a restricted circulation, aimed primarily at professional researchers. Many of them have been commissioned by party or government offices seeking to understand and govern an increasingly complex and heterogeneous society. They represent a small fraction of the hundreds, if not thousands, of studies published by China's social scientists to determine the attitudes and opinions of Chinese youth. They range from large-scale national samples of tens of thousands to local surveys encompassing no more than a single classroom. [2]

The interpretation of Chinese surveys is hindered by a number of constraining factors. Because they began to appear only in 1979, we have little in the way of time-series data. Chinese social scientists have sought to compensate for this by offering their impressions of the Maoist period when reporting attitude and opinion data from the 1980s. The most numerous and reliable surveys tend to come from large cities—particularly Beijing, Shanghai, Tianjin, and Guangzhou—making it difficult to draw conclusions about the vast interior of the country. Local surveys of outlying areas and national surveys—for example, on peasant youth attitudes—do exist. National surveys, however, often present findings that are not sufficiently disaggregated to be sociologically revealing, while the quality of local studies tends to be questionable. Still, many generalizations can be gleaned from this vast survey output.

VALUE CHANGE AMONG YOUTH

Several cautionary notes are in order when discussing Chinese value change over time. In addition to the lack of time-series data noted above, some readers may also protest that we are measuring only changing political norms, not values—that in post-Mao China it is finally acceptable to report openly what one has always believed. Moreover, youth opinions, particularly those of college students, may be highly volatile. Surveys done while political reform is a "hot" topic or soon after student demonstrations tend to exaggerate the political commitment of respondents. Surveys done prior to the large demonstrations of 1985 and 1986 tend to show much less interest in political commitment. More recent surveys have shown a marked decline in the desire of students to study and a growing interest in making money.[3] Despite such caveats, Chinese social scientists are surely correct in asserting that the values of youth in the 1980s are very different from those of their counterparts in the 1950s, 1960s, and 1970s. Indeed, when one combines survey results with interview data and actual behavior, a strong case in favor of value change can be made.

Judging from recent surveys, China's open policy and expansion of market opportunities have contributed to an interest in events outside China and a "privatization" of values, reflected in a concern with lifestyle issues. Surveys also reveal a skepticism regarding some of the core principles on which the legitimacy of the party-state rests—part of the more general independence of belief shown by youth—and on uncertainty about the future. In at least some localities where economic development is rapid, such independence and privatization have led to an open rejection of collectivist values and even a return to some pre-1949 behavioral patterns. It is interesting to examine some recent data from Beijing and Wenzhou, a city that has become nationally known because of its success in creating wealth through private economic ventures.

A large-scale survey (20,000 questionnaires distributed; 12,000 ana-

TABLE 1 Ten News Items of Greatest Interest to Youth

News Item	% of Youth (N = 12,000)
Summer time change carried out nationally	88.5
Explosion of *Challenger*	85.9
Ascension of Corazon Aquino as president of Philippines	84.6
Thirteenth World Cup soccer tournament	82.1
China's winning of Uber Cup and Thomas Cup (badminton)	78.2
Chernobyl nuclear accident	76.9
Convictions of Chen Xiaomeng and Ye Zhifeng[a]	75.6
China's launching of communications satellite	75.6
Criticism in news organs of Beijing's commercial services	75.4
Big rainstorms in Beijing in July	74.4

Source: Wang Qun, "Beijing qingniande xinxi yishi" (Beijing youths' consciousness of news), *Qingnian yanjiu* (Youth research) 6:20 (1987).

a. Chen Xiaomeng, convicted of raping many women, was the son of Chen Guodeng, the former first secretary of the Shanghai Municipal Party Committee; Ye Zhifeng, guilty of economic corruption, is the daughter of Ye Fei, former minister of communications and former PLA navy commander.

lyzed) conducted in the last half of 1986 by the Youth League in Beijing asked young people, inter alia, their sources of information, news stories of interest to them, and the subjects they most enjoyed discussing. Forty-nine news stories from the first half of 1986 were listed, and respondents could choose five expressions, ranging from "familiar and concerned" to "I don't know and I don't care," to reflect their opinions. As Table 1 shows, four of the news items garnering the most interest concerned foreign events. Youth also showed an interest in sports news, Chinese achievements, events affecting daily life, and cadre corruption. As Table 2 reveals, of least interest were stories on cultural research and the economy. By a wide margin, the topics considered most enjoyable and most frequently discussed concerned "one's income and life," followed by literary and art works, personal relations, sports, and world affairs.[4]

Another recent survey, part of a massive effort (30,000 questionnaires were distributed) to investigate the effects of political-ideological education among Beijing's university students, uncovered rather similar results. For example, when asked the activities in which they had an interest, the lowest ranked were political study (51.1 percent not interested), activities of the party and Youth League (44.4 percent not interested), and voluntary labor (33.5 percent not interested).[5] A survey at four of

TABLE 2   Ten News Items of Least Interest to Youth

News Item	% of Youth (N = 12,000)
Craze for research on Chinese and foreign culture	46.2
Research on strategy of urban cultural development in Shanghai	32.1
Commencement of Spark Plan	30.8
Intention of U.S. and China to have weapons interchanges	29.5
First draft of Enterprise Bankruptcy Law	28.5
27th Soviet party conference	26.9
Shakespeare festival in China	25.6
Slow development of industry in Beijing from January to May	23.1
Price reform took a big step forward last year	23.1
Chinese edition of complete works of Marx and Engels now complete	23.1

Source: Wang Qun, "Beijing qingniande xinxi yishi" (Beijing youths' consciousness of news), *Qingnian yanjiu* (Youth research) 6:20 (1987).

China's most famous universities found the students most concerned with making China strong, making full use of their talents, and getting married. For example, in a sample of 344 Qinghua University students, 85.7 percent felt that university students should not only take study as their major task but also be concerned with society and politics; 59.3 percent thought that the first task of university students is to develop their abilities; and 86.3 percent felt that the university should not restrict the romantic activities of the students.[6]

Even students concerned with society and politics are now not necessarily willing to follow the lead of the party on these issues. One survey of 132 students at a "famous" (unnamed) university found that 53.1 percent saw Marxism as only one school of thought, not a guiding ideology; 44.7 percent did not agree that a thriving social science needed Marxism as a guide; and 37.5 percent felt that the statement that socialism is better than capitalism was only a worn-out cliché. A student forum at two other "famous" universities offered strong support for student demonstrations, and even for the democracy wall. At one of these schools only 5.3 percent agreed that big-character posters were not conducive to stability and unity and should not be used.[7]

Earlier surveys done in Shanghai had shown that college students valued respect for talent, patriotism (which was independent of party leadership), and creativity much higher than political commitments. As the authors of one survey report put it, "the students were concerned with talent and ability rather than ideals; knowledge rather than politics; and independent thought rather than obedience."[8]

In areas where economic growth has been particularly rapid, surveys reveal that youth are generally upbeat, creative, bold, and independent. Less frequently the "negative" face of the same attributes offers a more complete and balanced view of these changes. One recent study of Wenzhou youth is a good example.[9] To be sure, the survey demonstrates the creativity, independence, and success of these youth, but it also explicitly notes the relationship between such independence and a rejection of state and party influence. For example, "not a few" youth are characterized as undisciplined and unwilling to engage in civic voluntary labor; 71 percent of the crimes in the area are committed by 14- to 28-year-olds; 7.1 percent have become interested in Western religion; and so forth. Because this locality was particularly hard hit by Cultural Revolution policies, the newly rich youth have developed a strong spirit of "retaliation" against values of the recent past. They see no virtue in collectivism and nothing negative about the old traditions. Thus those with money will not contribute to schools or aid the government in road repair. Their money goes to rebuild temples and restore gravesides. For Wenzhou the "three goods" are a good private home, a good temple, and a good grave.[10]

Finally, a series of surveys among college students have revealed substantial uncertainty concerning the future. Recently students at eighteen universities in Shanghai were asked to comment on the statement, "It has already become very difficult to say what is right and what is wrong." About 23 percent agreed, 15 percent partially agreed, 24 percent found it difficult to agree or disagree, 11 percent partially disagreed, and 26 percent disagreed.[11] Quasi-time-series data confirm that this is a continuation of earlier trends. A 1987 survey of 887 students at twelve Shanghai universities compared the results with a 1981 survey of Fudan University students and a 1984 survey of East China Normal University students.[12] Whereas 59 percent in the 1981 survey expressed complete confidence in their own futures, only 47.5 percent were so confident in the 1987 survey; those who expressed confusion about their futures increased from 23 percent to 38 percent. When asked about their confidence in the continuation of current policies, fewer than 30 percent expressed such confidence in 1987, compared with around 33 percent in

1981. To be fair, over 50 percent in 1981 had expressed skepticism, a significantly higher figure than the 1987 total. However, almost 37 percent would not answer the question in 1987, not surprising since the survey was conducted in April–May 1987, during the campaign against "bourgeois liberalism."

Many forums have addressed the issue of college student malaise. In April 1988 universities in Hangzhou held a debate entitled "What Is Wrong with Contemporary College Students?" One official publication summed up the situation as follows: "Now there is no particularly dominant trend of thought among college students. Many 'hot issues' have also tended to become scattered. In 1985, college students focused on the theme of 'patriotism.' Two years ago, the students agitated under the banner of 'democratic freedom.' Now it is very difficult to find an idea that can call all college students to action." [13]

Reformers engaged in youth work have cited such survey results to show that university students "who hold positive views of values such as 'striving for the realization of communism and the Four Modernizations' and 'making contributions for the country and society' . . . are in the minority." Rather, they are shown to be concerned with improvements in their living conditions, eager "to obtain (and not sacrifice) all that they are entitled to . . . in the course of making contributions to society." As one young reformer, Yang Dongping, notes, this transformation of youth attitudes from the "strongly political," when "one billion people (were) all great critics," to the more personal is rather similar to developments in industrialized countries and may simply be "a normal phenomenon of a society of peace and prosperity focused on economic construction." Under these conditions some wonder how political socialization can be carried out effectively.

In the course of answering, Yang provides a devastating critique of current political education in China, which may produce apparent compliance in external behavior but has not touched the students' internalized value systems. When even the external compliance breaks down—as perhaps occurred in the student demonstrations in 1985, 1986, and particularly 1989—political education is inevitably "reduced to a case by case, fire-rescue type of preaching." What is needed, Yang argues, is to bring the students more directly into the political process, "to provide them with better political treatment than other members of society." [14] Yang's acknowledgment of the special place students occupied in Chinese society and his barely concealed suggestion that a mechanism for consultation, even cooptation, be devised had generated some support in the first half of 1986, during a high tide of reform.

Despite such appeals from reformers, however, more "conservative" party leaders have used similar surveys to argue that ideological education needs to be strengthened, that Chinese youth are subject to too little control. Thus, after the 1986 student demonstrations, Lei Feng, the deceased young soldier from the early 1960s whose greatest ambition was to become a "rust-free screw" concerned only with serving the people, was revived as a model; the State Education Commission announced regulations in April 1987 that called for paying greater attention to the political attitudes and behavior of prospective college and university students; and commentaries in the press began to argue that training in skills was secondary to the primary educational task of fostering "correct political orientation." [15]

If the 1986 demonstrations effectively curtailed the ability of the reformers to bring the students on board politically, the results of the demonstrations were no less frustrating to the ideological hard-liners and the students themselves. Students had originally taken to the streets in support of the reform movement but became more critical when the state-controlled media began to distort their activities. The sense of betrayal the students felt began to transform their movement from a progovernment to an antigovernment position. In their turn, the aging orthodox Marxists had been able to engineer the removal of Party General Secretary Hu Yaobang, but their anti-bourgeois-liberalism campaign lasted only four months, with Deng Xiaoping calling it off to protect China's economic reforms and the opening to the West. Indeed, as I have argued elsewhere, the roots of the 1989 student demonstrations—and the harsh response of the hard-liners—can be found in the incomplete resolution of the 1986–87 student movement, with the frustrations experienced by virtually all the major actors. [16]

ATTITUDES TOWARD THE PARTY

The independence of thought and uncertainty about the future also find expression in the assessment of the CCP and its cadres. Surveys of college students reveal a skepticism that the party can improve its work style in the near future. Moreover, recent trends in party recruitment suggest that the impasse in early post-Mao China—there was very little rejuvenation of the CCP from 1976 to 1983—has been broken, but that the

TABLE 3 Views of University Students in Beijing about Party Work Style

Views	% of Youth (N = 2,723)
Very confident	9.7
Believe it will basically improve, but not confident improvement will take place in next few years	44.6
As far as improvement in Party work style, believe one can only move a step at a time and see the results	26.1
Lack confidence in any basic improvement	12.2
No confidence	6.5

Source: Wang Dianqing et al., "Daxuesheng sixiang zhuangkuang de diaocha fenxi" (An investigation and analysis of the ideology of university students), in Beijing Municipal Party Committee Research Office, ed., Xin shiqi daxuesheng sixiang zhengzhi jiaoyu yanjiu (Research on ideological and political education of university students in the new period, Beijing, Beijing Normal University Press, 1988), p. 65.

new recruits may be joining for instrumental reasons, which they are sometimes willing to disclose openly.

A survey of students in management and social science classes at a "famous" (unnamed) university found several sources of dissatisfaction, one of which was party corruption. Many felt that it was common for party members to use their power for private gain and particularly noted the increasing promotion of and reliance on children of high-level cadres. As many as 83.1 percent of the students thought that party work style had not significantly improved, and an additional 3.1 percent saw it as becoming worse.[17] The results of a more detailed survey of university students in Beijing are presented in Table 3, which shows that over 90 percent of the students lacked confidence that party work style would soon improve. Indeed, when queried about political cadres who control their lives—those who decide job allocations, screen applicants to the party, compile dossiers, and so forth—some students have revealed particularly negative views. When students at Shandong Maritime Institute were asked their deepest impression of current cadres, the largest number (41.9 percent) chose "contemptible, hateful, detestable," followed by "none of the above" (41 percent) and then "frightening" (10.2 percent). Only 2.5 percent chose "worthy of respect and approachable."[18]

The recent surge in party recruitment began in 1984 and reflected a recognition that the CCP needed rejuvenation. In such a general atmosphere of skepticism, however, it is perhaps not surprising that many students are suspicious of those who seek party membership, and that the applicants themselves may see little need to cloak their true feelings. For their part, CCP officials have been concerned with recruiting China's best and brightest—particularly those in the elite universities—into party ranks.

China's leaders by the 1980s were sitting atop a party apparatus that had been steadily aging since 1949. Whereas party members 25 years old and younger had made up 26.6 percent of all party members in 1950, by 1983 the equivalent figure was 3.36 percent. In Shanghai the change was even more stark, going from 41 percent just after 1949 to 2.25 percent in 1983. The change in values among university students described in the previous section is congruent with party membership figures for university students in the 1980s, compared with the 1950s and 1960s. An internal report from the Ministry of Education in 1983 contrasted the situation with the eve of the Cultural Revolution by saying that things were so bad that

in a few schools there is not a single student who has applied to join the party. Moreover, the schools' party and Youth League committees have not placed this issue on the agenda . . . At Beijing Normal University, where student party members made up 12.5 percent in the first half of 1966, the number is down to 2 percent. At Qinghua University the equivalent figures have gone from 13 percent to 1.9 percent. At other schools the numbers are lower . . . At many colleges and universities the percentage of student party members is the lowest since the founding of the People's Republic of China . . . and in some schools with long histories there are fewer student party members now than the number of underground party members there in the pre-Liberation period.[19]

The impasse in recruitment work reflected a generation gap pitting contemporary youth, holding 1980s values, against conservative party members, still seeking the ideal youth of the 1950s. The problem came from two directions. On the one hand, Chinese authorities have recognized that the traditional criteria associated with party membership (for example, selflessness, discipline, obedience) reflected neither current youth norms nor current youth values. As a number of surveys show, professional or academic success is given top priority by young people, who calculate that early party membership may constrain the pursuit of more materialistic goals. At the same time, they realize that they are more likely to become the objects of party courtship *after* they achieve academic or professional success.[20] There is in fact evidence of this. Some Youth League organizations have reported that applicants to the party with a higher educational background are treated as activists and allowed to take part in the party's organizational activities. Those workers with little educational background who apply, however, are denied access to such activities.

At the same time that youth have been less than eager to join, local party leaders at the grass-roots level have been reluctant to absorb the "new youth" into the party; some cadres have argued that they "would not rest assured if they should allow this crop of university students to take over from them." In effect, they have been looking for Lei Feng and finding instead independent, critical individuals closer to those Liu Binyan wrote about in *The Second Kind of Loyalty*. Under these conditions a large number of "veteran comrades" have argued that, since the "university students of the 1980s are inferior to those of the 1950s," the "conditions are unripe" for recruiting any college students into the party.[21] Young workers have complained in surveys that the leadership disparages young people who "dare to think," since such independence is "unlikely to accomplish anything but likely to spoil everything."[22]

Facing an increase in independent student activity in the 1980s—ranging from small group salons to boycotts of cafeteria food to campus demonstrations—the party in universities began in 1984 a major recruitment campaign that has, at least in terms of numbers, already paid dividends. In Beijing the number of university students recruited in 1984 was more than double the 1983 recruits; similarly, 1985's recruits were double the 1984 figure. By 1984, 2.5 percent of Beijing's undergraduates were party members; the 1985 figure climbed to 4.4 percent and by 1986 the figure had reached 5.5 percent.[23] Despite the increased numbers, there is widespread recognition—and complaints—about the "impure" motives of those who join. Table 4, from the survey of students at eighteen Shanghai universities cited earlier, suggests that party membership may offer little indication of a person's value system. Other surveys present rather similar findings. For example, when rural youth in a county outside Shanghai were asked about motivations to join the party, 50.6 percent saw it as a "refueling station" on the individual's road of advancement; 31.7 percent felt it would facilitate the quest for personal gain; and 15.4 percent held that joining the party was not very important. Of those who had applied to join, 56.1 percent felt that "in recent years if you don't get in, it doesn't matter," and "if you run into complications,

TABLE 4 Question: Some of Your Friends Have Joined the Party, Others Are Striving to Do So. What Is Your Observation and Understanding of This?

Responses	% of Youth (N = 2,063)
They believe in communism and want to make a contribution.	4
They think the party is good and are joining in order to be further educated.	10
In reality they want a "party card" they can use as capital to receive future benefits.	59
Other responses.	—

Source: Zhao Yicheng, "Jiazhide chongtu" (Value conflict), *Weidinggao* (Manuscripts not finalized) 8:29 (1988).

forget it."[24] These results suggest the tentative generalization that party membership remains desirable and offers clear benefits, but that youth also perceive they can succeed outside of party ranks.

Once again, some of these conclusions might need modification as a result of the 1989 unrest. There are some indications that a shift in the criteria for party membership is likely, as political loyalty and discipline reemerge as primary standards for CCP entrance. In terms of class composition, the CCP may find it more difficult to recruit students and intellectuals in the immediate future. Indeed, that may not be a high priority. There has been a reaffirmation of the working class as the "main force" in the country, which "some people" had "disputed." Although intellectuals are part of this class, it has nevertheless been acknowledged that industrial workers in large and medium-sized enterprises have created most of the country's social wealth but have felt slighted, a situation causing frustration and resentment. Not long ago it was the intellectuals who were being appealed to in these terms. Moreover, the Chinese press has criticized the emphasis on "privatization" of the economy under Zhao Ziyang, with Jiang Zemin, the new general secretary of the party, suggesting that individuals engaged in private enterprise may be making too much money. This is likely to reduce the party's flirtation with the rural rich and to promote the chances of poor but ideologically orthodox peasants. Another target group for recruitment may be young soldiers, most of whom are poorly educated peasant youth. Those who were killed clearing the square have been posthumously admitted into the CCP.

While it is demonstrably true that at least some of the current attitudes and opinions of Chinese youth—for example, the skepticism regarding political commitments—can be traced to the political twists and turns of the 1960s and 1970s, additional survey data reveal a more direct impact of post-Mao *economic* reforms on social change. For examples we turn next to surveys of a less overtly political nature, on military recruitment from the rural areas and on education.

MILITARY RECRUITMENT AND THE IDEOLOGY OF YOUNG SOLDIERS

The People's Liberation Army (PLA) faces an even greater challenge than the CCP as a result of the reforms. The Chinese press has openly acknowledged that youth have become more and more indifferent about serving in the military.[25] This seems to be particularly true of those areas that have benefited from the increasing market orientation of the economy. Some townships in the Wenzhou area, for example, have gone several years without a single youth registering for military service. Given the economic prosperity of the area, young people have been quite willing to pay the fines assessed for noncompliance with the conscription law. One self-employed businessman, with assets of several hundred thousand yuan, showed up at the conscription office, plunked 150 yuan on the table, and boldly announced, "Don't bother me for the next three years!"[26]

It has likewise been difficult to recruit soldiers from Beijing's high schools. In autumn 1984 fewer than one-third of the Western District's planned quota registered for the physical examination. At some of the key high schools, where it had previously been commonplace to have around 100 outstanding students a year apply for military service, virtually no one has joined up since 1980. Even in the interior of the country, entering the military has lost a good deal of its luster. In an effort to enhance recruitment, particularly in economically successful areas like Guangzhou and Shenzhen, a variety of perquisites have been preferred, including work promotions and housing benefits, for those willing to serve.

Many surveys on military recruitment explicitly take the new economic reforms as their starting point. Perhaps because of the difficulty in recruiting soldiers from wealthy rural areas, a seemingly disproportionate number of these surveys analyze the motivations, attitudes, and behavior of those who joined despite their economic success at home.

Although presumably not representative of the majority of recruits, PLA officials have explicitly recognized the potential advantages of attracting these beneficiaries of the economic reforms. The most intriguing is a 1986 survey of 1,109 new recruits by the Youth Division of the PLA General Political Department. In addition, panel discussions were held with 73 cadres at the regimental, battalion, company, and platoon levels. The authors of the survey focus particularly on an interesting subsample of 628 soldiers (56.6 percent) who had been engaged in commodity production or trade before enlistment; 96 percent were from the rural areas.

The findings are very revealing. First, we note that these youth are joining the military in an effort to parlay military service into enhanced status or wealth. About 38 percent of the subgroup of 628 hoped to increase their status (over 90 percent of them "had their eye on party membership"); over 40 percent wanted to learn a trade (over 80 percent of these wanted to learn truck driving, a lucrative occupation in the countryside). Some of the recruits were particularly forthright, as the following passage shows:

A new recruit of a certain regiment had been in the transportation business at home. The village cadre extorted money from him and they were at odds with each other. His purpose in enlisting was to gain admission to the party so that he could stand up against the village cadre when he returned home after discharge. A soldier of rural origin was enlisted to a certain regiment in 1986. He had been driving a truck at home, but had been unable to obtain a driver's license despite his many efforts at finding connections and giving out gifts. He declared: "My purpose in enlisting is to get a driver's license." What is new is not that soldiers joined partly for personal desires but that they could now openly disclose their personal intentions.[27]

Second, influenced by their business practices, these recruits explicitly placed a high value on building a *guanxi* [connections] network. Rather than saluting when passing an officer, some would offer cigarettes. When the larger sample of 1,109 recruits was asked, "What kind of people do you admire most in society?" 28 percent responded, "Those who are able to cultivate relations." Of this 28 percent, the subsample of 628 made up 18 percent. As one soldier noted on the back of his questionnaire, "I worship heroes and models, and I worship even more those who are able to make money and cultivate relations, because they fare well wherever they go."

Third, given their specific reasons for joining the military, it was not uncommon for the new recruits to become disheartened if they felt they had "overinvested" in becoming a soldier, endured more hardships than the gains they derived. Among the 628 surveyed, 113 (17.9 percent) had developed an unfavorable impression of the army. The large majority of them had either not been assigned to tasks that would allow them to acquire the skills they desired (e.g., driving a truck), felt they had no chance to be admitted to the party, or could not get along with their leaders. The survey also showed that 53 percent had not been assigned tasks that utilized their talents and were unhappy with their jobs.

Fourth, despite their low level of education, the recruits had little desire to upgrade their formal educational level. When asked, "Do you want to learn a skill or study some culture?" 99.3 percent of the 628 opted for learning a skill.

While recognizing certain obvious shortcomings, the authors of the survey argue that these economically independent recruits "are the biggest contingent of talent in the history of our army." But many cadres within the military criticize the new-style rural recruits arriving from a more prosperous countryside as "slick, speculative operators," "the dregs of society," "profiteers," and imbued with a "merchant mentality."

Another survey, contained in a lengthy collection of essays analyzing conditions among young soldiers in the Nanjing military district, sheds additional light on the attitudes of new military recruits from the countryside.[28] In a study of 127 recruits from the countryside, supplemented by discussions with more than 20 cadres, several "disturbing" trends were noted. The level of dissatisfaction with military life was high; 54.3 percent of those surveyed wanted to return before the end of their three-year tour of duty. "Several years earlier," the equivalent figure had been 20–30 percent. Interest in learning a specialty or a technical skill had increased, but concern with politics had decreased. Company-level cadres reported that in the early 1980s more than 80 percent of the young soldiers wanted to join the party or receive certificates of merit. But survey results show that only 52.8 percent desired party membership, and only 30 percent were seeking to obtain such moral rewards as certificates of merit.

The soldiers' families reinforced the recruits' lack of commitment; 41.7 percent of the family heads wanted the recruits to return home as early as possible. Although the survey does not correlate opinion with income level, by providing detailed tables on the rising income levels, occupations, ownership of agricultural machinery, and so forth of the soldiers' families since the December 1978 plenum, it does make the more general point that the above changes in outlook were closely related to the flour-ishing economic situation in the home areas of the recruits. Peasant youth no longer relied on the military just to leave the countryside. Another survey, on the material demands of soldiers, showed both a strong desire for material goods and a dissatisfaction with the quality of food, cloth-ing, housing, and so forth provided in the army.[29]

YOUTH ATTITUDES AND EDUCATION

The post-Mao stress on economic development accepts differential treat-ment of geographic areas—based on preconditions for development—and individuals. Thus it allows coastal provinces like Guangdong to prosper before the more backward interior provinces, and the most qualified stu-dents to be concentrated in the better schools. This strategy has had an important impact on the social mobility opportunities of Chinese youth and, in turn, has influenced their attitudes and behavior.

In accordance with Deng Xiaoping's views of the role of education in economic development, China has created an essentially bifurcated edu-cational system beginning in elementary school. A small "elite" sector trains first-class bureaucrats, managers, scientists, and engineers needed to meet the ambitious targets of the Four Modernizations program. A large "mass" sector provides basic educational skills, with the possibility of additional vocational training, for the majority. In the past decade the gap between the two sectors has become wider and wider, with less and less interchange possible.[30]

For students able to work their way up through key schools in the elite sector, the reward is often entrance to a top university. For those who get tracked out of the elite sector somewhere on the educational ladder, the realization sets in early that none of the potential benefits of academic success—advanced graduate training; overseas study; allocation of a secure, desirable job on the frontiers of Chinese modernization—will be likely. This is particularly true of those channeled into "middling" or "slow" classes in high school. The desire to "invest" in one's education, therefore, is often directly proportional to one's place within this educa-tional hierarchy. Many studies have documented the seriousness of the problem. For example, a study of two "slow" senior high classrooms in a Wuhan school found that 60 percent of the students did not want to be in school; a broader study of students in several different Tianjin schools came up with a figure of 18.1 percent. The equivalent figure for key schools was said to be 6 percent.[31] The unanticipated consequences of this hierarchical educational model have been substantial. Some of the more visible effects are discussed below.[32]

The dropout rate among primary and secondary school students became a major problem as early as 1979, and by 1983 it had become a common theme in the Chinese press. The situation is especially serious at schools where students, with little hope of advancing up the educational ladder, consider early entry to the job market an attractive alternative. The issue has been frequently discussed in forums in newspapers for youth, under such titles as "Is It True that Studying Is Not as Good as Selling Popsicles?" and "Is It Worth It to Leave School to Go into Business?"[33] A letter to the editor from a group of high school students illustrates their confusion amidst China's rapid social change:

We are students from an ordinary middle school in Jiabei district. Last semester, two classmates who had poor study achievements and felt they could not catch up, dropped out of school. Now, one works as a contract worker in a barber shop and makes about 90 yuan a month. The other has set up a fruit stall and makes about 150 yuan a month. When this news reached us, the whole class became excited. A great many became disheartened about studying, asking, What's the use? Those who are uneducated can follow this model to make money, and make more than the intellectuals! The study atmosphere in the classroom has become worse and worse. As class cadres, seeing more and more students failing, we have become very worried, and have tried our best to persuade everyone. But we are at a loss as to what to say to them.[34]

The official response, of course, is to urge students to stay in school; however, the reasons given—for example, to improve one's spiritual life or to give one a greater competitive advantage in the job market—often seem unconvincing. As one letter writer put it: "Even those who love to read books can't buy them on low salaries . . . teahouses where they play music tapes and other such (entertainment) places belong to the world of the private entrepreneur. Therefore, we can see that the happiness of the higher spiritual life is inseparable from money."[35]

The dropout rate appears to be particularly high in those parts of the country where the economy is expanding. Studies in Beijing and Wenzhou show that the major reason for leaving school is to return to suburban and rural areas to help out in family enterprises or to seek a job and increase family income. Wenzhou's rapid development has been fueled, in part, by child labor. According to surveys, this accounts for 20 per-

TABLE 5 Plans of Graduating High School Seniors in Guangzhou and Xian

Plans	% of Seniors in Guangzhou	% of Seniors in Xian
Take the university entrance examination again if I don't succeed this time.	33.6	73.5
Study at a spare-time university if I don't get into a regular university.	35.8	16.8
Feel at ease in getting a job if I don't get into university.	26.2	8.4
Strive to study abroad.	4.4	1.5

Source: Yang Xianjun, "Xuesheng guxiang yu jiaoyu sixiang gaige" (Student choice and the reform in educational thinking), *Zhongguo jiaoyu xuehui tongxun*, (China Education Society bulletin) 2:28 (1987).

cent of the workers hired in the countryside around Wenzhou, and about 85 percent of these 10- to 16-year-olds are girls. Their families are reportedly quite satisfied to sacrifice their schooling, even their literacy, for early employment.[36] There have been reports in some cities that units have gone directly to high schools to recruit students in the graduating classes prior to graduation. In Guangzhou it has become serious enough that the Labor Bureau and the Education Bureau issued a joint notice opposing this practice.[37]

Comparative data, while still limited, have shown the differences between coastal and interior provinces and cities, county seats, and rural townships in terms of job opportunities and youth attitudes toward education. Noting that the pressure on employment had been eased in large and medium-sized cities, one study found that the proportion of people waiting for employment in county seats and towns relative to the total number of people waiting for jobs throughout the country had risen from 38 percent in 1980 to 50 percent in 1986.[38] Table 5 examines the graduating plans of high school seniors in Guangzhou and Xian and shows that entering a university may not have the overriding importance in Guangzhou that it has in Xian. Job opportunities for those who are not university graduates appear to be prevalent in Guangzhou. Articles in Guangzhou youth magazines have for at least several years been publishing surveys on the relatively high rate of labor mobility of young workers and on the changing job perceptions of youth in various parts of Guang-

TABLE 6   First Choices for Further Schooling of Junior High
Graduates in Guangzhou, June 1986

First-Choice Schooling	% Junior High Graduates (N = 20,000 +)	Ratio of Students Accepted to Applicants
Regular senior high	33.4	1:1.20
Provincial and municipal key	11.8	1:1.84
District key	5.0	1:1.29
Nonkey	16.6	1:0.99
Secondary technical (zhongzhuan)	38.2	1:2.60
Skilled worker training (zhongji)	14.1	1:1.70
Vocational (zhizhong)	14.3	1:1.30

Source: Yang Xianjun, "Xuesheng guxiang yu jiaoyu sixiang gaige," (Student choice and the reform in educational thinking) Zhongguo jiaoyu xuehui tongxun, (China Education Society bulletin) 2:32 (1987).

dong.[39] Table 6 further supports this argument by revealing the actual choices made by Guangzhou's junior high graduating class in 1986. It shows that places in secondary technical schools, which do not lead to university entrance, were scarcer than those at key senior highs and that only one of three junior high graduates chose a regular academic senior high, which prepares students for university entrance, as a first choice.

The Guangzhou data become more meaningful when compared with data from Shaanxi Province in China's interior. Each year about half the senior high students studying for the university entrance examinations are repeaters from previous years, studying in tutorial classrooms along with current-year graduates. As the head of the provincial educational bureau noted, the pressure to run these classes often comes from party and government leaders.[40]

A detailed study of a poor district in Shaanxi Province showed how a lack of educational funding and a severely limited job market had structured the options—and behavior—of junior high graduates.[41] Of the 33,800 junior high graduates in 1986, only 6,900 (20.4 percent) were recruited to regular senior highs, 1,030 (3 percent) were recruited to secondary technical schools, and 1,500 were recruited to vocational schools (4.4 percent); thus only 28 percent went on to the senior middle level. The large majority of the 72 percent who were not accommodated sought to return to their junior highs to prepare for the next year's examination; in the end, 12,000 students (50 percent of those not promoted) were allowed to do so. The lack of an expanding job market compelled students to concentrate on squeezing into a secondary technical school or a teacher training school, since this led to a guaranteed job assignment. Other forms of senior high were considered virtually useless dead ends. Since opportunities for higher education were minimal, ordinary academic senior highs had trouble attracting students. Vocational schools were considered the worst option; the 1,500 students recruited were only a third of the number sought. Local labor bureaus, knowing the poor quality of these schools, simply did not recruit workers or cadres from them.

In the course of pursuing economic development and "Chinese-style socialism," China is witnessing major social changes. The overall reform process, far more than any particular reform, has created an environment that accepts, and even encourages, the freedom of the individual to pursue materialistic goals. The expansion of market opportunities has begun to "open up" the system. The Maoist emphasis on creating a new socialist man and woman glorified individuals like Lei Feng, who would selflessly aspire to be "rust-free screws" in the service of the party's and the nation's needs. Indeed, all work was said to serve the revolution equally. Deng Xiaoping's reform program could not succeed with a nation of Lei Fengs. The post-Mao emphasis on the creation of a new "economic man," competitive and innovative, justifies job distinctions and differential rewards. It is no longer a sin to become wealthy; indeed, until the military crackdown, there were open debates on whether the party should recruit millionaire entrepreneurs who hire hundreds of workers.[42] No one can yet say what form a modernized, "socialist" China is likely to take. Still, the transitional period has already provided enough hints to indicate the direction of social change and the challenges now faced by some of China's most hallowed institutions. The analysis has suggested a number of points.

First, society presents youth many options other than continued schooling. Decisions of school youth may be seen as "investment" options. For example, if one fails to enter a key junior or senior high, one has little chance of entering a good university, and therefore continuing one's schooling may be considered a poor investment. Hence dropping out to find a well-paying job or to help one's family prosper becomes an attractive possibility. Such options, however, are clearly much more available in areas where economic development has created an expanding job market. Large parts of interior China have not yet begun this transition. In 1986 the government introduced a nine-year compulsory education law to reduce or at least delay some of these options, but it is too early to evaluate the effectiveness of this measure.

Second, the "freedom" of individuals to choose among options reflects a clear decline in the state's ability to control social change. The new environment supports a "privatization" of values. Moreover, the post-Mao ideological vacuum, created by policies pushing whatever helps economic development, contributed to the use of money as the overwhelming standard for success. The encouragement of private entrepreneurship, the daily floating population in virtually all Chinese cities, and increased opportunities for labor mobility are all products of the economic reforms, while the large numbers of school-leavers and the increases in juvenile delinquency, premarital abortions, divorces, and so forth all reflect the decline in social control.

Third, institutions that have long provided the best opportunities for upward social mobility—the party, the military, state enterprises, the schools—are forced to adjust to new socioeconomic conditions. For the party, Youth League, and military, there are questions of *who* to recruit and *how* to socialize them. Peasant youth, their major source of recruits in the past, are becoming more economically independent and no longer look to the military as a possible escape route from a backward countryside. Rather, they often see military service as a necessary price to pay for joining the party so they can protect their wealth or for learning a valuable skill to expand their wealth. Should the military recruit these newly rich peasants and seek to convert them into political "Reds," socializing them to support "communist" values? Is it not more probable, given the prevailing ideological climate, that the institutions themselves will be resocialized away from such values, following an influx of these new recruits?

The Communist Youth League (CYL) has also felt the stresses of economic development. In many localities, particularly in the countryside, it has become moribund or been infected by the economic ambitions of its members and potential recruits. Chinese authorities have sought to revive and reorient the CYL by tying its future to the success of the economic reforms and their beneficiaries. Thus a report from the Central CYL Secretariat went so far as to explain that the primary task of rural league branches is to help youth get rich. CYL cadres from newly rich peasant households, the report went on, made up only 10 percent of all league cadres in the countryside; the goal was to bring this figure up to 50 percent.[43] Some localities were criticized for carrying the message too far, such as the regulation reported in parts of Hubei Province which stipulated that only youth from households in which the average income per person was 300 yuan would be considered.[44] The party and military are not likely ever to reach this point, but they do face some of the same dilemmas of adjustment to an increasingly market-oriented society as faced by the CYL.

Fourth, concern with politics has inevitably declined. Before the Cultural Revolution it was common for Chinese youth to adopt "strategies" that led them either to seek academic or professional success (the "expert" path) or to engage in political activism (the "Red" path).[45] During the Cultural Revolution, of course, concern with politics was necessary for all youth who sought upward mobility. Now, political interest *follows* success in other areas. Newly rich peasants will seek party membership or military entrance *after* economic success. Students who apply for party membership often do so only *after* achievements in their academic and professional careers. The declining interest of young people in politics is not surprising. What is ironic, however, is the party's own contribution to this decline. While the media were emphasizing the crucial importance of fostering a communist value system, party recruitment in recent years has been concentrated heavily on the achievers, that is, on those with university degrees, professional positions, and so forth. With the party reaching out to the expert, those who are only Red had nowhere to go. It remains to be seen whether the events of 1989 will reverse these trends.

Chronology
Notes
Glossary
Bibliography
Index

PRELUDE TO REFORM

1976

January	Death of Zhou Enlai
February	Hua Guofeng named acting premier
April	Tiananmen Incident over commemoration of Zhou Enlai
	Deng Xiaoping removed from all posts by Politburo
	Hua Guofeng confirmed as premier
July	Tangshan earthquake
September	Death of Mao
October	Arrest of Gang of Four: Jiang Qing, Zhang Chunqiao, Yao Wenyuan, and Wang Hongwen

RETURN OF DENG XIAOPING AND LAUNCHING OF ECONOMIC AND LEGAL REFORMS

1977

March	Hua Guofeng agrees to return of Deng
August	Eleventh CCP Congress
	confirms Hua as party chairman
	appoints Deng vice chairman of CCP, vice premier, and People's Liberation Army chief of staff

December	Restoration of university entrance exams

1978

February	Fifth National People's Congress (NPC)
	approves Hua's Ten-Year Plan
	confirms 1978 constitution, which
	retains "Four Bigs" (speaking out freely, airing views fully, holding great debates, and writing big-character posters)
	retains right to strike of 1975 constitution
	retains role of Mao and Mao Zedong Thought
	restores procuracy
May	*People's Daily* editorial: "Practice is the sole criterion of truth"
June	Army Political Work Conference, where Deng advocates "seeking truth from facts"
September	Deng criticizes Hua's unquestioning support of Mao as "two whatevers"
October	Pilot scheme for profit retention in state industry

DENG'S FIRST CONSOLIDATION OF ECONOMIC AND LEGAL REFORMS

December	Third Plenum of Eleventh Central Committee
	launches the Four Modernizations: in agriculture, industry, science and technology, and national defense
	establishes Central Discipline Commission under Chen Yun to oversee rectification of CCP
	rehabilitates Peng Dehuai
	reverses verdicts on 1976 Tiananmen Incident
	replaces Wong Dongxing with Yao Yilin

1979

January	Arrest of Fu Yuehua, advocate of rural petitioners
	Wei Jingsheng publishes call for "Fifth Modernization"
	Retirement Law of 1978 goes into effect nationwide
	Explicit policy of nondiscrimination toward children of landlords and rich peasants
	First announcement of One-Child-Family policy
February	Shanghai youth demonstrate against returning to countryside
	China invades Vietnam
	Regulations of 1957 for arrest and detention reaffirmed
March	Deng reaffirms "Four Basic Principles":
	Keep to the socialist road
	Uphold the dictatorship of the proletariat
	Uphold the leadership of the Communist party
	Uphold Marxism-Leninism and Mao Zedong Thought
	Democracy wall restricted to certain areas
	Arrest of Wei Jingsheng

April	State raises grain prices 35%
	Lawyers Association restored in Beijing
June	Hua Guofeng amends his Ten-Year Plan because of huge trade deficit and inflation
July	One-Child-Family policy to be intensified
	Second Session of Fifth NPC
	adopts first Criminal Law and Law of Criminal Procedure, new Organic Laws for people's courts and procuracy, new Election Law allowing direct election to county congresses
	abolishes revolutionary committees
September	Fourth Plenum of Eleventh Party Congress
	reverses 1955 charges against writer Hu Feng
	Zhao Ziyang and Peng Zhen join Politburo
	NPC restores Ministry of Justice (abolished in 1958)
	adopts China's first Environmental Protection Law
October	NPC endorses return of private plots
	Trial of Wei Jingsheng
	Trial of Fu Yuehua
November	Fourth Workers' and Artists' Congress reaffirms principles of Mao's Yan'an forum as guidelines for literary work
	Wei Jingsheng's appeal rejected
	State Council amends 1957 regulation on labor reform to limit punishment but also affirms extrajudicial punishment
December	Closing of democracy wall

POLITICAL CONSOLIDATION UNDER DENG

1980

January	New Criminal Law and Election Law go into effect
February	Fifth Plenum of Eleventh Central Committee
	rehabilitates Liu Shaoqi
	appoints Hu Yaobang general secretary
	abolishes lifetime jobs for cadres
	reestablishes party secretariat
	purges "little Gang of Four" (Chen Xilian, Wu De, Ji Dengkui, Wang Dongxing) for supporting "two whatevers"
	rescinds article 45 of 1978 constitution protecting free speech
March	Foreign exchange coupons issued for first time
June	Attack on Dazhai model brigade and resignation of Chen Yonggui
August	Enlarged Politburo meeting
	launches reform of party and state leadership
	offers special inducements for cadre retirement *(lixiu)*
September	Third session of Fifth NPC
	approves new Marriage Law, Nationalities Law, income tax for joint ventures, individual income tax, law on duties and training of lawyers

reaffirms validity of laws enacted after 1949

endorses State Council decision to make Shenzhen a special economic zone

establishes Committee for Revision of Constitution

Hua announces scrapping of his Ten-Year Plan

Zhao Ziyang replaces Hua as premier

October– Conflicts at local elections for people's congresses
November

November   Trial of Gang of Four begins

FUNDAMENTAL REFORMS IN AGRICULTURE AND EXPERIMENTS IN INDUSTRY

1981

January   CCP Military Commission announces defense cuts

New Marriage Law permitting easier divorce in effect

Sentencing of Gang of Four

State Council regulation to curb bonuses

February   *People's Daily* calls for expansion of new towns

March   Xue Muqiao announces need to cut capital expenditures

April   Attack on Bai Hua for "Unrequited Love"

Arrests of democracy "activists" begin

Central Committee attacks "illegal publications"

State units allowed to negotiate profit retention

June   Sixth Plenum of Eleventh Central Committee

approves Hua's resignation as premier

promotes Hu Yaobang to chairmanship of Central Committee

approves "Resolution on Certain Questions in the History of our Party since the founding of the People's Republic," criticizing Mao Zedong

July   Deng attacks "bourgeois liberalization as opposition to CCP"

November   Fourth Session of Fifth NPC

approves sixth Five-Year Plan (1981–1985)

passes Economic Contract Law

December   73% of rural households use a form of new household contracting system

80% of state industries use profit retention

1982

January   Document No. 1 of Central Committee supports new contracting systems but continues to subordinate market mechanism to central planning and the collective

March   Twenty-second Session of Standing Committee of Fifth NPC

simplifies structure and staff of State Council

cuts staff from 49,000 to 32,000

approves promotion of more-educated cadres

modifies Criminal Code to punish economic criminals more severely, to permit death penalty, and to weaken access to mandatory high-court review

adopts Civil Code (draft)

April   Constitution of 1982 replaces one of 1978

reestablishes *xiang* to replace commune

prohibits frame-ups

eliminates freedom to strike and "Four Bigs"

adds State Central Military Commission

allows fully owned foreign enterprises

strengthens duty to practice birth control

May   State Council establishes Economic System Reform Commission

FUNDAMENTAL RESTRUCTURING GOES FORWARD

September   Twelfth CCP Congress

ratifies most of Deng's reform

dismisses Hua from Politburo

adopts new CCP constitution

December   Fifth Session of Fifth NPC

adopts 1982 constitution

ends communes as political units

1983

January   Document No. 1 of Central Committee fully endorses rural decollectivization

Supreme People's Court reduces Jiang Qing's death sentence to life
imprisonment

One-Child-Family policy goes into more intense phase

February   97% of rural households use household contracting system

March   New Criminal Laws go into effect

April   Taxes replace profits as revenue from state industries to state

June   Zhao's report at Sixth NPC criticizes urban reform, citing budget
deficit, excessive investment, excessive bonuses

August   Labor reform for criminals shifted from public security to judiciary

September   Second Session of Sixth NPC

announces harsher measures for economic crimes

adds new Ministry of State Security

October   Second Plenum of Twelfth Central Committee

initiates party rectification

launches attack on "spiritual pollution"

December   Expansion of metropolitan authority over *xian* and *qu*

replacement of prefecture by metropolitan region

1984

January	Document No. 1 of Central Committee advances rural reforms
	land to be contracted for fifteen years
	capital may flow freely
	labor may be hired
	families may concentrate land and specialize output
	Document No. 7 announces exceptions to One-Child quota, signaling retreat from 1983 extremism
	Wang Ruoshui, leading dissident writer, dropped as deputy editor from *People's Daily*
March	*Der Spiegel* correspondent Terziani expelled
April	CCP political rectification reaches provinces
May	Factory Director Responsibility System begins
June	Document No. 9 of Central Committee calls for continued party rectification

REFORMERS TURN TO THE URBAN ECONOMY AND PACE OF CHANGE QUICKENS

October	Third Plenum of Twelfth Central Committee
	endorses urban reforms and attacks "iron rice bowl"
	endorses "commodity economy"
	states goal to learn from capitalist nations
	endorses further substitution of tax for profit
	State Council Regulation permits migration of peasants to small towns, legitimates massive rural out-migration
November	NPC endorses Hong Kong agreement, "One country, two systems"

1985

January	Document No. 1 of Central Committee initiates further decollectivization and privatization of agriculture
	end of mandatory sales of grain to state
	70% of grain tax can be paid in cash
	Fourth National Congress of Chinese Writers' Association
	Hu Qili calls for freedom of art and literature
	Liu Binyan elected to leadership on secret ballot
	People's Daily, 3 January, "Four Modernizations must be accompanied by political democracy"
February	Decision to cut People's Liberation Army ranks by one million
April	Abolition of unified purchase price for grain
	Central Committee promises wage and price reforms
	NPC endorses China's first Inheritance Law that allows inheritance of means of production
	endorses new Patent Law
May	State Council announces goal to universalize nine-year education
July	Deng Liqun retires as director of propaganda

September   Fifth Plenum of Twelfth Central Committee
        starts with a new Central Committee with 50% new members
        sets up Central Political System Reform Group
November   CCP rectification reaches village members
        Further liberalization of rural commodity markets

1986

January   NPC endorses General Principles of Civil Code (still incomplete) to go into effect January 1987
March   Fourth Session of Sixth NPC adopts seventh Five-Year Plan (1986–1990)
August   NPC endorses Bankruptcy Law
        announces contract labor system for all new state workers hired after 1 October 1986
September   Sixth Plenum of Twelfth Central Committee
        issues "Guiding Principles for Building a Socialist Society with Advanced Culture and Ideology"
        identifies bourgeois liberalism, not feudalism, as chief threat
        gives factory directors new authority
October   "Twenty-two Articles on Foreign Trade" creates generally more secure environment for foreign business but holds back on repatriation of profits
December   Students in Hefei, Shanghai, Wuhan, and Beijing rally for democracy
        NPC passes new Banking Law (on three-month trial)
        revises NPC Electoral Law again

FIRST CRACKDOWN AND PARTIAL RETREAT

1987

January   Enlarged meeting of Central Committee–Politburo
        self-criticism and resignation of Hu Yaobang
        election of Zhao Ziyang as acting CCP secretary
        dismissal of Fang Lizhi, Wang Ruowang, and Liu Binyan from CCP
March   Campaign against bourgeois liberalism continues
April   NPC endorses Zhao's work report on government
October   Thirteenth Party Congress
        Li Peng appointed acting premier
        Zhao Ziyang confirmed as general secretary
        return of Hu Yaobang and failure of Deng Liqun to be elected to either Central Committee or Central Advisory Commission
        adoption of theoretical perspective: "China in the early stages of socialism"
November   Draft Organic Law governing village committees

1988

January   Sixth NPC standing committee supplementary provisions on corrup-
               tion and bribery add death penalty
               Rationing of pork, eggs, and sugar returns in many cities
February   Rural Development Research Center announces twelve areas to test
               different forms of agricultural ownership and management
March   Second Plenum of Thirteenth Central Committee
               Zhao's report announces "that everyone must learn to swim in the
                  ocean of the commodity economy"
April   Seventh NPC
               71% of delegates newly elected
               confirms Li Peng as premier
               adopts Bankruptcy Law
               amends constitution to permit transfer of land-use rights
               allows private business to hire more than seven employees
               adopts State Enterprise Law, granting enterprises standing as "legal
                  persons"
July   New regulations on private business take effect, removing CCP from
               daily management
               90% of large state units use *chengbao* contracts
September   NPC strengthens State Secrets Law, adding death penalty
               Third Plenum of Thirteenth Central Committee
               announces slowdown on price reform
               agrees to maintain dual-track pricing

HIGH-LEVEL DIVISIONS THREATEN REFORM

October   Full meeting of State Council
               Li Peng announces cuts of investment and price control
               Fourth session of Seventh NPC Standing Committee
               demands some recentralization
December   Central Committee Secretariat meets on corruption

1989

February   Central Committee calls for more politics in literature
               Riots in Tibet begin
March   Second session of Seventh NPC
               Li Peng speaks out against privatization
April   Death of Hu Yaobang
               Students rally in Tiananmen and other urban centers
May   Demonstrations persist
               Gorbachev visits Beijing
               Zhao Ziyang resigns

DECLARATION OF MARTIAL LAW

June   Troops fire on demonstrators and bystanders in Beijing

NOTES

The following abbreviations are used for frequently cited works:

CQ	*China Quarterly*
FBIS	*Foreign Broadcast Information Service (China)*
GRRB	*Gongren ribao* (Workers' daily)
JJRB	*Jingji ribao* (Economics daily)
JPRS	*Joint Publications Research Service*
RMRB	*Renmin ribao* (People's daily)
ZGFZB	*Zhongguo fazhibao* (China's legal gazette)
ZGTJNJ	*Zhongguo tongji nianjian* (Statistical yearbook of China; Beijing, State Statistical Bureau)
ZGWSNJ	*Zhongguo weisheng nianjian* (Health yearbook of China; Beijing, People's Medical Publishing House)

Introduction: The Social and Political Consequences of Reform, by Deborah Davis and Ezra F. Vogel

1. Janos Kornai, "Bureaucratic and Market Coordination," *Osteuropa* (December 1984), pp. 306–319.
2. Ivan Szelenyi, "The Prospects and Limits of the East European New Call Project," *Politics and Society* 15:103–144 (1986–87).

Chapter 1. The Fate of the Collective after the Commune, by Jean C. Oi

Earlier versions of this paper were presented at "China in a New Era: Continuity and Change," Third International Congress of Professors World Peace Academy, Manila, the Philippines, 24–29 August 1987, and "Social Consequences of the Chinese Economic Reforms," John King Fairbank Center for East Asian Research, Harvard University, 13–15 May 1988.

1. The details of the responsibility system have been examined elsewhere. See Kathleen Hartford, "Socialist Agriculture Is Dead; Long Live Socialist Agriculture," in Elizabeth J. Perry and Christine Wong, eds., *The Political Economy of Reform in Post-Mao China* (Cambridge, Mass., and London, Harvard Contemporary China Series, no. 2, Council on East Asian Studies, Harvard University, 1985), pp. 31–62. For an overview of the economic problems that led to the reforms as well as the reforms themselves, see Carl Riskin, *China's Political Economy: The Quest for Development since 1949* (New York, Oxford University Press, 1987).

2. For details, see Jean Oi, "Peasant Grain Marketing and State Procurement: China's Grain Contracting System," *CQ* 106:272–290 (1986).

3. For a more detailed discussion of this process, see Jean Oi, *State and Peasant in Contemporary China: The Political Economy of Village Government* (Berkeley, University of California Press, 1989), chap. 9.

4. The name for this level of administration varies significantly. In Shandong, for example, the former teams are now called *pian* (piece [of land]). In some villages this level does not exist at all.

5. Grain rationing technically still exists in that each person is allowed to procure a limited amount of grain at state prices. But for those peasants who grow grain, the system for all intents and purposes is defunct. There are no limits on the amount that they can keep. Those who do not grow grain are, however, still limited by the rationing system, but now large supplies exist on the open market, if at higher prices.

6. For details on the struggle over the harvest during the Maoist period, see Oi, *State and Peasant,* esp. chaps. 2–4.

7. "Dui gaige nongye shuide shexiang" (Tentative plans on reforming the agricultural tax), *Nongye jingji wenti* (Problems of agricultural economics) 4:36 (1985).

8. "Caizhengbu jueding bing guiding shishi banfa jinyibu jianqing nongcun shuishou fudan" (The Ministry of Finance decides and stipulates procedures to further decrease the rural tax burden), *RMRB* 2:1 (October 1979).

9. On continuing problems, see Oi, "Peasant Grain Marketing," and *State and Peasant,* chap. 8. For a detailed discussion of problems in grain prices, see Terry Sicular, "Agricultural Planning and Pricing in the Post-Mao Period," *CQ* 116:671–705 (1988). Some of the most recent problems with regard to grain procurements center on the state's insufficiency of funds to pay peasants for its purchases. The result has been the issuance of "white slips" (i.e., IOUs). To prevent this problem, local granaries in some localities simply stop buying grain when they run out of funds. See, for example, *FBIS,* 6 November 1989, p. 51.

10. The bulk of the research was done from April to August 1986 and June to September 1988. I interviewed at district, county, township, and village levels

near Tianjin, Shenyang, Dalian, Chengdu, Chongqing, and Jinan about changes in the planning process and the degree of government involvement in the management of the rural economy, focusing on the management and finance of rural enterprises. At the district *(qu)* and county *(xian)* levels, I met representatives from township management bureaus; planning and economic commissions; agricultural and forestry offices; commerce, tax, price, and finance bureaus; sales cooperatives; agricultural banks; and industrial and commercial management bureaus. At the township *(xiang)* level, I interviewed township heads and vice heads, the economic commissions *(jingwei)*, township industrial companies *(xiang qiye gongsi)*, heads of saving cooperatives, and factory managers of *xiang*-run industry. At the village *(cun)* level, I interviewed village party secretaries and village heads *(cunzhang)* as well as factory directors. Unless otherwise indicated, the material for this paper is based on these interviews. I want to stress that I am laying out rather preliminary findings. The propositions sketched here will be further tested and no doubt modified as I continue to research this topic.

11. For a detailed discussion of the different claimants on the collective harvest during the Maoist period and the changes that took place with the post-1978 reforms, see my *State and Peasant.*

12. See William A. Byrd and Lin Qingsong, eds., "China's Rural Industry: Structure, Development, and Reform" (unpublished manuscript), esp. chap. 15 by Song Lina and Du He, "The Role of Township Governments in Rural Industrialization."

13. As Whyte, Parish, and others have shown, considerable income inequality has always existed in the rural areas. See, for example, Martin K. Whyte, "Social Trends in China: The Triumph of Inequality?" in A. Doak Barnett and Ralph Clough, eds., *Modernizing China* (Boulder, Colo., Westview Press, 1986), pp. 103–123.

14. For example, the village in Shenyang that provides impressive subsidies had twenty-six village-level enterprises. According to the World Bank study, the national average per village in 1985 was less than one. Byrd and Lin, "Market Interactions and Industrial Structures," in their "China's Rural Industry," p. 38.

15. This aspect of the reforms has received little attention. See, for example, the otherwise useful volume on reform in China by Perry and Wong, eds., *Political Economy of Reform.* To date, the World Bank study edited by Byrd and Lin cited earlier, the most comprehensive treatment of the operation and impact of rural industry.

16. See, for example, Graham E. Johnson, "The Fate of the Communal Economy: Some Contrary Evidence from the Pearl River Delta," paper presented at Annual Meeting of the Association of Asian Studies, Chicago, 21–23 March 1986.

17. There is some disagreement on the exact date this occurred. Christine P. W. Wong, in "Interpreting Rural Industrial Growth in the Post-Mao Period," *Modern China* 14:3–30 (1988), dates this development to 1986. The World Bank dates it to 1987. "China's Rural Industry: An Introduction," in Byrd and Lin, "China's Rural Industry," p. 22.

18. "Rural Industry Provides Base for Economic Growth," *China Daily,* 5 August 1987, p. 1, in *JPRS* 87-045, 9 September 1987, pp. 41–42.

19. "Broad and Profound Impact of the Development of China's Township Enterprises," *Ching-chi tao-pao* (Economic reporter), 20 October 1987, pp. 34–35, translated in *JPRS* 87–061, 31 December 1987, pp. 23–25.

20. See Oi, *State and Peasant,* chap. 9, for details on the differences in wages between those in agriculture and those in industry.

21. *ZGTJNJ 1988,* p. 293. According to Wong, "Interpreting Rural Industrial Growth," the figures from the State Statistical Bureau on this item tend to undercount the number of persons actually working in rural industry. Regardless of the precise number, the trend is clearly toward peasants moving into nonfarm activity.

22. This figure includes all nonagricultural jobs. Huang Qingde, Wang Chengde, and He Daofeng, Rural Development Research Center of the State Council, "The Relationship between Agriculture and Industry in China's Economic Development: Economic Growth and Structural Change," *Shijie jingji daobao* (World economic herald), 11 January 1988, p. 7, translated in *JPRS* 88–011, 8 March 1988, pp. 26–29.

23. Byrd and Lin, "China's Rural Industry," p. 18.

24. As Wong, "Interpreting Rural Industrial Growth," cautions, the absolute numbers should not be taken too literally. There are systemic incentives, such as tax breaks, for the creation of new enterprises. Officials have admitted in my interviews that it is not uncommon for an enterprise to close and reopen under a new name in order to qualify for the exemptions. Moreover, there is the problem of definition. See below.

25. *China Agricultural Yearbook 1988,* p. 296; *Zhongguo xiangzhen qiye nianjian 1978–1987* (Chinese rural township enterprise yearbook 1978–1987; Beijing, Nongye Chubanshe, 1989), p. 569. The growth of these industries between 1978 and 1986 has been uneven. It was not until 1984 that take-off really began.

26. China Interview 72886.

27. China Interview 11888.

28. *JPRS* 87-061, 31 December 1987, p. 24.

29. Zhang Lin, "The Theory of the Initial Stage of Socialism and the Practice of Rural Economic Development at Wenzhou," *Nongmin bao* (Peasant gazette), 3:4 (June 1987) translated in *JPRS* 87–019, 15 July 1987, pp. 96–97. For detailed discussion of these points, see Du Haiyan, "Causes of Rapid Rural Industrial Development," in Byrd and Lin, "China's Rural Industry."

30. Deng Yiming, "Analysis of Surplus Rural Labor," *Jingjixue zhoubao* (Economic studies weekly), 5 April 1987, p. 3, translated in *JPRS* 87-037, 24 August 1987, pp. 59–61. Du Runsheng, director of the Rural Development Research Center of the State Council, announced in 1985 that the state planned to transfer over 50% of the surplus labor from agricultural production to nonagricultural departments by the end of the century. *Beijing Review,* 24 June 1985, p. 17.

31. Guowuyuan Banshiting Diaoyanshi, eds., *Geti jingji diaocha yu yanjiu* (Investigation and research on the individual economy; Beijing, Jingji Kexue Chubanshe, 1986), pp. 296, 301–302.

32. *ZGTJNJ 1988*, p. 286.

33. *ZGTJNJ 1988*, p. 287.

34. The management fee seems to vary. In parts of Sichuan, for example, it is 1% of total income. This money is collected by the tax office from both village and township enterprises. The township receives the money but then gives a portion to the *qu*. China Interview 81786. In one county near Jinan, 1% of total sales is levied by the township management bureau as the management fee. Different portions are then allotted to the township and county governments. China Interview 53188. In yet another county in Shandong, the township government levies a fee of 20% of enterprise profits and then pays the township management bureau a percentage as the management fee. China Interview 72388.

35. Wong makes a similar point. See her "Interpreting Rural Industrial Growth."

36. See Jean Oi, "Commercializing China's Rural Cadres," *Problems of Communism* 35:1–15 (1986), for examples of this problem. See also David Zweig et al., "Law, Contracts, and Economic Modernization: Lessons from the Recent Chinese Rural Reforms," *Stanford Journal of International Law* 23:319–364 (1987).

37. Wong, "Interpreting Rural Industrial Growth," p. 23.

38. Du Haiyan, "Causes of Rapid Rural Industrial Development," in Byrd and Lin, "China's Rural Industry," p. 31.

39. China Interview 6488.

40. "Township Enterprises Should Also Implement Reforms," *Jingji cankao* (Economic reference news), 18 November 1987, p. 1, translated in *JPRS* 88–005, 18 February 1988. Wong, "Interpreting Rural Industrial Growth," p. 23, also refers to this problem.

41. China Interview 71886.

42. Ibid.

43. Some local governments, usually only at the township level and above, help by investing in factories that produce raw materials required by local industries. This guarantees needed supplies for their enterprises and provides profit for the local authorities.

44. Chaps. 15 and 16 in Byrd and Lin, "China's Rural Industry," also strongly make this point.

45. See Jean Oi, "Peasant Households between Plan and Market: Cadre Control over Agricultural Inputs," *Modern China* 12:230–251 (1986), and Oi, "Commercializing China's Rural Cadres," for further details in this regard. These articles deal primarily with agriculture, but the problems faced by rural industry are similar.

46. I was struck by the similarities when Andrew Walder and I conducted interviews in urban state-owned industry. For a published description of the continued "soft budget constraint" in state-owned factories, see Andrew G. Walder, "The Informal Dimension of Enterprise Financial Reforms," in U.S. Congress Joint Economic Committee, *The Four Modernizations*, vol. 1 of *China's Economy Looks toward the Year 2000* (Washington, D.C., U.S. GPO, 1986), pp. 630–645.

47. There are exceptions to this, such as the exhaust-fan factory mentioned earlier. The factory itself sold its products. This was not a problem, because the fans were required in certain types of factories and so demand was high.

48. China Interview 81386.

49. The national average of profits used for reinvestment in 1985 was 46.3%. In 1986 it was 49.8%. *ZGTJNJ 1987*, p. 205. Whether in fact factories actually follow their local guidelines is another issue. For an account of the illegal use of profits see *JPRS* 88–005, 18 February 1988, pp. 21–22.
50. China Interview 72388.
51. This is paid sometimes to the village, sometimes to the township. In Nanjiao, outside Tianjin, village industry pays nothing to the village, only to the township, which then distributes the funds to all its villages. Local officials said that this ensures fairer distribution. The township in this area also takes care of the five guaranteed households. China Interview 71886.
52. The precise method varies from village to village. Tom Bernstein provides details of the process in two counties in Shandong and Anhui. See his "Local Political Authorities and Economic Reform: Observations from Two Counties in Shandong and Anhui, 1985," paper presented at "Conference on Market Reforms in China and Eastern Europe," Santa Barbara, Calif., 8–11 May 1986. Graham Johnson describes the process for villages in the Pearl River Delta. See his "Fate of the Communal Economy."
53. If it is a village enterprise, the village industrial company *(gongye gongsi qiye guanli weiyuanhui)* sets the ratio and determines the percentage of over-quota profits each party will receive; at the township level this is done by the economic commission *(jingwei)*.
54. China Interview 72986.
55. Some contracts are very comprehensive and specify the amount of profit the factory manager gets, the amount for workers, etc.; others are less specific.
56. China Interview 21688.
57. China Interview 72388.
58. Some villages have what is called an industrial enterprise management committee that oversees all its industries. Often it is headed by the village party secretary.
59. China Interview 71886.
60. China Interview 6488.
61. China Interview 72388.
62. China Interview 11888.
63. Pu Changxing of the Department of Agricultural Engineering, Jiangyin County, Zhejiang, "Several Problems of the Township Enterprise Contract Responsibility System in Urgent Need of Resolution," *Nongye jingji wenti* 12:25–27 (23 December 1986), translated in *JPRS* 87–014, 2 July 1987, pp. 24–29.
64. For all these reasons, his village planned to extend this system to all its enterprises, including those owned by former production teams and now contracted out on the simple profit-quota system. In this particular village, once the change was instituted there was decreased demand for the enterprises. China Interview 72986.
65. Graham Johnson found that villages in the Pearl River Delta also provided substantial funds for collective welfare. See his "Fate of the Communal Economy."
66. China Interview 6488; China Interview 72886; China Interview 81786.
67. China Interview 81786; China Interview 6488.

68. China Interview 72886.
69. China Interview 6488. This particular village has the added problem of land being taken away by urban sprawl.
70. China Interview 11888.
71. *ZGTJNJ 1987,* p. 205; *ZGTJNJ 1988,* p. 287.
72. Wong, "Interpreting Rural Industrial Growth," pp. 18–19.
73. Ibid., p. 19.
74. "Town and Township Enterprises Grow Rapidly amid Reform and Decontrol," *Jingjixue zhoubao,* 15 November 1987, p. 3, translated in *JPRS* 88–006, 19 February 1988, p. 29.
75. *JPRS* 87-045, 9 September 1987.
76. China Interview 72886.
77. "Broad and Profound Impact of the Development of China's Township Enterprises."
78. China Interview 81786.
79. Wong, "Interpreting Rural Industrial Growth," p. 25.
80. William Byrd and Alan Gelb, "Why Industrialize? The Incentives for Rural Community Governments," in Byrd and Lin, "China's Rural Industry."
81. China Interview 6688.
82. See, for example, *JPRS* 88–005, 18 February 1988, pp. 20–21.
83. China Interview 72388.
84. China Interview 17788.
85. See, for example, *JPRS* 88–005, 18 February 1988, pp. 20–21; also Xu Hao and Wang Qingshan, Research Department, Agricultural Bank of China, "China's Rural Financial Markets: Current Situation and Strategy," *Nongye jingji wenti* 9:39–43 (23 September 1987), translated in *JPRS* 88–002, 5 February 1988, pp. 54–57.
86. My use of the terms *corporation* and *corporatism* implies the existence of a body—in this case either a township or a village—that has diverse interests, different components, some profitable, some less profitable; but the interests of the body are taken as the most important and overriding concern, with the political heads of the body, the party secretaries and leaders, making the final decisions.
87. Kathleen Hartford, in a much earlier article written shortly after the reforms were started, points to the need for cadres to increase their control over finances if they are to keep the collective alive and their power strong. See her "Socialist Agriculture," p. 60. The rules for rural industry seem to be key to this strategy.
88. China Interview 72188.
89. Outside Shenyang, a village official (head of the economic company) had to return some of his bonus pay because it was so much more than the average village member's income. China Interview 72886.
90. Byrd and Lin, "China's Rural Industry." This conflict of interests also helps explain the even rates of subsidy to agriculture discussed above.
91. I have dealt here only with the collective's ability to extract and redistribute funds from collective enterprises, but there are also numerous ways in which the village is able to extract money from individual entrepreneurs. These methods, however, are less open and rely on more informal, subtle, and sometimes not so

subtle methods. I have described some of these methods in my discussion of cadre envy *(yanhong)*. See "Commercializing China's Rural Cadres" and *State and Peasant,* chap. 9. For an interesting account of the social-leveling process from an anthropologist's perspective, see Ann Anagnost, "Prosperity and Counter-prosperity," October 1986, unpublished manuscript.

Chapter 2. Political Reform and Rural Government, by Tyrene White

Research for this paper was supported by the Ohio State University–Wuhan University Exchange Program, the Committee on Scholarly Communication with the People's Republic of China (CSCPRC), and the Swarthmore College Faculty Research Support Fund. Thanks to Thomas Bernstein, Deborah Davis, Lisa Rofel, Ezra Vogel, and David Zweig for comments on earlier drafts, and to Rachel Klingensmith for research assistance. I bear sole responsibility for the final product.

1. Although these sources support the findings presented here, the lack of more recent field data, the standard problems with Chinese newspaper and journal articles, and the great diversity of the Chinese countryside demand a cautious reading. At best, I hope to set forth several propositions that can be tested by future fieldwork.

2. For a comparison of the people's commune and the postcommune structure, see Frederick W. Crook, "The Reform of the Commune System and the Rise of the Township-Collective-Household System," in U.S. Congress Joint Economic Committee, *The Four Modernizations,* vol. 1 of *China's Economy Looks toward the Year 2000* (Washington, D.C., U.S. GPO, 1986), pp. 354–375. For a description of the experimental reform site of Guanghan County, see Vivienne Shue, "The Fate of the Commune," *Modern China* 10: 259–283 (1984). For a comparative investigation of several localities, see J. Bruce Jacobs, "Political and Economic Organizational Changes and Continuities in Six Rural Chinese Localities," *Australian Journal of Chinese Affairs* 14:105–130 (1986).

3. By 1985 the organizational changes resulted in an increase by nearly two-thirds in the number of commune-level units, a 30% increase in the number of brigade-level units, and a 20% decline in the number of team-level units. By 1986, however, the number of towns and townships had declined by nearly 20,000, and the number of administrative villages by nearly 100,000. Although these figures suggest great volatility across rural China, three provinces account for the vast proportion of the 1985 increase and the 1986 decrease: Hubei, Guangdong, and Yunnan. Unlike the standard pattern of converting one commune into one town or township, in Hubei communes were divided into an average of three rural townships, and in Guangdong and Yunnan production brigades were converted into township governments. As a result, these three provinces combined accounted for most of the increase in local-level governmental units between 1983 and 1985. By 1986, however, Guangdong had moved to reduce the number of local governmental units by replacing rural administrative districts *(qu)* with town and township governments and creating administrative villages at the level of the prereform production brigade. This move resulted in a precipitous drop in the number of township- and village-level units nationwide

and a sudden increase in the number of rural towns. When this instability in Guangdong is discounted, changes in Hubei and Yunnan alone account for most of the total increase between 1982 and 1986 in the number of township- and village-level units. A description of the three patterns of conversion, based on former communes, districts, or brigades, can be found in Wang Zhenyao, "Nongcun jiceng zhengquande zhineng fenhua taishi yu zhengce xuanju" (The state of the functional division of rural grass-roots political power and policy options), *Zhengzhixue yanjiu* (Political science studies) 4:29–33 (1987). See also Guangdong Provincial Service, 26 June 1986, in *FBIS*, 2 July 1986, P1.

4. For excellent discussions of the process of implementing the responsibility system and cadre reactions, see David Zweig, "Context and Content in Policy Implementation: Household Contracts and Decollectivization, 1977–1983," in David M. Lampton, ed., *Policy Implementation in Post-Mao China* (Berkeley, University of California Press, 1987), pp. 255–283; Thomas P. Bernstein, "Reforming China's Agriculture," paper prepared for conference, "To Reform the Chinese Political Order," Harwichport, Mass., June 1984; Richard J. Latham, "The Implications of Rural Reforms for Grass-Roots Cadres," in Elizabeth J. Perry and Christine Wong, eds., *The Political Economy of Reform in Post-Mao China* (Cambridge, Mass., and London, Harvard Contemporary China Series, no. 2, Council on East Asian Studies, Harvard University, 1985), pp. 157–173; John P. Burns, "Local Cadre Accommodation to the 'Responsibility System' in Rural China," *Pacific Affairs* 58:607–625 (1986); Jonathan Unger, "The Decollectivization of the Chinese Countryside: A Survey of Twenty-Eight Villages," *Pacific Affairs* 58:585–606 (1986).

5. Bernstein, "Reforming China's Agriculture"; Latham, "Implications of Rural Reforms," pp. 157–173.

6. *Hebei ribao* (Hebei daily), 12 November 1981, in *FBIS*, 9 December 1981, R1; "Bringing into Full Play the Economic and Political Functions of Rural Grass-Roots Organizations," *Hebei ribao*, 19 March 1982, in *FBIS*, 31 March 1982, R1–3; Henan Provincial Service, 17 March 1982, in *FBIS*, 18 March 1982, P3.

7. *Ningxia ribao* (Ningxia daily), 8 April 1982, in *FBIS*, 30 April 1982, T2; "It Is Necessary to Show More Concern for and Assist Grassroots Cadres in Rural Areas," *RMRB* 15 July 1981, in *FBIS*, 23 July 1981, K8; "Hebei Provincial CCP Committee Rural Work Department's 'Opinions on Regularly Grasping the Work of Perfecting the Agricultural Production Responsibility System,' " *Hebei ribao*, 12 June 1981, in *FBIS*, 9 July 1981, R7.

8. Zhang Chunsheng and Song Dahan, "Separation of Government Administration from Commune Management Required by the Development of the Rural Economy and the Buildup of State Power," *RMRB*, 30 July 1982, in *FBIS*, 5 August 1982, K2–6; *Xinhua* (New China news agency), 1 June 1982, in *FBIS*, 3 June 1982, K2.

9. *Xinhua*, 1 June 1982, in *FBIS*, 3 June 1982, K4.

10. Jacobs, "Political and Economic Organizational Changes."

11. "Separation of Government Adminstration from Commune Management Is Imperative," *JJRB*, 26 October 1983, in *FBIS*, 10 November 1983, K15. See also

"Conscientiously Do a Good Job in Building Townships," *RMRB*, 30 March 1984, in *FBIS*, 4 April 1984, K1.

12. Huang Changlu and Xiong Xiaowei, "Zhengshe fenkai liangnianjian" (Two years of the separation of government administration and commune management), *Liaowang* (Outlook) 22:14 (1984).

13. *Xinhua*, 22 January 1985, in *FBIS*, 24 January 1985, K20.

14. Two periods of fieldwork were conducted in Huashan. The first, February–December 1982, was sponsored by the Ohio State–Wuhan University Exchange Program. The second, January–June 1984, was supported by a fellowship from the CSCPRC, National Academy of Sciences. During these two periods interviews were conducted with a range of commune officials, and field visits and interviews were arranged in twelve of Huashan's nineteen brigades. Three brigades were visited in both 1982 and 1984, before and after decommunization. For background on Huashan and the process of rural reform in this locality, see my Ph.D. dissertation, "Population Policy and Rural Reform in China, 1977–1984: Policy Implementation and Interdependency at the Local Level," Ohio State University, 1985, chap. 2. The commune is located in the northeastern corner of Wuhan Municipality and in 1984 had a population of approximately 30,000. Its nineteen brigades and the suburban location make it anything but representative of the rural "norm," but unlike many suburban communes, rice production was an important part of the diversified economy. In 1981 average rural per capita income for Hubei Province was 102 yuan, while Huashan averaged 209 yuan. Compared with other suburban communes ringing Wuhan, however, Huashan was the poorest at that time.

15. Appearances were maintained for my benefit, however. The deputy party secretary who had been my escort in 1982 was said to be away "studying," and I was hosted instead by a newly installed deputy township director.

16. Interview File, 1984.5.14.

17. For details on the leadership transition, including background and personal characteristics of all commune cadres, see my unpublished manuscript, "Impediments to Commune Structural Reform: The Case of Huashan," 1985.

18. Interview File, 1984.3.13; 1984.3.17.

19. *RMRB*, 14 November 1986; Investigation Group of Zunyi County Committee, Guizhou Province, "Dangde nongcun zhengce xuanchuanzhongde 'shenlou xianxiang' qianshe" (An initial inquiry into the "seepage phenomenon" in the propagation of the party's rural policies), *Nongcun gongzuo tongxun* (Rural work bulletin) 11:42–43 (1987).

20. Zunyi County Committee, "Initial inquiry," p. 42; Bai Yihua and Tang Pusu, "Gaige xiangzhen tizhi jianqiang jiceng zhengquan" (Reform the town and township system, strengthen grass-roots political power), *Nongcun gongzuo tongxun* 11:42 (1986).

21. *Xinhua*, 26 November 1988, in *FBIS*, 27 November 1988, p. 14.

22. Wang Zhenyao, "Nongcun jiceng zhengquande zhineng fenhua," p. 32.

23. Ibid., p. 31.

24. *RMRB*, 14 November 1986.

25. Li Sanyuan, "Lun jingjiao xiang zhengquan jianshede wanshanhua" (On perfect-

ing the construction of the political power in Beijing's suburban townships), *Zhengzhixue yanjiu* 5:61 (1986).

26. See, for example, Bo Guili, "Woguo zhen zhengfu guanli jingjide zhineng he zhen zhengfude jigou gaige" (The economic management functions of our town governments and the reform of town governmental organs), *Zhengzhixue yanjiu* 3:45 (1986). He criticizes "the establishment of a local economic committee of equal rank to the local government." This article can be found in translation in Benedict Stavis, ed., "Reform of China's Political System," *Chinese Law and Government* (1987), pp. 93–96.

27. Wang Zhenyao, "Nongcun jiceng zhengquande zhineng fenhua," p. 32.

28. *Xinhua,* 22 January 1985, in *FBIS,* 24 January 1985, K20.

29. *RMRB,* 14 November 1986, in *FBIS,* 26 November 1986, K10.

30. Bo Guili, "Woguo zhen zhengfu guanli," p. 45. See also CASS Study Group, "Ideas for the Midterm (1988–1995) Reform of China's Economic Structure," *Social Sciences in China* 10:39–73 (1989).

31. See, for example, *JPRS* 84–077, 20 November 1984, p. 72; *Xinhua,* 29 March 1983, in *FBIS,* 1 April 1983, O1–2; *Zhongguo xinwenshe* (China news agency), 14 November 1984, in *FBIS,* 15 November 1984, P2; Jiangxi Provincial Service, 29 December 1984, in *FBIS,* 4 January 1985, O1.

32. Li Shenglin, "Strengthen the Building of Township Government," *Guangming ribao* (Guangming daily), 19 September 1983, in *FBIS,* 4 October 1983, K15.

33. Rural Economic Survey Leading Group of the Rural Policy Research Center, Secretariat, CPC Central Committee, and the Rural Development Research Center of the State Council, "Rural Primary Organizations, Party Members, and Cadres," *Nongmin ribao* (Farmers' daily), 16–17 May 1986, in *JPRS* 86–064, 19 August 1986, pp. 31–37.

34. The total number of township, village, and small-group cadres covered by the survey was 25,159, which indicates a fairly large sample.

35. *JPRS* 86–064, 19 August 1986, p. 32.

36. Interview File, 1984.5.14; 1984.6.16. This number does not include any members of the party committee unless they hold a post in the township government or the economic management committee. More recently, a suburban Changchun village with a population of 2,040 was reported to have twenty-two "village cadres and planning cadres" and a cadre wage bill of 30,000 yuan, suggesting that increases in staff size were not confined to the township level. See Yang Zhimin, "The Burdens Are Increasing All the Time—Thoughts on Lightening the Peasants' Burdens," *Nongmin ribao,* 23 September 1988, p. 2, in *FBIS,* 5 October 1988, p. 26.

37. Zweig, "Content and Context," pp. 255–283; Bernstein, "Reforming China's Agriculture"; Latham, "Implications of Rural Reforms," pp. 157–173; Burns, "Local Cadre Accommodation," pp. 607–625; Unger, "Decollectivization of the Chinese Countryside," pp. 585–606.

38. For a discussion of these new opportunities and cadre behavior, see Jean Oi, "Commercializing China's Rural Cadres," *Problems of Communism* 35:1–15 (1986).

39. As noted above, in 1983 Huashan had not yet undergone commune structural reform. The brigades were formally converted to administrative villages in 1984.

40. Wang Zhenyao, "Nongcun jiceng zhengquande zhineng fenhua," p. 31.

41. Xu Xingguan, "Fazhan cunji jingji, wanshan shuangceng jingji tizhi" (Develop the village-level economy, perfect the two-level management system), *Nongcun gongzuo tongxun* 8:24 (1987).

42. Zhu Liansheng and Li Chunshan, "Wanshan shuangceng jingying tizhi, qianghua shehuihua fuwu" (Perfect the two-level system of economic management, strengthen socialized services), *Nongye jingji* (Agricultural economics) 6:15 (1987).

43. *RMRB,* 19 November 1985, p. 1, in *FBIS,* 22 November 1985, K19.

44. Xu Xingguan, "Fazhan cunji jingji," p. 24.

45. Zhang Dexi and Jin Xitian, "Jiaqiang cunji jianshede jizhong banfa" (Several ways to strengthen village-level construction), *Nongcun gongzuo tongxun* 5:41 (1988).

46. Five yearbooks constitute this sample. Of the five, Fujian, Liaoning, and Sichuan all give figures for the small groups, whereas Hebei and Jiangsu do not. It is unclear whether the failure to report figures implies the dissolution of this administrative level.

47. I arrived at this standard by my own calculations; it was not reported to me as the operating standard.

48. Other sources of income and nonmaterial benefits from cadre service may offset this disincentive, of course.

49. Louise do Rosario, "Bound by Red Tape," *Far Eastern Economic Review,* 9 November 1989. See also, *ZGTJNJ 1989,* p. 108.

50. Ibid., pp. 108, 120.

51. *Xinhua,* 13 December 1984, in *FBIS,* 17 December 1984, Q1; Mo Ruo, "Streamlining Government Administration by Higher Staff Capability Is Imperative," *Liaowang* 42:4 (1986), in *JPRS* 87–008, 18 February 1987, pp. 10–12. See also Tang Tian, "The Readjustment of the Cadre Distribution Structure Is Imperative," *Liaowang* 36:18 (1987), in *FBIS,* 18 September 1987, p. 18; He Daofeng et al., "Dui xianji zhengfu xingweide chubu fenxi" (A preliminary investigation of the activities of county-level government), *Nongye jingji wenti* (Problems of agricultural economics) 4:19–22 (1987).

52. Tang Tian, "The Readjustment of the Cadre Distribution Structure," p. 18; Zhou Guohua and Zhou Deguang, "Wuwei Shi gaige nongcun guanli tizhi" (Reform of the system of rural management in Wuwei Municipality), *Liaowang* 52:16 (1986); Shaanxi Provincial Service, 8 September 1985, in *JPRS* 85–099, 24 September 1985, pp. 111–112; Zhang Dexi and Jin Xitian, "Jiaqiang cunji jianshede jizhong banfa," pp. 41–42.

53. Bai Yihua, Song Zhiqiang, and Tang Pusu, "Jinyibu wanshan xiangzhen zhengfu zhineng gaige ti tiaokuai fenge xingzheng guanli" (Go a step further in perfecting the functions of town and township governments, reform the system of vertical and horizontal division of administrative management), *Zhengzhixue yanjiu* 6:57 (1986).

54. Jiang Chunyun and Gao Changli, "Develop Political Advantages to Alleviate Rural Economic Contradictions," *Liaowang* 13:12–13 (1989), translated in *JPRS* 89–086, 16 August 1989, pp. 32–35.

55. Bai Yihua, Song Zhiqiang, and Tang Pusu, "Jinyibu wanshan xiangzhen zhengfu," p. 57. Even villages have been affected. In 1988 a suburban village in Changchun

with a population of 2,040 was reported to have twenty-two cadres drawing wages, constituting a total annual wage bill of 75 yuan per household. Yang Zhimin, "The Burdens Are Increasing All the Time," p. 26.

56. Bai Yihua, Song Zhiqiang, and Tang Pusu, "Jinyibu wanshan xiangzhen zhengfu," pp. 57–58.

57. Ibid., p. 57.

58. Liu Shunguo, "The Worries of Township and Town Cadres," *Nongmin ribao,* 20 September 1988, p. 3, in *FBIS,* 5 October 1988, p. 24.

59. Hua Guiqin, "Putting the Rural Contradictions in Proper Perspective," *Banyuetan* (Fortnightly chats) 14:17–19 (1988), in *FBIS,* 16 August 1988, pp. 39–41.

60. *The Constitution of the People's Republic of China,* 1982, chap. 3, sec. 5, art. 111.

61. Party Central Committee and State Council, "Circular on Separating Government Administration and Commune Management and Setting up Township Governments," translated in *Chinese Law and Government* 19:36 (1986–87).

62. Yang Haikun, "Brief Discussion on Self-Management of Community Affairs by the Masses at the Grassroots Level in the Urban and Rural Areas," *Guangming ribao,* 24 September 1984, in *FBIS,* 5 October 1984, K18.

63. Interview File, 1984.3.13, 1984.2.28, 1984.3.3.

64. Bao Xin, "Concerning the Villagers' Committee Organization Law," *Liaowang* (overseas ed.) 16:1 (1987), in *FBIS,* 24 April 1987, K10–12; Gong Miao, "Reform of Political Structure, Autonomy for Peasants—NPC Deputies Argue over Draft of Villagers' Law," *Zhongguo tongxunshe* (China news agency), 11 April 1987, in *FBIS,* 14 April 1987, K24–25; *Xinhua,* 19 November 1987, in *FBIS,* 20 November 1987, pp. 12–13.

65. *Xinhua,* 24 November 1987, in *FBIS,* 25 November 1987, p. 11.

66. Shouguang County Committee Office, "Cun chou xiang guan jiti tiliu" (Village planning and township management of collection withholding) *Nongcun gongzuo tongxun* 1:41 (1988).

67. Bao Xin, "Concerning the Villagers' Committee Organization Law," K10–12.

68. Ibid., K10; "Give Full Play to the Role of Villagers' Committees," *RMRB,* 26 November 1987, p. 3, in *FBIS* 30 November 1987, p. 16.

69. Hua Guiqin, "Putting the Rural Contradictions in Proper Perspective," pp. 39–41; Yang Zhimin, "Burdens Are Increasing," pp. 25–27.

70. *Xinhua,* 10 March 1987, in *FBIS,* 11 March 1987, K4.

71. Art. 12, Trial Law, in *FBIS,* 27 November 1987, p. 22.

72. Certainly the failure of the national media to take note of the law's trial implementation on 1 June 1988 or after raises doubts about the seriousness with which it will be pursued.

73. For reports of the scandal and response, see *Xinhua,* 2 July 1987, in *FBIS,* 7 July 1987, K14–15; *RMRB,* 17 June 1987, in *FBIS,* 19 June 1987, K26–27.

74. "No Withholding of the Party's Concern for Peasants," *RMRB,* 17 June 1987, p. 1, in *FBIS,* 19 June 1987, K26. This problem persisted into 1988, prompting a State Council decision to regulate strictly the supply, distribution, and prices of chemical fertilizers, insecticides, and vinyl mulch. *Xinhua,* 13 October 1988, in *FBIS,* 18 October 1988, p. 42.

75. *Xinhua,* 19 May 1988, in *FBIS,* 23 May 1988, pp. 48–49.

76. Zhou Qiren, "Land System: Valid Property Rights, Long-Term Tenancy, and Paid Transfer," *Jingji cankao* (Economic reference news), 2 November 1988, p. 4, in *FBIS,* 23 November 1988, p. 43.

77. Su Suining, "There Are Many Causes of Strained Relations between Cadres and Masses in the Rural Areas," *Nongmin ribao,* 26 September 1988, p. 1, in *FBIS,* 7 October 1988, p. 13.

78. Rural Survey Office, "Report Analyzing Particular Data from 1987 National Rural Survey," *Nongye jingji wenti* 4:40–45 (1989), translated in *JPRS* 89–080, 31 July 1989, pp. 46–53.

79. Li Demin, "Soldiers Are at the Head of Their Generals—Three County Party Secretaries on the Way to Treat Basic-Level Cadres," *RMRB,* 27 October 1989, p. 5, in *FBIS,* 8 November 1989, pp. 23–24.

80. Zhou Zuohan, "Thoughts Concerning the Building of Villagers' Committees, *Guangming ribao,* 4 January 1988, p. 3, in *FBIS,* 1 February 1988, p. 34.

81. This is a loose translation for the saying, *Shangmian qiantiao xian, xiamian dian ge yan.* Wang Zhenyao, "Nongcun jiceng zhengquande zhineng fenhua," p. 32.

82. Latham, "Implications of Rural Reforms," pp. 157–173.

83. One beleaguered township party secretary, complaining of the hard work and low pay, expressed fears that soon township party secretaries and government heads would have to be chosen by drawing lots, a phenomenon that has already occurred at the village level. Liu Shunguo, "Worries of Township and Town Cadres," p. 24.

84. Ibid., p. 24. One report from Suining County, Jiangsu Province, noted that there had been 381 "incidents of revenge" in twelve towns and townships over the course of a year and a half. Of the five basic categories for these incidents, two—family planning and grain and tax requisitions—accounted for 61% of the total (32% and 29%, respectively). The incidents themselves were not detailed, but destruction of cadre property and beatings were mentioned. See Su Suining, "Many Causes of Strained Relations," p. 13.

85. Ren Weijie, "A Profound Call," *Nongmin ribao,* 12 September 1988, p. 1, in *FBIS,* 29 September 1988, pp. 47–49; Yang Zhimin, "Burdens Are Increasing," pp. 25–27.

86. Ren Weijie, "A Profound Call," p. 47.

87. Liu Shunguo, "Worries of Township and Town Cadres," p. 23.

88. Ibid., p. 23.

89. Ren Weijie, "A Profound Call," p. 48.

90. There are obvious parallels here with Janos Kornai's use of the parent-offspring model to interpret the relationship between the state and the firm in centrally planned economies. See his "Degrees of Paternalism," in *Contradictions and Dilemmas: Studies on the Socialist Economy and Society* (Cambridge, Mass., MIT Press, 1986), pp. 52–61.

Chapter 3. The Politics of Migration in a Market Town, by Helen F. Siu

1. In my recent book, *Agents and Victims in South China: Accomplices in Rural Revolution* (New Haven, Yale University Press, 1989), I argue that the peasants were confined in rural communities that had been made more cellular and isolated

from the cities. This view agrees with the observations of William L. Parish and Martin K. Whyte, *Village and Family in Contemporary China* (Chicago, University of Chicago Press, 1978); Martin K. Whyte and William L. Parish, *Urban Life in Contemporary China* (Chicago, University of Chicago Press, 1984); and Vivienne Shue, *The Reach of the State* (Stanford, Calif., Stanford University Press, 1988). See also the debate between Audrey Donnithorne, "China's Cellular Economy: Some Economic Trends since the Cultural Revolution," *CQ* 52:605–619 (1972), and Nicholas Lardy, "Centralization and Decentralization in Chinese Fiscal Management," *CQ* 61:25–61 (1975).

2. At this town level there are few state-sector jobs. In a recent paper I describe the history of the buildup of Nanxi Town (a pseudonym) in the Pearl River Delta and the problems it faces in an age of reform. See Helen Siu, "Socialist Peddlers and Princes in a Chinese Market Town," *American Ethnologist* 16:195–212 (1989). The town has been an independent collective unit since 1952. *Jianzhi zhen* (incorporated town), as this category of market town is called, was administratively a commune-level unit in Guangdong. Its population is entitled to commodity grain and engages in nonagricultural occupations, but the people do not have the security of the employees in the state sector.

3. See Fei Xiaotong, *Xiao chengzhen siji* (Four chapters on small towns; Beijing, Xinhua Chubanshe, 1985); Qiu Zhuohua et al., eds., *Zhujiang sanjiaozhou jingji kaifangqu touzi zhinan* (Investment guide for the open economic zones of the Pearl River Delta; Hong Kong, Xinhua Chubanshe, 1986); and Jiangsu Sheng Xiao Chengzhen Yanjiu Ketizu, ed., *Xiao chengzhen, xin kaituo* (Small towns, new growth; Jiangsu Renmin Chubanshe, 1986).

4. All names in this essay are pseudonyms.

5. This paper is based on fieldwork conducted in 1986, when I received a year-long grant from the Committee on Scholarly Communication with the People's Republic of China. I made subsequent trips in 1987 and 1988.

6. The third district was basically the town proper and the surrounding twenty or so *xiang* (townships or village clusters). Among the townships close to Nanxi Town, there was also a sizable nonagricultural population, such as that of Yongding Xiang at the western edge of Nanxi.

7. A 1971 record of the "five black categories" *(wulei fenzi)* in the town reveals a total of 683 persons, of which 482 were landlords and 57 were rich peasants.

8. Even today the output of these enterprises constitutes over 70% of Nanxi Town's total industrial output.

9. In 1985 the nonagricultural population of the Nanxi Rural Commune was 10,809, from a total of 111,313; most resided in the suburban area.

10. Up to 1979 Nanxi Rural Commune was required to devote 68,000 *mu* (out of 92,410 *mu* of cultivable land) for grain production. Its procurement quota for grain was 3 million catties in 1964 but was raised to 7 million in 1968 and 9 million in 1969. It leveled out at 7 million catties in 1976.

11. For the competition between the two collectives, see Helen Siu, "The Politics of Growth: Pearl River Delta Experiences," in Ri Yin-wang Kwok et al., eds., *Chinese Urban Reforms: What Model Now?* (Armonk, N.Y., Sharpe, 1990).

12. This was a general policy of Guangdong in the mid-1980s to build town-centered local and regional economies. It was an effort to correct the Maoist bias

against commerce, which had created cellularized and stagnant economies in both town and countryside. David Zweig, in "Rural Small Towns and the Politics of Planned Development" (paper presented at Fortieth Annual Meeting of the Association of Asian Studies, San Francisco, March 1988), observes similar problems in Jiangsu, where the merger established a more centralized bureaucracy.

13. Similar ideas are noted in Liu Bang, ed., "Xuexi Zhongyang yihao wenjian zhengce yibai ti" (A hundred answers for studying the number-one document of the Party Central Committee; Beijing, Xinhua Chubanshe, 1985).

14. If they had made arrangements with their resident villages about grain rations, they were allowed to buy from the town's grain stations at a flexible price (around 25 yuan per picul in 1986).

15. The drop did not show in the town statistics, but I managed to copy the non-aggregated data from the records of the fifteen neighborhood committees, and confirmed them with the neighborhood-committee directors who worked with me in the surveys.

16. In 1986 the per capita land-man ratio was less than four-fifths of a *mu* for the Nanxi Rural Commune, including private plots. This also means that the ratio for these townships was half as much.

17. Some of them also became sharecroppers in the outlying villages, contracting with farm families whose sons had moved to better job opportunities.

18. As expected, the populations of the two provinces have been linked to the Pearl River Delta through a history of trade and migration up and down the West River.

19. For similar situations in Hunan, see Li Jiang et al., "Guanyu jiasu Hunan Sheng xiao chengzhen fazhan de jige wenti" (On accelerating the development of small towns in Hunan Province), *Jingji yanjiu cankao ziliao* (Reference materials for economic research; Beijing, Jingji Kexue Chubanshe, 1985).

20. Some join labor gangs to work on construction sites or contract with individual households for "the mean trades" (for example, carrying coffins or digging graves). Cadres in the town government say that employment of these laborers is occasional, and they are not able to obtain statistics on them.

21. One can compare such mentality with Hong Kong in the 1980s, where residents of the congested colony, nervous over their political and economic futures, heap negative images on recent immigrants, particularly those of rural origins. See Helen Siu, "Immigrants and Social Ethos: Hong Kong in the 1980s," *Journal of the Hong Kong Branch of the Royal Asiatic Society* 26:1–16 (1988).

22. Ezra Vogel and Deborah Davis note that many of the towns in Jiangsu do not accept migrant laborers. I suspect that for the enterprises in Nanxi that do accept migrants, there is pressure from overseas investors to hire the cheapest laborers available.

23. I found the cost of living here was higher than that in Guangzhou. Residents attributed the inflation to the sudden wealth from rural areas and from the lavish spending of individual entrepreneurs.

24. These are not unrealistic numbers. I was given such figures by a range of cadres and workers as a wage slightly above the average. In the highly successful elec-

tric switch factory formerly operated by the Nanxi Rural Commune (now under the Nanxi Zhen No. 2 Industrial Corporation after the merger in 1987), the wages of its 1,200 workers range from 300 to 800 yuan. The deputy manager for the factory's overseas section earns an annual income of 60,000 yuan on the books. In Yongding Xiang, incentives for the managers and workers are stimulated by large bonuses. The *xiang* government contracts with the managers for an annual amount of output, profit, and taxes. Once the output target is reached, the managers' wages are doubled. On top of that, they can expect approximately 5,000 to 10,000 yuan of year-end bonus. Taxes over and above the contracted amount are distributed to the workers as bonuses.

25. Peasants complain that bride price has become extremely high in their villages. In the town and the periurban villages, the going rate for the bride price was 800 to 1,000 yuan in 1987; in the outlying villages, it ranged from 2,000 to 5,000 yuan.

26. See Siu, "Socialist Peddlers and Princes."

27. For a comparison of Nanxi Town and Yongding Brigade, see Siu, "Politics of Growth."

28. Even the town's tricycle peddlers find their daily earnings dropped by a third, from 50–60 yuan to 30–40 yuan. One told me in August 1989 that since the beginning of 1989, expeditors from outside the delta stopped coming because of the shortage of credit. After 4 June the volume of travelers dropped to a trickle.

29. This information was collected during fieldwork in July and August 1989.

30. Migration studies have fallen into three broad categories. A conventional economics approach assumes a priori the unequal distribution of factors of production in society and then builds models of individual choices based on marginal utility assumptions. See Michael Todaro, "A Model of Labor Migration and Urban Unemployment in Less Developed Counties," *American Economic Review* (March 1969), and John Caldwell, *African Rural-Urban Migration* (Cambridge, Cambridge University Press, 1969).

    This is countered by a political economy approach that emphasizes the structure of state power, which determines overall development strategies setting the pace and direction of migration. See Samir Amin, "Modern Migrations in Western Africa," in Samir Amin, ed., *Modern Migrations in Western Africa* (London, Oxford University Press, 1974), pp. 65–124, and Bernard Magubane, *The Political Economy of Race and Class in South Africa* (New York, Monthly Review Press, 1979).

    Social anthropologists have also made considerable contributions to migration studies. They put into context individual choices by highlighting cultural dimensions in the strategies of migration and assimilation such as kinship networks, voluntary associations, and ethnicity. See Kenneth Little, *West African Urbanization* (Cambridge, Cambridge University Press, 1965); Clyde Mitchell, "Distance, Transportation, and Urban Involvement in Zambia," in Adian Southall, ed., *Urban Anthropology* (London, Oxford University Press, 1973), pp. 287–314; J. A. Jackson, ed., *Migrations* (Cambridge, Cambridge University Press, 1969); Josef Gugler, "Migration and Ethnicity in Sub-Sahara Africa: Affinity, Rural

Interests and Urban Alignments," in Helen Safa and Brian Du Toit, eds., *Migration and Development* (Hague, Mouton, 1975), pp. 295–311; and Janice Perlman, *The Myth of Marginality* (Berkeley, University of California Press, 1976). See also Ulf Hannerz, *Exploring the City* (New York, Columbia University Press, 1980), and Nancy Graves and Theodore Graves, "Adaptive Strategies in Urban Migration," *Annual Review of Anthropology* 3:117–151 (1974), for a summary of urban anthropology. The case of Nanxi Zhen can be used to illustrate an analytical perspective that fruitfully integrates these approaches.

31. See Philip Abrams, *Historical Sociology* (Ithaca, Cornell University Press, 1982), on the concepts of human agency and structuring; Anthony Leeds, "Locality Power in Relation to Superlocal Institutions," in Southall, ed., *Urban Anthropology*, pp. 15–42, on a theoretical statement of the interface between local and superlocal analysis; and Shue, *The Reach of the State*, on a similar theoretical statement for Chinese politics.

Chapter 4. Urban Job Mobility, by Deborah Davis

1. *RMRB*, 14 August 1988, p. 8.

2. In 1980 the urban population was distributed among large, medium, and small cities in the ratio of 1 : 1.5 : 2.4. By December 1986 it had shifted to 1 : 1.8 : 4.0. *RMRB*, 9 June 1988, p. 2. In Guizhou Province, for example, by December 1986, 160,000 legally registered workers had emigrated to Guiyang from rural areas. Half came from Sichuan Province alone, and in 1986, 15% of the city's wage bill was remitted to that province through the Guiyang post office. *RMRB*, 17 November 1987, p. 2. In 1986 Beijing reported 1 million and Shanghai 1.16 million rural workers in the city labor force. Zhou Weixin, "Zhongguo chengshi fanzui xianguang pouxi" (A dissection of current crimes in Chinese cities), *Shehui* (Society) 5:12–15 (1988); Wang Sigang, "Wailai renkou de kunrao" (The puzzle of immigration), *Shehui* 6:16–17 (1988). Guangzhou already had more than 1 million emigrants as early as 1984. *Beijing daxue xuebao* (Newsletter of Beijing University) 6:37–43 (1986).

3. In 1983 the State Council granted any peasant with the ability to start a business a temporary resident's certificate. In October 1984 in *Guofa* No. 141 all sixty thousand market towns below county level in practice abandoned any serious effort to keep rural workers and entrepreneurs out of the towns. In a marked departure from the prereform era, these rural residents were even allowed to build housing in the towns. D. Solinger, "Temporary Resident's Certificates," *CQ* 101:98–103 (1985); *Guowuyuan gongbao* (Bulletin of the State Council; 1984), pp. 919–920; *FBIS*, 23 October 1984, K18–19.

4. Migration as a means of allowing the most-impoverished areas to share in the new affluence was endorsed as official policy for all of Guangdong in 1987 and for Yunnan in 1988. *RMRB*, 19 April 1987, p. 2; 26 April 1988, p. 2.

5. On the success of the Chinese in using market mechanisms in areas other than labor, see David Granick, "The Industrial Environment in China and the CMEA Countries," in Gene Tidrick and Chen Jiyuan, eds., *China's Industrial Reform*

(New York, Oxford University Press, 1987), pp. 103–131; Gene Tidrick, "Planning and Supply," in Tidrick, ed., *China's Industrial Reform,* pp. 175–209; and William Byrd. "The Role and Impact of Markets," in *China's Industrial Reform,* pp. 237–275.

6. *RMRB,* 25 May 1988, p. 1.

7. In 1987 in the large city of Xian the overall ratio of job turnover among all *zhiyuan* was 0.1%, and nationwide among all technical staff it was 1%. *RMRB,* 13 March 1988, p. 2; 10 July 1988, p. 3.

8. Paul Osterman, ed., *Internal Labor Markets* (Cambridge, Mass., MIT Press, 1984).

9. Abram Bergson, "Income Inequality under Soviet Socialism," *Journal of Economic Literature* 22:1052–99 (1984); Granick, "Industrial Environment," pp. 103–132; T. W. Hu, M. Li, and S. Z. Shi, "Analysis of Wages and Bonuses among Tianjin Workers," *CQ* 113:78 (1988).

10. Andrew Walder, *Communist Neo-Traditionalism: Work and Authority in Chinese Industry* (Berkeley, University of California Press, 1986), p. 11.

11. For a general discussion of this 1983–84 innovation, see Laodong Renshibu Ganbu Jiaoyuzu (Cadre education group of the Ministry of Labor and Personnel), eds., *Laodong gongzi renshi zhidu gaige de yanjiu* (Inquiry and research on reform of wage and labor system; Beijing, Laodong Renshi Chubanshe, 1985), pp. 401–410; *FBIS,* 8 June 1984, K15–16, and 23 October 1984, K18.

12. *FBIS,* 23 October 1984, K18.

13. *RMRB,* 9 August 1988, p. 1.

14. *RMRB,* 10 July 1988, p. 3.

15. Christine P. W. Wong, "Between Plan and Market," *Journal of Comparative Economics* 11:385–398 (1987); Barry Naughton, "The Decline of Central Control over Investment in Post-Mao China," in David M. Lampton, ed., *Policy Implementation in Post-Mao China* (Berkeley, University of California Press, 1987), pp. 51–80.

16. I have as yet found no specific discussion of the principles that guided these manpower policies adopted in the 1950s, but my hypothesis is that they were de facto application of the personnel practices that the CCP had used when fighting the Japanese and the Nationalists, and that therefore military practices shaped CCP manpower policy as much as socialist and communist ideals.

17. Walder, *Communist Neo-Traditionalism,* chap. 2.

18. For a good, lengthy discussion, see Xu Yulong and Wang Yongjiang, *Zhongguo shehuizhuyi laodong wenti* (China's socialist labor problems; Anhui Chubanshe, 1985), p. 15.

19. *Tingxin liuzhi* seems to have first appeared in June 1983. While available to any worker or staff, it required in most cases approval of a supervisor and thus quickly failed to meet the goal of increased mobility since supervisors only wanted "poor" staff to leave. In particular, after shops found their wages and bonuses tied to group productivity, supervisors became especially unwilling to let the most efficient, best educated, or most ambitious transfer. Zhuang Qidong, ed., *Laodong gongzi shouce* (Handbook on labor salaries; Tianjin Renmin Chubanshe, 1984), pp. 123–125.

20. *Zhongguo laodong* (Chinese labor) 9:23 (1985).
21. *RMRB,* 3 April 1985, p. 3; *Zhongguo laodong renshi bao* (Chinese labor and personnel news), 7 April 1986, p. 3.
22. *RMRB,* 10 July 1988, p. 3.
23. The transfer described here is a "negotiated transfer" *(shangdiao).* After 1987, when work units were allowed to keep the wages of those who had left the unit in the unit's general wage pool, this type of transfer became even more difficult, and preference was given to "exchange transfers" *(shuangdiao)* whereby a worker in one unit switches with a worker in another, thus keeping the total number of workers in each unit constant.
24. *RMRB,* 4 April 1987, p. 3; 12 November 1987, p. 3; *Laodong bao* (Labor news), 22 May 1986, p. 3.
25. "Questions and Answers on Party Organization," originally issued in January 1983, partially translated and published in *Chinese Law and Government* (Fall 1984), p. 98.
26. Zhuang, *Laodong gongzi shouce,* pp. 129–140.
27. *RMRB,* 12 July 1987, p. 8.
28. *RMRB,* 23 April 1988, p. 3; 10 July 1988, p. 3.
29. *RMRB,* 12 March 1986, p. 2; 21 July 1986, p. 3; 5 November 1986, p. 5; 2 December 1986, p. 3; 10 December 1986, p. 3; 23 April 1987, p. 4; 21 July 1987, p. 3; 26 July 1987, p. 8; *Hubei ribao* (Hubei daily), 5 January 1987, p. 1; *Laodong bao,* 6 January 1987, p. 1.
30. *RMRB,* 20 April 1987, p. 3.
31. For example, in Hebei Province the provincial government passed a regulation stipulating that not more than 2% of cadres and 6% of workers could transfer in 1985. *GRRB,* 8 June 1985, p. 1. In Shanghai the restrictions were within *xitong. Laodong bao,* 13 June 1985, p. 1. In one report on Hubei factories, each unit set percentages. *Changjiang ribao,* (Yangzi daily), 19 August 1985, p. 1.
32. The date and direction of this shift vary among different cities. The year 1980 is a decisive turning point for Shanghai, but in Guangzhou job control had shifted from schools to the parents' unit as early as 1973. Jonathan Unger, *Education under Mao* (New York, Columbia University Press, 1982), pp. 164–168.
33. *Guowuyuan gongbao* (1986), pp. 739–750.
34. In June 1987 I had two interviews with cadres from Putuo District, who explained that although some jobs might be posted in all district labor offices, in practice each district office allocates jobs only within its jurisdiction. In 1988 a cadre in a Wuhan street committee described the same pattern for that city.
35. In the first eighteen months, approximately 10% of the 270,000 contract workers in Shanghai applied for and received unemployment aid. *RMRB* (overseas ed.), 2 June 1988, p. 1.
36. This summary draws primarily from D. Davis-Friedmann. *Long Lives: Chinese Elderly and the Communist Revolution* (Cambridge, Mass., Harvard University Press, 1983), chap. 5, and D. Davis, "Unequal Chances, Unequal Outcomes," *CQ* 114:223–241 (1988).
37. In eight enterprises I visited in 1979, 80% of all retirees used *dingti.* Of the

132 Shanghai women I interviewed in 1986 and 1987, 77% (N=37/48) of those who had retired in 1979 or 1980 used *dingti,* whereas among those retiring in 1982 and 1983 only 44% (N=8/18) used it.

38. Based on visits to a variety of units between 1979 and 1988, it appears that 1980 and 1981 marked the turning point for this type of job creation. Examples of such hiring at Wuhan University in 1981 were a gardening brigade, a fish pond brigade, and several small canteens staffed entirely by children of faculty and staff. In the large textile, radio, and electric cable factories I visited in Shanghai in 1986 and 1987, the initial efforts of 1980 and 1981 had diversified and expanded, growing to include over one thousand staff children, all of whom were collective workers "outside the plan."

39. Between 1962 and 1979, 17.7 million urban teenagers were sent to work in the countryside, and by December 1979, 14.9 million had returned, of which 6.5 million returned in 1978 and 1979 alone. *Zhongguo laodong gongzi tongji ziliao 1949–1985* (Statistical materials on Chinese labor and wages 1949–1985; Beijing, Zhongguo Tongji Chubanshe, 1987), pp. 110–111. Overall official rates of urban unemployment fell from 5.4% in 1979 to 2.3% in 1983. Ibid., p. 109.

40. In 1978 there were 850,000 students in colleges and universities. By 1983 the number had risen to 1.23 million in full-time regular schools. *ZGTJNJ 1981,* p. 441, and *1985,* p. 581. Furthermore, new age restrictions on who could take the college entrance exam as well as an increased number of university places meant that by 1983 the ratio of college enrollments among those who took the entrance exam rose from 4% in 1978 and 5.8% in 1979 to 23% in 1983. World Bank, *China: Socialist Economic Development* (Washington, D.C., 1983); *Xinhua* (New China news agency), 16 September 1979, translated in *JPRS China Report: Political, Sociological, and Military Affairs,* 30 October 1979, p. 43. *China Exchange News,* December 1984.

41. In a 1985 survey in nine major cities, researchers found that as of 1983, 38.2% of the young adults aged 15–28 had entered their workplace on *dingti* or *neizhao. Dangdai Zhongguo qingnian zhigong qingkuang* (Employment situation of today's Chinese youth; Wuhan Gongren Chubanshe, 1986), p. 6. In my 1987 survey of 100 Shanghai families, I found that 52% of first-born sons and 37% of first-born daughters had used *dingti* between 1978 and 1987.

42. *RMRB,* 12 November 1984, p. 3; 21 April 1985, p. 3; 4 September 1987, p. 3; 15 October 1987, p. 3.

43. *Guowuyuan gongbao* (1985), pp. 771–776; *Guowuyuan gongbao* (1986), pp. 227–234; *Hongqi* (Red flag) 19:10–15 (1986); *Zhongguo jiaoyu bao* (Chinese educational news), 28 May 1987, p. 1; *Zhongguo jiaoyu bao,* 6 June 1987, p. 3; *Wenhui bao,* 22 May 1987, p. 1; *RMRB,* 7 August 1987, p. 3; *RMRB,* 1 September 1987, p. 1.

44. *Zhongguo jiaoyu bao,* 16 July 1985, p. 1; *RMRB,* 15 July 1985, p. 3.

45. *Guowuyuan gongbao* (1986), pp. 739–745.

46. Walder, *Communist Neo-Traditionalism,* pp. 48–54.

47. For a fuller discussion, see Davis, "Unequal Chances, Unequal Outcomes," and Gordon White, "The Politics of Economic Reform in Chinese Industry," *CQ* 111:365–389 (1987).

48. *RMRB,* 20 February 1987, p. 2; *RMRB,* 5 August 1987, p. 1; *Zhongguo funü bao* (Chinese women's news), 13 May 1988, p. 1.

49. *Zhongguo tongji zhaiyao 1987* (China statistical abstract 1987; Beijing, Zhongguo Tongji Chubanshe, 1987), p. 17; *Zhongguo funü bao,* 13 May 1988, p. 1.

50. The same reluctance is described in published accounts. *Zhongguo laodong renshi bao,* 1 July 1987, p. 1; 19 August 1987, p. 3; *RMRB,* 20 February 1988, p. 5.

51. *RMRB,* 21 January 1987, p. 1; *Zhongguo laodong renshi bao,* 18 February 1987, p. 1; 18 March 1987, p. 2.

52. Similar trends were reported in the press for firemen and medical technicians. *RMRB,* 22 January 1987, p. 5; 19 August 1987, p. 3.

53. This research was sponsored by a grant from the Committee on Scholarly Communication with the PRC and made possible by the generosity and cooperation of the Retirement Committee of the Shanghai Municipal Union. The 100 families were selected by a random sample from a name list of all households in one residential area that included one woman born between 1925 and 1935. This last qualification was used in order to increase the likelihood that in each interview I would gather work histories of at least two generations of urban workers.

54. For the analysis in this paper, I reviewed the careers of each first-born girl and each first-born boy. Thus in any family that had at least one boy and one girl, two children were observed; hence the number of children exceeds the number of mothers.

55. As a group women in the survey held lower-status jobs; 65% were production workers, 25% did routine white-collar work, and only 10% were professionals or administrators.

56. Ten of the women and four of the men migrated to Shanghai with their parents.

57. Thirty-two percent ($N=31$) of the men and 38% ($N=37$) of the women worked in only one unit between 1949 and their retirement, 62% of men and 66% of women worked in only one or two units, and only 5% worked in five or more units.

58. Thus among the fifty-four men who did move at least once and whose route of mobility is known to me, and among the fifty women who met these same criteria, only four men and five women moved for professional advancement on their own initiative.

59. Walder, *Communist Neo-Traditionalism,* chap. 1.

60. For a full statement of this argument, see Davis, "Unequal Chances, Unequal Outcomes," pp. 223–241.

61. A very similar outcome resulted in the 1950s when the central government also advocated decentralization. On the 1950s, see Franz Schurmann. *Ideology and Organization in Communist China* (Berkeley, University of California Press, 1968); Christopher Howe, *Employment and Economic Growth in Urban China, 1949–1957* (Cambridge, Cambridge University Press, 1971), pp. 87–137.

62. A 1988 article estimated that the lifetime value of subsidies to state workers was 200,000 yuan for housing, 15,000 for medical care, and 15,000 for pension benefits. *RMRB,* 11 July 1988, p. 1.

63. Thomas Rawski, "The Simple Arithmetic of Chinese Income Distribution," *Keizai Kenkyu* 33:12–26 (1982).

64. In 1987 they equaled 85% of remuneration. *Beijing Review* 3:30 (1988).
65. In 1978, 6.5% of funds earmarked for wages of state employees went to subsidies (*jintie*). In 1980 the percentage rose to 14.1%, and by 1987 it had reached 18.9% *ZGTJNJ 1988*, p. 182.

Chapter 5. Micropolitics and the Factory Director Responsibility System, 1984–1987, by Yves Chevrier

1. Many Chinese social scientists study the "cultural background of reforms" in this perspective, by attributing both China's traditional communal structures and Mao's neocommunal ones to "feudalism." See, for instance, Bai Nanfeng and Yang Guansan, "Gaige de shehui xinli huanjing" (The social-psychological environment of the reforms), in Zhongguo Jingji Tizhi Gaige Yanjiusuo (Economic System Reform Institute), eds. *Zhongguo: Fazhan yu gaige* (China: Development and reform; Chengdu, Sichuan Renmin Chubanshe, 1986), pp. 568–579.
2. J. Kornai's concept is convincingly discussed in relation to the Chinese situation by Andrew G. Walder, "The Informal Dimension of Enterprise Financial Reforms," in U.S. Congress Joint Economic Committee, *The Four Modernizations*, vol. 1 of *China's Economy Looks toward the Year 2000* (Washington, D.C., U.S. GPO, 1986), pp. 630–645.
3. For a clear statement, see *Jingji guanli* (Economic management) 8:44–48 (1982), and comments in Claude Aubert and Yves Chevrier, "Réformer ou ne pas réformer: Le dilemme de l'expérience chinoise," *Revue française de gestion* (Winter 1982–83), pp. 9–46.
4. Quoted from Walder, "Informal Dimension of Reforms," p. 632.
5. The fact that the social setting emerging from Deng's reforms is far from being fully emancipated from communist and traditional patterns is analyzed in Yves Chevrier, "Une société infirme: La société chinoise dans la transition modernisatrice," in Aubert et al., *La société chinoise après Mao: Entre autorité et modernité* (Paris, Fayard, 1986).
6. Andrew G. Walder, "Factory and Manager in an Era of Reform," *CQ* 112:242–264 (1989), gives a detailed description of the local institutions encompassing state enterprises and of the informal dimension of power relations within and around them.
7. This is Heath B. Chamberlain's approach in "Party-Management Relations in Chinese Industries: Some Political Dimensions of Economic Reform," *CQ* 112:631–661 (1987), an accurate and useful analysis to which my many quotes will show that I am greatly indebted.
8. As it is currently done for describing the outcome of reforms in Eastern Europe, where Kornai speaks of recurrent "bargaining" and bureaucratic patterns governing the market. In addition to information gathered in the national and provincial media, my data come from interviews of managers and officials in Sichuan and Wuhan (November–December 1985) and in Beijing and Shanghai (February 1988). I also had useful discussions with members of the Economic System Reform Research Institute (Zhongguo Jingji Tizhi Gaige Yanjiusuo; for

short, Tigaisuo) in Beijing and with several economists and social scientists in both Beijing and Shanghai in February 1988.

9. See the example of Hubei, *GRRB,* 19 August 1986. On the unfolding of the FDRS, see Chamberlain, "Party-Management Relations," pp. 644ff., and also *China News Analysis* 1344:2 (1987). For examples of individual contracts for managers including economic penalties (on wages) and status penalties (loss of directorial function), see *Wenhuibao* (Cultural newspaper; Shanghai), 14 February 1985, and *Zhongguo qingnianbao* (China youth), 4 June 1985.

10. Chamberlain, "Party-Management Relations," p. 640. The contractual rights of the managers include hiring their technical staff, managing the enterprise work force, and deciding on output, prices, investments, borrowing, and development, in accordance with the obligations of the enterprise regarding planning and the overall economic policies of the local and central authorities.

11. The "industrial economic responsibility system" *(gongye jingji zerenzhi)* that crowned the first wave of industrial reforms failed to raise labor discipline and productivity standards in state enterprises, but it was generalized in 1982 because officials realized that it helped consolidate state revenues after profit sharing had significantly reduced the amount of resources transferred to the center. See Yves Chevrier, "Les politiques économiques de la démaoïsation, 1977–1982," *Revue d'études comparatives Est-Ouest* 14:40–54,56 (1986), and Peter Nanshong Lee, "Enterprise Autonomy Policy in Post-Mao China: A Case Study of Policy Making," *CQ* 105:68 (1986).

12. *Zhengzhi yu falü* (Politics and law) 3:3–4 (1984). One analysis, while criticizing the collective (collegiate) system of decision making in higher administrative bodies, referred favorably to the individualistic principles set by "bourgeois thinkers" such as Montesquieu and Rousseau. *Faxue yanjiu* (Law studies) 3:5–10 (1984).

13. *Liaowang* (Outlook) 47:27 (1984).

14. See a sketch of these images and a preliminary assessment of the rejuvenation program in Yves Chevrier, "Gestion et modernisation: L'entreprise chinoise face à l'Etat," *Tiers-Monde* 17:777–779 (1986).

15. Point 10 of the "Decision," *RMRB,* 21 October 1984.

16. Numerous examples can be found in the press. See that of Sichuan, *RMRB,* 14 October 1985. On the importance of "intellectuals" as party members, see the analysis and data in *Banyuetan* (Fortnightly chats) 23:10–11 (1984).

17. Examples are set by Shenyang industries, notably by the party committee of the Bureau of Metal Industries, *Liaoning ribao* (Liaoning daily), 14 May 1985. *Hubei ribao* (Hubei daily), 16 July 1985, spoke of "entente cordiale."

18. Where twenty-seven elder *ganbu* had to be "persuaded" during individual interviews with the party secretary. *GRRB,* 3 May 1985.

19. Preliminary report on this activity drafted for the central government *(guowuyuan), JJRB,* 21 March 1985.

20. Good example of such a charter for the No. 3 Bicycle Factory in Shanghai. *Wenhuibao* (Shanghai), 23 August 1985.

21. This argument is also made by Chamberlain, "Party-Management Relations," p. 653.

22. Ibid. quotes the "Propaganda outline regarding the three sets of regulations on industrial enterprises owned by the whole people," published by *Qiye guanli* (Enterprise management) 11:22 (1986): "Party management cadres, unlike others, are appointed directly by the party organization."
23. *ZGFZB,* 7 January 1985.
24. Ibid., 12 May 1986.
25. Numerous examples crop up in the press after mid-1985, answering the official line. Tax evasion is also given much negative publicity (see an "experimental investigation" revealing that 54.8% of the 1,799 enterprises surveyed between July and September 1985 practiced evasion, as reported in *Beijing ribao* [Beijing daily], 17 October 1985).
26. *GRRB,* 17 June 1985.
27. *JJRB,* 3 July 1985. By late 1985 I had surveyed several Sichuanese enterprises where party and union representatives sat as such in the management committee *(guanli weiyuanhui),* an institution that had initially been a management team chosen by the director among his deputies.
28. Section 3 of the "Decision" defines state enterprises as *shehuizhuyi shangpin shengchanzhe he jingguanzhe* (producers and operators [managers] of the socialist commodity production [economy] endowed with *faren*).
29. *ZGFZB,* 15 February 1985.
30. Model stories in *GRRB,* 7 January 1985, and *Wenhuibao* (Shanghai), 18 August 1985. See also the famous Ma Shengli in Shijiazhuang, *GRRB,* 8 February 1985.
31. See the report from a Shanghai factory in *Wenhuibao* (Shanghai), 18 August 1985.
32. *Liaoning ribao,* 14 May 1985.
33. On 29 June 1985, at a study session organized by the trade unions and the Economic Commission of the State Council. *GRRB,* 1 July 1985.
34. The voices, tuned to the official line, were heard in *GRRB,* 3 June 1985.
35. "It is all well and good to stress the political qualifications of factory directors, but you cannot rely solely on the spiritual qualities of the manager to reconcile the interests of the state, enterprise, and workers," said one manager in a group interviewed in late 1985 by *Jingji guanli,* as reported and quoted by Chamberlain, "Party-Management Relations," pp. 635–636. I use the quote in a slightly different context and thus reach different conclusions.
36. As "responses to decline in firms, organizations, and states." I am entirely responsible for using Hirschman's conception in the context of the FDRS.
37. On 16 August 1985 *Hubei ribao* gave voice to the voluntary (but in fact forced) exit of Chang Jiaxiang, the "intellectual" manager of a small collective enterprise in Wuhan. The stories I refer to in the following paragraphs and notes show that relations between officials and managers display an arbitrary ruthlessness that is all too common. Many of the factory directors I interviewed hinted at this ruthless behavior.
38. See an intricate story in *GRRB,* 23 April 1985. In the context of Eastern Europe, Alec Nove once remarked, "Never forget that party secretaries know how to use a telephone." A report from Anshan illustrates these words at the expense of a manager. *RMRB,* quoted in *Guangming ribao* (Guangming daily), 11 August

1985. On factory directors being reinstated by party organizations without legal procedures, see *GRRB,* 19 June 1986.

39. I heard in Beijing in February 1988 the equivalent of the couplet quoted by Walder ("Informal Dimension of Reforms," p. 643): *Shangmian you houtai, xiamian you bangpai* ("Above are the backers, below are their cliques"). Chamberlain ("Party-Management Relations," pp. 643–644) concurs in this view by quoting enterprise executives who declared, in 1984, that the "existing system of 'factory director under Party committee leadership' is probably best. At least now, when difficulties arise, the enterprise Party committee can step in and take charge, where the factory director might otherwise have to back off."

40. Examples of intraparty splits and factions: secretary against committee (over management matters), *GRRB,* 23 April 1985; two factions in the same committee, with bureau committee interfering at municipal level, and corruption, *Zhongguo qingnianbao,* 4 June 1985; industrial bureau and enterprise party committee in a coalition against a new director, *GRRB,* 19 June 1986.

41. *GRRB,* 31 January 1985.

42. The political culture and style inherited by party cadres and state officials from Maoism is never far from the surface. The story, reported from Anhui (*GRRB,* 23 April 1985), also exemplifies the arbitrary power of party organizations over legal organs.

43. For an example of a small enterprise in Sichuan, see *GRRB,* 13 May 1985. Even the restructured People's Liberation Army (PLA) is not immune from squeeze. *JJRB* reported (11 February 1988) that it had been "forced" to donate more than 70 million yuan to local construction projects in 1986–87. Of course, the pre-reform PLA was organized to do just that, as enterprises and other segments of the Maoist organic organization were. And the PLA, ancient and new, is also vulnerable to corruption and micropolitical factional conflicts. See the report about a busy ring in Shenyang in *Xinhua* (New China news agency), 25 April 1988 (Summary of World Broadcasts [SWB] FE/0137 B2/1, 28 April 1988).

44. The grievances of the Henan managers against bureaucratic privilege and squeeze (including feasts and travels) were given some publicity in *GRRB,* 7 January 1985, 16 May 1985, and 7 June 1985, following an investigation of 100 enterprises in Zhengzhou. The municipal party committee and government observed that these outside interferences in enterprise management were mostly violations of official regulations.

45. Severe diagnoses can be found in *ZGFZB,* 7 January 1985, and *Nanfang ribao,* 1 May 1985. The latter criticized the "peasant," "archaic" mentality behind squeeze, amounting to the ancient wisdom of "killing the rich and equalizing wealth."

46. On these ventures started and run by cadres (and forbidden as well as constantly criticized since 1985), see Chevrier, "Gestion et modernisation," p. 788, and W. Zafanolli, "A Brief Outline of China's Second Economy," *Asian Survey* 25:715–736 (1985). China had already witnessed the impact of economic growth and commercialization of the economy on the bureaucratic-communal structure at the end of the sixteenth and eighteenth centuries, when corruption, in E. Balazs's words, left its "normal" level to reach an "extraordinary stage." For our

time Thomas Gold has pointed out the strong impact of post-Mao economics on the reemergence of *guanxi* networks (see his "After Comradeship: Personal Relations in China since the Cultural Revolution," *CQ* 104 (1985).

47. *ZGFZB,* 18 September 1985, and, more explicitly, 5 July 1986. The rise of economic crime is also attributed to the changing nature of economic management: more economic responsibilities, new, untrained managers, and more contracts to negotiate mean more occasions to cheat—and to be cheated. Together with the lack of experience (and even education), incompetence and naïveté are cited. See Chevrier, "Gestion et modernisation," pp. 788–789.

48. *ZGFZB,* 12 May 1986.

49. *Nanfang ribao* (Nanfang daily), 17 August 1985. Since June 1989, conservative attacks against Zhao Ziyang have reproached him with giving a free hand to localism and local "feudal" powers—ideological variations on a common theme.

50. Andrew G. Walder, "Wage Reform and the Web of Factory Interests," *CQ* 109:22–41 (1987). Bridging the gap separating workers from management was one of the duties of the "ideal" manager portrayed in 1984 and, ironically, one area where "enlightened secretaries" were expected to help management reforms by reconciling divergent interests through education and persuasion.

51. Individualizing, in this case, does not mean separating and functionalizing social relations but, in Confucian or communist fashion, moralizing power relations.

52. This was argued during interviews and work sessions at Tigaisuo in Beijing in February 1988. See Walder's comments on these patterns in "Factory and Manager," *passim.*

53. One factory director in Changchun, faced with intense factional strife, finds backing for recruiting supporters into his *danwei* and arranges for their families to follow them, i.e., for housing. *GRRB,* 16 August 1985.

54. Chamberlain, "Party-Management Relations," pp. 637, 650.

55. According to a survey of 300 managers in the Beijing electronics industries, 16% wanted to resign in 1986 because of outside interferences. *JJRB,* 14 October 1986. Similar attitudes keep being reported (see *JJRB,* 4 April 1988).

56. On the various forms of this "management contract system" (or contracted managerial responsibility system, *chengbao jingguan zerenzhi*), see *China News Analysis* 1344:4–6 (1987).

57. Interviews in Beijing, February 1988. The various forms of the management contract system launched after May 1987 recall, by their adaptation to specific situations (profits or losses, profitable sector, etc.) and the possibility of constantly readjusting contracted objectives according to performance, the contractual evolution of the profit-sharing system initiated in 1978–79 that led to the first version of the industrial economic responsibility system in 1981, that is, less actual financial autonomy to enterprises and more power to local officials. On this evolution, see Aubert and Chevrier, "Réformer ou ne pas réformer," pp. 33–34. As before, the result was not to cut losses (30% of state enterprises were running in the red in 1987) but to consolidate the shortcomings of short-term management. Thus the editors of *China News Analysis* (1344:4 [1987]) wrote at the end of 1987 that "the short-term ethic of enterprises has become a household word in the press. Managers do not look farther than the end of the year. Plan-

ning is no planning, but only bargaining between parties who are perfectly aware that their plans may be undone overnight."

58. Example of contradictory statements in the same issue of *GRRB*, 12 June 1986: If party secretaries oppose factory directors against the letter of the contracts, they should be removed; and counterstatement.

59. *Xinhua*, in English, 20 October 1986.

60. Tony Saich, "The Chinese Communist Party at the Thirteenth National Congress: Policies and Prospects for Reform," in King-yuh Chang, ed., *Political and Social Changes in Taiwan and Mainland China*, (Taipei, Institute of International Relations, 1989), p. 100. The National People's Congress formal vote, however, also formalized the legal status of managers by restating the 1984 identification of enterprise *faren* and director responsibility.

61. *GRRB*, 28 July 1986.

62. For the latter, the case is argued in *ZGFZB*, 20 September 1986. On the unfolding of the evaluation campaign, see *ZGFZB*, 6 January 1986 (on Jilin); 31 January 1986 (report on Shenyang Municipality); 4 June 1986 (on Anshan); 23 June 1986 (on Shanxi); 14 July 1986 (on Hubei); central government decision, 31 October 1986.

63. For an example in Shanxi Province, see *ZGFZB*, 23 June 1986.

64. At a brick factory in a Hubei *xian*, the nominee refused to start his mandate before an audit cleared him of any responsibility for more than 500,000 yuan of deficit. *ZGFZB*, 31 October 1986.

65. *China Daily*, 14 February 1985.

66. Chevrier, "Gestion et modernisation," pp. 776–777. By mid-1986, 40,000 large and medium-sized enterprises had used legal advisers (compared with 411 organizations with legal advisers in 1982). See Edward Epstein's report, "Law: Long March to the Present, Long Way to Go," in *Far Eastern Economic Review*, 18 March 1987, p. 104.

67. I developed this argument in "NEP and Beyond: The Transition to 'Modernization' in China (1978–85)," in Stephan Feuchtwang, Athar Hussain, and Thierry Pairault, eds., *Transforming China's Economy in the Eighties* (Boulder, Colo., Westview Press, 1988), I, 26–30. The weakening of central controls and the rise of local bosses have detrimental consequences not only in microeconomic management but also with the rise of runaway investment and inflation responsible for the overheating of the economy.

68. This scheme and its various political consequences (and requirements) were debated during work sessions with Chinese colleagues at Tigaisuo in Beijing (February 1988). The "commodity economy" (the market) should be regulated by the "plan" *(you jihua de shangpin jingji)*, using indirect controls and macroeconomic regulators, as the "commodity society" should be moderated by a renovated state (especially a welfare state) working on new social structures. Such speculations are totally phased out in the PRC for the time being, but current developments (April 1990) in the Soviet Union indicate that deeper economic reforms call for a global deregulation of socialist societies.

69. Epstein ("Law," pp. 106–107) remarks that "the type of civil disputes taken to

court is also changing. Divorce cases and property settlements once constituted more than half of all civic actions. Now divorce cases have given way to disputes over inheritance, property (especially housing disputes), and simple debts." The same author remarks that at the same time, "the relatively small decline in people's mediation tends to support China's very strong ideological and political commitment to mediation as an institution for dispute settlement."

70. Nonlitigious dispute settlement through "people's mediation" is one of these relations. The rehabilitation of selected aspects of the Confucian ethos belongs to the same strategy. See the discussion on the use of Confucian values of discipline, hierarchy, familial solidarity, and education at the conference on the educational thinking of Confucius, 21–26 September 1984, *Jiaoyu yanjiu* (Education studies) 11:27–33 (1984). Hua Chang-ming shows how the official treatment of old age relies on the cultivation of traditional filial piety *(xiao)* in order to offset the disintegration of the traditional family, while the state is unable to organize and finance a system of social security. "Le troisième âge," in Aubert et al., *La société chinoise,* pp. 131–153. This example shows that the modern treatment of traditional communal values subordinates them to the state and to the new atomistic social organization, as Liang Qichao had anticipated in his theory of modernization at the beginning of the twentieth century.

71. Zhao Ziyang's report at the Thirteenth Party Congress in October 1987 (*RMRB,* 4 November 1987) highlighted what was known in Chinese intellectual and policy debate as the "neoauthoritarian" process of modernization, inspired by Japan and Taiwan.

72. Banks, which were expected to play an essential role in the process of economic regulation, have, in the words of Daniel Brotman ("Reforming the Domestic Banking System," *China Business Review* 12:17–23 [1985]), "been assigned the task of increasing microlevel efficiency and at the same time guaranteeing balanced sectoral growth. These are responsibilities fit for an adult, whereas the Chinese banking system is still in its infancy." The fiscal system fares no better, and the remark can well be extended to the entire field of state building in China today.

73. This situation still prevailed in 1988, according to the report of Louise do Rosario, "Managers' Bruising Battles on the Shop Floor," in *Far Eastern Economic Review,* 8 September 1988, p. 131.

74. Ibid.

75. Saich ("Chinese Communist Party," p. 101) points out that in the wake of the April 1988 Enterprise Law, party officials have bullied factory directors into changing places with them.

76. *ZGFZB,* 23 August 1986.

77. A director charged and demoted by a party committee is reinstated by the *xian* control office. *GRRB,* 9 December 1986.

78. See the report of the Fourth Session of the Sixth National People's Congress, 8 April 1986 (SWB FE/8247/C1).

79. Example in *ZGFZB,* 23 August 1986.

80. Compare the attitude of Soviet authorities in coopting the new technical elites

at the same time as they destroyed the social pluralism of the NEP in K. E. Bailes, *Technology and Society under Lenin and Stalin: Origins of the Soviet Technical Intelligentsia* (Princeton, N.J., Princeton University Press, 1978).

81. Before 1989, "interest groups" were a favorite topic and concept in the Chinese academic community and media (see Luo Rongxing, Zhu Huaxin, and Cao Huanrong, "Different Interest Groups under Socialism," *Beijing Review,* 30 November–6 December 1987, pp. 14–15), and managers are often listed among the examples of new "interests" emerging from the reforms. In this light, they became one of the top priorities for sociological surveys and research programs assigned to research bodies in the PRC (the director of the Institute of Sociology of the Liaoning Academy of Social Sciences listed them in this position for his institute in Shenyang and across the country; personal communication, Paris, March 1988). Class struggle was reintroduced in party propaganda in the latter half of 1989.

82. "Civil society" means more than society versus the state. It does imply a political culture resting on the notion of individual rights, a nonparticularistic institutional and intellectual tradition crystallizing into collective forms of action and representative institutions. Activist intellectuals and public opinion are therefore not sufficient conditions for a modern civil society to emerge.

83. See Guan Guangmei's example, *Xinhua,* in English, 30 October 1987 (SWB FE/8715/C1/21), and Thomas Gold's chapter in this volume.

84. Personal communications, Beijing, February 1988.

85. These associations *(xiehui)* are either established by industrial branches *(hangye xiehui; Beijing ribao,* 6 May 1985), by provinces (on Zhejiang, see *Zhejiang ribao,* 31 March 1985), or according to age: the young managers *(qingnian qiye guanlizhe)* organized their own association on 4 February 1985 *(Zhongguo qingnianbao,* 5 February 1985). The Youth League has been especially active in promoting (and "guiding") this kind of organization, which serves the dual purpose of controlling new forces and establishing social counterweights. In the latter role, see the performance of the Shaanxi provincial *xiehui* against bureaucratic privilege in *Shaanxi ribao* (Shaanxi daily), 27 January 1985.

86. Such is the case with the Shanghai Zhongqingnian Qiye Fazhan Yanjiuhui (Shanghai Enterprise Development Research Society for Middle-Aged and Young Economists), founded 28 February 1987. The statutes and domination of the steering committees by local party and state officials exemplify the dual function of such organizations. However, a young member of the society underlined the importance of having lawyers as members and the determination of many nonofficial members to use them in order to support their interests. Personal communication, Shanghai, February 1988.

87. Six factory directors had been recruited (by public advertising) by the Second Bureau of Light Industries in Xiangtan (Hunan) in July–August 1984. Three were fired a few months later for insisting too much on their contractual rights. The provincial Association of Factory Directors voiced its anger, prompting a debate at the Municipal Assembly. *GRRB,* 19 May 1985.

88. Examples are *Jingji guanli* and *ZGFZB,* often quoted in these notes.

89. Thus in August 1985 *Yangcheng wanbao* (Yangcheng evening news) not only

exposed a local ring of corruption and protection feeding, so to speak, on adulterated milk powder. While other newspapers had done so since 1983, *Yangcheng wanbao,* through its reporters and "legal counsel," also mobilized public opinion against those who had blocked former investigations and frozen the legal organs into inaction (21–25 August 1985). The role of the press as the "voice" organ of a pluralistic society was discussed at the first session of the Seventh National People's Congress in April 1988.

90. *Yangcheng wanbao,* 14 September 1985.

91. See *Zhengming* (Contending) 4:1–4 (1985).

92. See Moshe Lewin's analysis in *The Gorbachev Phenomenon* (Berkeley, University of California Press, 1988).

93. On these business ventures and their relations to official policies, see Chevrier, "Gestion et modernisation," pp. 776, 788.

94. On the involvement of cadres and officials, see above, "Informal Resistances and Micropolitics," and note 43. "Industrial companies" set up in lieu of industrial bureaus have been denounced by enterprise directors and reformist economists as new "mothers-in-law" since the reform began. Aubert and Chevrier, "Réformer ou ne pas réformer," p. 22. The trend, nonetheless, is developing, as the authorities hope to channel the rising tide of enterprises trying to move out of local administrative channels by investing in other units far away. Thus seventy-seven industrial companies were dismantled in Shanghai between mid-1986 and March 1987, giving birth to more than two thousand economic organizations, including a hundred large industrial groups. Katsuhiko Hama, "Further Tightening of the Chinese Economy," *China Newsletter,* JETRO, July–August 1987, pp. 2–8. Companies belonging to officials and to official (state-party) organs have been a prime target of the anti-corruption and investigation drive that began in the fall of 1989.

95. Li Yining (*RMRB,* 26 September 1986; *JJRB,* 15 August 1987) insists on the fact that the industrial system cannot be transformed, because there are as yet no private interests in industrial management. The principle of "separating management from ownership" had been enshrined in the October 1984 decision on economic system reform. As opposed to management contracts, management leases give a complete *jus utendi* to individual managers (or individuals signing as a team) selected by public competition. As legal "owners" (under contract) of the enterprise, they have a free hand in running it (including staff and personnel) as they see fit; they must pay taxes to the state and a rent to the owner, and must give a share of the profits above taxes and rent (70% in Shenyang). If no profits are made or in case of losses, the contractors (or collaterals, also involved in the contract) must still pay the agreed amounts. In 1987 "asset management contracts" were developed by including the right to sell factory assets. On these various forms of leases, be they "leasing management" (*zulin jingguan*) or "asset management" (*zichan jingguan*), see *China News Analysis* 1344:8 (1987).

96. In Liaoning, a province that, together with Shenyang Municipality, has been a pioneer of the new system, of a total of 1,400 state enterprises, 827 small ones were under experimental management leases by spring 1987. *RMRB,* 29 March 1987, 18 May 1987. Central authorities have been careful to depict industrial

capitalists as good communists: Guan Guangmei (note 83) has become a politi-
cal-ethical model of the desired harmony, much as "good" factory directors were
supposed to emulate "good" party secretaries (note 30).

97. The best formulation of the resulting chaos has perhaps been given unwittingly
by the deputy director of the Economic, Technological, and Social Development
Research Center of the State Council at the time of the Thirteenth Party Congress in his comments on the new doctrine of the "initial stage of socialism."
Of the ten contradictory (and transitional) aspects listed by him as characteristic
of that stage, point 9 is especially relevant to microeconomic management: "The
rule of man coexists with the rule by law." *JJRB,* 21 October 1987.

98. In the wake of Tiananmen, there is evidence that they are also trying to block
(especially in the south) the new economic policies and anti-corruption campaign
decided on by the central authorities in Beijing.

99. In early 1990 the central government's retrenchment policies have all but phased
out structural reforms in the state sector of the economy. Central authorities
uphold the Enterprise Law of 1988 but stress cooperation between party secretaries and factory directors with renewed emphasis. At a symposium for managers of the Northeast held on 19 September 1989, Li Peng stated that the
leadership in state enterprises belonged to the working class, not to one individual. *Xinhua,* 24 September 1989. The meaning of "responsibility" is also changed
from individualizing functions to disciplining individuals and strengthening their
dedication to the "interests of the whole." *Jingji cankao* (Economic reference
news), 18 September 1989. The formula whereby factory directors are concurrently party secretaries in the enterprise is also commended. *Jingji guanli* 8:32–
34 (1989). Ideas are not entirely frozen, however, where theoretical debates are
confined. Thus the fall 1989 issue (in English) of *Social Sciences in China* was still
permitted to carry an article arguing for the separation of ownership rights and
management authority. *Social Sciences in China* 10:9–26 (1989).

Chapter 6. *Economic Reform and Income Distribution in Tianjin, 1976–1986, by Andrew G. Walder*

I would like to thank Yanjie Bian, Peter Blau, Deborah Davis, Nan Lin, Louis
Putterman, Carl Riskin, Danching Ruan, Ezra Vogel, and Jaeyeol Yee for their
comments on several earlier versions of this paper. Danching Ruan performed the
computer analysis, and was listed as coauthor, for the first draft, presented at Harvard
University in May 1988. The research was supported by National Science Foundation
Grant INT–86–15759.

1. See Martin K. Whyte, "Destratification and Restratification in China," in G.
Berreman, ed., *Social Inequality: Comparative and Developmental Approaches* (New
York, Academic Press, 1981).

2. Ivan Szelenyi, *Urban Inequalities under State Socialism* (New York, Oxford University Press, 1983), and Szelenyi, "Social Inequalities in State Socialist Redistributive Economies," *International Journal of Comparative Sociology* 19:63–87 (1978).

3. For a retrospective evaluation of this view, see Ivan Szelenyi and Robert Manchin, "Social Policy under State Socialism: Market, Redistribution, and Social

Inequalities in East European Socialist Societies," in Gosta Esping-Andersen, Martin Rein and Lee Rainwater, eds., *Stagnation and Renewal in Social Policy* (Armonk, N.Y., Sharpe, 1987).

4. See Henryk Flakierski, *Economic Reform and Income Distribution: A Case Study of Hungary and Poland* (Armonk, N.Y., Sharpe, 1986). Victor Nee's writings about China's agricultural reform draw inspiration from the work of Szelenyi. See his "A Theory of Market Transition: From Redistribution to Markets in State Socialism," *American Sociological Review* 54:663–681 (1989).

5. A series of studies of rural China in the 1970s showed a marked equality of incomes within villages. See the data summarized in Bingyuan Hsiung and Louis Putterman, "Pre- and Post-Reform Income Distribution in a Chinese Commune: The Case of Dahe Township in Hebei Province," *Journal of Comparative Economics* 13:406–445 (1989).

6. Martin K. Whyte, "Social Trends in China: The Triumph of Inequality?" in A. Doak Barnett and Ralph Clough, eds., *Modernizing China* (Boulder, Colo., Westview Press, 1986), p. 109.

7. See Nick Eberstadt, *The Poverty of Communism* (New Brunswick, N.J., Transaction, 1988), pp. 138–176; Eduard Vermeer, *Economic Development in Provincial China: The Central Shaanxi since 1930* (Cambridge, Cambridge University Press, 1988), pp. 410–415; Nicholas Lardy, *Agriculture in China's Modern Economic Development* (Cambridge, Cambridge University Press, 1983); Carl Riskin, *China's Political Economy: The Quest for Development since 1949* (New York, Oxford University Press, 1987), pp. 229–253; and Mark Selden, *The Political Economy of Chinese Socialism* (Armonk, N.Y., Sharpe, 1988), pp. 144–173.

8. William L. Parish, "Egalitarianism in Chinese Society," *Problems of Communism* 29:37–53 (1981), and Whyte, "Social Trends in China."

9. Whyte, "Social Trends in China," p. 109.

10. Nee, "Theory of Market Transition."

11. Vermeer, *Economic Development in Provincial China,* chap. 9 and p. 431, points to a lessening in the 1980s of income differentials between counties in Central Shaanxi, after they had increased from the 1930s through the 1970s. Selden, *Political Economy of Chinese Socialism,* chaps. 5 and 6, finds that some measures of rural inequality have risen, and others fallen, in the past decade.

12. We have data for 1986 on other aspects of inequality—housing space, delivery of workplace services, consumption of leading consumer items, and others—and also on characteristics of the firm, all important aspects of income inequality. We are forced to limit our analysis here only to those variables for which we have data for both 1976 and 1986. We shall present fuller analyses of stratification in 1986 in future publications.

13. Peter Blau, Andrew Walder, and Danching Ruan, then all at Columbia University, designed the questionnaire in collaboration with sociologists at the Institute of Sociology, Tianjin Academy of Social Sciences (primarily Zhou Lu and Ren Hong'en). The survey was conducted by the city government's District Affairs Department *(qujiechu)* under its director, Yang Hanzhang, and with the assistance of Zhang Yuchun, in collaboration with the academy sociologists. The survey procedures, questionnaire, and preliminary tabulations are described in

Andrew G. Walder et al., "The 1986 Survey of Work and Social Life in Tianjin, China: Aims, Methods, and Documentation," Working Paper No. 26, Center for Research on Politics and Social Organization, Harvard University Department of Sociology, 1989.

14. We asked about 1976 incomes because that was the last year before bonuses and pay raises were widely restored. Respondents had no difficulty recalling their income in 1976, because wages had not been raised since 1972 for the younger members of the work force and since 1963 for the older members. The 1976 data, readers will note, are not a representative sample of the Tianjin work force in that year. The age structure of those reporting incomes for 1976 is compressed: older workers are underrepresented because the respondents are all ten years younger than at the time of their interview in 1986, while a large proportion of the younger respondents disappear from the sample because they did not work at that time. Age, as we shall see shortly, is more strongly related to wage inequality than is any other factor; our sample therefore *underestimates* the degree of wage inequality in 1976. Were our 1976 data more representative, they would show an even greater decline in wage inequality than we report here.

15. Twenty-five individuals in our sample worked in "new collectives"; nine of them were retired and had incomes well above the city average. In many cases these "new collectives" do not differ greatly from family enterprises classified as "individual".

16. Tianjin Shi Tongjiju (Tianjin Municipal Bureau of Statistics), eds., *Tianjin tongji nianjian 1987* (Tianjin statistical yearbook 1987; Beijing, Zhongguo Tongji Chubanshe, 1987), p. 75. Official statistics for all of urban China in 1986 report that 3.6% more than double the official Tianjin figure were employed in the private sector. *ZGTJNJ 1987*, p. 115.

17. *ZGTJNJ 1987*, p. 688. Our question asked that respondents report their income on a monthly basis, and it may be that annual bonuses consequently are underreported. However, this is probably not a major problem. Annual bonuses, when granted, are usually equal to about one month's salary, and it is not known how prevalent this practice is today in the face of consistent government directives prohibiting them beginning in the early 1980s.

18. Ibid.

19. See Xia Xiaoxun and Li Jun, "Consumption Expansion: A Grave Challenge to Reform and Development," in Bruce L. Reynolds, ed., *Reform in China: Challenges and Choices* (Armonk, N.Y., Sharpe, 1987), p. 89. The data are from a survey of 429 enterprises in 27 cities, conducted by the State Council's Research Institute on the Reform of the Economic Structure.

20. See Susan L. Shirk, "Recent Chinese Labour Policies and the Transformation of Industrial Organisation in China," *CQ* 88:575–593 (1981).

21. See Andrew G. Walder, "Wage Reform and the Web of Factory Interests," *CQ* 109:22–41 (1987).

22. There is evidence of increased urban-rural differences in health care and other social services, for example. See the chapter by Gail Henderson in this volume, and Deborah Davis, "Chinese Social Welfare: Policies and Outcomes," *CQ*

119:577–597 (1989). Davis has also pointed to increasing differences in the life chances of generations (see Davis, "Unequal Chances, Unequal Outcomes: Pension Reform and Urban Inequality," *CQ* 114:223–241 [1988]) and related differences in social services available to employees in different sectors of the urban economy (see her chapter in this volume). Others, however, find evidence that there has been no significant change in *interprovincial* inequalities in health care and other services. See James Tong, "Fiscal Reform, Elite Turnover, and Central-Provincial Relations in Post-Mao China," *Australian Journal of Chinese Affairs* 22:1–28 (1989). Our Tianjin survey includes information about housing and other goods and services delivered by urban workplaces, but these data are available only for 1986 and will be analyzed elsewhere.

23. Cost of living index is from *ZGTJNJ 1987*, p. 648. We shall use real incomes for 1986 whenever we analyze the trend of change below; otherwise we shall use nominal 1986 incomes. Each table will note whether nominal or real incomes are used.

24. We have used a variation on the alternative computational formula in Peter M. Blau, *Inequality and Heterogeneity: A Primitive Theory of Social Structure* (New York, Free Press, 1977), p. 58, and have grouped the wage data into twenty-five categories of equal size. Nancy Williamson kindly wrote and tested a computer program to calculate these indices.

25. See Martin K. Whyte and William L. Parish, *Urban Life in Contemporary China* (Chicago, University of Chicago Press, 1984), p. 44.

26. We cannot speculate about the divergence of our figures for bonuses and total incomes from theirs, but we note that for unexplained reasons their coefficients for these two items were based on a subset of only 300 respondents. See Tehwei Hu, Ming Li, and Shuzhong Shi, "Analysis of Wages and Bonus Payments among Tianjin Urban Workers," *CQ* 113:77–93 (1988).

27. Wen Xie, "Structural Changes and Individual Earnings in Urban China," paper presented at Annual Meeting of the American Sociological Association, Chicago, 1987.

28. All individual data pertain to the respective year. Because we do not have information about occupation, rank, and many other individual characteristics in 1976, we are limited to the handful of variables that we analyze here.

29. Andrew G. Walder, *Communist Neo-Traditionalism: Work and Authority in Chinese Industry* (Berkeley, University of California Press, 1986), chap. 6.

30. Party membership here, and in Tables 7 and 8 in this chapter, does not indicate the advantages of party membership per se; rather, it reflects the fact that party members are concentrated in the higher job ranks. Until we reach Table 9, we shall not be able to separate the effects of party membership and rank, because we have no data on jobs held in 1976. Party membership should be understood for the time being as a general indicator of high social rank.

31. The zero-order correlation coefficient between years of education and 1976 income is $-.197$, significant at the .001 level.

32. See Thomas P. Bernstein, *Up to the Mountains and Down to the Villages: The Transfer of Youth from Urban to Rural China* (New Haven, Yale University Press,

1977), pp. 33–59, and Jonathan Unger, *Education under Mao: Class and Competition in Canton Schools, 1960–1980* (New York, Columbia University Press, 1982), chaps. 2 and 3.

33. The zero-order correlation coefficient for years of education and 1986 income is −.101, significant at the .001 level.

34. See Riskin, *China's Political Economy,* pp. 250–253.

Chapter 7. Urban Private Business and Social Change, by Thomas B. Gold

1. "Guowuyuan guanyu chengzhen feinongye geti jingji ruogan zhengce xing guiding" (Some policy regulations concerning the urban and township nonagricultural individual economy), in Guojia Gongshang Xingzheng Guanliju Geti Jingjisi and Beijing Ribao Lilunbu, eds., *Geti laodongzhe shouce* (Handbook for individual laborers; Beijing, Beijing Ribao Chubanshe and Gongshang Chubanshe, 1984), pp. 5–9.

2. See Lynn T. White III, *Careers in Shanghai* (Berkeley, University of California Press, 1979), esp. chap. 3.

3. Feng Lanrui and Zhao Lukuan, "Urban Unemployment in China," *Social Sciences in China* 1:131 (1982). Of 7 million middle-school graduates, 4% (280,000) went to institutions of higher education and the same number went to technical or vocational schools.

4. John Philip Emerson, "Urban School-Leavers and Unemployment in China," *CQ* 93:7 (1983). Emerson says that an additional 5 to 10 million family members must be included in this figure.

5. Thomas P. Bernstein, *Up to the Mountains and Down to the Villages: The Transfer of Youth from Urban to Rural China* (New Haven, Yale University Press, 1977), esp. chap. 2. At the same time, over 10 million rural people moved to the cities and gained permanent residence, taking away job opportunities from city youths. Feng Lanrui and Zhao Lukuan, "Urban Unemployment," pp. 131–132.

6. Thomas B. Gold, "Back to the City: The Return of Shanghai's Educated Youth," *CQ* 84:755–770 (1980).

7. Emerson, "Urban School-Leavers," pp. 1–2.

8. For a summary of the classic formulation, see David Stark and Victor Nee, "Toward an Institutional Analysis of State Socialism," in Victor Nee and David Stark, eds., *Remaking the Economic Institutions of Socialism* (Stanford, Calif., Stanford University Press, 1989), pp. 9–11. An excellent summary of the economic problems facing the reformers can be found in Carl Riskin, *China's Political Economy: The Quest for Development since 1949* (New York, Oxford University Press, 1987), esp. chap. 11.

9. Two other forms encouraged at this time were "people-run enterprises" (*minban qiye*) and labor-service companies. The former were cooperatives formed by young people waiting for work who raised their own funds. Labor-service companies helped to train youths and provide temporary jobs. See Feng Lanrui and Zhao Lukuan, "Urban Unemployment," pp. 134–135, and Liu Jialin and Mao Fenghua, eds. *Zhongguo laodong zhidu gaige* (Reform of China's labor system; Beijing, Jingji Kexue Chubanshe, 1988), pp. 77–98.

10. Not coincidentally, permitting private business could serve as a signal to Hong Kong, Macao, and Taiwan that the communists were sincere about reforms and that they could tolerate diversity of economic forms. This could thereby allay fears about reunification.

11. This is the theme of Linda Hershkovitz, "The Fruits of Ambivalence: China's Urban Individual Economy," *Pacific Affairs* 58:427–450 (1985).

12. Published in Chinese in Guojia Gongshang Xingzheng Guanliju Geti Jingjisi and Beijing Ribao Lilunbu, eds., *Geti laodongzhe shouce*, pp. 5–9. For a discussion of other documents and experiences between the Third Plenum and 1981, see Susan Lynn Muth, "Private Business under Socialism: An Examination of the Urban Individual Economic Sector in China," Ph.D. diss., George Washington University, 1987.

13. In Guojia Gongshang Xingzheng Guanliju Geti Jingjisi and Beijing Ribao Lilunbu, eds., *Geti laodongzhe shouce*, pp. 10–13.

14. Thomas B. Gold, " 'Just in Time!' China Battles Spiritual Pollution on the Eve of 1984," *Asian Survey* 24:947–974 (1984).

15. These are discussed in Liu Jialin and Mao Fenghua, *Zhongguo laodong*. Many of these reforms grew out of a conference on labor and employment held by the CCP Central Committee in August 1980. See Feng Lanrui and Zhao Lukuan, "Urban Unemployment," pp. 136–137.

16. Deng Xiaoping, *Build Socialism with Chinese Characteristics* (Beijing, Foreign Languages Press, 1985), p. 37. See also "Our Work in All Fields Should Contribute to the Building of Socialism with Chinese Characteristics," pp. 10–13, in the same book. Many of Deng's themes are illustrated in Orville Schell, *To Get Rich Is Glorious* (New York, New American Library, 1986).

17. Zhao Ziyang, "Advance along the Road of Socialism with Chinese Characteristics," *Beijing Review* (North American ed.) 45:23–49 (1987).

18. Guojia Gongshang Xingzheng Guanliju Geti Jingjisi and Beijing Ribao Lilunbu, eds., *Geti laodongzhe shouce*, pp. 80–83; Hu Guohua, Liu Jinghuai, and Chen Ming, *Duo setiao de Zhongguo geti jingyingzhe* (China's multicolored individual managers; Beijing, Jingji Xueyuan Chubanshe, 1988), p. 217.

19. See Marcia Yudkin, *Making Good: Private Business in Socialist China* (Beijing, Foreign Languages Press, 1986).

20. The data in this table come from the State Statistical Bureau. The State Administration for Industry and Commerce has published a set of figures at variance with these. I have included them here for reference.

Unit	1981	1982	1983	1984	1985	1986	1987
Number of households (in thousands)	1,829	2,636	5,901	9,304	11,710	12,111	13,725
Urban	868	1,132	1,706	2,222	2,799	2,910	3,383
Rural	961	1,504	4,195	7,082	8,911	9,201	10,342
Number of employees (in thousands)	2,274	3,198	7,465	13,031	17,660	18,459	21,583

Unit	1981	1982	1983	1984	1985	1986	1987
Urban	1,056	1,358	2,086	2,911	3,849	4,076	4,923
Rural	1,218	1,840	5,379	10,120	13,811	14,383	16,660

Source: "The Individually Owned Economy," *Beijing Review* (North American ed.) 9:27 (1989). The benefit of these figures is that they illustrate the small percentage of urban individual enterprises in the total.

In November 1989 the total number of households dropped from a high of 14.5 million to 12.3 million, owing mainly to the crackdown on illegal businesses and tax evasion that began in August. "State to Set Private Businesses Straight," *China Daily,* 7 November 1989, p. 1.

21. Calculated from tables on pp. 131 and 141 in State Statistical Bureau, *Statistical Yearbook of China 1988* (Beijing, 1988).
22. Ole Bruun, "The Reappearance of the Family as an Economic Unit: A Sample Survey of Individual Households in Workshop Production and Crafts, Chengdu, Sichuan Province, China," Copenhagen Discussion Papers No. 1, Center for East and Southeast Asian Studies, University of Copenhagen, 1988.
23. "Call for Action on Moonlighters," *South China Morning Post,* 6 September 1989, p. 10. The article cites a Chinese survey which showed that 15 million people moonlighted. Temporary layoffs in late 1989 sent numerous workers onto the streets to earn money. In December 1989 I saw many of them selling Christmas cards and shashlik and other food items in Kunming and Shanghai.
24. Beijingshi Renmin Zhengfu Yanjiushi and Beijingshi Laodongju, eds., *Beijing chengzhen de siren gugong* (Private hiring of labor in Beijing city and municipality; Beijing, Jingji Xueyuan Chubanshe, 1989), p. 31.
25. "Campaign Cleans up Street Trade," *China Daily,* 6 November 1989, p. 3.
26. Interview in Lhasa, 7 October 1988.
27. Yuan Enzhen, ed., *Wenzhou moshi yu fuyu zhi lu* (Wenzhou model of economy and the road to affluence; Shanghai, Shanghai Shehui Kexueyuan Chubanshe, 1987).
28. Interview on boat to Wenzhou, 26 May 1988.
29. Yueyang Shiwei Zhengce Yanjiushi, eds., "Yiwanduo geti gongshang hu weihe xieye?" (Why did more than ten thousand individual industrial and commercial households cease operation?), *Shehui* (Sociology) 10:13–14 (1988). *Xieye* actually means temporarily stopping business but keeping one's license and paying certain administrative fees. Closings increased with the crackdown after August 1989. During a late December trip to Kunming and Shanghai, however, I was impressed with the continued vigor of urban enterprises. A restaurateur in Shanghai summed up a common attitude when he told me that as long as he could earn more than in the state job from which he was on leave, he would not abandon the private sector.
30. *Beijing Review* (North American ed.), 4 May 1987, p. 8.
31. Beijingshi Renmin Zhengfu Yanjiushi and Beijingshi Laodongju, eds., *Beijing chengzhen,* p. 3.

32. Shanghaishi Gongshang Xingzheng Guanliju, eds., "Shanghaishi geti gongshang-ye fazhan zhuangkuang de diaocha" (Investigation into the current situation of the development of Shanghai's individual industrial and commercial sector), in Guowuyuan Banshiting Diaoyanshi, eds., *Geti jingji diaocha yu yanjiu* (Investigation and research on the individual economy; Beijing, Jingji Kexue Chu-banshe, 1986), p. 20.

33. Table 4, p. 298, Guowuyuan Banshiting Diaoyanshi, eds., *Geti jingji diaocha;* 1987 figures from "Taking Stock of Commercial Reform," *Beijing Review* (North American ed.) 52:21 (1988–89).

34. State Statistical Bureau, *Statistical Yearbook of China 1988,* pp. 165, 169.

35. Table 6, Guowuyuan Banshiting Diaoyanshi, eds., *Geti jingji diaocha,* pp. 300–302.

36. Liu Zheng et al., *Siying jingji wenti jieda* (Answers to questions about the private economy; Beijing, Dizhi Chubanshe, 1988), pp. 8, 39. See also Susan Young, "Policy, Practice and the Private Sector in China," *Australian Journal of Chinese Affairs* 21:57–80 (1989).

37. Huang Jian, "Guanyu geti laodongzhe xiehui de jige wenti" (Some questions concerning the Self-Employed Laborers Association), in Guowuyuan Banshiting Diaoyanshi, eds., *Geti jingji diaocha,* pp. 281–288; Yang Zhengwen and Ye Cuihua, "Wuhan yikao geti xiehui jiaoyu geti hu" (Wuhan relies on the Self-Employed Association to educate individual entrepreneurs), *Liaowang* (Outlook) 9:24 (1986).

38. Chen Jian, "An Effective Way to Increase Employment," *Chinese Economic Stud-ies,* Part 1, 21:43–71 (1987), table 4, p. 50.

39. Interview in Guangzhou, 26 May 1982.

40. Hu Guohua, Liu Jinghai, and Chen Ming, *Duo Setiao,* p. 23.

41. "Geti hu de youle yu fazhi guan" (The worries, happiness and legal system views of individual businessmen), *ZGFZB,* 23 July 1986, p. 2.

42. Stanley Rosen, ed., "The Private Economy," pt. 2, *Chinese Economic Studies* 21: 120 (1987–88).

43. Chen Jian, "An Effective Way," table 4, p. 50.

44. Shanghaishi Gongshang Xingzheng Guanliju, eds., Shanghaishi geti gongshang-ye," p. 21. In the Shanghai survey, social idlers constituted 49% and prisoners another 9%. In the national survey in 1985, idlers constituted 66%, and in the Beijing survey in 1984, 43%.

45. Liu Jialin and Mao Fenghua, *Zhongguo laodong,* p. 134. Most of the youths in this period went into collective enterprises.

46. For instance, pp. 84–86 in Guojia Gongshang Xingzheng Guanliju Geti Jingjisi and Beijing Ribao Lilunbu, eds., *Geti laodongzhe shouce.*

47. Interview in Changsha, 16 May 1985.

48. Interview in Kunming, 8 May 1985.

49. Interviews in Guiyang, 12 May 1985, and Quanzhou, 27 May 1985.

50. Interview in Chengdu, 13 April 1989.

51. Adi Ignatius, "Beijing Finds High-Tech Success Story," *Asian Wall Street Jour-nal,* 7 June 1988, p. 1.

52. For example, Tang Qiwei, "My Way: Young Entrepreneur Shuns the Easy Life," *Chinese Youth* 9:16–18 (1988), about a computer science major starting his own business. Tang's essay barely conceals his disdain for state employees.

53. Zhao Wentao, "Daxuesheng de 'jingshangre' " ('Commercial fever' among university students), *Zhongguo qingnian* (China's youth) 7:13 (1988).

54. Interview in Xian, 10 April 1989.

55. For example, "Hu chuxian shoujia minban wenyansuo" (The first private cultural research institute appears in Shanghai), *RMRB* (overseas ed.), 22 February 1989, p. 4.

56. "Rengxia shubao de xiaoshangren" (Little merchants who have thrown down their schoolbags), *RMRB* (overseas ed.), 25 February 1989, p. 4.

57. Andrew G. Walder, *Communist Neo-Traditionalism: Work and Authority in Chinese Industry*, (Berkeley, University of California Press, 1986), p. 40.

58. Jean C. Oi, "Commercializing China's Rural Cadres," *Problems of Communism* 35:1–15 (1986).

59. Julia Leung, "Beijing Purge of Profiteers Sparks Alarm," *Asian Wall Street Journal*, 7–8 October 1988, p. 1.

60. "Jinqi zuo qijian qunzhong guanxin de shi" (In the near future do seven things the masses are concerned about), *RMRB*, 29 July 1989, p. 1.

61. "Ren Zhonglin on Company Screening," *FBIS*, 30 August 1989, pp. 7–8.

62. Xie Peihui, *Qian, fengkuang de kunshou* (Money, the mad cornered beast; Changsha, Hunan Wenyi Chubanshe, 1988).

63. English in *FBIS*, 12 July 1989, pp. 15–20.

64. For example, "Quanguo jiang kaizhan geti shuishou zhixu da jiancha" (The whole nation will launch a major investigation of the tax collection system of individual business), *JJRB*, 2 August 1989, p. 1. My visit in December 1989 showed little progress in record keeping.

65. Stanley Rosen, "Public Opinion and Reform in the People's Republic of China," *Studies in Comparative Communism* 22:153–170 (1989); Liu Yuejin, "Shinian gaigezhong jiazhiguan de shige zhuanbian" (Ten changes in values in the decade of reform), *Xinhua wenzhai* (Xinhua digest) 2:13–16 (1989).

66. Ye Guang, "Wan Runnan banqi 'shitou' yao za shei?" (Who does Wan Runnan want to smash when he throws a 'stone'?), *RMRB*, 17 August 1989, p. 1.

67. Andrew Watson, "The Reform of Agricultural Marketing in China since 1978," *CQ* 113:1–28 (1988).

68. An important statement is Huang Youguang and Yang Xiaokai, "Weihe Zhongguo ying yitiao guohe de jinxing minyinghua?" (Why should China carry out privatized management in one leap?), *Shijie jingji daobao* (World economic herald), 6 February 1989, pp. 12–13; 20 February 1989, p. 15.

69. Jin Guang, "Ping 'siyouzhi xuanyan' " (Criticize the 'declaration of privatization') *RMRB*, 2 December 1989, p. 1.

Chapter 8. Changes in Mate Choice in Chengdu, by Martin King Whyte

1. This survey was designed to be a substantial replication of a study I directed in the Detroit area in 1984, in which 459 ever-married women were interviewed.

In this chapter, comparative results from this American study will be noted occasionally. My collaborators in the Chengdu survey were Yuan Yayu and Xu Xiaohe, from the Sociology Research Office of Sichuan University, although they bear no responsibility for the particular interpretations offered here. Face-to-face interviews were conducted by sociology students from Sichuan University, usually in the homes of respondents, but in some cases in the workplace or elsewhere. The response rate for the survey was 87.7%. Chengdu is, of course, not "typical" of all urban China, but there is no reason to think that it is especially unusual in comparison with other major cities in China. Chengdu is China's tenth-largest city, with a population estimated at 2.6 million in 1985, and it is also the capital of Sichuan Province. See State Statistical Bureau, *China: A Statistical Survey in 1986* (Beijing, New World Press, 1986), p. 24.

2. This custom, combining elements of a bride-price payment and a dowry, is technically referred to as an "indirect-dowry" custom. See Jack Goody and S. J. Tambiah, *Bridewealth and Dowry* (Cambridge, Cambridge University Press, 1973).

3. No detailed discussion of these earlier changes will be offered here, given the ample writings on this topic by others. See Olga Lang, *Chinese Family and Society* (New Haven, Yale University Press, 1946); Marion Levy, *The Family Revolution in Modern China* (Cambridge, Mass., Harvard University Press, 1949); and William J. Goode, *World Revolution and Family Patterns* (New York, Free Press, 1963).

4. In some periods there were attempts to replace ritual practices, such as the couple bowing to ancestral tablets and the new bride serving tea to or washing the feet of her mother-in-law or both, which conveyed filiality and familial subordination, with new ritual elements, such as bowing to a portrait of Mao and pledging loyalty to the CCP, which express subordination instead to the new political system.

5. Occasionally articles have appeared in the press pointing to the advantages of matrilocal postmarital residence, and these became more common in the 1970s when it was increasingly recognized that the patrilocal custom posed obstacles to the government's family-planning goals. The 1980 revision of the 1950 Marriage Law of the People's Republic of China, unlike the original, stipulates that the couple can live after marriage with either the bride's family or the groom's family. See "The Marriage Law of the People's Republic of China (1980)," *Pacific Affairs* 57:266–269 (1984). Interestingly, the new law makes no mention of the possibility of the couple living neolocally, even though we shall see that this is the most common option in urban Chengdu and, no doubt, in other large cities. On balance, though, no major effort has been made since 1949 to alter the patterns of postmarital residence.

6. Not all aspects of official family-policy enforcement fit this campaign-cycle pattern, however. Aspects of family life related to birth control have come under increasing pressure since about 1970, and this pressure has not relaxed in the reform era. The most stringent policy in this realm, the "one-child-per-couple" campaign, was first proclaimed in 1979 and continues to be pursued. Of more direct relevance to the discussion here is official policy on minimum marriage ages. The 1950 marriage law stated that the minimum marriage age for females

was 18 and for males 20. By the 1970s administrative pressure was being used to foster late marriage, even though the 1950 law had not been repealed. Generally in urban areas this meant that females were supposed to wait until 25 to marry, and males until 27 or 28. The 1980 revised version of the marriage law proclaimed new legal minima of 20 for females and 22 for males. So while on paper the new minima were later, in reality they involved legal limits substantially below what local authorities had been trying to enforce.

7. The terminology of "convergence" is drawn from modernization theory, which argues that it is not socialism versus capitalism, but simply the extent to which structural changes associated with modernization (industrialization, urbanization, commercialization, etc.) have occurred that will determine the pace of change toward more "conjugal" family forms. See the discussion in Goode, *World Revolution*.

8. In this and subsequent tables, the marriage customs of respondents are compared in terms of the years in which they first got married. Ninety-four percent of our respondents had been married only once, and in our questionnaire we asked all interviewees to recall and report a series of features of that first experience. The time divisions used here correspond roughly to the conventional political watersheds used in the study of the PRC. Finer or slightly altered time divisions (such as using 1950 in place of 1949 as a dividing line, since Sichuan fell to the CCP only late in 1949) could be tried, but they would not substantially affect the conclusions offered here.

9. It must be acknowledged, however, that respondent and other biases may exaggerate the changes. For example, it may be politically acceptable to say that your parents arranged your marriage if you married before 1949 but not if you married more recently. Even though precautions were taken to assure respondents that this was an academic study, that their answers would be strictly confidential, and that participation was voluntary, still in the context of recent Chinese history, in which survey research is new and unfamiliar and the political risks of unacceptable expression are old and familiar, we cannot be certain how frankly our respondents answered questions such as these. See the general discussion of these and other problems in Stanley Rosen and David Chu, *Survey Research in the People's Republic of China* (Washington, D.C., USIA, 1987). Still, since I am primarily interested here not in the pre-1949/post-1949 transition, but in the contrast across the periods in the PRC, and particularly between prereform and postreform eras, this sort of bias should not affect my conclusions on trends in these later periods. Even if respondents are overstating somewhat the degree of freedom of choice in post-1949 marriages, there is no reason to expect that respondents who married in one of the latter four periods should exaggerate more than those in the other periods. One other factor that may produce an exaggerated impression of change over time in these results is the fact that our sample is composed of women currently resident in Chengdu, but not necessarily resident in that city when they married. Thus the earliest marriage cohorts have more members who grew up outside of Chengdu, and often in rural areas, where their marriage customs would not be expected to reflect urban customs at that time. (The percentages of women who were married in

Chengdu are 56%, 50%, 74%, 72%, and 91% in the five marriage cohorts.) Preliminary examination of comparable tables with only those who married in Chengdu included indicated that only for the second marriage cohort is the "traditionalism" of marriage customs somewhat exaggerated by the presence of women who married in rural areas. The results for the first cohort do not change much if I consider only urban marriages prior to 1949, which indicates that urban and rural customs were not as different before 1949 as they were to become afterward.

10. Unfortunately, since we interviewed only women, we do not have information on how the degree of freedom of choice looked to the grooms involved.

11. One other aspect we thought might be relevant to freedom of mate choice was also investigated: the degree of parental approval versus disapproval of the mate chosen. We assumed that with the greater freedom of mate choice, more women would end up marrying men whom their parents did not approve of. Questions about both approval from the mother and the father, however, showed little sign of change across marriage cohorts, with roughly 80–90% of parents said to have approved or have strongly approved of the mate chosen in all periods. Since in the Detroit survey reports of parental approval are almost this high, I conclude that these items are not a good indicator of the degree of freedom of mate choice.

12. On both the definition of a dating culture and the evolution of the same in American society, see John Modell, "Dating Becomes the Way of American Youth," in L. Moch and G. Stark, eds., *Essays on the Family and Historical Change* (College Station, Texas A&M University Press, 1983).

13. For comparison purposes, 66% of the women interviewed in the Detroit survey had had more than one romance, and 45% had had more than one man they seriously considered marrying.

14. For elaboration on aspects of a sexual double standard in dating and mate choice in contemporary China, see Emily Honig and Gail Hershatter, *Personal Voices* (Stanford, Calif., Stanford University Press, 1988).

15. Included were items 1, 2, and 3 from Table 1 and items 1, 2 and 4 from Table 2, all scaled so that a high value indicated more freedom of choice, dating experience, romantic feelings, and so on. The items were chosen based on the strength of their mutual intercorrelations, with the average among all six items being $r = .42$. The scale was computed based on the mean of the standardized (or Z) scores on each item.

16. A three-year moving average calculates the mean of one year and the years before and after it—for example, the value for 1957 would be an average of the means computed for 1956, 1957, and 1958. The reason for using this moving-average procedure is to smooth out fluctuations that would occur from year to year, especially in the early years represented in the graph, where the number of respondents used to compute the average is fairly small. As a result of this smoothing process, the primary trends in the data can be more readily seen. Even with this smoothing, the number of cases in the early years is so small that the precise level of the left end of the curve should not be interpreted too literally.

17. For comparison purposes, only 69% of the women in the Detroit survey were working at the time they first married, and only 17% expected to have lifelong careers. Even among recent marriage cohorts in the Detroit sample, the modal expectation is to work some of the time after marriage, rather than to have a lifetime career.

18. In our questionnaire we asked about dates of the first marriage and of the birth of the first child, and the results reported in item 1 are simply based on a comparison of those dates and are of course subject to error. For an example of the use of this sort of indicator to trace historical trends, see Daniel S. Smith and Michael Hindus, "Premarital Pregnancy in America, 1640–1971: An Overview and Interpretation," *Journal of Interdisciplinary History* 4:537–570 (1975). Even if this method of estimation were very accurate, it would still yield a conservative picture of the extent of, and trends in, premarital sex. This is the case not only because women who are sexually active prior to marriage may not become pregnant, but also because even if they do, they may be able to arrange to get an abortion. One study in a Tianjin hospital reported that the percentage of abortions there involving unmarried women rose from 9% in 1977 to 16% in 1979. See Katherine Lyle, "Planned Birth in Tianjin," *CQ* 83:551–567 (1983). A press report claimed that in 1986, 27.9% of all the abortions performed in Peking involved unmarried women. See Honig and Hershatter, *Personal Voices,* p. 114. If more and more premarital pregnancies are ending in abortions, then figures based on the date of birth of the first child would not reveal the full measure of any trend toward increases in premarital conceptions. For comparison purposes, overall in the Detroit survey 6% of the first births occurred prior to marriage and 15% within eight months after the wedding.

19. See, for example, Li Xianfu, "Weihun tongjuzhe yongtiandiao" (The aria of premarital cohabiters), *Wenhui yuekan* (Cultural contact monthly) 12:2–9 (1987), and Honig and Hershatter, *Personal Voices,* pp. 114–116. However, this trend is still modest in comparison with the West. In our Detroit survey fully 40% of those women who married within the period 1979–1984 had cohabited prior to marriage.

20. This estimate is conservative because women who lose their virginity prior to marriage but do not have another birthday before marrying would be erroneously classified as virgins at marriage. Of course, these estimates may also be conservative because women may lie about when they first had sex. There was a disturbing tendency for some respondents to report ages of first sexual experiences that were later—sometimes substantially later—than the ages at which they got married. Although part of this tendency—which was not visible in the Detroit survey—may be attributable to traditional Chinese age-reckoning practices, which yield ages one or two years above the actual age, I suspect that overzealous efforts to conceal premarital experiences may also play a role. Loss of virginity prior to marriage is still a matter of considerable shame and personal risk in China, primarily for women. These sources of conservative bias, however, should be roughly constant across marriage cohorts, so any trend detected is probably genuine.

21. For comparison purposes, overall in the Detroit sample 62% of the women were

estimated to be nonvirgins at marriage (using the indicator reported in item 3a), and among women who married in recent times, the figure rises to well over 80% nonvirgins.

22. The even lower figures shown for the years prior to 1935 are probably a fluke produced by the small number of cases and a phenomenon known as "age truncation bias"—only women who married at unusually young ages at that time would still qualify under the age 70 maximum we used in sampling. In other words, I would not argue that the average female prior to 1935 was marrying younger than 15.

23. Data from a national fertility survey reveal trends in urban marriage ages that are very similar to those shown in Figure 2—both in terms of the dominant trend and in regard to the secondary dips in marriage ages. See Judith Banister, *China's Changing Population,* (Stanford, Calif., Stanford University Press, 1987), pp. 156–157. Broadly similar trends over time are visible if we examine male instead of female ages of first marriage. For males the late 1970s peak in marriage age among Chengdu respondents was above 29, and by 1987 the average had dropped below age 26.

24. I considered one other possible explanation of this most recent reversal of the trend. There has been a substantial reduction in secondary school enrollments in the reform era, a reduction that perhaps affects the educational attainment of rural women most of all. Other things being equal, reduced years of schooling should promote earlier marriage. However, I discovered that women in the Chengdu sample who married in the mid-1980s tended to have had slightly more, not fewer, years of schooling than women who married at the end of the Mao era. Therefore the dip in marriage ages of females since 1979 cannot be attributable to reductions in years of schooling. (Interestingly, this examination also revealed that even in recent years women have not regained the high average educational attainment levels they had achieved just prior to the onset of the Cultural Revolution, when at marriage the average woman in our sample had an upper-middle-school education or slightly more.)

25. In our questionnaire we asked respondents to estimate the amounts that were spent on these various aspects of the wedding in terms of today's currency. How accurately they were able to make such estimates may be questioned, but the intent was to come up with figures that would not be distorted by inflation and currency changes. The attendance and expenditure averages given in Table 5 (in items 2, 4, 10, 12, and 14) are averages for only those who reported having the activity or exchange in question. If I had computed averages for all women in the sample, the resulting means would, of course, have been lower. Because of the small number of cases for which bride-price figures were given, the trends in expenditure on this item (see item 12) are not very reliable, especially for the pre-1957 period.

26. Another curious finding that is not shown in Table 5 is that an officially preferred form of "socialist" wedding designed to inhibit excessive expenditures has never been widely followed and is even less so in recent times. This is the "collective wedding," in which large numbers of couples are married in a single, simple ceremony. The percentages of weddings that took this form in the four

PRC marriage cohorts were 9%, 5%, 0%, and 2%. In this case the apparently most doctrinaire era, the Cultural Revolution decade, was least likely to follow this preferred form of wedding, perhaps owing to the organizational chaos of the period.

27. In popular discussions of this topic one also hears the demands for gifts from the male to the bride stressed, and there are a variety of set phrases—"three rounds and one sound," "thirty legs," and so forth—that are used to denote the consumer durables and furniture that are expected. See the discussion in Honig and Hershatter, *Personal Voices,* chap. 4. The figures here also provide evidence for the point made earlier in Martin K. Whyte and William L. Parish, *Urban Life in Contemporary China* (Chicago, University of Chicago Press, 1984)—that in contemporary large cities, unlike in rural areas, "true" bride-price payments from the groom's family to the bride's are rare.

28. The distinction between the gifts to the bride and bride prices is that the latter go from the groom or his family to the bride's family and not directly to her.

29. The major difference between rural and urban areas in how the earnings of women are handled has been described in my two books coauthored with William L. Parish, *Village and Family in Contemporary China* (Chicago, University of Chicago Press, 1978) and *Urban Life in Contemporary China* and is also treated in my article "Family Change in China," *Amsterdams Sociologisch Tijdschrift* 6:399–417 (1979).

30. See Goody and Tambiah, *Bridewealth and Dowry;* Rubie Watson and Patricia Ebrey, eds., *Marriage and Inequality in Chinese Society* (Berkeley, University of California Press, 1990).

31. Dowry exchanges also entail a conception of marriage as a union of families more than of individuals and some substantial parental influence on the mate-choice process. With increasing freedom of mate choice, any sort of substantial interfamily marriage-finance exchanges can be expected to decline. See Goode, *World Revolution.* Clearly this has not happened yet in urban Chengdu. Unfortunately, we did not inquire and thus do not know whether the contemporary dowries are the result of explicit negotiations between families, as was traditionally the case, or are simply unilateral bequests from the families of brides.

32. Our questionnaire asked about what items were included in the various kinds of wedding gifts, as well as about their value, although the information on specific items is not displayed in Table 5.

33. Of course, it could be noted that the 12% in the final cohort who married matrilocally are not being very traditional, since they are not moving in with the groom's parents. Still, they are establishing an extended family, rather than the sort of nuclear family that is the dominant form in competitive and individualistic modern societies.

34. I have not included figures in Table 5 on the gifts—usually in cash—that couples received from guests at their weddings, but these have also increased and help to meet the costs of an elaborate wedding. To be specific, 100% of the Great Leap era weddings involved receipt of less than 400 yuan from guests, but this was the case for only 45% of reform-era weddings.

35. The methods used to construct this scale were the same as those described earlier in regard to the freedom-of-mate-choice scale. The average item-to-item correlation among these seven wedding items was $r = .32$.

36. It may be the case that this "early" trend toward wedding elaborateness reflects peculiarities of Sichuan as a test area for the policies of Deng Xiaoping and Zhao Ziyang in the 1970s. No comparable data on other cities in China are available to test this supposition. However, I am embarking on new survey projects on mate choice and family life in northern Chinese cities, and when these are completed, I should be able to examine how distinctive this trend and other patterns in the Chengdu data are.

37. The logical exercise I am trying to complete here is inherently a difficult one in the study of social change in any society. It involves the attempt to link changes in larger social conditions to the evolving behavior of individuals and families—in the jargon of the trade, to link "macro" changes with "micro" changes. Since our survey data reflect only individual circumstances, and since generalizations about conditions in the social environment come not from these data but from a general awareness of historical developments in the PRC, this linkage effort ends up resting on plausibility rather than on systematic proof.

38. This sort of uneven transition has been observed in East Asian development in Japan and Taiwan. For Japan, see Ezra Vogel, "The Go-Between in a Developing Society: The Case of the Japanese Marriage Arranger," *Human Organization* 20:112–120 (1961); for Taiwan, consult David Schak, *Dating and Mate Selection in Modern Taiwan* (Taipei, Asian Folklore and Social Life Monographs, 1974).

39. The ideal of freedom of mate choice has had some influence since the time of the May Fourth movement, but only after 1949 was this ideal vigorously communicated to all sectors of the Chinese population.

40. On the growing wariness in relations between male and female students as they get older, see Ann-ping Chin, *Children of China* (New York, Knopf, 1988). For university students an additional factor is the bureaucratic job-assignment system, which means that individuals who have surreptitiously become romantically involved may be assigned to work in different locales after graduation. Given the unpredictability of the job-assignment process, many feel it is better to avoid romantic involvement until one begins work. But then many workplaces have more lopsided male/female sex ratios than do schools, making meeting eligible individuals difficult. An official ban on romance also applies to industrial apprentices in factories.

41. See Whyte and Parish, *Urban Life in Contemporary China*.

42. In some cases "sent-down" youths were offered a cruel choice. They could languish with their sweethearts in the villages, or they could agree to marry urban prospects located by kin in exchange for having transfers back to the city arranged through the contacts of those prospects. See the discussion of the experience of the writer Yu Luojin, as described in Emily Honig, "Courtship, Love, and Marriage: The Life and Times of Yu Luojin," *Pacific Affairs* 57:252–265 (1984).

43. The regulations of the movement to send urban youths to the countryside specified that one child would be allowed to remain in the city in order to provide

care to the parents, and in the case of families with several children, the parents had some discretion in deciding who would go and who would stay. During this period the practice of a parent retiring so that a child would be given employment by their work unit was formalized, although this practice was criticized and formally abolished in the 1980s.

44. In this regard, it is interesting to note that a more fine-grained analysis of several premarital-intimacy variables than is shown in Table 2 indicated that a temporary "peak" in loss of virginity prior to marriage occurred among those marrying in 1955 and 1956, with women who married in subsequent years less likely to have lost their virginity before marriage, details not shown here. This pattern hints that the consolidation of socialist organizational forms in the mid-1950s actually reversed a trend toward greater youth autonomy and premarital intimacy right after 1949.

45. See the commentary in Honig and Hershatter, *Personal Voices;* Zhou Xiao, "Virginity and Premarital Sexual Behavior in Contemporary China," *Feminist Studies* 15:279–288 (1989).

46. For comparison purposes, survey data from Taiwan indicate that premarital sexual experience for women and premarital pregnancy have both increased in a more linear fashion. The percentage of married women surveyed on Taiwan who were not virgins at marriage went from about 12–13% for those born just prior to the end of World War II to 38% for those born in the years 1956–1960, with premarital conceptions increasing over the same period from about 9% of such women to 26% of such women. In Taiwan the female marriage age never got as high as it did in Chengdu, remaining between 22 and 23. See Arland Thornton, Ming-Cheng Chang, and Te-Hsiung Sun, "Social and Economic Change, Intergenerational Relationships, and Family Formation in Taiwan," *Demography* 21:475–499 (1984); Chang Jui-shan, personal communication concerning 1986 KAP–6 survey on Taiwan.

47. Many of these influences foster late marriage for men as well, but since the data examined in Figure 2 concern women, the discussion here is couched in terms of females. Youth initiative fosters late marriage only when the previous system of arranged marriage often produced "early" marriages. This was the case in China, although less so than in some other societies, such as India. Where arranged marriages typically occurred very late, as in rural Ireland, increasing youth initiative would have the opposite effect, of fostering younger marriage. See Goode, *World Revolution.*

48. As indicated earlier, the late-marriage policy was itself strengthened by being made more and more mandatory in later years (but prior to 1980). When that shift occurred, the mechanisms existed to discourage marriage below administratively set minimum ages, particularly by refusing to issue the required work-unit introduction letter to take to the marriage registration office or to approve requests for housing.

49. It may seem puzzling why, in a period of massive new housing construction (since 1978), the tendency to live with parents after marriage would increase (as we saw in Table 5). The answer is that newlyweds were generally not eligible for the new apartments that were constructed, which went mostly to older cou-

ples who had suffered a shortage of housing for years. But as such couples moved into new quarters, they sometimes found they had more than enough space for their own needs, and in fact enough to provide room to allow a child to marry and start a family in the same space.

50. No systematic data on this point are available, and modernization theories such as William Goode's do not deal with realms like wedding elaborateness. It is useful to note, however, that in general the Detroit weddings studied in my companion survey showed a tendency to become somewhat more elaborate in recent times.

51. Officially, the authorities are still on record as preferring frugal weddings and condemning "excessive" spending on gifts, feasts, and other activities. But at the same time, the reformers promote the notion that it is good to get rich, and that envy of the new prosperity of others will "trickle down" and provide motivation for others to work harder and be more entrepreneurial. Thus official policies have acted to make conspicuous consumption acceptable, and the authorities cannot really protest too much if the population engages in such behavior. I do not have a very clear impression of how some of the factors mentioned earlier were changing over the years after 1949—in particular, whether the extensiveness of people's social ties and obligations to reciprocate through wedding invitations has changed over time. One could construct an argument that the need to rely extensively on "connections" and mobilize social networks to cope with the difficulties of life in the post–Cultural Revolution era may have contributed to the growing elaborateness of weddings, but I have no concrete evidence to support this scenario.

52. It might be argued that the modest reduction in official interference in private life that is a part of the reform program contributed to this change. But the most direct impetus, the revised 1980 marriage law, is not inherently linked to the reform effort, and the specific changes involved in the reforms—development of markets and private enterprises, the open-door policy, encouragement of income and status competition, for example—do not appear to have logical links to this change in marriage ages.

53. See the discussion in Goode, *World Revolution*. As noted earlier, modernization theory does not yield very precise predictions about marriage age—only that it will tend to occur in young adulthood, rather than in, say, the teens or the thirties. Wedding celebrations are not dealt with at all, although there is no basis for expecting that modernization will lead to weddings becoming extremely simple.

Chapter 9. New Options for the Urban Elderly, by Charlotte Ikels

1. This title is that of an article published in the 23 January 1984 *Beijing Review* commenting on a letter that had appeared earlier in the recently founded magazine *Elderly Chinese*. The basic problem is that the 1982 census revealed that the proportion of the Chinese population over age 60 was growing very rapidly.

2. For a comparative perspective on the differing circumstances of the urban and rural elderly since 1949, see Charlotte Ikels, "Family Caregivers and the Elderly

in China," pp. 270–284, in David E. Biegel and Arthur Blum, eds., *Aging and Caregiving: Theory, Research and Policy* (Newbury Park, Calif., Sage, 1990).

3. For an overview of the reforms, see Ezra F. Vogel, *One Step Ahead in China: Guangdong under Reform* (Cambridge, Mass., Harvard University Press, 1989), esp. pp. 76–122.

4. See, for example, Wei Hengcang, "Growth of the Aged Population in China: Trends and Policies," pp. 10–18; Wu Cangping, "Family Planning and Population Aging in China," pp. 47–56; and Wu Yuanjin and Xu Qin, "The Impact of an Aging Population on Socio-economic Development and Families in China," pp. 19–35, translated in James H. Schulz and Deborah Davis-Friedmann, eds., *Aging China: Family, Economics, and Government Policies in Transition* (Washington, D.C., Gerontological Society of America, 1987). See also Jersey Liang, Edward Jow-Ching Tu, and Xiangming Chen, "Population Aging in the People's Republic of China," *Social Science and Medicine* 23:1353–62 (1986).

5. The splits at ages 14 and 65 reflect Western modes of calculating dependency ratios. Although these splits may make some sense for China's rural population, they are not valid indicators for the urban population, in which retirement generally occurs by age 55 for women and 60 for men.

6. Deborah Davis, "Unequal Chances, Unequal Outcomes: Pension Reform and Urban Inequality," *CQ* 114:223–242 (1988).

7. Interviews with officials of the Guangdong Public Health Department, June and July 1987.

8. *Asia 1978 Yearbook* (Hong Kong, Review Publications, 1978), p. 166.

9. *Guangdong tongji nianjian 1986* (Guangdong statistical annual; Guangzhou, Zhongguo Tongji Chubanshe, 1986), p. 350.

10. *Asia 1989 Yearbook* (Hong Kong, Review Publications, 1989), p. 111.

11. Indeed, as Davis, "Unequal Chances, Unequal Outcomes," points out (pp. 228–230), the decision to create jobs for youth led directly to the broadening of criteria for retirement eligibility.

12. See, for example, Ralph L. Cherry and Scott Magnuson-Martinson, "Modernization and the Status of the Aged in China: Decline or Equalization?" *Sociological Quarterly* 22:253–261 (1981); Deborah Davis-Friedmann, "Intergenerational Inequalities and the Chinese Revolution," *Modern China* 11:177–201 (1985); Judith Treas, "Socialist Organization and Economic Development in China: Latent Consequences for the Aged," *The Gerontologist* 19:34–43 (1979); and Peter Yin and Kwok Hung Lai, "A Reconceptualization of Age Stratification in China," *Journal of Gerontology* 38:608–613 (1983).

13. See, for example, Harry Harding, *China's Second Revolution* (Washington, D.C., Brookings Institution, 1987), and Melanie Manion, "Remaking Policy: Cadre Retirement in the People's Republic of China," paper presented at conference, "The Structure of Authority and Bureaucratic Behavior in China," sponsored by the Joint Committee on Chinese Studies of the American Council of Learned Societies and Social Science Research Council, Tucson, 19–23 June 1988.

14. Yuan Jihui, "The Reform of the Social Security System for the Aged in China," translated in Schulz and Davis-Friedmann, eds., *Aging China*, pp. 244–245.

15. Davis, "Unequal Chances, Unequal Outcomes," pp. 238–239. In interviews

with officials of the Guangdong Province Labour Bureau in July 1987, I was told that the contributory jurisdictions in Guangzhou City proper were the eight city districts. Each jurisdiction sets the proportion of the enterprises' wages it will collect, which, by provincial regulations, was supposed to fall between 15% and 20%. In fact, provincewide, the proportion actually collected the previous year was on the order of 12% of total wages. In 1986 the upper limit was raised to 22% because the ratio of workers to retirees had dropped to approximately 7 : 1. Officials feared that they would have to raise the upper limit again as the ratio became even more lopsided, and were concerned that enterprises would not be able to tolerate such an increase. In consultation with pension experts from West Germany and Japan, they had been told that an upper limit of 23.9% was the absolute maximum an enterprise could bear.

16. See Davis, "Unequal Chances, Unequal Outcomes," pp. 231–233, for a fuller discussion of *lixiu* status.

17. Interview with an official of the Guangdong Province Central Labor Union, 4 January 1988.

18. Since 1983 a host of monthly and bimonthly magazines—e.g., *Lao tongzhi zhi you, Tuixiu shenghuo, Laonian shijie, Zhongguo laonian* (the leading national publication of this genre)—all aimed at the elderly, have begun publishing articles on model retired people, health tips, and fiction and other works by the elderly themselves.

19. It is nevertheless true that periodic cases of elder abuse surface in the newspapers and that the Chinese government considered it desirable to write into the state constitution that care of parents is a filial obligation.

20. See, for example, Deborah Davis-Friedmann, *Long Lives: Chinese Elderly and the Communist Revolution* (Cambridge, Mass., Harvard University Press, 1983), and Wen-Hui Tsai, "Life after Retirement: Elderly Welfare in China," *Asian Survey* 27:566–576 (1987).

21. For a fuller discussion of the problems inherent in the use of subjective evaluations of health and physical status, see Charlotte Ikels, "Aging and Disability in China: Cultural Issues in Measurement and Interpretation," *Social Science and Medicine,* in press.

22. See, for example, "Finding Older Love Second Time Around," *Beijing Review,* 3 March 1986, pp. 7–8, and innumerable articles in *Zhongguo laonian* (Elderly Chinese).

23. Lu Panqing and Li Ning, "Remarriage Still Causes Controversy," *Beijing Review,* 21 September 1987, pp. 16–18.

24. Deng Weizhi, "Children Should Not Interfere in the Marriage of Parents," *Shehui* (Society) 1:40–41 (1981); translated in *Chinese Sociology and Anthropology* 16:127–129 (1983–84).

25. Liu Nanchang, "Guangzhou's Aged: Life Begins at 60," *Beijing Review,* 2 September 1985, pp. 23–25, 29.

26. See, for example, Edgar Cahn, "Service Credits: A Market Strategy for Redefining the Elderly as Producers," in Robert Morris and Scott A. Bass, eds., *Retirement Reconsidered* (New York, Springer, 1988), pp. 232–249.

Chapter 10. The Spiritual Crisis of China's Intellectuals, by Richard Madsen

1. *RMRB* (overseas ed.), 25, 26, 28, 29 March 1987. (The same article was printed in the domestic ed. in two parts, 23–24 March.) Translation of part 2 of the domestic ed. is in *FBIS,* 15 April 1987.
2. The material in this paragraph is based on Lowell Dittmer, "China in 1986: Domestic Politics," John Major and Anthony Kane, eds., *China Briefing 1987* (Boulder, Colo., Westview Press, 1987), pp. 1–25.
3. Robert N. Bellah et al., *Habits of the Heart: Individualism and Commitment in American Life* (Berkeley, University of California Press, 1985), p. viii.
4. Fang Lizhi, "The Social Responsibility of Today's Intellectuals," *China Spring Digest,* March–April 1987, p. 35.
5. For a summary and discussion of this television series, see Frederic Wakeman, Jr., "All the Rage in China," *New York Review of Books* 36:19–21 (1989).
6. Michael Ignatieff, *The Needs of Strangers* (New York, Penguin, 1986), p. 53.

Chapter 11. Increased Inequality in Health Care, by Gail Henderson

1. *Medical China Newsfile,* 5 December 1987, p. 1.
2. William C. Hsiao, "The Incomplete Revolution: China's Health Care System under Market Socialism," manuscript prepared for Meeting of the Association for Asian Studies, Boston, spring 1987.
3. William C. Hsiao, "Transformation of Health Care in China," *New England Journal of Medicine* 310:932–936 (1984).
4. Martin K. Whyte, "Social Trends in China: The Triumph of Inequality?" in A. D. Barnett and R. N. Clough, eds., *Modernizing China* (Boulder, Colo., Westview Press, 1986), pp. 103–123.
5. Henry J. Aaron and William B. Schwartz, *The Painful Prescription: Rationing Hospital Care* (Washington, D.C., Brookings Institution, 1984).
6. Nicholas Prescott and Dean T. Jamison, "The Distribution and Impact of Health Resource Availability in China," *International Journal of Health Planning and Management* 1:45–56 (1985).
7. Data for this chapter are drawn from a variety of Chinese- and English-language secondary sources and from several collaborative studies conducted over the past three years. These include studies on the acquisition of new medical technology (Gail Henderson et al., "The Rise of Technology in Chinese Hospitals," *International Journal of Technology Assessment in Health Care* 3:253–263 [1987]); the role of urban insurance systems in the funding of expensive high-technology medicine (Henderson et al., "High-Technology Medicine in China: The Case of Chronic Renal Failure and Hemodialysis," *New England Journal of Medicine* 318:1000–04 [1988]); and investigations on rural medical care and insurance programs in two locations in Guangdong and Shandong provinces. It should be noted at the outset that no definitive study exists that provides evidence for the position taken in the title of this chapter. Rather, the thesis is built on diverse sources and types of studies addressing different aspects of an extremely complex subject.

8. Robert J. Blendon, "Can China's Health Care Be Transplanted without China's Economic Policies?" *New England Journal of Medicine* 300:1453–58 (1979).
9. Gail Henderson and Myron S. Cohen, *The Chinese Hospital: A Socialist Work Unit* (New Haven, Yale University Press, 1984).
10. Dean T. Jamison et al., *China: The Health Sector* (Washington, D.C., World Bank, 1984).
11. Gail Henderson, "Issues in the Modernization of Medicine in China," in Denis Simon and Merle Goldman, eds., *Science and Technology in Post-Mao China* (Cambridge, Mass., Harvard Contemporary China Series, no. 5, Council on East Asian Studies, Harvard University, 1988).
12. Hu Teh-Wei, "Diffusion of Western Medical Technology in China since the Economic Reform," *International Journal of Technology Assessment in Health Care,* in press.
13. Ministry of Health, "Woguo weisheng shiye de jiben qingkuang ji cunzai de wenti" (The basic conditions and current problems in China's health sector), Ministry of Health document, 1986.
14. Robert Crowell, Shao Xia-Hong, and Richard O. Cummins, "Emergency Medicine in China—1987," *Annals of Emergency Medicine* 17:1069–73 (1988).
15. Hu Teh-wei, "Diffusion of Technology."
16. Henderson et al., "High-Technology Medicine in China."
17. Ministry of Health document, 1986.
18. Zhang Yifang, "Shoudu yiyuan gaige shidian gongzuo qingkuang" (A summary of pilot tests in the reform of Capital [PUMC] Hospital), *Zhongguo yiyuan guanli* (Chinese hospital management; February 1985), pp. 28–33.
19. "Gaibian yiliao weisheng shiye de kuisun zhumian bixu cong gaige yiliao shoufei zhidu xiashou" (In order to change the deficit aspect of health work, it is necessary to start to reform the system of medical charges), *Jingjixue zhoubao* (Economics weekly), 16 March 1986, p. 11.
20. "Shortages Hit Medicine Production," *China Daily,* 16 May 1987, p. 4.
21. Henderson et al., "A Rise of Technology in Chinese Hospitals,"; John Lewis and Deborah Diamond-Kim, "Hospital Care in China," *China Business Review,* November–December 1987, pp. 26–28; Henderson et al., "High-Technology Medicine in China."
22. "Jiang CT shebei fahui zuida xiaoyi" (Discussing the great benefit of the CT), *Jiankang bao* (Health news daily), 31 March 1986.
23. *Medical China Newsfile* 21:1 (1987).
24. Ibid., p. 6.
25. Crowell et al., "Emergency Medicine in China."
26. "Bribery Is Rampant in Hospitals," *China Daily,* 23 March 1988, p. 4.
27. Henderson et al., "High-Technology Medicine in China."
28. Zhong Shi, "Yiyuan buzheng zhi feng de qingkuang diaocha" (An investigation into irregularities in hospitals), *Shehui* (Society) 3:40–44 (1982), translated in *Chinese Sociology and Anthropology* (1984), pp. 36–48.
29. Henderson et al., "High-Technology Medicine in China."
30. Hsiao, "Transformation of Health Care in China,"; Jamison et al., *China: The Health Sector.*

31. *ZGWSNJ 1987*, p. 497.

32. Gail Henderson, "Health and Health Care in Zouping County, Shandong Province," unpublished manuscript.

33. Liu Yuanli, "Dui woguo shixing jiankang baojian ruogan wenti de shentao" (Discussion of issues involved in the implementation of health insurance in China), *Zhongguo weisheng jingji* (Chinese health economics) 2:22–24 (1988).

34. Prescott and Jamison, "Health Resource Availability," p. 52.

35. Ibid., p. 45.

36. There is substantial variation in the bed-to-population ratio among provinces. Although the average is 2.10:1000, Beijing and surrounding countryside has 3.65, and Guangxi has 1.43. The range in cities is from Qingdao with 9.11 to Tianjin with 3.83. *ZGWSNJ 1986*.

37. *Medical China Newsfile* 19:1 (1987).

38. *ZGWSNJ 1987*, pp. 496–497.

39. Liu Zongxiu and Yu Xiucheng, "Shilun weisheng jihua gongzuo gaige" (Discussion of the reform of health planning work), paper presented at Zhongguo weisheng jingji yanjiuhui (Research conference on Chinese health economics), December 1984.

40. Jiang Guohe, "Xiangzhen weishengyuan 'ru bu fu chu' de yuanyin ji duice" (Causes and recommendations regarding the township hospital's being unable to make ends meet), *Zhongguo weisheng jingji* 7:51–53 (1987).

41. Jamison et al., *China: The Health Sector.*

42. "Woguo gongfei yiliao jingfei langfei yanzhong" (Serious waste in medical expenditures for the public insurance program) *JJRB*, 6 May 1986.

43. Guangzhou Yearbook Committee, *Guangzhou Yearbook 1985*, p. 471.

44. "Gongfei yiliao yaoping feiyong yanzhong" (Serious waste of medicines under the public insurance system), *Jiankang bao* (Health daily), January 1986; "Gankuai duzhu gongfei yiliaozhong de da loudong" (Quickly block the big leak in public insurance), *RMRB*, May 1986.

45. Henderson et al., "High-Technology Medicine in China."

46. Jamison et al., *China: The Health Sector.*

47. Zhu Aorong, "Nongcun hezuo yiliao baojian zhidu de xilie yanjiu" (Theoretical investigation of the rural health insurance system), *Zhongguo weisheng jingji* 4:13–19 (1988).

48. Zhao and Wang, "Heilongjiang Fengdongxian nongmin yiliao feiyong fenxi" (Analysis of farmers' health expenditures in Fengdong County), *Zhongguo weisheng jingji* 4:31–34 (1987).

49. Henderson et al., "High-Technology Medicine in China."

50. Jamison et al., *China: The Health Sector.*

51. During research conducted in China in 1985, E. Murphy and S. Sockwell found this to be the case in Guangzhou and the surrounding countryside in screening for nasopharyngeal cancer (personal communication).

52. Judith Banister, *China's Changing Population* (Stanford, Calif., Stanford University Press, 1987).

53. Banister (p. 105) describes a variety of mistakes in the Chinese reporting system that lead to startling conclusions. For example, the infant mortality rate of Inner

Mongolia in the mid-1970s was reported to be lower than that of any nation in the world.

54. See Judith Banister, "A New Survey of Infant Mortality in China: A Research Note," and a translation by Florence L. Yuan of excerpts from Zhou Youshang et al., "Zhongguo Ying'er Siwanglü" (An analysis of infant mortality rates in China), *Zhongguo renkou kexue* (Population science of China) 3: 35–46 (June 1989).

55. "China Baby-killing Theory Groundless," *China Daily* 1 November 1985.

56. Terence Hull, "Implications of Rising Sex Ratios in China," Unpublished research note, 15 December 1988.

57. Jamison et al., *China: The Health Sector,* p. 124.

58. Ibid.

59. State Statistical Bureau, "China In-depth Fertility Survey," Department of Population Statistics, October 1986.

60. Zhu Aorong, "Nongcun hezuo yiliao."

61. Henderson, "Health and Health Care in Zouping."

62. *Medical China Newsfile* 15:4 (1987).

63. Zhao and Wang, "Heilongjiang nongmin yiliao."

64. *ZGWSNJ 1985,* p. 56; Jamison et al., *China: The Health Sector,* p. 127.

65. *China Daily,* 4 January 1985, p. 3.

66. Ibid., 17 April 1986, p. 3.

67. *ZGWSNJ 1987,* p. 509.

68. Henderson, "Health and Health Care in Zouping."

69. The percentage of Chinese smokers, particularly males, has increased since the reforms. According to a report in 1987, 60% of Chinese men smoke 10–20 cigarettes per day. *Medical China Newsfile* 12:1 (1987). The incidence is directly related to income and is increasing among young people. Smoking is a major risk factor for heart, cerebrovascular, and respiratory diseases, which are all increasing in China. Lung cancer, for example, in Guangzhou has increased 206% in the past twelve years. *Medical China Newsfile* 19:1 (1987). Prevention efforts run counter to the state's investments. The tobacco industry in China is second only to oil, earning 11 billion yuan each year. *Medical China Newsfile* 12:2 (1987).

70. While the higher incomes and greater productivity of the reforms have provided more food and a greater variety of diet, there are problems with persisting nutritional deficits, a decline in breastfeeding in urban areas, and improper diets leading to risk for heart disease and the rise of obesity, especially among children. These problems have been featured in several press reports. In 1986 the average intake of calories in China was reported to be 2,485 (compared with 2,624 world average). The average proportion of meat and eggs in the urban Chinese diet rose from 3.5% to 10% in the past twenty-five years, while the proportion of cereals shrank to 39% from 54%. However, a recent Beijing survey found that 25.7% of the diet was fat, creating risk for obesity, high blood pressure, and heart disease. "Daily Diet Could Be Recipe for Health," *China Daily,* 16 June 1985, p. 5. In fact, "the incidence of high blood pressure and coronary heart disease is increasing. In Beijing, 5 percent of the children and 31 percent of the adults are overweight. In contrast, in some rural areas, malnutrition is still prevalent." *China Daily,* 16 July 1986, p. 5. One report notes,

"Chinese children get only half the calcium they need for normal growth and the Chinese diet is also low in protein, minerals and vitamins." "Chinese Diet Lacking," *China Daily,* 8 January 1986, p. 1. A survey of 660 children between the ages of 2 and 6 showed that 3% suffered from rickets resulting from lack of vitamin D, and in North China perhaps as many as one-third of all children suffered from mild rickets. *China Daily,* 4 July 1986, p. 3. Finally, breastfeeding, an important source of infant nutrition, has dropped from 80–90% in the countryside to 60–70%. It is much lower in urban areas, reportedly because cow's milk is freely distributed. "Human Milk Found Best for Babies," *China Daily,* 16 July 1986, p. 3.

71. The increase in air and water pollution has been linked to the modernization drive. Air pollution, particularly indoor air pollution, is a risk factor for respiratory disease. *China Environment News* recently reported that one-fifth of China's water resources have been seriously polluted, noting that no fish or shrimp live in rivers running through some cities. Eighty-two percent of China's waste water was not treated properly before disposal; 80% of annual industrial waste residue was also not treated properly; and 80% of urban tap waters were polluted to some extent. "Water Pollution a Threat," *China Daily,* 21 November 1986, p. 3. Several new laws setting environmental standards have been enacted since the late 1970s, but enforcement and long-term solutions are difficult.

72. Data on occupational injuries and illnesses are limited, particularly for the very rapidly growing small industries. Rural township industries, for example, grew from 1.35 million in 1983 to 15.1 million in 1986. *China Daily* (2 August 1986, p. 3), in an article entitled "Industrial Casualties Mount," cited a survey of nineteen provinces and municipalities that found labor casualties had increased in fourteen of them. In Tianjin, Beijing, and Xinjiang the number of worker deaths and accidents doubled. The total industrial death toll for the country rose by 9% from 1985 to 1986. The evident lack of safety was blamed on factory leaders not paying attention to safety regulations and putting production targets above the safety of workers. In the metallurgical industry 300 workers have died of accidents and 1,700–1,800 people suffer from occupational lung disease. "Move to Tighten Safety Rules," *China Daily,* 24 March 1987, p. 3. Noise pollution is also cited as a problem in textile factories, causing significant hearing loss. "Noise Pollution Vexes Shanghai Residents," *China Daily,* 19 February 1986, p. 4.

   Traffic accidents were on the rise as well. The road death toll rose 20% in 1985, with 42.3% more injuries. *China Daily,* 13 April 1986, p. 1. It was noted that Beijing added some 101,000 motor vehicles in 1985, while expanding road surface by only 2%. In 1985 there were 78% more traffic accidents in Guangdong than in 1984.

73. Karen Davis and Cathy Schoen, *Health and the War on Poverty: A Ten-Year Appraisal* (Washington, D.C., Brookings Institution, 1978).

Chapter 12. The Impact of Reform Policies on Youth Attitudes, by Stanley Rosen

1. This issue is discussed in Stanley Rosen and David S. K. Chu, *Survey Research in the People's Republic of China* (Washington, D.C., USIA, 1987), pp. 4–11.

2. For some large-scale studies, see *1983 Zhongguo nongcun qingnian diaocha ziliao* (1983 Chinese peasant youth investigation materials; Beijing, Zhongguo Shehui Kexueyuan Qingshaonian Yanjiusuo [Institute of Youth Studies, Chinese Academy of Social Sciences], 1984), in which about 25,000 rural youth from nine provinces were surveyed, and *Shehui diaocha yu yanjiu* (Social investigation and research) 4:32–42 (1985), in which 12,000 young workers from seven cities were surveyed.

3. *China Daily*, 20 August 1988, p. 4; *Liaowang* (Outlook), 21 November 1988, pp. 17–18, in *FBIS*, 2 December 1988, pp. 21–24; *Xinhua* (New China news agency), 25 August 1988, in *FBIS*, 29 August 1988, pp. 24–26.

4. Wang Qun, "Beijing qingniande xinxi yishi" (Beijing youths' consciousness of news), *Qingnian yanjiu* (Youth research) 6:18–23 (1987), p. 19.

5. Wang Sunyu et al., "Daxueshengzhong dangde jianshe gongzuo chutan" (A preliminary exploration of party construction work among university students), in Zhonggong Beijing Shiwei Yanjiushi (Beijing Municipal Party Committee Research Office), eds., *Xin shiqi daxuesheng sixiang zhengzhi jiaoyu yanjiu* (Research on ideological and political education of university students in the new period; Beijing, Beijing Normal University Press, 1988), p. 209.

6. Wu Mu, Li Yanjie, and Zhang Yideng, "Guanyu sisuo quanguo zhuming gaodeng yuanxiao bufen xuesheng sixiang qingkuangde diaocha" (Investigation on the thinking of some of the students at four national famous universities), *Qingnian gongzuo yanjiu yu cankao* (Research and reference work on youth work) 2:16–19 (1987).

7. The "Four Bigs" were part of article 45 of the Chinese constitution in 1978. It gave citizens the right to "speak out freely, air their views fully, hold great debates, and write big-character posters." At the Third Session of the Fifth National People's Congress in September 1980, a resolution to ban these "Four Bigs" was adopted, and they were removed from the constitution.

8. For more detail on these surveys, see Stanley Rosen, "The Impact of Reform on the Attitudes and Behavior of Chinese Youth: Some Evidence from Survey Research," in Donna Bahry and Joel Moses, eds., *Communist Dialectic: The Political Implications of Economic Reform in Communist Systems* (New York, New York University Press, forthcoming).

9. Hu Yongyue, "Kaifang, nifan, jingzheng, shizai: Wenzhou qingniande sida tezheng" (Openness, defiance, competitiveness, practicality: the four great features of Wenzhou youth), *Qingnian yanjiu* 2:10–14 (1987).

10. The "three goods" are normally applied to students who are good in study, morality, and health.

11. Zhao Yicheng, "Jiazhide chongtu" (Value conflict), *Weidinggao* (Manuscripts not finalized) 8:26–33 (1988), p. 30.

12. Mao En and Gong Haifeng, "Buke hushi de yidai" (A generation that cannot be ignored), *Qingnian yanjiu* 11:1–9 (1987).

13. *Liaowang,* 5 September 1988, in *FBIS,* 14 September 1988, pp. 30–33.

14. Yang Dongping, "Contemporary Chinese University Students: A New Epoch," *Shijie jingji daobao* (World economic herald), 23 December 1985, p. 12, translated in Stanley Rosen, ed., "Youth Socialization and Political Recruitment in Post-Mao China," *Chinese Law and Government* 20:9–17 (1987). On the privatization of youth values, see Stanley Rosen, "Prosperity, Privatization, and China's Youth," *Problems of Communism* 34:1–28 (1985).

15. *Guangming ribao* (Guangming daily), 3 April 1987, and Robert Delfs, "A Lesson for Students," *Far Eastern Economic Review* 14 May 1987, p. 16. It had been common before the 1985 and 1986 student demonstrations to deemphasize political study. For example, Beijing University, faced with student apathy, cut the number of hours for political study in half in 1985. See *Agence-France Presse,* 7 June 1985, in *JPRS* 85-067, 3 July 1985, pp. 103–104. For additional data on the conservative backlash in 1987, see Stanley Rosen, "Students," in Anthony J. Kane, ed., *China Briefing 1988* (Boulder, Colo., Westview Press, 1988), pp. 79–105.

16. Stanley Rosen, "Political Education and Student Response: Some Background Factors behind the 1989 Beijing Demonstrations," *Issues and Studies* 25:12–39 (1989).

17. Wu Mu, Li Yanjie, and Zhang Yideng, "Guanyu sisuo quanguo zhuming gaodeng yuanxiao bufen xuesheng sixiang qingkuangde diaocha," p. 17.

18. Tao Chounian, Sun Binggang, and Yu Chunxian, "Daxuesheng zai xiang shenma?" (What are university students thinking?), *Wengao yu ziliao* (Manuscripts and materials) 3:28–34 (1985). This is a publication of the Shandong Provincial Party Committee School.

19. *Jiaoyu tongxun* (Education bulletin) 42:6 (1983).

20. See, for example, the surveys on party recruitment of young intellectuals and university students in *Chinese Law and Government* 20.

21. Li Yongjin, "Stress Recruitment of Party Members among University Students," *Gaojiao yanjiu* (Research on higher education) 20:67–84 (1985), translated in *Chinese Law and Government* 20:67–84.

22. Research Group on Youth Education, Guangdong Glass Factory, "Pay Great Attention to Recruiting Outstanding Youth into the Party," *Qingnian tansuo* (Youth exploration) 4:16–25 (1984), translated in *Chinese Law and Government* 20:97–101.

23. Wang Sunyu et al., "Daxueshengzhong," pp. 186–187.

24. "Attitudes of Rural Youth toward Joining Party," *Shanghai zhibu shenghuo* (Shanghai party branch life), 14 June 1988, pp. 36–37, translated in *JPRS,* 30 November 1988, pp. 47–48. For Qinghua University in Beijing, see Zhang Yuzhou, "Muqian daxuesheng rudang dongji qianxi." (A superficial analysis of the motivations for joining the party of today's university students), *Sixiang lilun jiaoyu* (Education in ideology and theory) 2:24–26 (1988).

25. Much of the data in this and the following paragraph rely on Zhang Xingxing,

"Bingyuan weiji weixie Zhonggong," (A crisis of soldiers threatens the Chinese communists), *Zhengming* (Contention) 12:27 (1988).

26. Zhejiang Provincial Service, "More Zhejiang Youths Dodge Military Service," 21 September 1988, in *FBIS*, 27 September 1988, p. 54.

27. Zhang Wenrui et al., "The Great Changes and New Characteristics in the Composition of Our Troops," *Qingnian yanjiu* 6:19–23 (1986), translated in *Chinese Law and Government* 20:102–117. Quotation is from p. 110. For additional survey data on relatively affluent rural recruits, see Rosen, "Impact of Reform."

28. Nanjing junqu zhuanji (A special edition from the Nanjing Military District), *1984 budui qingnian yanjiu lunwenji* (A collection of research articles on youth in the military; Nanjing, 1984), pp. 205–214.

29. Ibid., pp. 191–204.

30. Stanley Rosen, "Recentralization, Decentralization, and Rationalization: Deng Xiaoping's Bifurcated Educational Policy," *Modern China* 11:301–346 (1985).

31. *Jiaoyu qingbao cankao* (Reference information on education; 1983–84), pp. 100–102.

32. A fuller discussion appears in Stanley Rosen, "The Impact of Educational Reform on Chinese Youth," *Interchange* 19:60–75 (1988).

33. *Qingnian bao* (Youth news), 22 February 1985, p. 2; 12 July 1985, p. 5; 21 December 1984, p. 5. *Beijing qingnian bao* (Beijing youth news), 18 June 1985, p. 1. Also see *Tianjin ribao* (Tianjin daily), 18 April 1986, p. 1, and *Wenhui bao*, 7 January 1986, p. 2.

34. *Qingnian bao*, 21 December 1984, p. 5

35. *Ibid.*, 12 July 1985, p. 5.

36. Zhu Qingfang, "On the Evolution and Changes of Individual Economy and Countermeasures," *Jingji yanjiu cankao ziliao* (Economic research reference materials) 66:33–40 (1986), translated in Stanley Rosen, ed., "The Private Economy (II)," *Chinese Economic Studies* 21:95–109 (1988) .

37. *Guangzhou ribao* (Guangzhou daily), 9 June 1986, p. 1.

38. Yan Guohua, "Accomplishments in Employing Workers in Townships and Cities and the New Situation We Face," *Qingnian yanjiu* 1:7–11,19 (1988), translated in Stanley Rosen, ed., "Issues in Employment," *Chinese Economic Studies* 21:69–91 (1988).

39. He Songjiang, "Guangzhou qingnian zhigong 'zhiye liudong re' chutan" (A preliminary exploration of the 'craze for professional mobility' among Guangzhou's workers and staff), *Qingnian tansuo* (Youth exploration) 3:13–23 (1985); Liang Jungang and Yang Rungui, "Zhuhai qingniande bianhua" (The changes in Zhuhai youth), *Qingnian tansuo* 2:2–6 (1987). On Guangdong province's booming economic growth, including the hiring of temporary workers from other provinces, see *Far Eastern Economic Review*, 8 December 1988, pp. 60–63.

40. *Guangming ribao*, 15 May 1987, p. 2.

41. *Shanxi jiaoyu tongxun* (Shanxi education bulletin) 2 (1987).

42. *Xinhua*, in English, 6 September 1988, in *FBIS*, 7 September 1988, p. 27.

43. Li Yuanchao, "Nongcun tuan zuzhi yao dailing qingnian zhifu" (The rural Com-

munist Youth League should lead youths to become rich), *Nongcun qingnian* (Rural youth) 3:5 (1984).

44. Rosen, "Prosperity, Privatization, and China's Youth," p. 10.
45. Susan Shirk, *Competitive Comrades* (Berkeley, University of California Press, 1982), and Stanley Rosen, *Red Guard Factionalism and the Cultural Revolution in Guangzhou* (Boulder, Colo., Westview Press, 1982).

GLOSSARY

bangshou	helper (employee)
bao	production responsibilities
baomu	nursemaid
baoxian fuli fei	insurance and welfare expenditures
biantai	abnormal, anomalous
bianzhi	rank, table of organization
bumen suoyouzhi	ownership by the branch unit

changzhang	factory director
changzhang fuzezhi	factory director responsibility system
chengbao jingguan zerenzhi	contracted managerial responsibility system
chengbao zhi	management contract system
Chenghuang	city god
chidun	slow in thought or action

chijo sin	to have become ridiculous or idiotic (Cantonese)
chuji	primary stage
cun	village
cunmin weiyuanhui	villagers' committee
cun xiaozu	village small group

da youji	guerrilla warfare
dai	lead
daiye qingnian	youth waiting for work
daling guniang	overage maidens
Dan	boat people
dang'an	personal dossier
danwei	work unit
danwei suoyouzhi	ownership by the unit
dazhuan	postsecondary technical institutes
diaodong	a transfer
dingti	substitute
dingti	take job in unit of retiring parent
dingyun ding'e	labor quotas

fahui caineng	bring talents into full play
fang	mobility
faren	legal personality
fen	decollectivization
fenpei	job assignment
fenxiao	branch school
fuli	benefit

gaogan zidi	children of high-ranking cadres
gaohuo jingji	enliven the economy
geti	individual
geti hu	private entrepreneurs

geti jingying hu	individual economy
geti jingyingzhe	individual manager
geti laodongzhe	individual laborer
geti laodongzhe xiehui	self-employed laborers' association
gong (vs. *si*)	public
gongfei yiliao	state medical-coverage program for cadres
gongren daizi ruchang	workers bring funds into the factory
gongye	industry
gongye gongsi	industrial corporation/company
gongye jingji zerenzhi	industrial economic responsibility system
guakao	attach to (collective enterprise)
guandao	civil service profiteer
guandu shangban	private management under state supervision
guanli weiyuanhui	management committee
guanlizhe	manager
guanlizhe xiehui	manager association
guanxi	interpersonal relations/connections
guding	permanent
guofa	national law
hengxiang lianhe	horizontal linkage
hetong gong	contract laborers
hongyanbing	jealousy ("red-eye disease")
hukou	household registration
hutu	confused, bewildered
jiguan	administrative agencies
jingji guanli weiyuanhui	economic management committee
jintie	subsidy
jumin	town resident
kending guanxi	fixed relationship

laodong baoxian	health insurance for state enterprise workers
laodong gongzike	labor office
lao mengdong	muddled, ignorant
leuhnjeuhn	clumsy in physical or mental performance (Cantonese)
lingshi gong	short-term workers
lirun baogan chaoli fencheng	profit responsibility, overquota system
lixiu	retired party cadre
minban qiye	people-run enterprises
neizhao	recruited from within
pibao gongsi	briefcase companies
popo	mother-in-law, supervising unit (colloquial)
qing	hire
qiye	enterprise
qu	rural district
quanmin suoyouzhi	state-owned
rencai jiaoliu zhongxin	centers for job exchanges
renshike	personnel office
sha	stupid, muddle-headed
shangdiao	negotiated job transfer
shangpin jingji	commodity economy
shangpin shehui	commodity society

shehui xiansan renyuan	socially idle persons
shehuizhuyi shangpin sheng-chanzhe he jingguanzhe	producers and operators (managers) of the socialist commodity economy
shuangdiao	job transfer by exchange
shuidao	paddy (rice)
shuiqian huankuan	repay loans before taxes
shuishang dadui	boat brigade
si (vs. *gong*)	private
siying	private
siying qiye	private business
suishi	at any time

tan lian'ai	talk romance
tigao guanli shuiping	raise the level of management
tingxin liuzhi	unpaid leave of absence

waidi ren	outsiders
weiguan	enclosed compounds
wo bu yong, ye bu gei ni yong	"If I can't use it, I won't let you use it."

xiang	township
xiang zhengfu	township government
xiangzhen qiye	community (township or village-owned) enterprise
xin jiti	new collectives
xingzheng cun	administrative village
xitong	sector; system(s)
xuetu	apprentice

"yigong bunong"	"Use industry to subsidize agriculture"
you jihua de shangpin jingji	planned commodity economy
youhuan yishi	spirit of distress

zhen	market town; township
zhen zhengfu	town government
zhengdang	party rectification
zhengshe fenkai	separate government administration from commune management
zhengshe heyi	integrate government administration with commune management
zhidaoxing jihua	guidance plans
zhilingxing jihua	mandatory plans
zhiyuan	urban salaried worker
zhongzhuan	secondary technical schools
zichan jingguan	asset management
zililiang hu	households who take care of their own grain
zulin jingguan	leasing management

SELECTED BIBLIOGRAPHY

Aubert, Claude, Yves Chevrier, et al. *La société chinoise après Mao: Entre autorité et modernité*. Paris, Fayard, 1986.

Bai Nanfeng and Yang Guansan. "Gaige de shehui xinli huanjing" (The social psychological environment of the reforms). In Zhongguo Jingji Tizhi Gaige Yanjiusuo (Economic System Reform Institute), eds., *Zhongguo: Fazhan yu gaige* (China: Development and reform). Chengdu, Sichuan Renmin Chubanshe, 1986.

Bai Yihua, Song Zhiqiang, and Tang Pusu. "Jinyibu wanshan xiangzhen zhengfu zhineng gaige ti tiaokuai fenge xingzheng guanli" (Go a step further in perfecting the functions of town and township governments, reform the system of vertical and horizontal division of administrative management). *Zhengzhixue yanjiu* (Political science studies) 6:57 (1987).

Bai Yihua and Tang Pusu. "Gaige xiangzhen tizhi jiaqiang jiceng zhengquan" (Reform the town and township system, strengthen grass-roots political power). *Nongcun gongzuo tongxun* (Rural work bulletin) 11:42 (1986).

Bailes, Kendal E. *Technology and Society under Lenin and Stalin: Origins of the Soviet Technical Intelligentsia*. Princeton, N.J., Princeton University Press, 1978.

Banister, Judith. *China's Changing Population*. Stanford, Calif., Stanford University Press, 1987.

Beijingshi Renmin Zhengfu Yanjiushi and Beijingshi Laodongju, eds. *Beijing cheng-zhen de siren gugong* (Private hiring of labor in Beijing City and Municipality). Beijing, Jingji Xueyuan Chubanshe, 1989.

Bergson, Abram. "Income Inequality under Soviet Socialism." *Journal of Economic Literature* 22:1052–99 (1984).

Bernstein, Thomas. "Local Political Authorities and Economic Reform: Observations from Two Counties in Shandong and Anhui, 1985." Paper presented at "Conference on Market Reforms in China and Eastern Europe," Santa Barbara, Calif., 8–11 May 1986.

Blendon, Robert J. "Can China's Health Care Be Transplanted without China's Economic Policies?" *New England Journal of Medicine* 300:1453–58 (1979).

Bo Guili. "Woguo zhen zhengfu guanli jingjide zhineng he zhen zhengfude jigou gaige" (The economic management functions of our town governments and the reform of town governmental organs). *Zhengzhixue yanjiu* (Political science studies) 3:45 (1986).

Byrd, William A. and Lin Qingsong, eds. "China's Rural Industry: Structure, Development, and Reform." Oxford University Press, 1990.

Cahn, Edgar. "Service Credits: A Market Strategy for Redefining the Elderly as Producers." In Robert Morris and Scott A. Bass, eds., *Retirement Reconsidered*. New York, Springer, 1988.

Chamberlain, Heath B. "Party-Management Relations in Chinese Industries: Some Political Dimensions of Economic Reform." *China Quarterly* 112:631–661 (1987).

Cherry, Ralph and Scott Magnuson-Martinson. "Modernization and the Status of the Aged in China: Decline of Equalization?" *Sociological Quarterly* 22:253–261 (1981).

Chevrier, Yves. "Les politiques économiques de la démaoïsation, 1977–1982." *Revue d'études comparatives Est-Ouest* 14:5–74 (1983).

———. "Gestion et modernisation: L'entreprise chinoise face à l'Etat." *Tiers-Monde* 27:755–794 (1986).

——— and Claude Aubert. "Réformer ou ne pas réformer: Le dilemme de l'expérience chinoise." *Revue française de gestion* (Winter 1982–83), pp. 9–46.

Chin, Ann-ping. *Children of China*. New York, Knopf, 1988.

Crook, Frederick W. "The Reform of the Commune System and the Rise of the Township-Collective-Household System." U.S. Congress Joint Economic Committee. *The Four Modernizations,* vol. 1 of *China's Economy Looks toward the Year 2000*. Washington, D.C., U. S. Government Printing Office, 1986.

Dangdai Zhongguo qingnian zhigong qingkuang (Employment situation of today's Chinese youth). Wuhan Gongren Chubanshe, 1986.

Davis, Deborah. "Unequal Chances, Unequal Outcomes: Pension Reform and Urban Inequality." *China Quarterly* 114:223–241 (1988).

————. "Chinese Social Welfare: Policies and Outcomes." *China Quarterly* 119:577–597 (1989).

Davis-Friedmann, Deborah. *Long Lives: Chinese Elderly and the Communist Revolution.* Cambridge, Mass., Harvard University Press, 1983.

————. "Intergenerational Inequalities and the Chinese Revolution." *Modern China* 11:177–201 (1985).

Donnithorne, Audrey. "China's Cellular Economy: Some Economic Trends since the Cultural Revolution." *China Quarterly* 52:605–619 (1972).

Fei Xiaotong. *Xiao chengzhen siji* (Four chapters on small towns). Beijing, Xinhua Chubanshe, 1985.

Feuchtwang, Stephan, Athar Hussain, and Thierry Pairault, eds. *Transforming China's Economy in the Eighties,* vols. 1 and 2. Boulder, Colo., and London, Westview Press and Zed Books, 1988.

Flakierski, Henryk. *Economic Reform and Income Distribution: A Case Study of Hungary and Poland.* Armonk, N.Y., Sharpe, 1986.

Goode, William J. *World Revolution and Family Patterns.* New York, Free Press, 1963.

Guojia Gongshang Xingzheng Guanli Geti Jingjisi and Beijing Ribao Lilunbu, eds. *Geti laodongzhe shouce* (Handbook for individual laborers). Beijing, Beijing Ribao Chubanshe and Gongshang Chubanshe, 1984.

Guowuyuan Banshiting Diaoyanshi, eds., *Geti jingji diaocha yu yanjiu* (Investigation and research on the individual economy). Beijing, Jingji Kexue Chubanshe, 1986.

Harding, Harry. *China's Second Revolution.* Washington, D.C., Brookings Institution, 1987.

Hartford, Kathleen. "Socialist Agriculture Is Dead; Long Live Socialist Agriculture." In Christine Wong and Elizabeth Perry, eds., *The Political Economy of Reform in Post-Mao China.* Cambridge, Mass., and London, Harvard Contemporary China Series, no. 2, Council on East Asian Studies, Harvard University, 1985.

Henderson, Gail. "Issues in the Modernization of Medicine in China." In Denis Simon and Merle Goldman, eds. *Science and Technology in Post-Mao China.* Cambridge, Mass., Harvard Contemporary Chinese Series, no. 5, Council on East Asian Studies, Harvard University, 1988.

———— and Myron S. Cohen. *The Chinese Hospital: A Socialist Work Unit.* New Haven, Yale University Press, 1984.

Henderson, Gail, Elizabeth A. Murphy, Samuel T. Sockwell, Zhou Jiongliang, Shen Qingrui, and Li Zhiming. "High-Technology Medicine in China: The Case of Chronic Renal Failure and Hemodialysis." *New England Journal of Medicine* 318:1000–04 (1988).

Hershkovitz, Linda. "The Fruits of Ambivalence: China's Urban Individual Economy." *Pacific Affairs* 58:427–450 (1985).

Honig, Emily. "Courtship, Love and Marriage: The Life and Times of Yu Luojin." *Pacific Affairs* 57:252–265 (1984).

———— and Gail Hershatter. *Personal Voices*. Stanford, Calif., Stanford University Press, 1988.

Howe, Christopher. *Employment and Economic Growth in Urban China, 1949–57*. Cambridge, Cambridge University Press, 1971.

Hsiao, William C. "Transformation of Health Care in China." *New England Journal of Medicine* 310:932–936 (1984).

Hsiung, Bingyuang and Louis Putterman. "Pre- and Post-Reform Income Distribution in a Chinese Commune: The Case of Dahe Township in Hebei Province." *Journal of Comparative Economics,* in press.

Hu Guohua, Liu Jinghai, and Chen Ming. *Duo setiao de Zhongguo geti jingyingzhe* (China's multicolored individual managers). Beijing, Jingji Xueyuan Chubanshe, 1988.

Hu, T. W., M. Li, and S. Z. Shi. "Analysis of Wages and Bonuses among Tianjin Workers." *China Quarterly* 113:78 (1988).

Hu Yongyue. "Kaifang, nifan, jingzheng, shizai: Wenzhou qingniande sida tezheng" (Openness, defiance, competitiveness, practicality: the four great features of Wenzhou youth). *Qingnian yanjiu* (Youth research) 2:10–14 (1987).

Huang Changlu and Xiong Xiaowei. "Zhengshe fenkai liangnianjian" (Two years of the separation of government administration and commune management). *Liaowang* (Outlook) 22:14 (1984).

Ikels, Charlotte. "Family Caregivers and the Elderly in China." In David E. Biegel and Arthur Blum, eds., *Aging and Caregiving: Theory, Research and Policy*. Newbury Park, Calif., Sage, 1990.

————. "Aging and Disability in China: Cultural Issues in Measurement and Interpretation." *Social Science and Medicine,* in press.

Investigation Group of Zunyi County Committee, Guizhou Province. "Dangde nongcun zhengce xuanchuanzhongde 'shenlou xianxiang' qianshe" (An initial inquiry into the "seepage phenomenon" in the propagation of the party's rural policies). *Nongcun gongzuo tongxun* (Rural work bulletin) 11:42–43 (1987).

Jacobs, J. Bruce. "Political and Economic Organizational Changes and Continuities in Six Rural Chinese Localities." *Australian Journal of Chinese Affairs* 14:105–130 (1986).

Jamison, Dean et al. *China: The Health Sector*. Washington, D.C., World Bank, 1984.

Jiangsu Sheng Xiao Chengzhen Yanjiu Ketizu, eds. *Xiao chengzhen, xin kaituo* (Small towns, new growth). Jiangsu Renmin Chubanshe, 1986.

Johnson, Graham E. "The Fate of the Communal Economy: Some Contrary Evidence from the Pearl River Delta." Paper presented at Annual Meeting of the Association of Asian Studies, Chicago, 21–23 March 1986.

Kornai, Janos. "Bureaucratic and Market Coordination." *Osteuropa* (December 1984), pp. 306–319.

————. *Contradictions and Dilemmas: Studies on the Socialist Economy and Society.* Cambridge, Mass., MIT Press, 1986.

Lang, Olga. *Chinese Family and Society.* New Haven, Yale University Press, 1946.

Laodong Renshibu Ganbu Jiaoyuzu (Cadre Education Group of the Ministry of Labor and Personnel), eds. *Laodong gongzi renshi zhidu gaige de yanjiu* (Inquiry and research on reform of wage and labor system). Beijing, Laodong Renshi Chubanshe, 1985.

Lardy, Nicholas. "Centralization and Decentralization in Chinese Fiscal Management." *China Quarterly* 61:25–61 (1975).

Latham, Richard. "The Implications of Rural Reforms for Grassroots Cadres." In Elizabeth J. Perry and Christine Wong, eds., *The Political Economy of Reform in Post-Mao China.* Cambridge, Mass., and London, Harvard Contemporary China Series, no. 2, Council on East Asian Studies, Harvard University, 1985.

Levy, Marion J. *The Family Revolution in Modern China.* Cambridge, Mass., Harvard University Press, 1949.

Lewin, Moshe. *The Gorbachev Phenomenon.* Berkeley, University of California Press, 1988.

Li Jiang et al. "Guanyu jiasu Hunan Sheng xiao chengzhen fazhan de jige wenti" (On accelerating the development of small towns in Hunan Province). *Jingji yanjiu cankao ziliao* (Reference materials for economic research). Beijing, Jingji Kexue Chubanshe, 1985.

Li Sanyuan. "Lun jingjiao xiang zhengquan jianshede wanshanhua" (On perfecting the construction of the political power of Beijing's suburban townships). *Zhengzhixue yanjiu* (Political science studies) 5:61 (1986).

Lin Nan and Wen Xie. "Occupational Prestige in Urban China." *American Journal of Sociology* 93:793–832 (1988).

Liu Yuanli. "Dui woguo shixing jiankang baojian ruogan wenti de shentao" (Discussion of issues involved in the implementation of health insurance in China). *Zhongguo weisheng jingji* (Chinese health economics) 2:22–24 (1988).

Liu Zheng et al. *Siying jingji wenti jieda* (Answers to questions about the private economy). Beijing, Dizhi Chubanshe, 1988.

Mao En and Gong Haifeng. "Buke hushi de yidai" (A generation that cannot be ignored). *Qingnian yanjiu* (Youth research) 11:1–9 (1987).

Muth, Susan Lynn. "Private Business under Socialism: An Examination of the Urban Individual Economic Sector in China." Ph.D. dissertation, George Washington University, 1987.

Nanjing junqu zhuanji (A special edition from the Nanjing Military District). *1984 budui qingnian yanjiu lunwenji* (A collection of research articles on youth in the military, 1984).

Naughton, Barry. "The Decline of Central Control over Investment in Post-Mao China." In David M. Lampton, ed., *Policy Implementation in Post-Mao China.* Berkeley, University of California Press, 1987.

Nee, Victor. "A Theory of Market Transition: From Redistribution to Markets in State Socialism." *American Sociological Review* 54:663–681 (1989).

Oi, Jean C. "Commercializing China's Rural Cadres." *Problems of Communism* 35:1–15 (1986).

———. "Peasant Grain Marketing and State Procurement: China's Grain Contracting System." *China Quarterly* 106:272–290 (1986).

———. "Peasant Households between Plan and Market: Cadre Control over Agricultural Inputs." *Modern China* 12:230–251 (1986).

———. *State and Peasant in Contemporary China: The Political Economy of Village Government*. Berkeley, University of California Press, 1989.

Parish, William L. "Destratification in China." In J. L. Watson, ed., *Class and Social Stratification in Post-Revolution China*. Cambridge, Cambridge University Press, 1984.

——— and Martin King Whyte. *Village and Family in Contemporary China*. Chicago, University of Chicago Press, 1978.

Party Central Committee and State Council. "Circular on Separating Government Administration and Commune Management and Setting up Township Governments." Translated in *Chinese Law and Government* 19:34–37 (1986–87).

Prescott, Nicholas and Dean T. Jamison. "The Distribution and Impact of Health Resource Availability in China." *International Journal of Health Planning and Management* 1:45–56 (1985).

Qiu Zuohua et al., eds. *Zhujiang sanjiaozhou jingji kaifengqu touzi zhinan* (Investment guide for the open economic zones of the Pearl River Delta). Hong Kong, Xinhua Chubanshe, 1986.

Riskin, Carl. *China's Political Economy: The Quest for Development since 1949*. New York, Oxford University Press, 1987.

Rosen, Stanley. *Red Guard Factionalism and the Cultural Revolution in Guangzhou*. Boulder, Colo., Westview Press, 1982.

———. "Prosperity, Privatization, and China's Youth." *Problems of Communism* 34:1–28 (1985).

———. "Recentralization, Decentralization, and Rationalization: Deng Xiaoping's Bifurcated Educational Policy." *Modern China* 11:301–311 (1985).

———, ed. "The Private Economy," Parts 1 and 2. *Chinese Economic Studies* 21 (1987–88).

———. "Political Education and Student Response: Some Background Factors behind the 1989 Beijing Demonstrations." *Issues and Studies* 25:12–39 (1989).

———, ed. "Youth Socialization and Political Recruitment in Post-Mao China." *Chinese Law and Government* 20:9–17 (1987).

——— and David Chu. *Survey Research in the People's Republic of China*. Washington, D.C., United States Information Agency, 1987.

Rural Economic Survey Leading Group of the Rural Policy Research Center, Secretariat, CPC Central Committee, and the Rural Development Research Center of the State Council. "Rural Primary Organizations, Party Members, and Cadres." *Nongmin ribao* (Farmers' daily), 16–17 May 1986, in *JPRS* 86–064, 19 August 1986, pp. 31–37.

Saich, Tony. "The Chinese Communist Party at the Thirteenth Party Congress: Policies and Prospects for Reform." In King-yuh Chang, ed. *Political and Social Changes in Taiwan and Mainland China.* Taipei, Institute of International Relations, English Monograph Series No. 35, 1989.

Shirk, Susan. *Competitive Comrades.* Berkeley, University of California Press, 1982.

Shue, Vivienne. "The Fate of the Commune." *Modern China* 10:259–283 (1984).

———. *The Reach of the State.* Stanford, Calif., Stanford University Press, 1988.

Sicular, Terry. "Agricultural Planning and Pricing in the Post-Mao Period." *China Quarterly* 116:671–705 (1988).

Siu, Helen. "Immigrants and Social Ethos: Hong Kong in the 1980s." *Journal of the Hong Kong Branch of the Royal Asiatic Society* (1987).

———. *Agents and Victims in South China: Accomplices in Rural Revolution.* New Haven, Yale University Press, 1989.

———. "Socialist Peddlers and Princes in a Chinese Market Town." *American Ethnologist* 16:195–212 (1989).

———. "The Politics of Growth: Pearl River Delta Experiences." In Ri Yin-wang Kwok et al., eds., *Chinese Urban Reforms: What Model Now?* Armonk, N.Y., Sharpe, 1990.

Szelenyi, Ivan. "Social Inequalities in State Socialist Redistributive Economies." *International Journal of Comparative Sociology* 19:63–87 (1978).

———. "The Prospects and Limits of the East European New Call Project." *Politics and Society* 15:103–144 (1986–87).

——— and Robert Manchin. "Social Policy under State Socialism: Market, Redistribution, and Social Inequalities in East European Socialist Societies." In Gosta Esping-Andersen, Martin Rein, and Lee Rainwater, eds., *Stagnation and Renewal in Social Policy.* Armonk, N.Y., Sharpe, 1987.

Thornton, Arland, Ming-Cheng Chang, and Te-Hsiung Sun. "Social and Economic Change, Intergenerational Relationships, and Family Formation in Taiwan." *Demography* 21:475–499 (1984).

Tidrick, Gene, and Chen Jiyuan, eds. *China's Industrial Reform.* New York, Oxford University Press, 1987.

Treas, Judith. "Socialist Organization and Economic Development in China: Latent Consequences for the Aged." *The Gerontologist* 19:34–43 (1979).

Tsai, Wen-Hui. "Life after Retirement: Elderly Welfare in China." *Asian Survey* 27:566–576 (1987).

Vogel, Ezra F. "The Go-Between in a Developing Society: The Case of the Japanese Marriage Arranger." *Human Organization* 20:112–120 (1961).

————. *One Step Ahead in China: Guangdong Under Reform.* Cambridge, Harvard University Press, 1989.

Walder, Andrew G. *Communist Neo-Traditionalism: Work and Authority in Chinese Industry.* Berkeley, University of California Press, 1986.

————. "The Informal Dimension of Enterprise Financial Reforms." In U.S. Congress Joint Economic Committee, *The Four Modernizations,* vol. 1 of *China's Economy Looks toward the Year 2000.* Washington, D.C., U.S. Government Printing Office, 1986.

————. "Wage Reform and the Web of Factory Interests." *China Quarterly* 109:22–41 (1987).

————. "Factory and Manager in an Era of Reform." *China Quarterly* 112:242–264 (1989).

Wang Qun. "Beijing qingniande xinxi yishi" (Beijing youths' consciousness of news). *Qingnian yanjiu* (Youth research) 6:18–23 (1987).

Wang Sunyu et al. "Daxueshengzhong dangde jianshe gongzuo chutan" (A preliminary exploration of party construction work among university students). In Zhonggong Beijing Shiwei Yanjiushi (Beijing Municipal Party Committee Research Office), eds. *Xin shiqi daxuesheng sixiang zhengzhi jiaoyu yanjiu* (Research on ideological and political education of university students in the new period). Beijing, Beijing Normal University Press, 1988.

Wang Zhenyao. "Nongcun jiceng zhengquande zhineng fenhua taishi yu zhengce xuanzu" (The state of the functional division of rural grass-roots political power and policy options). *Zhengzhixue yanjiu* (Political science studies) 4:29–33 (1987).

Watson, Rubie S. and Patricia B. Ebrey, eds. *Marriage and Inequality in Chinese Society.* Berkeley, University of California Press, 1990.

Wei Hengcang. "Growth of the Aged Population in China." Translated in James H. Schulz and Deborah Davis-Friedmann, eds., *Aging in China: Family, Economics, and Government Policies in Transition.* Washington, D.C., Gerontological Society of America, 1987.

White, Gordon. "The Impact of Economic Reforms in the Chinese Countryside: Towards the Politics of Social Capitalism." *Modern China* 13:411–440 (1987).

————. "The Politics of Economic Reform in Chinese Industry." *China Quarterly* 111:365–389 (1987).

Whyte, Martin King. "Family Change in China." *Amsterdams sociologisch tijdschrift* 6:399–417 (1979).

————. "Social Trends in China: The Triumph of Inequality?" In A. Doak Barnett and Ralph Clough, eds., *Modernizing China.* Boulder, Colo., Westview Press, 1986.

———— and William L. Parish *Urban Life in Contemporary China.* Chicago, University of Chicago Press, 1984.

Wong, Christine P. W. "Between Plan and Market." *Journal of Comparative Economics* 11:385–398 (1987).

————. "Interpreting Rural Industrial Growth in the Post-Mao Period." *Modern China* 14:3–30 (1988).

Wu Mu, Li Yanjie, and Zhang Yideng. "Guanyu sisuo quanguo zhuming gaodeng yuanxiao bufen xuesheng sixiang qingkuangde diaocha" (An investigation on the thinking of some of the students at four nationally famous universities). *Qingnian gongzuo yanjiu yu cankao* (Research and reference on youth work) 2:16–19 (1987).

Xie Peihui. *Qian, fengkuang de kunshou* (Money, the mad cornered beast). Changsha, Hunan Wenyi Chubanshe, 1988.

Xu Yulong and Wang Yongjiang. *Zhongguo shehuizhuyi laodong wenti* (China's socialist labor problems). Anhui Chubanshe, 1985.

Young, Susan. "Policy, Practice, and the Private Sector in China." *Australian Journal of Chinese Affairs* 21:57–80 (1989).

Yuan Enzhen, ed. *Wenzhou moshi yu fuyu zhi lu* (Wenzhou model of economy and the road to affluence). Shanghai, Shanghai Shehui Kexueyuan Chubanshe, 1987.

Yudkin, Marcia. *Making Good: Private Business in Socialist China.* Beijing, Foreign Languages Press, 1986.

Zafanolli, Wojtek. "A Brief Outline of China's Second Economy." *Asian Survey* 25:715–736 (1985).

Zhang Dexi and Jin Xitian. "Jiaqiang cunji jianshede jizhong banfa" (Several ways to strengthen village-level construction). *Nongcun gongzuo tongxun* (Rural work bulletin) 5:41–42 (1988).

Zhao Yicheng. "Jiazhide chongtu" (Value conflict). *Weidinggao* (Manuscripts not finalized) 8:26–33 (1988).

Zhong Shi. "Yiyuan bu zheng zhi feng de qingkuang diaocha" (An investigation into irregularities in hospitals). *Shehui* (Society) 3:40–44 (1982). Translated in *Chinese Sociology and Anthropology* (1984), pp. 36–48.

Zhongguo Jingji Tizhi Gaige Yanjiusuo (Economic System Reform Institute), eds. *Zhongguo: Fazhan yu gaige* (China: Development and reform). Chengdu, Sichuan Renmin Chubanshe, 1986.

Zhongguo laodong gongzi tongji ziliao 1949–85 (Statistical materials on Chinese labor and wages). Beijing, Zhongguo Tongji Chubanshe, 1987.

1983 Zhongguo nongcun qingnian diaocha ziliao (1983 Chinese peasant youth investigation materials). Beijing, Zhongguo Shehui Kexueyuan Qingshaonian Yanjiusuo (Institute of Youth Studies, Chinese Academy of Social Sciences), 1984.

Zhongguo weisheng nianjian 1985, 1986 and 1987 (China health yearbook). Beijing, People's Medical Publishing House, 1985, 1986, and 1987.

Zhou Xiao. "Virginity and Premarital Sexual Behavior in Contemporary China." *Feminist Studies* 15:279–288 (1989).

Zhu Aorong et al. "Nongcun hezuo yiliao baojian zhidu de xilie yanjiu" (Theoretical investigation of the rural health insurance system). *Zhongguo weisheng jingji* (Chinese health economics) 4:13–19 (1988).

Zhuang Qidong, ed. *Laodong gongzi shouce* (Handbook on labor salaries). Tianjin Renmin Chubanshe, 1984.

Zweig, David. "Rural Small Towns and the Politics of Planned Development." Paper presented at Fortieth Annual Meeting of the Association of Asian Studies, San Francisco, March 1988.

————, Kathy Hartford, James Feinerman, and Deng Jianxu. "Law, Contracts, and Economic Modernization: Lessons from the Recent Chinese Rural Reforms." *Stanford Journal of International Law* 23:319–364 (1987).

Abortions, 68, 276, 304

Age: and income inequalities, 142, 147-150, 155; of marriage, 182, 190, 192, 193; of first marriage, 194, 209-210, 211. *See also* Elderly, the

Agriculture: reforms in, 2; and grain quotas, 5; vs. industry in rural areas, 18, 20-21, 34, 49, 76; income from, 20, 76; subsidies for, 30-31; decollectivization of and health, 268-269, 271

Anti-intellectualism, 250

Anti-rightist campaign, 255

Artisan craftsmen, 4

Authoritarianism, problems of, 131-132

Autonomy, of villages, 53-57

Banister, Judith, 274-275

baomu (nursemaid), costs of for the elderly, 234

Barzun, Jacques, 246

Beijing: demonstrations in, 2; suburban townships of, 45; and the FDRS, 112; urban individual laborers in, 165, 169, 172; health care in, 270; mortality in, 277; surveys of youth in, 285-287, 292; re-cruitment by CCP in, 294; military recruitment in, 296; school dropout rate in, 300

Beijing Normal University, 293

Bell, Daniel, 247

Bellah, Robert, 245

Birth control, 58; campaigns for, 68

Boat people *(Dan)*, 63, 64; in Yangjiang County, 75-76

Bonuses: unfair distribution of, 120; growth of, 140-141, 219; as source of income inequality, 143-144, 153, 156

Bourgeois liberalism: and intellectuals, 245-248; aftermath of repression, 255-256; campaign against, 291

Brigades: subsidies from, 50-51; in Nanxi Rural Commune, 67

"Build Socialism with Chinese Characteristics" (Deng Xiaoping), 164

Bureaucracies: in rural administration, 52-53, 80; above township level, 57; control over urban employment, 86-87; local, 110; and the FDRS, 116, 118, 119, 121, 130; economic vs. political levers for change of, 128-129; and mate choice, 208-209, 212

Bureaucratism, effect of in Eastern Europe, 10
Byrd, William, 35

Cadres: rural, 38, 45; reform of, 46-48; promotion of younger, 46, 58; subsidies for,
48-49; as scapegoats, 59-60; and rural
migrants, 77; in management of town
industry, 79-80; income after retirement, 228; health care for, 264, 266,
272, 281; children of, 292; youth attitudes toward, 292-293
Cancer, 229, 264, 273, 277; persisting infectious disease, 280
Cancer Epidemiology Survey, 273, 277
Capitalism: and development of private sector, 154; conditions for mate choice under, 204-205; and bourgeois liberalism,
246
Cerebrovascular disease, 280
Changzhou, 19, 112
Chemical fertilizers, scandal concerning, 56
Chengdu: marriages in, 8; mate choice in, 181-
213; dating in, 186, 212; wedding celebrations, 196-200, 202; dowries, 199;
housing for newlyweds, 200-201; con-
clusions concerning mate choice in, 211-
213. *See also* Mate choice; Weddings
Chevrier, Yves, 6-7, 109-133
Child care, under Mao, 265
Child labor, 300-301
Childless elderly, 224-225
Children, infectious diseases of, 277-278
"Children Should Not Interfere in the Marriage of Parents" (Deng Weizhi), 238
China: departures from communism in, 1, 283,
303; regional economics in, 88; state
building in, 123-126; family in, 181;
problems of aging population in, 217-
220. *See also* State
Chinese Communist Party (CCP): consolidation of power, 3; and economic reform,
7; and the new youth, 9-10; in rural enterprise, 34-35; and rural administrative
reform, 44-46, 59; and town industries,
79-80; on labor markets, 87-88; and job
mobility, 102-104; and the FDRS, 110,
112, 114; formal resistance to FDRS,
115-117, 121; and statecraft of modernization, 129-133; income of members,
142, 147-151, 153; and private business, 162; on marriage customs, 183; and
bourgeois liberalism, 246; on role of intellectual, 249; loss of control over intellectuals, 253-254; confrontation with,
254-255; loss of control over youth, 284,

288, 289, 291-296, 304; aging of, 293;
recruitment campaigns of, 294
Cohabitation, premarital, 193, 208
Collectives: after the commune, 15-36; changes
in ownership, 16; and village sources of
income, 18; use of term defined, 19; industry as new basis of, 20-29; new redistributive socialism, 29-33; emergence of
redistributive corporatism, 33-36; income of workers in, 169. *See also* Rural
enterprises
Commerce: employment in, 21; individual
operators in, 168-169
Commodification, 4, 105; consequences of, 5
Commodity economy *(shangpin jingji),* 124
Commodity society *(shangpin shehui),* 124, 125;
attempt at, 131
Communist Youth League (CYL), 293-294,
304-305
Community leaders, in management of state
enterprises, 120
Confucianism, 259
Connections *(guanxi):* for rural industry, 26;
in the military, 297
"Conscientiously Eliminate Unfair Phenom-
ena in Social Distribution" (Jiang Zemin),
176-177
Construction, employment in, 21
Consumers, rise of wealthy, 7
Contract laborers *(hetong gong),* in state industry, 99-101
Contract system for rural enterprise, 23-26;
term *contract,* 24
Corporatism, redistributive, 5, 33-36
Counties, power of vs. township, 54
Crime: among the unemployed, 160; among
youth, 289, 304
Cultural Revolution, 3, 68, 243; employment
during, 92, 159-160; retirement during,
95; contract labor during, 99; reforms
after, 158; family-change efforts in, 183,
186, 188; and marriage patterns, 196,
202, 211; and intellectuals, 250; health
care during, 266, 270, 277; and youth
attitudes, 289; and concern with politics, 305
Culture: changes in, 243, 244; Zhao Fusan on
change, 253. *See also* Social change

Dalian, 112
Dating practices: in the West, 186; in China,
186-187, 188, 205-206, 212
Davis, Deborah, 1-12, 85-108, 217
Decentralization, 2; effects of, 88-89, 109-110;
and job mobility, 105-106

"Decisions on Reform of the Economic Structure" (Oct. 1984), 116, 129, 164
Decollectivization, 2; consequences of, 5-6; effect on rural areas, 49
Democracy: at the village level, 53-54; demonstrations for, 245
Democracy Wall, 3, 288
Demonstrations: student, 245, 288; use of telecommunications in, 256; in 1989 Beijing Spring, 256; and state's loss of control, 284; of 1986–87, 291
Deng Liqun, 116
Deng Pufang, 176
Deng Weizhi, 238
Deng Xiaoping: economic reforms of, 1-2, 3, 11-12, 87, 111-112, 113; consolidation of CCP by, 3-4; rural reforms of, 59-60; efforts to increase job mobility, 88; emphasis on decentralization, 89, 105; and the FDRS, 111-112; effect of archaic power structure under, 130-131, 132; on socialism, 164; and bourgeois liberalism, 291; on education, 299; growth of individualism under, 303
dingti ("substitution") option, 95-97, 99
Disintegration, social, and the FDRS, 130
Doctors, "barefoot," 271. *See also* Medicine
Dropouts, and private enterprise, 174. *See also* Education

East China Normal University, 289
Eastern Europe: departures from communism in, 1, 256; radicals of, 8; decollectivization compared to China's, 10; labor markets in, 87
Economic Management Committee (EMC) in Huashan, 43
Economic reform: in pre-existing economic order, 1, 128-129; in rural China, 37; separation from politics, 38-46; primacy of, 58; in Tianjin, 135-156; and changes in culture, 244, 296, 304; irrationality of, 251; and health care, 266
Economy, impact of aging population on, 217-220
Education: changes in, 9-10; enrollment, 94; and job mobility, 102; and income, 142-144, 147-150, 151-153, 155; of a sample of elderly, 226-227; political, 290-291; and youth attitudes, 299-303, 304; hierarchies of, 299-300; dropout rate, 300
Egalitarianism: repudiation of, 135-136; in Tianjin, 138
Elderly, the, 8; new options for urban, 215-242; impact of on economy, 217-220; sharing costs of increases in, 220-226; health care financing for, 223-224, 232-235; targeting selected segments of, 224-225; in a Guangzhou neighborhood, 226-241; income of, 226-229; physical status of, 229-232; family life of, 235-237; new options for, 237-241; remarriage for, 238-239; organizations for, 240; policy options of, 241-242; mortality of, 277
Employment: shift from agriculture to industry, 20-22; in township enterprise, 23, 25; distribution, 30-31; effects of decentralization on, 89-90; reform of transfer procedure, 90-93; hiring procedures, 93-101; effect of *dingti* on, 97; partial reform of, 105; length of, and income, 147-151, 152-153; private vs. state, 155; on coast vs. interior, 301
Enterprise Law of April 1888, 111
Entrepreneurs *(geti hu)*: encouragement of, 4, 164; rise of, 7; in Eastern Europe, 11; in services, 22; rural, in Nanxi Town, 73-74; dilemma of in Nanxi, 81-82; social background of, 170-174; life style of, 174-178; intellectuals as, 254
Environment: sanitation control under Mao, 265; new challenges of, 281
Epidemic hemorrhagic fever (EHF), 279, 280
Ex-prisoners, as entrepreneurs, 171
Extortion ("squeeze"), and the FDRS, 118-119

Factories: rural, 22, 27-28; importance of planning in, 25; compensation for managers of, 28; in Nanxi Town, 65, 73, 77; in Yongding, 74-75; rural labor shunned by, 76-77; and the FDRS, 110
Factory director responsibility system *(changzhang fuzezhi;* FDRS), 110; purposes of, 110-111; difficulties of, 111-112; rise of, 112-115; erosion of, 115-121; significance of failure, 121; compromise and consolidation, 121-129; microeconomic management and the statecraft of modernization, 129-133. *See also* Managers; Micropolitics
Family: new importance of, 17; in individual enterprises, 166, 172-173; as central, 181; reduction of importance of, 205; and marriage of children, 184, 188, 190, 196-200, 210, 212; and the elderly, 216, 217, 225, 235-237; of military recruits, 298-299
Fang Lizhi, 245-246, 259; on intellectuals, 251-252; later career, 256
Farmers, health care for, 269, 272
fenpei (job assignment), 95, 97-99, 284

Feudalism, and Marxism, 245-246
Four Modernizations, 162, 216; role of intel-
lectuals in, 250; effect on education, 299
French Revolution, 254
Fu Yuehua, 3
Fudan University, 98, 289
Fujian, 19; urban individual laborers in, 165

Gang of Four, 4, 160
Gender, and income, 148-150, 152, 155. *See
also* Women
geti hu (entrepreneurs), 7. *See also* Entrepreneurs; Urban private business and social
change
Gini coefficient, 142
Gold, Thomas, 7, 157-178
Gong Chong, 171
Gongren ribao, 115
Gorbachev, M. S., 115, 128
Grain: after end of collectives, 16; requisition
of, 58
Great Leap Forward, 183, 188; and marriage
patterns, 196, 201, 206, 211; mortality
during, 274
Guangdong, 19; urban individual laborers in,
165; elderly in, 216; inflation in, 219;
costs of health care in, 223
Guangzhou (Canton): families of, 8; elderly
in, 216-242; homes of respect for aged
in, 225; elderly in a neighborhood of,
226-241; health care for cadres in, 272;
surveys in, 285; military recruitment in,
296; child labor in, 301; employment in,
301-302
guanxi. See Connections
"Guiding Principles for Building a Socialist
Society with an Advanced Culture and
Ideology," 246
Guofa No. 104 (1978), 95
Guofa No. 137 (1983), 96
Guofa No. 91 (1985), 98, 99
Guofa No. 34 (1986), 98

Habits of the Heart (Bellah, Sullivan, Swidler,
Tifton, Madsen), 245, 246-248, 258, 259
Hangzhou, 290
Health care: for the elderly, 216, 217; costs
of, 217-219, 266, 267, 271; financing
of, 223-224; after retirement, 232-235;
increased inequality in, 263-282; new
problems for, 263-264; resources for, 265,
269-271; and health status, 265, 273-
281; from Maoist to market, 265-273;
insurance, 266, 269, 271-273; urban-
rural differences in resources for, 269-271;
changes in health status, 273-278

Health status, 265, 281-282; changes in, 273-
281; mortality, 273-277; infant mortality, 274-277; urban-rural mortality differentials, 277; morbidity, 277-280;
chronic conditions post-Mao, 280-281;
inequality in, 281-282
Heart disease, 280
Hebei, infant mortality in, 275-276
Henderson, Gail, 263-282
Hengyang Medical College, 174
Hepatitis, 279; vaccination for, 279
Hiring procedures, reform of, 93-101; pension reform and *dingti,* 95-97; employment of university graduates, 97-99; expanded use of contract labor, 99-101
Hirschman, A. O., 117
Hong Kong: criticism in, 127; and the elderly, 216-217
Hospitals: costs of, 223, 233, 267; care in
during Maoism, 265; beds in, 266, 269-
270; shortages in urban areas, 268; for
persisting infectious diseases, 280
Household: new unit in agricultural production, 16; relief household, 225
Housing: as impediment to mobility, 106;
quality of, 161; for newlyweds, 199, 206,
209-210; for childless elderly, 225; and
coresidence of elderly with children, 235-
236
Hu Qili, 98, 170
Hu Teh-wei, 142
Hu Yaobang, 124-125, 164, 291
Huashan Commune, 38, 42; personal characteristics of cadre force in, 47; villagers'
committees and township government in,
54-55
Hubei, 5-6
hukou (household registration), 6
Hull, Terence, 276
Hungary, economic change in, 11, 136
Hypertension, 280

Ignatieff, Michael, 258
Ikels, Charlotte, 8, 215-242
Immunization, 277-278; and UNICEF, 278-
279
Income: inequalities in, 7, 150, 176; redistribution of, 31-33, 35; of peasants, 67; in
Minlong, 75; survey in Tianjin, 138-141;
changing pattern of inequality in, 141-
144; sources of leveling, 144-145; outside, 145-147; changing social determinants of inequality in, 147-151; expanded model of, 151-155; in old age,
226-229; and health, 277

"In-depth Fertility Survey" (State Statistical Bureau), 275
Individual: new importance of, 17, 303; as entrepreneur, 22; in Maoist labor market, 89
Individual enterprise: legitimization of, 163-165; growth of urban, 165-174; licenses for, 166-167; closings of, 167-168; income of operators of, 169. *See also* Private business; Urban private business
Individual sector *(geti)*, incomes in, 138-139
Individualism: in American society, 246-247; Zhao Fusan on, 253, 259; vs. coercion, 259
Individualization, and the FDRS, 114
Industrialization, of villages, 18
Industry: reforms in, 2; in rural areas, 17-19, 21, 49; and village services, 18; as new basis of collective, 20-29; in Yongding vs. Nanxi Town, 76; in town vs. rural areas, 79-80
Inequality: and economic reforms, 135-138; changing pattern of incomes, 141-144, 178; changing social determinants of, 147-151; and expanded model of incomes, 151-155; conclusions concerning, 155-156
Infanticide, of females, 274-275, 276
Infants: mortality rate of, 273, 274; mortality by sex, 275-277; immunization of, 279
Infectious diseases, 273, 277; measles, 277; rural vs. urban, 277-278; hepatitis, 279; EHF, 280; persisting, 280-281
Inflation, 11, 176; in Nanxi Town, 82; and modernization, 125, 131; effect on wages, 219; and medical costs, 271
Inner Mongolia, 18-19
Inoculation, mass programs for, 265
Insurance: health care, 266, 269, 281; and access to health resources, 271-273; and infectious diseases, 278
Intellectuals: ambivalence of, 8-9; new professionals as, 126; spiritual crisis of, 243-261; and "bourgeois liberalism," 245-248; identity crisis of, 248-252; role of, 249; political-economic disorganization and confusion of, 252-255; international outlook of, 253-254; and the future of China, 255-260; and the CCP, 295
Interest groups, intellectuals in, 126-127
Internationalism, importance of to intellectuals, 258
Interpersonal networks *(guanxi wang)*: of managers, 118; as cause of "evil tendencies," 119; and legal profession, 126; attempt to bypass, 131. *See also* Connections *(guanxi)*

Investment: in rural enterprises, 32-33, from overseas, 81
"Iron rice bowl," 86, 89
"Is It True that Studying is Not as Good as Selling Popsicles?" 300
"Is It Worth It to Leave School to Go into Business?" 300

Jamison, Dean, 269
Japan: as model, 131; and the aged, 221
Jiang Zemin, 176, 295
Jiangsu, 30, 32; industrial output of, 19; rural subsidies in, 49
Jilin, 170
Jobs, *see* Employment

Kanghua Development Corporation, 176
Kornai, Janos, 10-11

Labor: jobs in rural areas, 22; earnings of, vs. factory managers, 29; in state-owned urban enterprises, 86-88, 99-101; reform of urban employment practices, 89-101, 105; effect of decentralization on, 89-90; reform of transfer procedures, 90-93; reform of hiring practices, 93-101; experience of 100 families, 101-105. *See also* Employment; Mobility
Labor office *(laodong gongzike)*, 91
Laborers, urban undividual, 168-170
Land: decisions on use of, 17; ratio of to population, 22; reform of in Nanxi Town, 65
Lang, Olga, 188
Legal profession, protection by, 124, 125-126
Lei Feng, 291, 294, 303
Lenin, Nikolai, 165
Levy, Marion, 188
Lewin, Moshe, 128
Lhasa, 167
Li Peng, 125
Li Wanfen, 238
Li Yining, 128
Liaoning, 19
Liberalism, and privatization, 177; *See also* Bourgeois liberalism
Licenses: for individual enterprises, 166-167; requirements for, 170-171
Life expectation, 273
Linghai Old People's Society, 240; retirement home of, 240
Liu Binyan, 245-246, 256, 259, 294
Liu Shaoqi, 3

Loans, to rural enterprises, 32-33
Longevity Hospital, 241

Macropolitics: and the ideology of reform, 3-4; and the FDRS, 112, 114, 133; debate on state enterprises, 121-122; state building, 123-126, 131
Madsen, Richard, 8-9, 243-260
Management: and contract workers, 101; modernization of, 122; microeconomic, 129-133. *See also* FDRS; Managers
Managers: of factories, 6-7; and negative decision making, 106-107; rise of and FDRS, 112-115; Party resistance to FDRS, 115-117; effect of bureaucracies on, 118; subject to "squeeze," 119; "economic crimes" of, 120; as moral community leaders, 120-121; evaluation of, 122-123; lack of legal protection for, 125-126; professional associations of, 127
Mao Zedong, 1; reversal of policies of, 3; on people's communes, 38; legacy on labor markets, 87, 89
Maoism: and the FDRS, 130; egalitarianism of, 135; inequalities under, 136, 156; and wedding celebrations, 202; and intellectuals, 250; health care under, 264, 265-273, 266, 273
Market towns: politics of migration in, 61-82; Nanxi Town as, 63. *See also* Nanxi Town
Marriage: practices, 8; in Chengdu, 182-213; delays in, 212; marital status in old age, 235; remarriage for the elderly, 238. *See also* Mate choice
Marriage Law (1950), 183
Marxism: and private-business class, 174; attitude of youth toward, 288
Marxism-Leninism: and feudalism, 245-246; loss of faith in, 254
Mate choice, changes in, 181-213; overview, 182-184; trends in marriage customs in Chengdu, 184-203; and parental choice, 184, 188, 190; timing of, 186; and women working outside the home, 190; and age, 190, 192, 193, 196, 211; and sex experience, 190, 192, 193, 207-209, 211; age of first marriage, 194, 196; and wedding celebrations, 196-200, 202, 210-211; and continuing dependence on family, 201; interpreting trends in, 204-211; reliance on romantic love, 206-207; conclusions, 211-213
Materialism, of new youth, 9-10, 303
May Fourth Movement: and attacks on ar-

ranged marriages, 182; anniversary of, 254
Medical care, inequalities in, 9, 263-282. *See also* Health care
Medicine: research in, 263, 266; preventive, 265; under Maoism, 265-266; professionalization of, 266-267; equipment for, 267-268
Mental impairment: in the elderly, 231-232; terms for, 232
Micropolitics: and factory director responsibility system, (FDRS), 109-133; informal resistance to FDRS, 117-121
Migrants: invisible boundaries for, 76-82; prejudice against rural, 77-78, 79-81
Migration: politics of in a market town, 61-82; restrictions on, 70; to town enterprises, 73-76; from rural to urban areas, 85. *See also* Mobility
Military, the: recruitment by, 296-299; motivations for service, 297-298; dissatisfaction with, 298; new problems of, 304
Ming Li, 142
Minlong Rural Commune, new enterprises in, 75
Mobility: government restraints on, 3, 61; and rise of nonagricultural enterprises, 20-21; in urban jobs, 85-108; effects of decentralization on, 89-90; and the contract laborer, 101; of families interviewed, 102-105; of the elderly, 230-231; of labor, 304. *See also* Migration
Modernization: and political control, 7; statecraft of, 111-112; and the FDRS, 114-115; and state building, 123-126; statecraft of, 129-133; of marriage practices, 212-213; and the elderly, 222; vs. Westernization, 247; and social responsibility, 259
Money: new role of, 11, 119, 304; effects of importance of, 175
Montesquieu, 259
Morbidity: changing patterns of, 223; and health status, 273; causes of, 277; infectious diseases, 277-280
Morning Strollers, The (Li Wanfen), 238
Mortality: causes of, 229, 264, 277; and health resources, 265; and changing health status, 273-277; infant, 274-277; urban-rural differentials in, 277. *See also* Health care
Mulberries, 69-70

Nanjing, 298
Nanxi Rural Commune, 67, 76; and Town

Commune, 68-69, 79; dynamism of, 80-81

Nanxi Town: history of, 62-69; population movements in, 69-76; invisible boundaries, 76-82; and state enterprises, 80; effect of party ideology on, 81

Nanxi Town Commune, 66-67; and Rural Commune, 68-69, 79; stagnation in, 79-80

Nanxi Zhen, 66

National Writers Conference, 3

Naughton, Barry, 89

Nee, Victor, 138

News items, of interest to youth, 287-288

Newspapers, in chains of protest, 127

Nongye jingji wenti (Problems of agricultural economy), 29

Nursing care, for the elderly, 225

Oi, Jean C., 5, 15-36

One-child family, 6, 68; and the elderly, 224, 225

"One Percent Population Survey," 275-276

Opinions, new diversity of, 177

"Organic Law Governing Village Committees of the PRC," 55

Overseas Chinese, 216-217

Parents: role in job mobility, 103-105; mate choices by, 184, 188, 190

Parish, William, 136-137; on income inequality, 142

Party rectification *(zhengdang):* and the FDRS, 112, 113, 114; targets of, 115, 119

Pearl River Delta, 6, 61-62; mobility in, 62-82

Peasants: estrangement of, 6, 58; after the end of collectives, 16; income of, 20, 50; and rural reform, 38, 59-60; vulnerability of, 56; prejudices against, 67-68; restrictions on migration, 70; and the CCP, 295; and the military, 299, 304

Peng Dehuai, 3

Pensions: reform of, 95-97, 222-223; and party membership, 104; for the elderly, 216, 219-220; disparities in, 227

People's communes: replaced, 4; effect of industrialization on, 5; transformation of, 38; structural reform of, 42

People's Daily, see Renmin ribao

People's Liberation Army (PLA); problems of, 296; recruitment by, 296-299; dissatisfaction with, 298-299

People's Republic of China (PRC): constitution of 1982, 54; anniversary of founding, 254

Personnel: introduction of younger cadres, 46-48; difficulties in transfer of skilled, 91-93. *See also* Cadres; Managers; Party rectification

Plans: "guidance" *(zhidaoxing jihua)*, 25; mandatory *(zhilingxing jihua)*, 25

Pluralism, social: after economic reforms, 111-112, 114; and state building, 123-126; and social counterweights, 126-128; economic levers for, 128-129; challenge of, 131-132; and entrepreneurs, 176, 177

Poland, economic changes in, 136

Political reform in rural China, 37; separation from economics, 38-46, 58; reform of cadre administration, 46-48; stabilization of rural leadership, 48-52; streamlining of administration, 52-53, 58; strengthening of village autonomy, 53-57; and changes in culture, 244; demonstrations for, 245

Politics: reporting of, 286; student interest in, 288-289; declining interest in, 305

Population: ratio to land, 22; movements in Nanxi Town, 69-76; aging, and the economy, 217-220

Pornography, 164, 176

Poverty, and health, 281-282

Pregnancy, pre-marital, 193

Prejudice, against rural migrants, 77

Prescott, Nicholas, 269

Prices: controls, 3; changes in structure of, 11

Private business *(siying qiye):* in urban areas, 157-178; creation of class for, 157, 158-162; creation of suitable environment for, 162-165; category of, 170; class for, and social change, 174-178

Privatization, 4, 105; consequences of, 5; and individual enterprise, 177, 178, 304

Production teams, end of, 16

Profiteers, civil-service, 176

Profits, from rural enterprises, 26, 27

Protection, of economic projects by the state, 123-126

Protest, chains of, 127

Provinces: industrial output in, 19; hospitals in, 271

Qing dynasty, 127

Qinghua University, 288, 293

Qiushi (Seeking truth), 176

Radicalism, confusion in, 8-9

"Red-eye disease" *(hongyanbing):* jealousy, 175

Red Guards, 160
Reforms: in urban China, 6-7, 85-108; and national-level constituencies, 9-10; and bureaucratic power, 10-11; in rural China, 37-60, 61-82; and state building, 123-126; irrationality of, 251; dilemmas of, 253; impact on health care, 263, 265, 266, 268, 280, 281; impact on youth attitudes, 283-305. *See also* Economic reform; Political reform
Remarriage, for the elderly, 238-239
Ren Zhonglin, 176
Renmin ribao, 43, 45, 93, 245, 246, 285
Rents: determination of in rural enterprises, 27-29; fixed, 27; floating, 27, 29; factory-manager responsibility system, 27-29
Respiratory disease, chronic, 280
Retirement: activities for, 215-216; early, 217; work activities after, 224; income after, 226-229; physical status during, 229-232; health care in, 232-235; family life in, 235-237; new options for the elderly, 237-241. *See also* Elderly, the
Retirement benefits: growth of pensions, 95-97; and loosening of generational bonds, 205
Reward structures, as impediment to mobility, 106
Riskin, Carl, 156
River Elegy (He shang), 256
Rosen, Stanley, 9-10, 283-305
Rural areas: reforms in, 4, 37-60, 61-82; government services in, 6, 18; agriculture vs. industry in, 16-19; political reform in, 37-60; administrative organization, 39-42; commune structural reform, 42-46; stabilization of leadership in, 48-52; village autonomy in, 53-57; emigration from, 85; incomes in, 136; health care in, 264, 265, 266; health problems of, 268-269; hospitals in, 269; differences in health resources in, 369-371. *See also* Agriculture; Villages
Rural Development Research Center of the State Council, 46
Rural enterprises: growth of, 21; importance of, 21-22; contract system, 23-26; determination of rents, 27-29; workers' "loans" to, 32; loans and investment in, 32-33. *See also* Collectives; Industry; Rural areas
Rural industry, 21
Rural Policy Research Center of the Party Secretariat, 46

Salaries: in rural cadres, 48-49; of intellectuals, 250. *See also* Wages
Second Kind of Loyalty, The (Liu Binyan), 294
Self-confidence, lack of among intellectuals, 252
Self-Employed Laborers Association *(geti laodongzhe xiehui;* SELA), 170
Sexual experience: premarital, 190, 192, 193, 207; influence of bureaucracy on, 208
Shaanxi: infant mortality in, 275-276; educational opportunities in, 302
Shandong: industrial output of, 19; bureaucracy in, 52
Shandong Maritime Institute, 292
Shanghai, 112; interviews with families in, 101-105; quality of life in, 161; urban individual laborers in, 165, 169, 172; infant mortality in, 275-276; student surveys in, 285, 288-289; views of CCP in, 294-295
Shanghai University, 98
Shenyang, 112; talent exchange centers in, 90-91
Shenzhen, military recruitment in, 296
Shenzhen University, 98
Shi Shuzhong, 142
Shue, Vivienne, 131
Sichuan, 32
Singapore, 162
Siu, Helen F., 5, 6, 61-82, 87
Smoking, 280-281
Social change: and private-business class, 174-178; and freedom to choose mate, 205-206, 212; toward individualism, 303
Social Development Research Institute, 177
Social problems, in urban areas, 161
Social services, as factor in income, 141
Socialism: new redistributive, 29-33; direct subsidies, 29-31; indirect subsidies, 31-33; reconceptualization of, 158; Deng Xiaoping on, 164; conditions for mate choice under, 205; "Chinese style," 283, 303
"Some Policy Regulations Concerning the Urban and Township Nonagricultural Individual Economy" (1981), 163
"Some Thoughts on Certain Aspects of Modern Western Culture" (Zhao Fusan), 245
Soviet Union: departure from communism in, 1; labor markets in, 87
State, the: and peasants' harvests, 17, 18; economic reforms and state building, 123-126, 131; demands of aging population on, 217; loss of control by, 253, 284, 289, 304; sponsorship of health care, 265,

268; loss of national-level planning by, 268

State-owned enterprises *(quanmin suoyouzhi):* immobility of labor in, 86-87, 105-108; expanded use of contract labor in, 99-101; resistance to FDRS in, 110-111; management reorganization in, 112; party leadership in, 115-117, 120, 129; as nexus of power, 129-133; wages of employees in, 141, 168; pension burdens of, 222-223

Stock markets: and power of managers, 128-129; introduction of, 164

Stone Group, 173, 177

Students: subsidies for, 30; in private business, 173-174; demonstrations by, 245; attempts to control, 284; interests of, 286-289; uncertainty over future, 289-290; attitudes toward CCP, 291-296. *See also* Education; *fenpei;* Youth attitudes

Su Shaozhi, 256, 259

Su Xiaokang, 256, 259

Subsidies *(jintie):* direct, 29-31; indirect, 31-33; ability to provide, 35; and job mobility, 106

Sullivan, William, 245

"Supplementary Regulations to 'Policy Regulations Concerning the Urban and Township Nonagricultural Individual Economy,' " (1983), 163

Surveys: research based on, 285; reliability of, 285; use of, 285-286; results of, 286-290; of military recruitment, 297

Suzhou, 19

Swidler, Ann, 245

Szelenyi, Ivan, 10-11

Taiwan, as model, 131, 132, 162

Talent exchange centers *(rencai jiaoliu zhongxin),* 90-91

Taxation, 58; on agriculture, 16; exemptions from, 68; of individual entrepreneurs, 177

Technology, 263, 267, 270; medical, 267, 272, 279; costs of, 272-273

Television, intellectuals' use of, 256

"Temporary Provisions for Private Business" (1988), 170

Textile work, and job mobility, 102

Thirteenth Party Congress (Oct. 1987), 124; managers at, 127

ti-yong controversies, 244

Tian Jiyun, 170

Tiananmen Square, 2; incident of 1976, 3

Tianjin, 112, 299; economic reform in, 138-156; survey of incomes in, 138-141; changing pattern of income inequality in, 141-144; sources of income leveling, 144-145; outside income, 145-147; social determinants of income inequality, 147-151; expanded model of 1986 incomes, 151-155; conclusions, 155-156; surveys in, 285

Tibet, 165-166, 167, 230

Tipton, Steven, 245

Tocqueville, Alexis de, 247, 259

Town resident *(jumin),* 61

Towns *(zhen),* 39

Township enterprises *(xiangzhen qiye),* 22-23; profits from, 24; function of "plans" in, 25; importance of connections in, 26; use of profits from, 26

"Township Hospitals are Unable to Make Ends Meet," 271

Townships *(xiang),* 39; use of term, 20; Huashan, 42; role between party and enterprise, 44-46; and villagers' committees, 54; and "Organic Law," 55-56; health care in, 268-269, 271

Transfers, reform of procedures for, 90-93

Transportation, employment in, 21

Tuberculosis, 279

Unemployment: and creation of urban private business, 158-159; in rural areas, 301. *See also* Employment

United Nations International Children's Emergency Fund (UNICEF), 278-279

United States, residence of elderly in, 236-237

Universities, desirability of attendance at, 302

University graduates, employment of, 97-99

Urban areas: reforms in, 4, 6-7, 85-108; government services in, 6; workers in, 7; intellectuals of, 8-9; reform of employment practices in, 89-101, 105-108; interviews with families in, 101-105; income in vs. that of rural areas, 136; private business in, 157-178; unemployment in, 158-160; social problems in, 161; growth of individual economy in, 165-170; changes in mate choice in, 181-182, 205; options for elderly in, 215-242; health care in, 264, 265, 266; shortages of health care in, 268; vs. rural areas in health resources, 269-271

Urban private business: and social change, 157-178; creation of private business class,

Urban private business (*continued*)
158-162; creation of suitable business
environment, 162-165; growth of urban
individual economy, 165-170; social
background of operators, 170-174; private-business class and social change, 174-
178

Vaccination, for hepatitis B, 279
Vietnam, 1
Village-owned enterprises: employment in, 23;
contracts in, 24
Village small groups (VSGs), 49; after end of
collectives, 16; subsidies for, 50; and
county control, 53; and "Organic Law,"
55-56
Villagers' committees (*cunmin weiyuanhui*), 39;
dual role of, 54; "Organic Law" governing, 55-56
Villages (*cun*), 24; sources of income in, 18,
21-22; use of term, 20; use of subsidies
from industries, 29-31; loans and investment by, 32-33; as diversified corporations, 34; structural reforms in, 48; subsidies for, 48-49; strengthening autonomy
of, 53-57; health care in, 268-269
Vision: of the elderly, 229-230; cataracts, 230
Vogel, Ezra F., 1-12

Wages: of migrant laborers, 75; in Nanxi
Town, 78; reforms in, 141, 219, 228;
raises as source of inequalities, 143-144
Walder, Andrew, 7, 135-156; on status
groups, 175
Wan Runnan, 173
Wang Luxian, 256
Wang Ruoshui, 256
Wang Ruowang, 245-246, 256
Wealth, redistribution of, 11
Weber, Max, 174-175
Weddings: celebration of, 196-200, 210-211;
gifts at, 199-200; feasts, 200; payment
for, 201
Wei Jingsheng, 3
weiguan (enclosed compounds), 64
Wen Xie, 142
Wenzhou: entrepreneurs from, 167; youth
values in, 286, 289; and military re-
cruitment, 296; school dropout rate in,
300-301
West, the: dating practices in, 186; influence
of ideas from, 243; and bourgeois liber-
alism, 245; spiritual pollution from, 246;

Zhao Fusan on, 246-248; role of intellectual in, 250; traditions of moral responsibility of intellectuals in, 257;
medical advances from, 266
Westernization: of marriage customs, 183, 200;
opposition to, 249
White, Tyrene, 5-6, 37-60
Whyte, Martin, 7-8, 181-213; on income inequality, 137, 142
Women: job immobility of, 102; income inequalities of, 142; work outside home,
190; age at marriage, 190, 192, 193,
196; and dowries, 199; education of, 226-
227, 301; family life of in old age, 235-
237; maternal health care for, 265
Wong, Christine, 32, 89
Work units: place of, and income, 151-153;
and health insurance, 272
Workers: urban, 6-7; health insurance for, 272
Working class, importance of, 295
World Bank: studies by, 18, 32, 272, 277;
on employment outside agriculture, 21;
on infant mortality, 274-275
World Economic Herald, 177
Wuhan, 6; rural reform in, 38; educational
problems in, 299
Wuxi, 19, 24, 30; pension expense in, 222

Xian, 301
Xiang Zhongyang, 20

Yan'an forum (1942), 3
Yang Dongping, 290
Yang Jingren, 170
Yangcheng wanbao, 127, 240
Yangjiang County, 75-76
Yantai, 19
Ye Xuanping, 81
Yongding: industry in, 74-75, 76; vs. Nanxi
Town, 76-79
Youth: attitudes of, 9-10; impact of reform
policies on, 283-305; options for, 303-
304
Youth attitudes: impact of reform policies on,
283-305; value change among students,
284, 286-291; toward CCP, 284, 291-
296; toward the military, toward labor
market, 284; and education, 299-303;
toward politics, 305
Youth League, *see* Communist Youth League
Yu Qiuli, 219
Yuan Jihui, 222
Yueyang, business closings in, 167-168

Zhao Fusan, 245, 246-248; explanations of work of, 248-249; positive aspects of, 253; resignation of, 259

Zhao Ziyang, 124, 125; on private business, 164, 295; and SELA, 170

Zhejiang: rural enterprises in, 18; rural subsidies in, 49; urban individual laborers in, 165

Zhixi Xiang, 75

Zhongguo fazhibao, 116, 122

Zhou Enlai, mourning for, 3

Zhujiang Delta, 9

zililiang hu ("households who take care of their own grain"), 72-73

1, 2, 3, 4, 5, 6, 7, 8, 9